*Second Edition*

# Contemporary Community Corrections

Thomas Ellsworth

*Illinois State University*

WAVELAND
PRESS, INC.
Prospect Heights, Illinois

For information about this book, write or call:
    Waveland Press, Inc.
    P.O. Box 400
    Prospect Heights, Illinois 60070
    (847) 634-0081

# Contents

*Preface*   vii

**Part I Corrections in the Community**.....................1

   **1** The Emergence of Community Corrections............3
     *Thomas Ellsworth*

   **2** The Goals of Community Sanctions.................13
     *M. Kay Harris*

   **3** The Goal Orientation of Adult Probation Professionals:
     A Study of Probation Systems.....................34
     *Thomas Ellsworth*

   **4** Community Corrections and Diversion: Costs and
     Benefits, Subsidy Modes, and Start-Up
     Recommendations ...............................50
     *James McSparron*

**Part II Investigation and Offender Supervision**.........75

   **5** Have Community Supervision Officers Changed
     Their Attitudes Toward Their Work?...............77
     *Patricia M. Harris, Todd R. Clear, and*
     *S. Christopher Baird*

   **6** A Typology of Presentence Probation Investigators....91
     *John Rosecrance*

   **7** Difficult Clients, Large Caseloads Plague Probation,
     Parole Agencies................................108
     *Randall Guynes*

   **8** Screening Devices in Probation and Parole:
     Management Problems..........................123
     *Todd R. Clear and Kenneth W. Gallagher*

   **9** Probation Supervision: Mission Impossible..........141
     *John Rosecrance*

**Part III  Alternative Sanctions**...........................157

   **10** The Control Controversy: A Preliminary Examination
        of Intensive Probation Supervision Programs in the
        United States.....................................160
        *James M. Byrne*

   **11** Stated and Latent Functions of ISP.................185
        *Michael Tonry*

   **12** The Future of Intensive Probation Supervision and
        the New Intermediate Sanctions....................203
        *James M. Byrne*

   **13** What Punishes? Inmates Rank the Severity of
        Prison vs. Intermediate Sanctions.................240
        *Joan Petersilia and Elizabeth Piper Deschenes*

   **14** Intensive Rehabilitation Supervision: The Next
        Generation in Community Corrections?.............252
        *Paul Gendreau, Francis T. Cullen, and James Bonta*

   **15** Community Service: A Review of the Basic Issues....266
        *Robert M. Carter, Jack Cocks, and Daniel Glaser*

   **16** Electronic Monitors: Realistically, What Can
        Be Expected?.....................................279
        *Annesley K. Schmidt*

**Part IV  The Effectiveness Issue**..........................291

   **17** Predictors of Success in a Co-Correctional Halfway
        House: A Discriminant Analysis...................294
        *Patrick G. Donnelly and Brian E. Forschner*

   **18** Measuring the Performance of Community
        Corrections......................................312
        *Joan Petersilia*

   **19** Factors Influencing Probation Outcome: A Review of
        the Literature...................................327
        *Kathryn D. Morgan*

   **20** The Effectiveness of Institutional and Community-Based
        Programs for Juvenile Offenders..................341
        *Larry Webb and John R. Scanlon*

   **21** Evaluating Intensive Supervision Probation/Parole:
        Results of a Nationwide Experiment...............349
        *Joan Petersilia and Susan Turner*

**Part V  Legal and Ethical Issues in
          Community Corrections**......................373

  **22**  When Do Probation and Parole Officers Enjoy the
       Same Immunity as Judges?.....................375
       *Mark Jones and Rolando V. del Carmen*

  **23**  Legal Issues in the Use of Electronic Surveillance
       in Probation.................................387
       *Rolando V. del Carmen and Joseph B. Vaughn*

  **24**  The Ethics of Community-Based Sanctions.........408
       *Andrew von Hirsch*

**Part VI  The Future of Community Corrections**..........421

  **25**  Reintegrating the Concept of *Community*
       into Community-Based Corrections...............422
       *James M. Byrne*

     *Epilogue*  449

# Preface

It seems as though light years have passed since the 1967 Final Report of the President's Commission on Law Enforcement and the Administration of Justice, recommending substantially more funding for such prison and jail alternatives as probation, parole, diversion programs, halfway and residential facilities, including work release. Since the initial recommendation, we have found that funding has increased, though the reasons for the increase are a radical departure from its original intent. We have seen a transformation in criminal justice and corrections from the 1960s, where incarceration was used when all other community alternatives were exhausted or found impractical, to the present, where a greater number of Americans are receiving a taste of the corrections experience. Today, there is unprecedented growth in America's prison and jail population. There appears to be no end in sight as the American justice system surpasses the one million mark in the number of citizens incarcerated in our nation's correctional system. Legislators seem quite willing to continue to fight the war on crime with substantially tougher laws mandating punishment and incarceration.

Today, unlike the period of the 1960s and early 1970s, community corrections must be multifaceted, combining elements of deterrence, incapacitation, retribution, and rehabilitation. In earlier times, policymakers and practitioners in the field emphasized reintegration and rehabilitation as primary system goals. The change in philosophy and a rethinking about the relationship between the offender and society is not without a starting point. During the mid-1970s, alarmed over rising crime rates and a general slowdown in the economy, many Americans demanded a change. Seeking alternatives and solutions to the crime problem, legislators and policymakers sought solutions from the academic world. One scholar who made a substantial contribution and whose research findings moved correctional philosophy and practice down an entirely different path was Robert Martinson. His piece in the 1974 *Public Interest*, "What Works: Questions and Answers About Prison Reform" is believed to be the most frequently cited work on the subject of corrections to date. The student wishing to better understand the 25-year transformation of the corrections profession is advised to review this work in its entirety. In it, Martinson, using recidivism as the measure of correctional program effectiveness, found that within most programs, offender treatment services had little, if any, effect on offender rearrest rates. The reaction was almost immediate. In virtually every state politicians adopted the "get tough on crime" agenda. The rhetoric of getting tough was realized with tougher laws, abolishing of parole, mandatory minimum sentence, and of course, a growth in state prison populations. Incapacitation rates skyrocketed reflecting a 100 percent population growth in most state prison systems through the 1980s. Prisons dotted the American landscape so that today families traveling across the country receive regular reminders of America's response to the crime "problem." To many, prisons appear to be everywhere. Communities wage battles between and among themselves when new prison construction is contemplated. "Siting" of prisons, or the selection of prison sites, has received considerable attention in the criminal justice literature and in the media. Today, many states spend more taxpayer dollars to incarcerate than to educate their youth. In at least a handful of states, the cost of juvenile corrections is seven to eight times greater than that spent on education. During the 1980s and 1990s, the high cost of incarceration when compared to other alternatives became an insignificant variable when weighed against the need to protect society. Rehabilitation and reintegration concepts widely practiced throughout the history of community corrections were widely viewed as ineffective and as "soft" on crime and criminals. As we moved into the 1980s, it became apparent that the recommendations presented by the President's Commission almost a decade before would largely go unfulfilled.

Data from the 1980s reflected the rapid growth of the correctional enterprise to the extent that private industry entered the market. States such as Ohio and others turned over major responsibilities for running correctional facilities to the private sector. Other states soon followed. During the 1980s, many state corrections systems saw their budgets increase three- to fourfold but were still unable to keep up with the demand. Overcrowded conditions and conditions associated with overcrowding such as safety, medical care, and food, to name a few, caused 60 percent of state corrections systems to come under the review of the courts. Within some states the entire prison system was placed under federal court order; in others, specific prisons or jails within the state were directed to improve conditions and/or reduce crowding. Prison crowding and conditions became "front stage" issues in the media as well as in Congress and in the various statehouses. By 1985 a total of 14 states had abolished the system of parole in response to the "get tough" movement, thus eliminating an opportunity to control prison growth. In spite of the change, the national figures during the 1980s continued to show tremendous growth in the number of releases under parole in states that maintained this form of release. Little attention, on the other hand, was given to the field of community corrections, where there was an increase in the number of offenders placed on probation and parole in the 1980s and 1990s, and where today there are more than twice the number of offenders on probation and parole than there are in prison and jail. Today, more than 2.5 million Americans are under probation supervision with another 600,000 on parole. In the case of probation, we have coined the term "probation crowding" to indicate a set of supervision-related problems that resemble those experienced by workers in prisons and jails. As we entered the 1990s, 1 in 42 adults in the United States were under some form of correctional supervision (prisons, jails, probation, or parole). Almost one-third of the black male population between the ages of 20 and 29 is under a similar form of supervision, an increase of almost 10 percent since 1990.

As the early chapters will describe, probation as the largest segment of the community corrections system was never designed to accommodate high risk, dangerous, multiproblem offenders, nor to exert punishment. From its inception, probation officers supervised low risk, less problematic cases, many of whom were misdemeanants, where the giving of a "second chance" was considered acceptable by most segments of society. By the mid-1980s and through today, we are again witnessing a transformation in probation practice with the majority of offenders serving felony sentences in the community. Not only was this growing population of "felony probationers" entering our nation's probation systems with a greater need for service such as jobs, schooling, and treatment, they also carried with them certain risk factors, such as prior criminal records, drug and alcohol involvement and aggressive/assaultive behavior. These attributes, while familiar to many probation officers in the past, were less severe than those found today. In light of the added responsibility and mandate to assure public safety, many probation officials and legislators began looking for ways to toughen probation supervision standards and practices. Innovative programs and practices referred to as intermediate punishments were developed in many jurisdictions and have proven useful in supervising adult and juvenile offenders in a less restrictive environment such as in the community. There is growing consensus between practitioners and scholars that the two extremes of punishment, prison and probation are used excessively and that little exists in between. Intermediate sanctions, or alternate punishments, are designed to fill this void through the use of equivalent punishments. The use of fines, community service, probation, day reporting, electronic monitoring, and intensive supervision are to be used on a continuum and as alternatives to incarceration. Today, virtually every state utilizes one or more of these alternatives.

The change in practice has also resulted in changes in the role of the community corrections practitioner. Deterrence and punishment share dominance with reintegration and rehabilitation as system goals, in spite of rhetoric to the contrary. Probation and parole staff continue, as they have done for more than a century, to assist offenders who wish to improve themselves and to provide for their families. In the 1990s, these activities are increasingly being conducted within the framework of the need to increase public safety. Staff who have been schooled in treatment and social work practices are increasingly receiving training in the use of firearms and other self-defense strategies.

The field of community corrections continues to grow as a profession, but during a politically conservative era fails to command the respect it deserves from legislators, prosecutors and judges. The effectiveness of the field continues to be overshadowed by the earlier work of Martinson, whose legacy of "nothing works" has been difficult to displace, especially during the conservative era of the 1990s. In recent years several scholars have revisited the question of effectiveness and outcome measures in the field, some of which is quite encouraging, adding to the growing knowledge base in community corrections. Recently published selections have been added to enhance the quality of the second edition.

The reader will find that change and contemporary practice continue to be the themes of this book. Several selections focusing on alternate sanctions and the effectiveness issue have been added. In addition, several themes from the first edition have been consolidated so as to emphasize the key issues confronting today's system of community corrections.

Two gentlemen from the Missouri Division of Probation and Parole, Gail Hughes and Jim Markham, with whom I worked during my brief career as a probation and parole officer, maintain my utmost respect. My family, Kay, Corey and Jodi continue to be the source of happiness and joy.

# Part I

## Corrections in the Community

In recent years the field of community corrections has received increased attention by policymakers, administrators, and scholars who have attempted to resolve many of the problems faced by the criminal justice system today. As we approach a new century, community corrections has been called upon to supervise a larger, more problematic offender group while at the same time facing a reduction in resources. Community corrections, particularly probation, is clearly viewed as the disposition of choice by the courts as probation populations' growth far exceeds that of institutional corrections. At the present time, it is estimated that four million adults, or one in every forty-two citizens in the United States, are under some form of correctional supervision, whether it be probation, parole, prison, or jail.

Through its history, community corrections has been viewed as less punitive than institutional corrections, with many supporting the view that the goals of community corrections are rooted in rehabilitation and reintegration. Just what the goals of community corrections should be has been the subject of much debate. Clearly, changes in public and political attitudes have resulted in a shift in both policy and practice toward close supervision and an enforcement orientation.

The first selection, "The Emergence of Community Corrections," traces the historical roots and the philosophy that has served to direct policy formulation and the day-to-day activities of those who work in the field. The changes that have occurred throughout community corrections in recent years can be better understood within the context of its history. For example, probation was developed primarily for minor offenders or those whose offense did not warrant severe punishment or incarceration. Over the last two decades, however, probation has emerged as the most often used disposition, with even felony offenders

1

being placed under probation supervision. Parole, as a form of prison release, was the result of prison overcrowding and poor prison conditions. During the 1990s these same factors have caused state parole systems, presently experiencing extreme prison overcrowding, to re-evaluate parole.

In attempting to identify the goals of community corrections, the next selection from the National Institute of Corrections, "Goals of Community Sanctions," is particularly relevant. The major philosophies of just deserts, general deterrence, incapacitation, and rehabilitation are important to our study in that each has become the focus of debate for lawmakers and policymakers in community corrections. What purpose is served when offenders are sanctioned? What are the practical implications when each of the philosophies or goals are utilized? Both questions are answered within this selection. The theme that "differing goals and orientations may lead to differences in practice" is illustrated through an examination of the Victim Offender Reconciliation Programs. These programs were found to be of similar type, but having "distinctly different characteristics because of divergent priorities and goals." This discussion helps students understand how the goals and task responsibilities vary within neighboring jurisdictions.

The next selection, "The Goal Orientation of Adult Probation Professionals," views the seemingly conflicting goals of enforcement and rehabilitation as part of the everyday life of probation and parole professionals. The author reports that practices associated with both of these goals occur within each system. More important, the author notes, is that probation staff and administrators prefer a dual goal system in which offenders receive needed rehabilitative services while at the same time they are closely monitored.

In the selection by James McSparron, "Community Corrections and Diversion," while noting that community corrections has serious drawbacks, the author describes the desirability of continuing to use community correction as a part of the "process" of diverting offenders from institutional corrections. The author sees great potential for the future of community corrections if the system, including the community, is able to coordinate services. He uses such examples as the Community Corrections Acts in Oregon, Kansas, Minnesota, and Mississippi to illustrate how such coordination can occur. In addition, he recommends that states provide needed funding in the form of subsidies to local community corrections as a means of maintaining local autonomy. Imprisonment, he argues, has less potential for success.

# 1

# The Emergence of Community Corrections

## Thomas Ellsworth

Prisons and jails serve as the foundation on which the American correctional system is based. When an offender is sentenced to a period of incarceration, there are a variety of purposes being served, including incapacitation, retribution, deterrence, and rehabilitation. These multiple, often conflicting, goals have led many judicial systems to incorporate community-based programs into their range of sentencing alternatives. Such programs, known as **community corrections,** have been defined as "any correctional-related activity purposively aimed at directly assisting and supporting the efforts of the offender to establish meaningful ties or relationships with the community for the specific purpose of becoming reestablished and functional in legitimate roles in the community" (Doeren and Hageman, 1982:16). In many jurisdictions across the United States, community corrections programs have enabled criminal justice personnel to better deal with a large and varied offender population.

Both institutional and community corrections have evolved in conjunction with societal demands and expectations focusing on the

3

punishment of the offender. Views toward punishment have, for the most part, reflected the evolution of civilized society and the social issues confronted by its citizens. The concept of community corrections first gained widespread recognition in the 1960s, when the expansion of community alternatives received considerable support. Prior to this time, those programs placed under the community corrections umbrella were nothing more than a loosely coupled network of public and private agencies designed to aid the offender. Major components of community corrections and their historical basis are discussed in the following sections.

## Probation

Probation is defined as a sentence or adjudication of conditional and revocable release under the supervision of a probation officer. This concept was first applied in the United States in 1841 when John Augustus, a Boston philanthropist, agreed to supervise a minor offender placed under his care by the courts. Prior court practices loosely resembling probation included such English Common law traditions as benefit of clergy, judicial reprieve, and recognizance.

Probation as it is known today was created by statute in Massachusetts in 1878. By 1915, 33 states had adopted a system of adult probation. For juvenile offenders the probation system grew at a much faster rate due to the general acceptance of child care as the primary purpose of the juvenile justice system.

Almost from its beginning, probation was considered a form of reintegration and rehabilitation rather than a form of punishment. This ideology, however, was not met with total acceptance by all segments of society. Professionals in the field, particularly police chiefs and prosecutors, viewed probation as too lenient and an undeserved "second chance" for the offender. In addition, police officials feared that offenders placed in the community would continue their criminal ways and thus endanger the community. The federal probation system was not established until 1925, after detractors had previously defeated more than a half dozen attempts at creating such a system.

Today, probation is the most frequently utilized community sanction. Most adult probation is organized on the state level, often with parole supervision. In twelve states, probation remains a function of the judiciary or is a combination of state and judicial administration and funding. The challenge of probation professionals in the 1990s will be to respond to critics who charge that the system is ineffective in its efforts to adequately supervise the offender and protect the community. This criticism is especially leveled with regard to felony probation. Petersilia (1985) has reported that a significant number of offenders placed on probation for felony offenses were rearrested and reconvicted, again for committing such offenses as burglary/theft, robbery, or other violent crimes—those which most concern the public. In fact, as Petersilia reports, only 35 percent managed to "stay clean" during the 40 month period following their probationary sentence. As the number of probationers steadily increases, probation professionals will increasingly utilize such programs as close supervision, risk assessment, intensive supervision programs, electronic monitoring, and home detention to manage their caseloads.

## Diversion

Diversion is considered an alternative to formal processing. The definition formulated by the National Advisory Commission on Criminal Justice Standards and Goals describes diversion as "formally acknowledged and organized efforts to utilize alternatives to initial and continued processing into the justice system. To qualify as diversion, such efforts must be undertaken prior to adjudication and after a legally prescribed action has occurred." Many would acknowledge that the criminal justice system requires a certain degree of flexibility in order to meet the varied and complex needs of citizens. Diversion provides that flexibility.

Diversion as a formally recognized component of the community corrections system is a recent development, originating in 1965 in Genesee County, Michigan. Keeping in mind the need to create a more flexible criminal justice system, supporters of diversion viewed it as a means to reduce the stigma resulting from being processed through the system. Thus, deficiencies in the "system" became the impetus for establishing diversion programs.

Shortly after the initiation of this first adult diversion program, the President's Crime Commission Report in 1967 urged that "dispositional alternatives to adjudication must be developed for dealing with juveniles, including agencies to provide and coordinate services and procedures to achieve necessary control without unnecessary stigma" (President's Crime Commission, 1967:81). Supporters of pre-trial diversion programs argued that the creation of formal diversion programs would serve the multiple purposes of rehabilitating the offender while at the same time relieving lengthy court dockets, reducing commitments to probation and prison, and providing a more efficient system of service delivery to the offender.

Diversion programs for adults and juveniles flourished during the late 1960s and throughout most of the 1970s. The reduction in federal funds (which had supported the creation and operation of diversion programs) had a significant impact on program availability. Many diversion programs that operated on the local level were forced to seek sources of alternative funding. Some programs survived, others became part of probation systems, and others simply ceased to exist.

Today, many diversion programs are affiliated with the county prosecutor's office. Some such programs have gained public confidence and support by accepting low-risk, low-priority cases. However, critics have charged diversion with "widening the net of social control" over the offender and doing nothing more than serving the political interests of the jurisdiction (Matthews, 1988). The outlook for diversion programs is uncertain. It is quite likely that they will again take on importance as state after state seeks to limit the formal processing of offenders and to reduce the number of offenders entering prison.

### Prisons and Parole

Parole is generally defined as the conditional release of an offender from a correctional institution to serve part of the unexpired sentence in the community under the custody of the state and the supervision and treatment of a parole officer (Doeren and Hageman, 1982). Unlike probation supervision, parole requires that the offender must have first served a minimum period of time in a prison or correctional facility, that minimum sentence being set by statute. Parole is closely aligned with a system of indeterminate (indefinite) sentencing in which an administrative body, often referred to as a parole board, uses release guidelines or other eligibility criteria to determine the release date of the offender as well as the conditions of the parole.

As early as the seventeenth century, England transported prisoners to the American colonies as a means of dealing with severe economic pressures and an overcrowded labor market. Prisoners were sold to the highest bidder and were considered indentured servants rather than prisoners. In the mid-1800s Alexander Maconochie, superintendent of the Norfolk Prison Colony located of the coast of Australia, developed the "ticket of leave" system. Release was earned through a system of "marks" achieved through hard work and good behavior. A similar Irish system was developed a decade later by Sir Walter Crofton.

Early American prison sentences were *determinate* or definite terms. Prison release, when it occurred, was done by governors in order to relieve prison overcrowding. As American society moved into the mid-1800s and as immigration, industrialization, and urbanization accelerated, prisons were characterized by overcrowding and poor conditions. Well-behaved inmates were first rewarded with a reduction in sentence under the "good time" laws of New York in 1817, a practice which allowed for a reduction of up to 25 percent of the inmate's sentence. By 1869, twenty-three states had similar "good time" laws.

It became clear that the same conditions which characterized early American prisons, overcrowding and poor conditions, would serve as the impetus for the rapid development of parole.

Throughout its history, parole has not been without its critics. Much of the dissatisfaction has focused on the performance of the decision-making body, the parole board. Until recently, selection for release was an arbitrary decision on the part of the board, relying on subjective data, moral judgments, and, as the critics charge, bias against certain types of offenders. Parole boards were further criticized for lacking professional expertise and training. With few exceptions, board members were political appointees. Moreover, large caseloads usually permitted the board to spend only a few minutes hearing each case, and in cases where parole was denied, the underlying reasons were not adequately explained to the inmate.

In 1971 the American Friends Service Committee published *Struggle for Justice*, which focused attention on the longstanding belief that parole and indeterminate sentences could be understood in light of individual pathology and could be best dealt with by treating the offender. This approach, known as the *correctional medical model*, considered offenders to be "sick," treated them within the confines of the institution, and released them when "cured." The job of corrections professionals was to diagnose the problem, and then administer an appropriate treatment program. The Committee, in its criticism, noted that the medical model ignored environmental factors such as economics, unemployment, and discrimination. Perhaps the most damaging finding, one which ultimately led to several states abandoning parole in favor of *determinate* sentencing, was that rehabilitative efforts had "no appreciable effect on recidivism" (Martinson, 1974:25). This conclusion was reached after an examination of 231 studies of correctional rehabilitative programs. The movement to limit the use of parole had begun. Fogel's *justice model* (1975) and von Hirsch's concept of *just deserts* (1976) pointed out the disparity of treatment of the criminal offender as well as the inequities in the sentencing process. To correct the inequities in sentencing and parole practice, state after state moved to limit judicial discretion and the powers of the parole board.

To date, fourteen states have abolished indeterminate sentencing and parole. An examination of national parole population trends, however, suggests that release on parole is still widely used, though the rate has declined significantly over the last 13 years. As Table 1 indicates, parole accounted for 40 percent of those released from prison in 1990. This is a significant decline from 1977, when almost 72 percent of all offenders released from prison were released under parole supervision. The fastest-growing type of release decision is *supervised mandatory release*, often used in states that have abolished parole and indeterminate sentencing.

Table 1

## State prison releases, by method, 1977-90

| Year | Total releases from prison | Percent of prison releases | | | | | | | | |
|---|---|---|---|---|---|---|---|---|---|---|
| | | | Conditional releases | | | | | Unconditional releases | | |
| | | All | Discretion-ary parole | Supervised mandatory release | Probation | Other* | Expiration of sentence | Commu-tation | Other |
| 1977 | 115,213 | 100% | 71.9% | 5.9 | 3.6% | 1.0% | 16.1% | 1.1% | .4% |
| 1978 | 119,796 | 100 | 70.4 | 5.8 | 3.3 | 2.3 | 17.0 | .7 | .5 |
| 1979 | 128,954 | 100 | 60.2 | 16.9 | 3.3 | 2.4 | 16.3 | .4 | .6 |
| 1980 | 136,968 | 100 | 57.4 | 19.5 | 3.6 | 3.2 | 14.9 | .5 | .8 |
| 1981 | 142,489 | 100 | 54.6 | 21.4 | 3.7 | 3.1 | 13.9 | 2.4 | 1.0 |
| 1982 | 157,144 | 100 | 51.9 | 24.4 | 4.8 | 3.6 | 14.4 | .3 | .6 |
| 1983 | 191,237 | 100% | 48.1% | 26.9% | 5.2% | 2.5% | 16.1% | .5% | .6% |
| 1984 | 191,499 | 100 | 46.0 | 28.7 | 4.9 | 2.7 | 16.3 | .5 | .9 |
| 1985 | 203,895 | 100 | 43.2 | 30.8 | 4.5 | 3.0 | 16.9 | .4 | 1.2 |
| 1986 | 230,672 | 100 | 43.2 | 31.1 | 4.5 | 4.6 | 14.8 | .3 | 1.4 |
| 1987 | 270,506 | 100 | 40.6 | 31.2 | 4.4 | 5.7 | 16.2 | 1.0 | .9 |
| 1988 | 301,378 | 100 | 40.3 | 30.6 | 4.1 | 6.0 | 16.8 | 1.0 | 1.2 |
| 1989 | 364,434 | 100% | 39.1% | 30.5% | 4.4% | 8.9% | 16.0% | .2% | .9% |
| 1990 | 394,682 | 100% | 40.5 | 29.6 | 5.3 | 10.6 | 13.1 | .1 | .9 |

Note: The data are from the National Prisoner Statistics reporting program. The total releases from State prison are those for which the method of release was reported. Deaths, unspecified releases, transfers, and escapes were not included. Altogether, 419,783 persons were released or removed from State prisons in 1990.

*Other conditional releases include prisoners discharged under special procedures that included early release because of crowding, supervised work furloughs, release to home detention, release to community residence, release to special programs with required supervision, supervised reprieves, and emergency releases. Approximately 93% of the 41,837 "other conditional releases" in 1990 occurred in 5 States: Arizona, Connecticut, Florida, Georgia, and Oregon.

Source: Bureau of Justice Statistics. Probation and Parole 1990. U.S. Department of Justice, 1991.

As reported by the U.S. Department of Justice, Bureau of Justice Statistics, "The percentage of supervised mandatory releases from prison increased five-fold over the past 12 years, from about 6 percent of all releases in 1977 to nearly 30 percent in 1990."

What the future holds for parole in view of national attention on prison overcrowding, poor conditions, and violence is a subject which will likely remain a significant political and criminal justice policy concern.

## Halfway Houses

A halfway house is a transitional residence for criminal offenders, usually upon release from a prison or jail. Originating in England and Ireland in the early 1800s, the concept spread to the United States but was not enthusiastically embraced by the public or the criminal justice system. While houses of refuge for juvenile offenders were established in New York in 1825 and in Boston the following year, consistent opposition curtailed the spread of the halfway house movement through much of the nineteenth century. Few publicly funded facilities existed. Opponents feared that residents might "contaminate" one another, spreading criminality as they would a virus. During this time, private groups, often religiously affiliated, initiated the development of some halfway facilities for offenders exiting prison. Shelters for ex-offenders were opened in Philadelphia in 1889, and were followed by similar developments in Illinois, California, Louisiana, Iowa, Ohio, Texas, and Florida. Local law enforcement opposed the shelters and, surprisingly, so to did parole authorities, since association with former prisoners was forbidden as a condition of parole.

The 1950s and 1960s saw a rapid development of halfway house facilities in both the public and private sector. Through the work of the International Halfway House Association (IHHA), halfway house programs developed high standards in both practice and management.

Today, most states either operate their own facilities or contract for offender residential services with a private organization, such as the Salvation Army. Like many residential programs based in the community, consistent opposition comes from neighbors who fear that the halfway house will be a negative influence on the community. Some studies have shown halfway houses to reduce recidivism while at the same time serving as a viable alternative to incarceration. The cost savings of keeping an offender in a halfway house versus the cost of incarceration in a state prison should increase the appeal of halfway house facilities. Yet, the literature on halfway houses has also shown that they can be plagued by poor planning and an inability to link with community resources designed to aid offenders. If such facilities are to survive they must engage in comprehensive planning in which the community plays a major role.

## Work Release

Temporary release programs, often referred to as *work release*, are designed to prepare an inmate for eventual release into the community. The focus is either on work or study and involves the release of the inmate to a job or schooling, followed by reincarceration during nonwork (nonschool) hours. During working hours, inmates labor in a manner similar to other workers. They are paid the prevailing wage for their work, though in many instances are required to reimburse the correctional system (prison or jail) for all or a portion of the cost of their confinement. The type of correctional facility and its location are important factors in the success of work release programs. Facilities located near urban areas usually have considerable employment opportunities for its inmates. Facilities in rural areas have limited employment opportunities and it is harder for inmates to become part of the community and to move about unnoticed.

The first work release legislation was passed in 1913 in Wisconsin to provide work release for misdemeanants in county jails. The pattern of growth was relatively slow, with only four states providing work release programs by the mid-1950s. In 1957, state legislation in North Carolina permitted work release for misdemeanant state prisoners, later to be extended to allow convicted felons to participate.

Correctional systems today are very sensitive to the type of offender placed on work release. A single offender who commits a serious crime while on work release can greatly affect the release opportunities for other inmates. Proper selection is a difficult task. Correctional systems tend to be very cautious in their selection process, often ruling out offenders who have committed aggressive/assaultive offenses, sex crimes, and drug-related offenses.

Unlike its halfway house counterpart, work release centers are most often publicly funded, operating on the federal, state, and local level. Despite the prison overcrowding faced by most state correctional systems, no more than 10 percent of a state's prison population is on work release at any given time, while on the average only 2 percent participate. States vary in their use of work release. For example, Florida, with a state prison population of more than 33,000 has almost 2,900 inmates on work release; on the other hand Texas, with a prison population of close to 40,000, has none. Recent figures report almost 15,000 state inmates on work release, while the number of local inmates, usually from county jails, is unknown. Approximately 900 inmates have access to study release programs, a low figure when one considers the number of people incarcerated nationwide. Perhaps limited state budgets for such programs, as well as the negative public attitude toward programs designed to treat or help inmates, may explain their limited use. Community resistance has done more to limit the growth of work release than any other obstacle faced by correctional administrators. The future of work release depends upon the ability of correctional administrators to properly integrate participants into the community. At this time it does not appear that any state is contemplating significant change in its use of work release.

## Intermediate Punishments

Many offenders are jailed or imprisoned because adequate and credible community punishments do not exist. In addition, judges often utilize jails and prisons for sentencing dispositions because they believe an offender's crime is too serious to warrant placement on ordinary probation. The 1980s ushered in a new concept in the punishment of offenders, known as *intermediate punishments*. This phrase refers to all punishments lying between prison and "ordinary" probation. Such punishments are important to the study of community corrections because they have, in most instances, been incorporated into existing community correctional agencies, particularly probation and parole agencies. Intermediate punishments include fines, community service orders, supervision fees, house arrest, intermittent imprisonment, split sentences, day reporting, electronic monitoring, and intensive supervision. Many have been established as a response to the problem of prison overcrowding and have been presented as a cheaper way of sanctioning the offender while at the same time protecting the community.

Supporters of intermediate punishments contend that these alternatives to incarceration are punitive, intrusive, and crime preventive. Yet, some critics are concerned that the use of intermediate punishments simply "widens the net of social control" over offenders who do not warrant such sanctions. For example, an offender who in the past may have received simple probation supervision may now be eligible for such sanctions as intensive supervision, electronic monitoring, and so on, simply because those alternatives are available in the sentencing jurisdiction.

Moreover, scholars such as Norval Morris and Michael Tonry have pointed out that, in the short run, intermediate punishments are not as cost effective as originally claimed. Further, and perhaps most important, is the contention that alternative punishments must be incorporated into comprehensive sentencing policies if they are to survive. Sentencing reform in the 1980s focused on eliminating or reducing unjustified disparities between punishments, a problem that is likely to reoccur with the inappropriate application of intermediate punishments. The question remains, when and on whom should intermediate punishments be imposed? The answer to this question may set the stage for community corrections in the next century.

## Refererences

American Friends Service Committee. 1971. *Struggle for Justice*. New York: Hill & Wang.

Bureau of Justice Statistics. 1991. *Probation and Parole, 1990*. U.S. Department of Justice.

Doeren, S. E., and Hageman, M. J. 1982. *Community Corrections*. Cincinnati: Anderson Publishing Co.

Fogel, D. 1975. *We Are the Living Proof: The Justice Model for Corrections*. Cincinnati: Anderson Publishing Co.

Martinson, R. 1974. "What Works? Questions and Answers About Prison Reform." *The Public Interest* 35 (Spring).

Matthews, W. G. 1988. "Pretrial Diversion: Promises We Can't Keep." *Journal of Offender Counseling, Services & Rehabilitation* 12(2), 191-201.

National Advisory Commission on Criminal Justice Standards and Goals. 1973. *Report on Corrections*. Washington, DC: U. S. Government Printing Office.

Petersilia, J. *Probation and Felony Offenders*. 1985. National Institute of Justice, U.S. Department of Justice.

President's Commission on Law Enforcement and the Administration of Justice. 1967. *The Challenge of Crime in a Free Society*. Washington, DC: Government Printing Office.

von Hirsch, A. 1976. *Doing Justice: The Choice of Punishments*. New York: Hill & Wang.

# The Goals of
# Community Sanctions

## M. Kay Harris

### Introduction

Suppose that as a probation supervisor, a community corrections administrator, or a correctional policymaker, you are called upon to carry out one of the following responsibilities:

- to establish criteria for selecting work sites for offenders ordered to perform community service;
- to design an intensive supervision program;
- to devise a means of reducing crowding in a local jail; or
- to propose a set of sentencing guidelines for the use of community sanctions.

Your response to any of these tasks would be influenced heavily by the views that you and other key actors hold about the goals of community sanctions. Consider some of the questions you would need to answer. Should community service work placements be tailored to enhance offender rehabilitation or to be punitive and unpleasant? Should

Source: National Institute of Corrections, U.S. Department of Justice, June 1986, 1-27.

intensive supervision be designed to control high risk offenders otherwise likely to be sent to prison or to provide a stronger deterrent to regular probationers? Would judges be more likely to use a halfway house or an electronic monitoring device as an alternative to a jail term? Should sentencing policy try to incorporate all of the various purposes for which community penalties might be employed or be centered around one aim?

This monograph is designed to assist policymakers, administrators, and program managers as they seek to resolve such questions. It stresses the value of clarifying underlying goals and philosophy when assessing current community sanctions or considering new programs and policies. More specifically, the monograph is intended to promote the following purposes:

- to highlight the importance of using a common language;
- to clarify distinctions among major sanctioning philosophies;
- to explore the implications of various philosophies for community sanctions;
- to illustrate how a given sanction can be put to various purposes; and
- to surface the importance of value questions.

Following the definition of community sanctions, the rest of this monograph is divided into two major sections and a conclusion. The first major section revisits the four traditional philosophies of sanctioning, describing their distinctive principles and key features. That section also illustrates how underlying philosophy is translated into practice by exploring how the major features of a sanctioning system — its basis and structure, its key actors, its dispositional criteria, and its characteristic sanctions — might vary depending on the philosophy used to develop it. The first section also notes the existence of other goals and values that need to be addressed in developing and assessing community sanctions.

The second major section moves to a more practical plane, offering examples of ways in which program design and operations can be influenced by the relative weight given to different goals. It also highlights the importance of assumptions made about how the components of a particular program contribute to attaining desired outcomes and suggests that these assumptions should be tested. The concluding section describes some of the ways that the material in this monograph might be utilized by those working to advance the state of the art in community sanctioning.

## Definition of Community Sanctions

The term "community sanctions" is used here to refer to what often are called community penalties, punishment in the community, alternatives to incarceration, field services, dispositional options and programs, and a variety of other names. "Sanctions" are the official responses levied or imposed by the criminal justice system on persons convicted of crimes. This term is broader than "sentences," encompassing such programs as parole or work release that constitute part of the official reactions to unlawful behavior but that are not generally thought of as "sentences." The term "sanctions" also is more neutral than the term "punishments" in that it does not imply what these official responses should be designed to achieve. Sanctions may be assigned for the purposes of punishment, treatment, public protection, deterrence, or a variety of other aims.

It is not always easy to agree on what constitutes a community sanction. In the correctional context, the term "community" may be used to refer to nonsecure environments, provision of services by noncorrectional personnel, the amount and types of offender movement allowed, the extent of citizen involvement, or other program features. Some people consider placement in a local jail a community sanction while others would include only programs that operate outside of institutional walls. For purposes of this monograph, the term "community" will be left intentionally broad, excluding only total confinement in state or federal institutions.

## The Traditional Purposes of Punishment

Many volumes have been written on the major philosophies of punishment. Virtually all discussions about sanctioning include reference to at least the four traditional purposes of punishment: just deserts (or retribution), deterrence, rehabilitation, and incapacitation. Each of the major sanctioning philosophies offers a justification for punishment, proposing reasons why we should punish offenders, and each philosophy carries implications for the nature of penalties that should be used and how they should be administered.

There are important differences among the major philosophies and a major distinction exists between utilitarian and desert perspectives. Deterrence, rehabilitation, and incapacitation are all utilitarian philosophies. Each looks forward to some good believed to follow from criminal sanctions: discouraging potential lawbreakers, helping offenders learn to avoid criminal behavior, or restraining those thought likely to commit future crimes. Each hopes to achieve reduction of crime.

Desert theory, on the other hand, is not future-oriented. Rather, it focuses on the harm done in the past by the offender's criminal act and holds simply that people who commit crimes deserve to be punished for them. This is so whether or not some future good can be expected to result from the punishment. The justification for punishment rests on moral grounds; punishment of offenders as they deserve is a moral imperative.

The relative merits of the utilitarian and just deserts perspectives have received renewed attention in recent years. Supporters of just deserts criticize utilitarian sanctioning goals as being difficult to achieve, likely to result in unfairness to individual offenders, and objectionable because they involve using persons as means to an end. Advocates of utilitarian aims object to the emphasis that just deserts philosophy places on the past and on the offense, arguing that society has a legitimate interest in seeking good consequences for the future when sanctions are imposed and that this requires considering a wider range of information. Many people find some appeal in each of the traditional philosophies, but also recognize that it is not easy to imagine a sanctioning system in which all are given equal weight. This section summarizes major characteristics of the four traditional sanctioning philosophies and suggests ways in which various philosophies may imply differing practices.

### Key Features of the Major Philosophies

*Just Deserts.* This theory also is referred to as retribution, a "justice model," or simply as punishment. If a just deserts theorist is asked, "Why do we punish?", the answer will be simply, "Because it is deserved." Just deserts theory emphasizes equity and proportionality of punishment, stressing that similar offenses should be punished similarly and that the penalty should be in balance, or commensurate, with the seriousness of the crime.

Because the focus is on the offense for which a person stands convicted as the basis for determining the punishment, desert philosophy holds that the amount of punishment should not be influenced by such factors as the offender's presumed need for treatment or predictions about what the offender or others might do in the future. Thus, under desert theory, the sanction imposed in a given case should be based on past proven acts, be similar to that imposed on others guilty of the same offense, and reflect in its severity the relative seriousness of the crime.

*General Deterrence.* This theory sometimes is referred to as general prevention, especially in Europe. It is a utilitarian, future-oriented theory. Specifically, general deterrence seeks to reduce crime by so punishing convicted offenders as to reduce the likelihood that other people will choose to commit crimes because of fear of the punishment. It is focused on mental processes in the sense that how a particular offender is punished does nothing to alter the *ability* of other people to commit crimes; the intent is to affect their *inclinations* to engage in crime.

Because it is concerned with how the punishment meted out to a known offender might affect the future behavior of other potential offenders, general deterrence theory requires the making of predictions. Because it involves prediction, the impact of policies and practices based on general deterrence theory can be assessed empirically. The extent to which the predicted results were achieved can be measured.

*Incapacitation*.    This theory of punishment also is called preventive restraint, isolation, and risk control. Like general deterrence, it is a utilitarian, future-oriented perspective with a crime reduction aim. However, incapacitation focuses on the individual offender rather than on potential offenders and seeks to affect *opportunities* rather than inclinations. Thus, incapacitative sanctions seek to reduce the offender's opportunity to commit additional crimes.

Incapacitation also involves the making of predictions. It requires predicting which offenders are likely to commit future crimes and the types of measures that might effectively restrict their opportunities to reoffend. There also may be a need to predict when restraints imposed safely could be reduced or eliminated. Although many people seem to equate incapacitation with incarceration, a variety of types and degrees of restraint are in common use. Execution results in complete and permanent incapacitation. Such practices as revoking drivers' licenses and providing intensive probation supervision yield partial, and generally temporary, incapacitation.

*Rehabilitation*.    Also called treatment, the third major utilitarian philosophy is aimed at reducing the inclination of individual offenders to commit crimes in the future. This theory is most commonly associated with efforts to meet the needs of offenders for education, vocational training, counseling, or other services. However, it sometimes is defined to include anything done to, with, or for the offender for the purpose of reducing the probability that he or she will choose to engage in criminal behavior. Thus, some people would put specific or individual deterrence—that theory of punishment aimed at reducing the individual offender's inclination to commit crimes through fear of the punishment—in the same category as rehabilitation.

Like the other utilitarian theories, rehabilitation involves making predictions. It requires predicting both whether or not a particular offender is likely to reoffend and how best to intervene in the lives of those believed to require treatment to alter their criminal proclivities. The focus is on what the offender is believed to need to keep him or her from choosing to commit crimes.

Major characteristics of the four traditional sanctioning philosophies are summarized in Chart 1.

### Implications of Different Philosophies for Practice

What would a community sanctioning system look like if any one of the major philosophies were to be used as the sole basis for designing it? Although it is unlikely that any jurisdiction would establish a system based exclusively on one sanctioning philosophy, the process of trying to specify what such a system might look like can help clarify central principles and what they imply for decision making and program design.

In designing a community sanctioning system, the following major issues would need to be addressed:

- What should be the *basis* for determining the sanction?
- What *information* should be used to determine the sanction?
- Who are the *key actors* that should play a role in determining the nature of the sanction?
- *When* (at what point(s)) should the sanction be established?
- What would be the *distinguishing features* of appropriate sanctions?
- What *sanctioning options* would be appropriate under this philosophy?

*Just Deserts.*   In a pure just deserts sanctioning system, the basis for determining the sanction would be primarily, if not exclusively, the seriousness of the conviction offense. Offenses would be ranked on the basis of seriousness and sanctions would be ranked according to severity. Then the intent would be to link the resulting scales so that sanctions would be prescribed that were proportionate to the various offenses.

If matching the seriousness of the crime with a penalty of commensurate severity were the major concern, the legislature, which defines crimes and punishments, clearly would play a major role. Under a pure just deserts philosophy, all sentences could well be fixed by law. If it seemed impractical for the legislature to prescribe the precise penalty to be assigned to each offense, a sentencing guidelines commission or similar body could be given the role of establishing policies to govern the imposition of sanctions in individual cases.

Once clear policies were developed, the task of the sentencing judge would be relatively straightforward. Given the focus back toward the offense, virtually all pertinent information would be known by the point

Chart 1

**Characteristics of Sanctioning Philosophies**

| | Sanctioning Philosophy | | | |
|---|---|---|---|---|
| | Just Deserts | General Deterrence | Incapacitation | Rehabilitation |
| Other Names for This Philosophy | Retribution; Punishment; Justice Model | General Prevention | Risk Control; Preventive Restraint | Treatment; Reformation |
| Justification | Moral Imperative | Crime Prevention | Crime Prevention | Crime Prevention |
| Type of Theory | Non-Utilitarian | Utilitarian | Utilitarian | Utilitarian |
| Crime Prevention Strategy | None | Reduce *Inclination* of *Potential Offenders* to Commit Crimes | Reduce *Opportunity* of *Convicted Offender* to Commit Crimes | Reduce *Inclination* of *Convicted Offender* to Commit Crimes |
| Time Orientation | Past | Future | Future | Future |
| Focus of Theory | Offense | Potential Offenders | Convicted Offender | Convicted Offender |
| Basis for Validity of Theory | Persuasiveness of Moral Argument | Accuracy of Prediction | Accuracy of Prediction | Accuracy of Prediction |

of conviction. If provided at all, presentence reports would be limited
to such issues as assessing the offender's blameworthiness or the harm
done by the crimes as provided in governing guidelines. It would not
be appropriate to include other information about offender risks, needs,
social history, or other characteristics.

A pure just deserts orientation also would carry significant implications for the types of sanctions to be employed. Whatever their nature,
sanctions would need to be unpleasant, with the amount or duration
of punishment reflecting the reprehensibility of the crime. To assure that
similar offenses would be punished similarly, sanctions used should be
relatively easy to standardize and they should not be subject to significant
variations or individualization. The nature and duration of sanctions
should be definite; allowing modification after sentencing would undermine equity and proportionality. Thus, there would be no role for parole
as a method of early release from prison or for other mechanisms that
allow for modifying the original sentence imposed.

Examples of what might be deemed appropriate sanctions under a just
deserts model would be financial penalties (geared to seriousness of
offense), community service work, specified periods of loss of leisure
time or loss of liberty, or other punitive conditions or requirements.

***Incapacitation.***   A sanctioning system based on a pure incapacitation
model would yield quite different answers to each of the questions posed
above. Sanctions would be determined on the basis of predictions about
an individual's likelihood of committing crimes in the future and what
it would take to effectively restrain or control that person. Thus,
considerable information would be needed about the offender (and/or
this *type* of offender) relevant to making such predictions, such as social
and criminal history, drug use, age, and psychological state.

Decisionmaking under a pure incapacitation model would need to be
ongoing; it would be difficult to determine once and for all what a given
offender required by way of controls. It would be preferable to give
personnel involved with offenders on a day to day basis considerable
leeway to vary the sanction as risk or need levels were deemed to have
changed. The legislature, working in the abstract, would be ill-suited
to playing a major role. Rather, persons able to focus on the individual
offender, such as probation officers, guards, caseworkers, psychologists,
psychiatrists, and parole board members would be key.

In determining the types of sanctions most compatible with an
incapacitation orientation, the critical dimension would be effectiveness
in controlling an individual's behavior. An array of physical, environmental, psychological, and social restrictions and controls should be
available, to be assigned on the basis of the individual offender's
proclivities. Appropriate sanctions under an incapacitation model might

include revocation of drivers' or occupational licenses, intensive supervision, curfews, home detention, electronic monitoring, and confinement.

*General Deterrence and Rehabilitation.* Just as there are significant differences between the two models discussed above, selection of any other philosophy as the sole basis for a sanctioning system would be apt to yield different characteristics.

The implications of adopting a general deterrence orientation would be similar in some respects to those consistent with a just deserts philosophy. To best frighten potential offenders, the legislature should make the dread consequences of various crimes vividly clear in advance by establishing mandatory, definite sentences. Unlike a desert perspective, however, a general deterrence thrust would exhibit more concern for the likely impact of penalties prescribed than for the seriousness of the conviction offense. If the community had been exhibiting great concern about prostitution or any other particular type of offense, it might be deemed appropriate to establish far more severe penalties for that crime than a just deserts model would allow.

Adoption of a pure rehabilitation emphasis would have many of the same implications for practice as adoption of an incapacitation model. In both models, the focus would be on individual offenders and how best to influence those deemed likely to reoffend. A great deal of information would be needed on an ongoing basis and considerable discretion should be given to personnel involved with offenders over the course of their correctional experience. However, the types of sanctions appropriate to these two models would be quite different. A rehabilitation focus would place greater emphasis on programs designed to meet offender needs and influence their future choices than on the restrictions and controls characteristic of an incapacitative orientation.

Chart 2 summarizes some of the similarities and differences that would be associated with adopting one or another of the four traditional sanctioning philosophies as the basis for developing a sanctioning system.

## Other Goals and Values

Although this discussion has focused on the four traditional philosophical goals of sanctioning, it is important to acknowledge that other types of goals are important. People involved in developing and administering community sanctions are concerned with a variety of more pragmatic interests. Among the other goals that may provide an impetus for developing or using a particular community sanction are the following: *cost minimization, reduction of prison and jail crowding, helping crime victims,* and *increasing public satisfaction* with the criminal justice system.

Chart 2

**Implications of Sanctioning Philosophies**

| Sanctioning Philosophy | | |
|---|---|---|
| | **Just Deserts** | **General Deterrence** |
| **Basis for the Sanction** | Seriousness of Offense | Predictions About How to Discourage Potential Offenders |
| **Information Needed to Determine the Sanction** | Offense Seriousness Ranking and Proportionate Penalty Ranking | Data About Calculations People Make in Deciding to Commit Crimes |
| **Key Actors** | Legislature; Sentencing Commission | Legislature; Judges; Researchers |
| **Best Time to Determine the Sanction** | Upon Conviction | Upon Conviction |
| **Characteristics of Appropriate Sanctions** | Unpleasant; Easy to Standardize; Definite; Proportionate to Offense | Uniform; Frightening; Definite |
| **Examples of Appropriate Sanctions** | Financial Penalties; Loss of Leisure Time or Liberty; Community Service | Mandatory Prison Terms; Stiff Fines; Shaming |

Chart 2

**Implications of Sanctioning Philosophies (continued)**

| Sanctioning Philosophy | | |
|---|---|---|
| | **Incapacitation** | **Rehabilitation** |
| **Basis for the Sanction** | Predictions of Offender Risk and How to Control Offender Behavior | Predictions of Offender Risk and How to Influence Offender Choices |
| **Information Needed to Determine the Sanction** | Offender Characteristics Related to Risk | Offender Characteristics Related to Treatment |
| **Key Actors** | Risk Assessment Specialists; Offender Supervisors; Parole Boards | Needs Assessment Specialists; Treatment Personnel |
| **Best Time to Determine the Sanction** | After Presentence Investigation; Ongoing | After Presentence Investigation; Ongoing |
| **Characteristics of Appropriate Sanctions** | Efficient in Monitoring and Controlling Behavior; Variable | Effective in Meeting Offender Needs; Variable |
| **Examples of Appropriate Sanctions** | License Revocation; Blood and Urine Testing; Intense Surveillance; Curfews; Confinement | Education; Training; Psychological Services; Individual Treatment Plan |

On another level, a number of personal and organizational goals can affect how community sanctions are conceptualized and administered. Personnel can be expected to have an interest in avoiding loss of power, influence, or discretion and disruptions of established routines and patterns of interaction. Concern for how a particular program will be perceived by the media, elected officials, and a variety of interest groups also may shape the way in which sanctions evolve.

Many important questions relevant to community sanctioning cannot be resolved by assessing effectiveness in achieving underlying goals or consistency with a particular philosophical orientation or practical constraints. Consider, for example, the debate occurring around electronic monitoring or surveillance. Many of the issues center around costs and effectiveness, but a variety of ethical and legal issues also need to be addressed. Some people are troubled by the Orwellian implications (a la 1984) associated with advancements in technological detection and control capabilities. Other people regard such advancements as the benchmarks of a brighter and safer future. The fact that different people view tradeoffs between privacy and crime control differently reflects differences in values.

A number of important value questions related to community sanctioning practices need to be confronted. Some issues concern the types of non-incarcerative sanctions communities will be willing to use. Besides electronic monitoring, other controversial sanctions proposed or in limited use include chemical or surgical castration, administration of electric shocks, and use of chemicals or drugs to influence behavior. Do such sanctions represent undue intrusions on bodily integrity and autonomy or reasonable alternatives to confinement? Are they sufficiently humane to comport with the evolving standards of decency that mark a civilized society? Would they be upheld by the courts?

Other issues involve what may be more subtle, but perhaps no less important, value questions. Consider, for example, concern for equity, an issue that has received considerable attention in discussions regarding such reforms as determinate sentencing, but one that has not been given much attention when community sanctions are being discussed.

Community sanctions have come to involve rather wide variations in terms of relative intrusiveness, intensity, and duration. There is quite a difference between non-reporting probation and a community sanction involving a residential commitment, community service obligations, restitution, payment of court and supervision fees, participation in group counselling, drug testing, and high level surveillance. Yet there has been limited debate about the grounds on which such differences in treatment justifiably can be made and the acceptable limits of variation.

Are decisionmakers comfortable with allowing sanctions to be tailored on the basis of differing offender needs when the result is that the

neediest receive the most punishment? To what extent is it appropriate
to vary sanctions according to perceived risks of recidivism? What if
an offender guilty of a minor offense is believed to present a higher risk
than an offender guilty of a serious offense? Is it justifiable to impose
a more onerous sanction on the lesser offender? Is it acceptable to include
in decisionmaking criteria offender characteristics associated with risk,
such as unemployment or criminal history, when such variables also
are highly correlated with race?

These are just a sample of the significant value questions surrounding
community sanctions and criminal justice practices in general. Although
normative issues are admittedly difficult to resolve, they cannot be
avoided. Failure to confront them directly means that they will be
decided by default, a result that those committed to developing
responsible programs and policies obviously want to avoid.

## The Influence of Goals on Programs

The preceding section described the basic characteristics and central
principles of the four traditional philosophies of punishment. To
illustrate the significant differences among those philosophical
orientations and how those differences might influence the structure,
operation, and programs within a sanctioning system, that section also
explored the implications of utilizing one or another of the philosophies
as the sole basis for dealing with convicted offenders. In reality, of
course, decisions about program design features, dispositional policies,
and other aspects of a sanctioning system rarely proceed from such a
theoretical, "blank slate" position.

New programs often are initiated by someone who has heard about
a restitution center or a community service work program in another
jurisdiction. The response to the suggestion that "we ought to have one
of those here" sometimes is to jump headlong into operational and
implementation questions before consensus has been reached as to why
such a program is needed or what it can be expected to achieve.
Discussion of philosophical goals and "pure" models might seem far
removed from the everyday world of criminal justice decisionmaking.
The truth is, however, that those everyday decisions are linked to, and
reflect, philosophical orientations and goals, whether or not those
connections are stated explicitly.

This section provides examples of how differing goals and orientations
may lead to differences in practice. Victim Offender Reconciliation
Programs are used to illustrate how programs of a given type may have
distinctly different characteristics because of divergent priorities and
goals. That even so practical a question as where an offender ought to
be sent to complete a community service work obligation depends on

philosophy also is discussed. In addition, the value of carefully thinking through and testing assumptions made about the connection between program components and expected outcomes is illustrated with reference to Intensive Supervision Programs.

### The Example of Victim Offender Reconciliation Programs

Programs referred to as Victim Offender Reconciliation Programs (VORPs) have been established in at least 15 American states, with a number of states boasting several such programs. VORPs typically involve efforts to arrange a meeting in a neutral setting between the victim(s) of a crime and the offender(s) who committed it, with a trained mediator present to facilitate a process of discussion aimed at achieving a mutually agreeable way of responding to the situation.

Those involved in operating VORPs generally evidence a high degree of enthusiasm for the concept of facilitating a resolution or reconciliation between victim and offender. They also tend to share a commitment to the goals of humanizing the criminal justice process and seeing to it that offenders make financial restitution to the victims of their crimes. Yet despite a general sense of shared mission and a high degree of consensus on certain goals, significant differences exist among those involved with respect to the priority attached to the goals of providing an alternative to incarceration, promoting reconciliation, and promoting system change.

Some VORP practitioners view reduction in the use of imprisonment as a dominant program aim. They regard VORP as a means of holding the offender accountable for his or her actions while avoiding the debilitating effects of imprisonment. Other VORP practitioners emphasize the value of the healing process believed to occur through reconciliation activities. Regarding crime as something that creates an injury to the community, they stress that social harmony only can be restored by an interpersonal process of involvement that takes seriously and responds to the attitudes, needs, and feelings of both victims and offenders.

Still other VORP practitioners are motivated by deep dissatisfaction with typical American responses to crime as manifested in standard criminal justice practices. They tend to reject the idea that the best way to respond to crime is for the state to take over the situation by seeking to affix blame and impose punishment. They see in the VORP process and the values on which it rests a framework upon which a fundamentally different, competing model of justice could be constructed.

These brief summaries of different emphases may be clarified by considering the relation between each of these orientations and punishment. Those who emphasize VORP as an alternative to incarceration think of participation in VORP as an alternative punishment. Those who emphasize reconciliation are relatively indifferent to the connection between VORP and punishment, seeing them as essentially separate interests. Those seeking system change or development of a new model of justice look to VORP as a means of promoting alternatives to punishment.

Although people emphasizing each of these orientations may see merit in the other positions, it is not easy to reconcile or combine these varied goals in practice. Consider some of the differing operational consequences likely to flow from having one or another of these perspectives as a dominant interest.

Those working to see that VORP is used as an alternative to incarceration need to identify and reach offenders who would be likely to be incarcerated in the absence of the VORP option. Thus, they need to be able to avoid selecting persons for program involvement who would be put on probation. This typically requires delaying intervention until offenders have progressed through several stages of the criminal justice process. It also calls for establishing good working relationships with judges, defense attorneys, prosecutors, probation officers, and others within the system.

People who believe that there is something intrinsically "good" or "right" about involving victims and offenders in a reconciliation process are likely to want to reach and involve as many people as possible. Thus, they would not want to target or limit participation to offenders who are jail- or prison-bound. Rather, they would be interested in receiving referrals from all stages of the criminal justice process, ranging from pretrial intervention with those unlikely to be prosecuted formally to convicted offenders already serving prison terms. Their aim would be maximum feasible participation.

Practitioners primarily interested in systems change are likely to have yet another orientation. Because of their interest in empowering people to take personal control over what happens in response to crime, rather than letting control be taken over by the government, they would not want to be closely associated with criminal justice officials. They would be more likely to want citizens to utilize VORP as an alternative to calling the police or otherwise invoking the formal criminal justice process. Indeed, people with this orientation are likely to see themselves in competition with the criminal justice system, hoping to reduce the system's reach and power by providing an alternative forum for resolving the problems it now takes on.

Thus, while various Victim Offender Reconciliation Programs may involve similar interactions among victims, offenders, and mediators, they also may reflect significant differences in the types of offenders they seek to involve, the way in which referrals are obtained, the timing of intervention, and other features.

## Philosophies Guiding Placements in
## Community Service Order Programs

Programs requiring offenders to perform work without pay as a penalty for their crimes often are promoted as serving multiple purposes. They may be described as advancing offender rehabilitation, making non-incarcerative sanctions more punitive, helping to satisfy community needs for services, enhancing victim satisfaction, or serving other interests. Since all of these objectives may appear to be reasonable, it may be tempting to avoid highlighting one or another as central. However, such an evasion can prove problematic when operational decisions must be made.

Consider as an example the issue of the philosophy under which community service work placements should be made. Some programs emphasize that "the punishment should fit the crime," asserting that the placement should be as unpleasant or as punitive as is warranted by the offense, or even that the penalty should "reflect" the offense, as in requiring drunk drivers to tend to victims of drunk drivers in hospital emergency rooms. Other programs operate with a preference for seeing that the placement is tailored so as to provide maximum benefit to the offender. Still other programs believe that community service placements should be made according to community needs and the skills that offenders offer, seeking to maximize benefits to the locale.

Operationally, these varying orientations would result in very different types of placements, ranging from assignment to such duties as shovelling garbage in a landfill under a punitive philosophy, to place-ment with a youth recreation or education program under a rehabilitation emphasis, to stuffing envelopes or answering the telephone for a non-profit agency under a community needs orientation. Guiding philosophy makes a difference.

## The Example of Intensive Supervision Programs

As the name implies, Intensive Supervision Programs (ISPs) involve more frequent contacts between offenders and their supervising officers and a greater number of restrictions than typically characterize regular probation. In general, ISPs also are intended to serve offenders who pose higher risks or have committed more serious crimes than traditional probationers.

Beyond these common elements, however, ISPs are being operation-alized to include a wide range of additional components. They may involve curfews, home detention, restitution requirements, community service obligations, supervision fee payments, development of self-improvement plans, participation in drug or alcohol programs, financial counseling, community sponsors, educational or employment requirements, stringent enforcement provisions, residential placements, regular urinalysis or breathalyzer tests, unannounced searches, and a variety of other conditions. The incorporation of the many elements beyond increased surveillance reflects the fact that ISPs are being asked to serve a wide range of goals.

Stated program goals may include reducing jail or prison crowding, providing better rehabilitative services, promoting public safety, restoring public confidence in probation, avoiding the costs of construction and facility improvement options, collecting more money from offenders, increasing victim satisfaction, facilitating early identification of offenders likely to get into further trouble, and allowing better matching of resources with offender risks and needs. As "intensive supervision" becomes an increasingly broad catch-all term for both activities and goals, it may be worthwhile to reassess the bases on which ISPs were established and the directions in which they have been evolving.

It is important to acknowledge that Intensive Supervision Programs rest more on assumptions than on empirically derived knowledge. ISPs reflect the assumptions that (1) more contacts between offenders and officers will lead to less unlawful behavior, and (2) more contacts will lead to better detection of unlawful behavior. These assumptions may well prove to be valid, but existing evidence in support of them is scanty.

As to the first assumption, research on New York's ISP, for example, found no significant relationship between the level of offender-officer contacts and probation outcomes. Thus, it may be that intensive supervision is inefficient, yielding no greater return than could be obtained through less monitoring. And even if it is true that "intensive supervision" is more effective than "standard supervision," how intensive does it have to be to yield the desired effects? Are 30 contacts a month more effective than 20?

As to the second assumption, earlier research suggested that intensive supervision led to increased revocations on technical violations but also to fewer convictions for new offenses. Unfortunately, the connection between revocation rates and crime reduction is unclear. It is frequently assumed that an offender who fails to abide by all of the technical conditions is more likely to engage in additional crimes than an offender who presents no difficulties. But if this assumption is not valid, institutional populations may be swelled with persons who would not in fact commit new crimes if retained under community supervision.

To complicate matters even more, it is important to consider the numbers and types of conditions that may be associated with various outcomes. It may be that violation of certain conditions is a good indicator of subsequent criminality, but that violation of other conditions is not. Or, there may be a "critical mass" of conditions, within which most people could successfully cope and comply, but beyond which almost anyone would be likely to get into trouble.

The point is that we know very little about the impact of imposing various numbers and types of conditions and it may not be safe to assume that more is better. For example, many ISPs assign high priority to requiring offenders to make financial restitution to victims, but also impose a number of additional requirements. However, research conducted in Minnesota suggested that adding on other conditions tended to hinder the restitution process.

There is a need for experimentation and research to better inform practitioners and policymakers about the impact of various conditions on various offenders in relation to various goals. This will require care in specifying the goals that are foremost and how various program elements are believed to be connected to attainment of those goals.

## Conclusion

Whenever goals are discussed, it is likely that at least one person present will say something to the effect of, "Well, that's all very interesting, but when are we going to get down to business?" Especially when the focus is on philosophical, as opposed to pragmatic goals, it is difficult for many people to make a meaningful connection between fundamental principles and day to day operational issues and problems. It is important, therefore, to illustrate some of the ways in which spending time thinking and talking about the goals of community sanctions might have a real "payoff" in practice.

The policymakers, program managers, and practitioners for whom this monograph is designed are apt to be involved with programs, policies, and problems, and in each of these areas, they are likely to be engaged in activities involving communication, design, assessment, and reform. This concluding section describes some of the ways in which knowledge and use of information about goals can be applied to each of these areas and activities.

How goal clarification can be helpful may be most readily apparent at the program level. Whether thinking about developing a new program or assessing an existing one, it is necessary to refer back to basic goals. This fact was illustrated above with reference to victim offender reconciliation, community service, and intensive supervision programs. Program managers can benefit by regularly making the effort to recall what their programs were originally designed to achieve, to review their own goals and expectations, and to reexamine the connections between ongoing activities and those goals.

If the jurisdiction adopted a community service program in order to provide an alternative to confinement, is a screening criterion that excludes felony and repeat offenders likely to be serving that aim? Can local resources, such as university faculty, be identified that could help the program develop selection and screening criteria that would distinguish jail-bound offenders more reliably? If revocation rates are rising because of failure of offenders to complete all of the financial obligations imposed on them, should the agency explore new ways of assisting offenders to satisfy such requirements? Would it be feasible to establish a program in which offenders could "work off" court costs and other fees? Could local businesses be persuaded to sponsor special programs to allow offenders to earn the amounts required?

Communication about goals also can be critical at the program level. A probation department's plan to utilize intensive supervision as a "last ditch" step before incarceration for high risk offenders can be sidetracked if sentencing judges decide to use the more intense surveillance as a means of punishing low risk, white collar defendants. A work release center designed to provide transition assistance to offenders nearing their parole dates can be quickly filled if judges use it for sentencing persons convicted of driving under the influence of alcohol. Early efforts to achieve consensus about purpose among those involved or affected by new programs can help minimize such difficulties.

Questions about goals also are key on the policy level. When a system-wide perspective is adopted, it often becomes clear that there is a lack of consensus among key actors throughout the system. The legislature may adopt a new penalty provision in order to frighten potential offenders of a certain type. Faced with a person who has committed such an offense, the sentencing judge may see involvement in a rehabilitation program as the most appropriate sentence. The person who completes the presentence investigation may believe that the offender fits the profile of a high risk offender and requires intensive supervision. Seeing that the offender is placed on probation, the general public may think that the offender has not been punished severely enough. Such divergent orientations often reflect the lack of clear and consistent sentencing policy.

Activities are underway in a number of jurisdictions that are aimed at developing system-wide sanctioning policies to guide the use of community penalties as well as prison terms. A Sentencing Accountability Commission in Delaware, for example, has developed a sanctioning model that incorporates a broader continuum of punishment options and specifies criteria for assigning offenders to one or another of the "accountability levels" established. Impact projections made on the basis of the model suggested a need for more mid-range sanctions between probation and incarceration, illustrating how a system-wide perspective can be of assistance in planning for the allocation of resources as well as in developing more uniform sentencing practices.

A focus on underlying goals also may be extremely useful in shorter-range problem solving. Consider, for example, a situation in which a federal court has ordered that a state's prison population be reduced substantially within a short period of time. All of the policymakers involved may have agreed that the best means of responding to the order is to expedite the release of enough prisoners to meet the cap imposed, and yet disagree about the basis on which such early releases should be made. Some of those involved may think that the best course of action would be for the legislature to act to cut prison terms across the board. Others may prefer a response involving case by case decisions, such as advancing dates of parole release eligibility. In such a situation, taking the discussion back to the philosophical level may be helpful in clarifying the issues and deciding how to proceed. The first option would be more compatible with a just deserts orientation and the second with a risk control or incapacitation orientation. When contrasted in this way, it may be easier for those involved to determine which approach would be more consistent with the overall policy orientation operative in that jurisdiction.

Many jurisdictions faced with crowding in their local jails have difficulty reaching agreement on the best ways of alleviating the problem. Should they try to develop community service orders, residential treatment programs, intensive supervision, electronic monitoring, bail guidelines, conditional release under supervision, or some other set of programs? In many cases, the difficulty encountered is related to failure to assess adequately the purposes the jail now is being asked to serve, as a basis for exploring alternative ways of meeting those interests. If, for example, what is most needed is a penalty more severe than probation for punishing petty offenders, options such as community service work, reparation fees, and victim restitution might fill the bill. Some of the other options, such as intensive supervision or electronic monitoring might be rated as less appropriate because they would involve greater control, and greater expense, than satisfying the primary interest would require. If the major motivation were to respond more effectively to offenders with drug or alcohol problems, then contracting for residential and non-residential treatment services might represent the best course. It is difficult to make sensible choices among all of the alternatives available unless the major goals are clear.

These examples were offered to highlight the significance of the goals of community sanctions at virtually every level of practice and to illustrate the value of taking time to clarify the dominant aims when decisions are being made. It is seldom possible in the criminal justice arena to resolve all conflicting interests, achieve full consensus, and link all activities precisely with agreed upon goals. But the process of exploring goals, philosophy, and values often can be of considerable benefit in efforts to communicate more effectively, improve program design and operations, reach satisfactory compromises on how to respond to pressing problems, and develop more clear and consistent policies.

# 3

# The Goal Orientation of Adult Probation Professionals
## A Study of Probation Systems
### Thomas Ellsworth

## Abstract

*Studies of probation officers over the last twenty years have emphasized the dual goal structure of the probation system. Various researchers have advocated enforcement and surveillance as the primary goal, while others have supported the helping, rehabilitation goal. The present research focuses on the actual and preferred goals of the adult probation systems in two states, one which maintains a centralized, state system, the other, a locally-administered system under the judicial branch. The findings point out that while enforcement is an important goal, so too is the rehabilitation of the offender. Respondents also preferred a dual goal system.*

## Introduction

Since its inception in 1841 when John Augustus first bailed offenders from jail and placed them under "supervision," there has been considerable debate as to what **is** and **should be** the primary purpose

Source: *Journal of Crime and Justice*, Vol. 13, No. 2, 55-76. Copyright © 1990 by Anderson Publishing Co. Reprinted with permission.

of adult probation. The reader would find that throughout probation history the concepts of both enforcement and rehabilitation have received considerable attention in the professional literature, with many authors citing one ideology or orientation as being superior to the other. The last 25 years have yielded a series of role typologies for probation professionals which attempt to reconcile the dichotomous roles played by probation officers as they attempt to cope with seemingly opposing goals. Empirical research which focuses on the implementation of enforcement and rehabilitation as goals of probation and the degree to which probation staff operationalize these goals has been given less attention by the scholars.

At the same time, since development as a formal component of the criminal justice system, there has not been total agreement as to the appropriate governmental level at which the probation system should exist. For example, there are presently 38 states in which the adult probation system is a function of the executive branch of government, with the remainder operating as part of the local judiciary (7 states) or as a state entity functioning exclusively under the judiciary.

Arguments involving the "one best way" to administer the system have been debated for the last 30 years (Killinger 1978). Whether it be the American Bar Association (1978) advocating judicial control or the National Council on Crime and Delinquency (1955) and the National Advisory Commission (1973) supporting a statewide system under executive control, the arguments presented by both sides have not resulted in major changes in the administrative alignment of the probation system.

As the discussion over which method of service delivery system is best has faded in the literature, with few probation systems likely to make radical changes in their configurations in the foreseeable future, more attention has focused on the need to develop a clear-cut mission for the probation system. In addition, various authors have presented new technologies in the probation and parole field which have gained the widespread acceptance of policy-makers, judges, staff, legislators, and the public. Among these have been a model classification system for adult offenders and more recently applied to juvenile offenders, programs of house arrest, electronic monitoring, intensive supervision, community work service, and probation supervision fees, to name just a few. Still other research has focused on offender supervision practices and decision-making by probation officers. For example, Erez (1989) recently pointed out that probation officers tend to stereotype probation offenders and such stereotypes guide the methods used in supervising the offender, especially when the treatment of the probationer is involved. The decisions made by probation staff, according to Erez, are influenced by "gender-role expectations" (p. 307). More recently, Harris,

Clear, and Baird (1989) reported that community supervision officers (probation and parole officers) have shifted their attitudes away from client assistance, with a new emphasis upon enforcement and surveillance.

The present study focuses on the extent to which adult probation professionals employed in two midwestern state probation systems support the ideologies of enforcement and rehabilitation as the actual and preferred goals of the profession in their respective states.

## Conceptual Framework

Like most components of the criminal justice system, the system of adult probation has undergone discernible change over the last 25 years. There are few who would argue that the dominant ideology in the 1980s for both institutional as well as community corrections is one of enforcement and punishment. This is exemplified through such changes as mandatory sentencing for specific offenses, abolishing of parole in several states, the drastic increase in prison and jail populations, and the implementation of more punishment-oriented and community protection-oriented programs such as intensive probation supervision, house arrest and electronic monitoring. The term "felony probation" aptly describes a growing number of offenders released into the community under probation supervision who in years past would have been incarcerated. In spite of the new attempts to punish the offender in the community, the critics continue to argue that probation remains "soft" on criminals. From its earliest beginning, probation has been viewed as a lesser sanction and certainly from its roots in the mid-1800s, as a more humane method of punishing the offender. More recently, the literature has become adept at pointing out the fact that the probation system suffers from an unclear statement of purpose and that the means to reach the desired goals of enforcement and rehabilitation are equally unclear (Gray 1986). Clear (1985) believes that the arguments over the purpose of probation basically occur on two levels. First, experts on probation and parole have not agreed as to what "should be" the purpose of probation. In addition, experts and practitioners alike have disagreed on "the philosophy that actually guides their efforts" (p. 35). Many analysts have attempted to separate the enforcement goal of probation from that of rehabilitation or treatment. The fact that both goals often conflict has been well documented in the literature (Ohlin, Piven, and Pappenfort 1956; Glaser 1969; Sigler and Bezanson 1970; Klockars 1972; Czajkoski 1973; Tomaino 1975; Studt 1978; McCleary 1978; von Hirsch and Hanrahan 1979; Lipsky 1980; Allen, Eskridge, Latessa, and Vito 1985).

The problem of what should be the goal(s) of the probation system has led several authors to suggest different and conflicting goals as the primary purpose of the system. Proponents such as Stanley (1978) and von Hirsch and Hanrahan (1979) argue that the primary goal of the probation system is treatment and rehabilitation. They view the enforcement goal as unfair and impractical.

Conversely, others have argued that the primary goal of the probation system is crime reduction and protection of the community, with treatment-oriented activities better left to agencies in the community better able to meet the social needs of the offender (Martinson and Wilk 1977; McAnany, Thomson and Fogel 1984; American Friends Service Committee 1971). Duffee has argued that a single dimensional model (enforcement or rehabilitation) provides no resolution to the conflict between the various models that support either the surveillance, law enforcement goal of probation service or the rehabilitation, treatment goal. Some have argued that since the probation system has been unable to reconcile the conflicting goals of enforcement and rehabilitation, probation should focus only on the enforcement role (Duffee 1984; Rosecrance 1986). As a means of reconciling the problem over purpose, Allen et al. (1979) and Fogel (1980) have emphasized the function of probation as a legal disposition, thus viewed as enforcers of the court's order granting probation. Focusing on the historical foundations on which probation was developed, Gray (1986) views probation as a "legislative grace," allowing for the co-existence of both the enforcement and rehabilitation models.

Within the correctional field, the conflict over the custody (enforcement) and treatment (rehabilitation) goals of the prisons has received ongoing attention from those who study organizations and the behavior of those who work in these settings. For example, Zald (1962) reports that goal conflict within a prison is the result of multiple goals, with vaguely defined means of reaching these goals. The correctional facility where security is the exclusive organizational goal is not likely to exist. Institutions by their nature are expected to balance the dual goal expectations of maintaining security while at the same providing programs to the inmate population. Goode (1960) points out that institutional staff who attempt to fulfill conflicting role expectations are likely to experience role strain, role conflict and, as reported by Kahn (1978), reduced satisfaction with their jobs and decreased confidence in the goals of the organization. In the field of juvenile justice, the choice between helping the child and protecting the public has become a common element of all detention decisions (Gottfredson 1968). Street, Vinter, and Perrow (1966) have earlier acknowledged the difficulty associated with developing organizational goals as arising from a lack of clarity coming from the parent organization. Within the mental health profession, King and Raynes (1968) present the conflict over patient control and patient care as a problem which must be resolved by professionals in the field. In the case of probation, the lack of clarity, appears to emanate from the legislature, the courts, the public, and the profession itself and has been part of the history of probation almost from its inception. In the 1980s this problem has been accentuated by a probation profession which has willingly accepted both goal orientations, appearing to be "all things to all people" for the sake of surviving during times when public support for community corrections is at a relatively low level when compared to institutional corrections.

There appears to be widespread consensus among researchers and practitioners that the adult probation system will not become "revitalized" until a clear-cut statement of mission is developed (Breed 1984; Harris 1984; McAnany 1984; Petersilia 1985). A 1985 Rand Corporation report stated that the mission of adult probation should be "redefined, limited, and explicitly stated, by statute, if necessary" (Petersilia et al. 1985: 388-89). While a discussion of which are the appropriate methods necessary to reach the goal(s) of probation are beyond the scope of this research, some would argue that the field had not and cannot achieve the status of a profession under conditions in which there is a "lack of clarity in organizational goals and little clear feedback and communication among administrative, supervisory, and line personnel" (Lawrence 1984:20).

When confronted with conflicting and ambiguous goals (as are found in most public bureaucracies), human service workers such as probation officers utilize the wide discretion given to them by the system. The result is that these "street-level bureaucrats" modify the agency's intended mission for the sake of coping with ambiguity, stress, large caseloads, and in some cases, danger (Lipsky 1980). Allen et al. (1985) conclude that probation officers are aware of the dichotomy which exists between the goals of enforcement and rehabilitation, but a clear consensus over which style of offender supervision "should dominate" has not emerged (p. 137). The focus of the present research is to determine the specific orientation toward practices of enforcement and rehabilitation and if a specific orientation is preferred by probation staff, supervisors, and administrators.

## Methodology

### Population and Sample

The population consisted of the 870 probation staff members, supervisors, and administrators employed in the state in which probation services are judicially controlled and the 536 staff members, supervisors, and administrators employed in the state in which probation is an executive function. A listing of all probation and court services staff, published by the state's professional probation organization and a staffing table were used to identify potential subjects in both states. Using a table of random numbers, 50 percent of the population was selected for a sample of 703 subjects. In one of the two states under study, a large metropolitan area employed one-third of all officers employed in that state. A cluster sample by geography reflecting the size of this office relative to the entire state probation population was drawn. This procedure was necessary because of the large proportion of the states' probation staff employed in one particular area.

**Instrumentation**

Data collection was accomplished with the use of a 49-item questionnaire, the Adult Probation Goal Inventory, constructed specifically for this project for the purposes of eliciting the perceptions of probation professionals relative to both the actual and preferred goals of the system. Items were drawn and classified from an extensive review of the literature, interviews with probation professionals, and the researchers' own experiences as an adult probation officer and supervisor. A preliminary step involved the piloting of the questionnaire to 33 professional staff from both states. Interviews with staff produced feedback which resulted in several changes reflected in the final draft. Efforts were made to eliminate jargon and descriptions of practices which were not easily understood by respondents. Since similar programs and duties may have dissimilar titles and names, it was important to provide descriptors which were understood by all subjects. For example, one state has developed an intensive supervision program while the other state, having similar goals and practices, referred to their program as community sentencing. The final instrument contained 30 goal statements, 17 of which were classified by probation professionals as typifying enforcement-oriented practices in probation work. For example, "The primary function of this office is the protection of the community" as well as "Have the same legal power of arrest as police officers" were two statements among the 17 which reflected a law enforcement orientation. An additional 13 items reflecting probation practice were agreed to reflect an offender rehabilitation orientation as a goal of the department. The rehabilitation orientation was reflective of such statements as, "The primary function of this office is the rehabilitation of the offender" and "Call to set employment interview for probationers" as goals of the department. Subjects were requested to respond to each of the 30 goal statements using the following six-level "Importance Scale":

Of Top Importance (TI)
Of Great Importance (GI)
Of Average Importance (AI)
Of Little Importance (LI)
Of No Importance (NI)
Don't Know/Can't Say (DK)

## Results

Of the 703 questionnaires mailed, 512 were returned and found usable (a return rate of 72 percent). Individual questionnaires in which the respondent failed to respond to at least 15 of the 30 goal statements were not used for analysis. The state in which probation is an executive function, or state controlled, had a return rate of 93 percent, while the state in which probation is judicially controlled on the local level had a return rate of 58 percent. The disparity in return rates between states was attributable to a low return from a large department in the state in which probation is judicially controlled. In addition, the researcher had once worked in the state which had the higher rate of return, and had gained the support of top administrators. The state with the higher return rate also maintained a research division, and was centrally administered. The other state did not have a research unit per se, and was more strongly administered at the local level.

Table 1 presents the demographic data of the respondents from the two states. Using the cross-tabulation procedure, several demographic variables were found to be statistically significant at the .05 level. Among these was gender, in which 47.5 percent of the state-run and 37.7 percent of the judicially-run staff were female. Fifty-two percent of the state-run staff and 61.9 percent of the judicially-run staff were reported as males. Race was determined to be statistically significant, with 89.8 percent of those employed in the state probation system and 85.8 percent of the staff in the judicial system reported as being White/Caucasian. Less than 10 percent of the respondents from the state system and judicial system were reported as being Black (9.8 and 9.7 percent, respectively). The judicial system reported 2.6 percent of the respondents being Hispanic, while the state system had no respondents in this racial group. The level of educational attainment differed among respondents from the two states. The staff employed in the state system reported a higher educational level than did respondents employed in the judicial system. No statistically significant differences were found to exist among respondents from the two states on the demographic variables of age, position, degree major, orientation of the respondents' degree program, years of probation experience, the presence of and type of previous work experience.

Table 1

**Characteristics of the Sample**

| | State system | | Judicial system | | Chi-square value |
|---|---|---|---|---|---|
| | N | Pct. | N | Pct. | |
| Total | 244 | | 268 | | |
| Gender | | | | | |
| Male | 127 | 52.0 | 166 | 61.9 | |
| Female | 116 | 47.5 | 101 | 37.7 | 5.10990[a] |
| Race | | | | | |
| White | 219 | 89.8 | 230 | 85.8 | |
| Black | 24 | 9.8 | 26 | 9.7 | |
| Hispanic | 0 | 0.0 | 7 | 2.6 | |
| Other | 0 | 0.0 | 4 | 1.5 | 10.2470[a] |
| Age | | | | | |
| 21-24 | 10 | 4.1 | 14 | 5.2 | |
| 25-34 | 116 | 47.5 | 131 | 48.9 | |
| 35-46 | 91 | 37.3 | 87 | 32.5 | |
| 47-55 | 18 | 7.4 | 20 | 7.5 | |
| 56-up | 8 | 3.3 | 11 | 4.1 | 3.79644[b] |
| Position | | | | | |
| Probation Officer | 191 | 78.2 | 199 | 74.3 | |
| Supervisor/ Admin. | 51 | 20.9 | 67 | 25.0 | 2.13347[c] |
| Caseload | | | | | |
| 0-50 | 28 | 11.5 | 40 | 14.9 | |
| 51-100 | 150 | 61.5 | 82 | 30.6 | |
| 101-150 | 16 | 6.6 | 55 | 20.5 | |
| 151-200 | 0 | 0.0 | 10 | 3.0 | |
| 201-up | 2 | .8 | 8 | 3.0 | 57.06903[d] |
| Experience (years) | | | | | |
| 0-2 | 116 | 47.5 | 132 | 49.3 | |
| 3-8 | 87 | 35.7 | 100 | 37.3 | |
| 9-15 | 35 | 14.3 | 32 | 11.9 | |
| 16-25 | 6 | 2.5 | 4 | 1.5 | 1.34829[b] |

Table 1 (continued)

**Characteristics of the Sample**

| | State system | | Judicial system | | Chi-square value |
|---|---|---|---|---|---|
| | N | Pct. | N | Pct. | |
| Educational level | | | | | |
| High school | 0 | 0.0 | 6 | 2.2 | |
| Some college | 8 | 3.3 | 23 | 8.6 | |
| College degree | 123 | 50.4 | 141 | 53.6 | |
| Some post-grad | 55 | 22.5 | 50 | 18.7 | |
| Master's degree | 48 | 19.7 | 38 | 14.2 | |
| Post-M.A. | 10 | 4.1 | 8 | 3.0 | 15.18768[d] |
| Office size | | | | | |
| 0-10 | 94 | 38.5 | 88 | 32.8 | |
| 11-25 | 88 | 36.1 | 61 | 22.8 | |
| 26-50 | 22 | 9.0 | 35 | 13.1 | |
| 51-110 | 15 | 6.1 | 31 | 11.6 | |
| 111-350 | 24 | 9.8 | 45 | 16.8 | 19.48750[d] |
| Office location | | | | | |
| Small town | 6 | 2.3 | 6 | 2.2 | |
| Town | 28 | 11.5 | 31 | 11.6 | |
| Small city | 55 | 22.5 | 71 | 26.5 | |
| City 50,000 | 36 | 14.8 | 65 | 24.3 | |
| City 150,000 | 22 | 9.0 | 18 | 6.7 | |
| Metro area | 68 | 27.9 | 52 | 19.4 | |
| Suburban | 27 | 11.1 | 24 | 9.0 | 12.02192[b] |

[a] $p < .05$

[b] $p > .05$

[c] $p = .05$

[d] $p < .01$

Organization and job-related demographics indicated several differences among the two states. Among the differences was caseload size, with the officers in the state system maintaining smaller average caseloads (81.73 in the state system and 97.04 in the judicial system). The number of staff employed in the office also differed, with more respondents from the state system (74.6 percent) working in smaller offices (those offices with 25 or fewer staff) than did those similarly employed in the judicial system (55.6 percent). The type of community setting, or the size of the area in which the office was located, did not differ among respondents from the two states.

Table 2 presents the rank order based on overall mean score (with 1 highest and 6 lowest) of the 13 actual enforcement and rehabilitation items ranked as being of "top importance" or of "great importance" by the respondents (mean of 1.00 to 2.99). Among this group, seven items of enforcement and six items of rehabilitation orientation are found. Table 2 also contains the ANOVA summary of each of the actual enforcement and rehabilitation items found to be of "top importance" and of "great importance" between states. The results report significant

Table 2

**Analysis of Actual Enforcement and
Rehabilitation Items by State**

| Item Descriptor | Mean | | Signifi-cance |
| --- | --- | --- | --- |
| | State system | Judic. system | |
| Notify courts/law violation[e] | 1.79 | 1.92 | NS |
| Require alcohol treatment[r] | 1.87 | 2.12 | .01 |
| Protection is office function[e] | 2.06 | 2.35 | .01 |
| Stringent rule application[e] | 2.37 | 2.12 | .01 |
| Rehab. is office function[r] | 2.20 | 2.30 | NS |
| Provide counseling[r] | 2.17 | 2.36 | NS |
| Provide close supervision[e] | 2.55 | 2.13 | .01 |
| Refer to voc. counseling[r] | 2.50 | 2.59 | NS |
| Notify courts/tech. violation[e] | 2.58 | 2.66 | NS |
| Refer vocational rehab.[r] | 2.35 | 2.93 | .01 |
| Permit violators doing okay to continue on probation[r] | 2.50 | 2.96 | .01 |
| Require testing for drugs[e] | 2.18 | 3.50 | .01 |
| Get permission from officer before leaving area[e] | 2.84 | 3.07 | .05 |

[e] Denotes item of actual enforcement orientation.
[r] Denotes item of actual rehabilitation orientation.

differences existing between states regarding the importance placed on the goal "of community protection," with the state probation staff identifying this goal as being more important than did the staff employed in the judicial system. Similar findings were achieved with the enforcement goals of "stringent application of probation rules," and "closely supervise all probationers" except this time the judicial probation staff viewing the goal as being more important than did staff in the state system. Of the remaining enforcement orientation items ranked as being of top importance or of great importance, the state probation staff ranked the goals of the "Use of urinalysis in offender supervision" and "Granting permission before leaving the state" as being more important than judicial probation staff. Finally, the ANOVA summary of the six actual rehabilitation goals which were identified by respondents as being of top importance or of great importance (mean of 1.00 to 2.99) are reported. The staff in the state probation system were identified as being statistically different from judicial probation in their orientation toward practices of rehabilitation. In three of the goals, the state probation staff viewed the goal as being more important than did the judicial staff. No statistical differences existed among respondents between states on the three remaining actual rehabilitation items.

Table 3 reports the mean rankings of the ten preferred enforcement and rehabilitation goal statements which were identified by respondents as being "of top importance" and "of great importance." From this list are found five items identified as reflecting practices of enforcement and five items of rehabilitation. Table 3 contains the results of the analysis of the ten preferred goals in which the probation staff from both systems were identified as being significantly different on three measures of goal orientation. First, the state probation staff identified one of the preferred goals ("Community Protection") as being more important, while the judicial probation staff viewed two goals ("Stringent Application of Probation Rules" and "Closely Supervise All Probationers") as being most important. The remaining goal statements, while seen as important, were not identified as being significantly different among respondents from the two states.

## Discussion

Based on this analysis, several conclusions can be drawn about the two probation systems who participated in the present research. First, probation professionals clearly identify the existence of a dual-goal system of probation in each state. In spite of the perceived public sentiment against rehabilitation, evidence exists that this goal holds considerable importance among probation professionals. Rehabilitation

Table 3

**Analysis of Preferred Enforcement and
Rehabilitation Items by State**

| Item Descriptor | Mean | | Signifi-cance |
| --- | --- | --- | --- |
| | State system | Judic. system | |
| Notify courts/law violation[e] | 1.64 | 1.67 | NS |
| Office function protection[e] | 1.49 | 1.82 | .01 |
| Require alcohol treatment[r] | 1.71 | 1.80 | NS |
| Stringent rule application[e] | 2.04 | 1.65 | .01 |
| Provide close supervision[e] | 2.00 | 1.71 | .01 |
| Office function is rehabilitation[r] | 1.88 | 1.90 | NS |
| Provide counseling[r] | 1.88 | 2.00 | NS |
| Require testing for drugs[e] | 1.97 | 2.18 | NS |
| Refer to voc. counseling[r] | 2.19 | 2.17 | NS |
| Refer voc. rehabilitation[r] | 2.02 | 2.42 | NS |

[e] Denotes item of actual enforcement orientation.
[r] Denotes item of actual rehabilitation orientation.

is an important goal which is shared by respondents from both states, regardless of the organizational structure of the probation system or its alignment with a particular branch of state government.

Next, while there was agreement among respondents about the importance of both goals, the present research identifies different strategies or practices designed to achieve the particular goal. Interesting was the fact that, except for one preferred goal statement, the order of importance placed on each goal was not the same for each state. The differences which existed among the two state probation systems when ranking the importance of the ten actual goal statements appear to reflect different methods or practices used to achieve the goals of enforcement and rehabilitation in the state. It can be assumed that the history of the probation system, its organizational culture, and perhaps the political, social, and economic climate in the state has had an impact on the way various goals are operationalized in that state. The goals of probation, especially in locally managed systems such as those found in one of the states under study, are not rooted in a singular set of beliefs, but are a combination of competing values and beliefs which have evolved over time (Smykla 1984). Based on the findings resulting from an analysis of the actual goals of probation, it can be concluded that when contrasting the two states, the system which is state administered was found to be more rehabilitation-oriented than the state which is judicially controlled. Why this was the case is not totally understood and is a question for future research.

The results point out a lack of clear direction among states as to the preferred goals of probation. State differences were not consistent in terms of support for either a preferred enforcement or a preferred rehabilitation orientation as a primary goal of the system. Differences among states, when they existed, did not occur in any consistent direction. When we examine the composite rankings of preferred goals by state, the same dual goal system appears. Of particular importance was the finding that, when given the opportunity to alter the goals of the probation system in their state (preferred goals), probation professionals again cited the desire to create a dual goal system. This finding differs from Harris, Clear, and Baird (1989) who reported that community service workers (probation and parole officers) in the 1980s show a greater concern for surveillance and authority as goals of the system. While not the focus of the present research, additional analysis concluded that probation professionals at all levels in the hierarchy, whether they be line officers or top administrators, agreed that a dual goal system was the preferred method of operation.

The results of this research confirm previous works by such scholars as Glaser (1969), McCleary (1978), and Studt (1978), who report that the probation officer has two simultaneous missions: to provide treatment and rehabilitative services to those offenders who wish it, while at the same time protecting the community from those probationers who are seen as representing a risk to community safety. It is apparent that probation staff from the two states have not operationalized the "Justice Model" presented by Fogel (1984) and Duffee (1984) by separating the two goals. These researchers have argued that probation should focus on enforcement of the court's order, leaving the service function to agencies in the community which are better able to handle the task. The present research lends support to the contention that service to the offender is an important part of probation work. Similarly, the results derived from the study of actual and preferred goals confirms part of the role typologies presented by Ohlin (1956), in describing the "protective officer" and Klockars (1972) the "synthetic officer," both of whom blend enforcement and rehabilitation practices. Further research is needed to determine how the probation officer assimilates both roles (goals) on a day-to-day basis, and the criteria which are used to determine the appropriate use of enforcement and rehabilitation in each case. Hall et al. (1986) argue that the conflict between the goals of protection (enforcement) and rehabilitation has been "virtually immobilizing" to the work of the correctional professional. There is little evidence in the present findings to support the belief that probation professionals have rejected both orientations. A more thorough examination of this effect is warranted. Previous research has reported the effect of the dual goal structure on such factors as job satisfaction, stress, burnout, and turnover (Whitehead 1986; Whitehead and Lindquist 1985), but these works have done little to explain how some probation professionals continue their careers for many years under the dual goal system while others do not. It is perhaps feasible that probation professionals adopt a yet unknown working style of offender supervision that helps maintain an equilibrium, especially when confronted by conflicting demands from supervisors, judges, and the public. From this analysis, it becomes apparent that a more in-depth study of organizational goals in criminal justice is necessary. In the probation field, knowing that the probation professional supports a particular goal or goals is not enough. How probation staff operationalize these goals should become the focus of our attention, given the fact that probation, similar to other components of the criminal justice system and the public sector, contain many ambiguous and conflicting directions, forcing the probation professional to make decisions which are in the best interest of everyone involved, including the officers themselves. Lipsky (1980) suggests than probation officers, as "street level bureaucrats," may implement the goals of the system in any way they feel best suits the needs of the case or their own personal safety. This position is supported by Petronio (1983), who applied Katz and Kahn's (1966) theory of role socialization to a juvenile probation setting. Judges and administrators conveyed the importance of the goal of community protection and offender accountability to line officers. Line staff, on the other hand, adopted whatever strategy they felt was necessary in each case, whether that strategy involved practices of enforcement or rehabilitation. The link between policy and practice remains somewhat unclear and is a topic suggested for further research.

## References

Allen, H., C. Eskridge, E. Latessa, and G. Vito. 1985. *Probation and Parole in America*. New York: Free Press.

American Bar Association. 1970. *Standards Relating to Probation*. Chicago: American Bar Association.

American Friends Service Committee. 1971. *Struggle for Justice*. New York: Hill and Wang.

Breed, A. 1984. "Foreword," in P. McAnany, D. Thomson, and D. Fogel (eds.), *Probation and Justice: Reconsideration of Mission*. Cambridge, MA: Oelgeschlager, Gunn, and Hain Publishers.

Clear, T. R. 1985. "Managerial Issues in Community Corrections," in L. F. Travis (ed.), *Probation, Parole, and Community Corrections*. Prospect Heights, IL: Waveland Press.

Czajkoski, E. 1973. "Exposing the Quasi-Judicial Role of the Probation Officer," *Federal Probation* 37:9-13.

Duffee, D. 1984. "Models of Probation Supervision," in P. McAnany, D. Thomson, and D. Fogel (eds.), *Probation and Justice: Reconsideration of Mission.* Cambridge, MA: Oelgeschlager, Gunn, and Hain Publishers.

Erez, E. 1989. "Gender, Rehabilitation, and Probation Decisions," *Criminology* 27(2):307-27.

Glaser, D. 1969. *The Effectiveness of a Prison and Parole System.* Indianapolis: Bobbs-Merrill.

Goode, W. 1960. "A Theory of Role Strain," *American Sociological Review* 25:483-96.

Gottfredson, D. 1967. *Critical Issues in Adult Probation.* Program for the Study of Crime and Delinquency, Ohio State University.

Gray, R. 1986. "Probation: An Exploration in Meaning," *Federal Probation* 50(4):26-31.

Hall, J. S., M. Williams, and L. Tomaino. 1966. "The Challenge of Correctional Change: The Interface of Conformity and Commitment," *Journal of Criminal Law, Criminology, and Police Science* 57:493-503.

Harris, M. K. 1984. "Rethinking Probation in the Context of the Justice Model," in P. McAnany, D. Thomson, and D. Fogel (eds.), *Probation and Justice: Reconsideration of Mission.* Cambridge, MA: Oelgeschlager, Gunn, and Hain Publishers.

Harris, P. M., T. R. Clear, and S. C. Baird. 1989. "Have Community Supervision Officers Changed Their Attitude Toward Their Work?" *Justice Quarterly* 6(2):233-46.

Kahn, R. L. 1978. "Job Burnout: Prevention and Remedies," *Public Welfare* 36:61-63.

Katz, D., and R. Kahn. 1966. *The Social Psychology of Organizations.* New York: John Wiley.

Killinger, G. G., H. B. Kerper, and P. F. Cromwell. 1976. *Probation and Parole in the Criminal Justice System.* St. Paul, MN: West Publishing Co.

King, R., and N. Raynes. 1968. "An Operational Measure of Inmate Management in Residential Institutions," *Social Science and Medicine* 2:41-53.

Klockars, K. B. 1972. "A Theory of Probation Supervision," *Journal of Criminal Law, Criminology, and Police Science* 63:550-57.

Lawrence, R. 1984. "Professionals or Judicial Civil Servants? An Examination of the Probation Officer's Role," *Federal Probation* 48(4):14-21.

Lipsky, M. 1980. *Street-level Bureaucracy.* New York: Russell Sage.

McAnany, P., D. Thomson, and D. Fogel (eds.). 1984. *Probation and Justice: Reconsideration of Mission.* Cambridge, MA: Oelgeschlager, Gunn, and Hain Publishers.

McCleary, R. 1978. *Dangerous Men: The Sociology of Parole.* Beverly Hills: Sage Publications.

Martinson, R., and J. Wilks. 1977. "Save Parole Supervision," *Federal Probation* 41(3):10-13.

National Advisory Commission on Criminal Justice Standards and Goals. 1973. *Corrections.* Washington, DC: US Government Printing Office.

National Council on Crime and Delinquency. 1955. *Standard Probation and Parole Act.* Paramus, NJ: National Council on Crime and Delinquency.

Ohlin, L., H. Piven, and D. Pappenfort. 1956. "Major Dilemmas of the Social Worker in Probation and Parole," *National Probation and Parole Association Journal* 11:211-25.

Petersilia, J. 1985. "Community Supervision: Trends and Critical Issues," *Crime and Delinquency* 31:339-47.

Petronio, R. 1983. "Role Socialization of Juvenile Court Probation Officers," *Criminal Justice and Behavior* 9(2):143-58.

Rosecrance, J. 1986. "Probation Supervision: Mission Impossible," *Federal Probation* 50(1):25-31.

Sigler, J., and T. Bezanson. 1970. "Role Perceptions Among New Jersey Probation Officers," *Rutgers Camden Law Journal* 2:256-60.

Smykla, J. O. 1984. *Probation and Parole: Crime Control in the Community.* New York: Macmillan.

Stanley, D. T. 1976. *Prisoners Among Us.* Washington, DC: Brookings.

Street, D., R. D. Vinter, and C. Perrow. 1966. *Organizations for Treatment.* New York: Free Press.

Studt, E. 1978. *Surveillance and Service in Parole.* U.S. Department of Justice. National Institute of Corrections.

Tomaino, L. 1975. "The Five Faces of Probation," *Federal Probation*, 39:41-46.

von Hirsch, A., and K. Hanrahan. 1979. *The Question of Parole.* Cambridge, MA: Ballinger.

Whitehead, J. T. 1986. "Job Burnout and Job Satisfaction Among Probation Managers," *Journal of Criminal Justice* 14:25-35.

Whitehead, J. T., and C. A. Lindquist. 1986. "Job Stress and Burnout Among Probation/Parole Officers: Perceptions and Causal Factors," *International Journal of Offender Therapy and Comparative Criminology* 29:109-19.

Zald, M. N. 1962. "Power Balance and Staff Conflict in Correctional Institutions," *Administrative Science Quarterly* 7:22-49.

# 4

# Community Correction and Diversion

## Costs and Benefits, Subsidy Modes, and Start-Up Recommendations

### James McSparron

*Community correction is fast becoming an undefinable cliché in the criminal justice community. To help create a uniform basis for discussion and study, I consider some structures and objectives common to many community correction efforts, and some of the pitfalls a correctional system may encounter in making a commitment to community correction. Mechanisms for subsidizing and implementing these programs and models for pretrial diversion are also discussed.*

The search for improvements in the manner which society deems appropriate to deal with those who have violated its laws makes for an understandably eager, and perhaps at times hasty, acceptance of correctional innovations. This eagerness can, on occasion, result in the acceptance of a concept with a less than full understanding of the results that can realistically be expected. The placing of more responsibility for correction within the community, with the attendant possibility of a variety of benefits — to wit, consolidation of the

*Source: Crime & Delinquency*, Vol. 26, No. 2 (April 1980), pp. 226-247. Copyright © 1980 Sage Publications, Inc. Reprinted by permission of Sage Publications, Inc.

*criminal justice system, a more cost-effective correction system, enhanced rehabilitation, and a more humane approach to correction — has immediate appeal. While such potential benefits may well exist, there are, as always, skeptics, critics, and, more important, systems having first-hand experience with a community correction program. A survey of some issues which have arisen in the community correction milieu will better equip one objectively to study and use it as a correctional tool. It is concluded that, although community correction programs have been less effective than hoped, their potential is preferable to the limited potential of traditional incarceration.*

## Introduction

A single term is seldom sufficient to describe a correction program or concept after the system has manipulated it for a few years. At this point there is much uncertainty and vagueness as to what *community correction* actually means — and equal vagueness about its purpose. Terms such as *rehabilitation* and *definite sentencing* have suffered a similar fate.

I propose to offer a working definition of community correction and briefly list its general objectives. I will then examine costs and benefits in terms of those objectives, look at various ways of subsidizing community correction programs, and discuss some of the mechanisms employed in their establishment and operation. Discussed separately will be pretrial diversion and nonadjudicatory dispute resolution — which, while not falling primarily within the correction bailiwick, parallel the community correction move from formal system to embedding community.

### Definition

The basic conditions of community correction are (1) placement of responsibility for correction within a political subdivision other than the state (e.g., counties, municipalities) and (2) less segregation of offenders from the "free world" than in more traditional dispositions. Note, however, that community correction frequently involves some degree of incarceration — for example, restrictions on movement and freedoms in halfway houses, group homes, and other residential settings — and is therefore not a total alternative to incarceration.

Alternative dispositions which avoid or supplement traditional incarceration in a jail or state prison can occur at any point in the criminal process, that is, from the time of arrest through conviction, sentencing, and sentence duration (parole and other conditional releases being examples of the latter).[1] Technically, actions taken in a pending criminal proceeding before a finding of guilt are judicial, not correctional, measures. However, for the purposes of this discussion, community-based and other alternative programs ordered before conviction will be included. Diversionary or evaluative programs used before the final disposition of a criminal proceeding often affect the outcome of the proceeding, and will provide the criminal justice system with more information about the accused, thus improving decisions made later in the process.

### Purposes

Upon conviction the state, through the criminal justice system, must decide what degree of social control it will impose upon the violator of its laws both to protect the public and to punish and/or rehabilitate the offender. The amount of control necessary to accomplish these objectives and the amount morally acceptable are an ongoing debate, with advocates of the death penalty and mandatory sentencing at one end of the spectrum and those of deinstitutionalization and community sentencing options at the other.[2] In addition to this important philosophical issue (rights and responsibilities of the individual versus those of society), certain practical considerations must be studied, including the fiscal implications of exercising various types or levels of control, and the effectiveness of various types of control in reducing criminal activity and protecting public security.

Community correction has been asserted to be more humane, cost effective, and generally a more successful approach to correction than traditional incarceration.

## Advantages and Disadvantages of Community Correction

Placing more responsibility for correction within counties or other political subdivisions of a state has been said to serve a number of purposes, including —

### Consolidation of Criminal Justice System

It has been argued that the use of community correction will bring correction into greater operational harmony with other facets of the criminal justice system (e.g., law enforcement and criminal adjudication, which now are almost exclusively the responsibility of counties or municipalities). As a result, fragmentation and bureaucratic indifference in the administration of criminal justice could be lessened.

## More Cost-Effective Correction

Most community correction programs emphasize that the use of community alternatives is not as costly as traditional incarceration. A program or proposal which can advertise fiscal savings in today's world has immediate appeal. There has been a tendency to oversell, oversimplify, and overaccept the money-saving angle of community correction—and to gloss over important substantive concerns. The lower costs of community programs must be weighed against rehabilitative quality, the uncanceled fixed costs of the remaining prisons, whether expenditures are really saved or merely postponed or displaced, and incapacitative effectiveness.

One of the harsher analyzers of community correction, David F. Greenberg, has noted that

> . . . cost arguments can be misleading, for some community alternatives may be less expensive only because of budgetary stinginess. If the goal of making educational and vocational opportunities or individual psychiatric counseling available to those who wanted these services were to be taken seriously, the cost might be considerable. In addition, much of the cost of running prisons is fixed and does not vary with a reduction in the number of inmates. For this reason, a diversion of some inmates to community dispositions may simply mean a higher per capita cost of imprisonment for those still incarcerated, with no overall savings. Indeed, the author knows of no Department of Corrections among those where extensive decarceration has taken place that has reduced its overall budget. Given organizational instincts for self-preservation and expansion, the prospects for substantial budget cuts through decarceration seem slight.[3]

It should be noted, however, that, as Greenberg pointed out, "While it is not universally true that the cost of a community disposition is less than that of imprisonment, frequently this is the case."[4]

The Minnesota Community Corrections effort has not evidenced any fiscal savings to date. The Minnesota Legislature has found it necessary to increase funding for community correction each year, and the Minnesota State Department of Corrections has received budget increases in each year since the Community Corrections Act was implemented. These increases are in part attributable to the addition of new counties to the program, inflationary cost increases, and changeover costs. As Kenneth Schoen, the Minnesota Commissioner of Corrections, put it, "In the long run, it just has to cost less. . . . But until the Act is fully implemented, we are running parallel systems." Schoen pointed out that per diem costs for community residential programs are much less than state institutional costs and even less for nonresidential community programs, concluding that the view that community correction programs are just as expensive to run is "absolute nonsense."[5]

A cost analysis study of a community correction center in Indiana reported that

> So-called "averted costs," e.g., savings associated with taking people from existing institutions and placing them in alternative programs need qualification and explanation.
>
> (a) Many of the components of institutional operating cost figures are "fixed" in nature (even as regards personnel) and would not be averted, or saved, through the construction of a facility such as the Community Corrections Center unless the old institution (or some portion of it) closed down.
>
> (b) The earlier in the criminal justice system that changes take place the greater the savings, other things remaining the same. Successful pre-trial diversion results in the aversion of prosecution, trial, and other related costs, including corrections. Most of these costs are not averted with a post-conviction alternative unless recidivism declines.
>
> For the moment and keeping the foregoing in mind, it is important to note that there appears to be no evidence of significant savings which will occur due to Community Corrections Center operation.[6]

A study of a residential community correction center in Minnesota found that "decreasing the level of social control from state incarceration to residential treatment has economic benefits."[7] The costs of supervising individuals diverted to the community program were approximately half the estimated costs of traditional incarceration. However, placement in a community residential center merely delayed traditional incarceration in many cases — 50 percent of those who were originally diverted to a community residential center were ". . . ultimately incarcerated and served extensive institutional time in addition to residential time in the [community] project."[8] As a result, correctional costs were only slightly less than they would have been had all originally diverted individuals been incarcerated initially.

The California Probation Subsidy Program (designed primarily to reduce commitments to state correctional facilities through the use of state fiscal incentives to expand the use of probation at the local level) did indeed result in an estimated $60 million savings to the state over six years — but, because of increased jail incarceration and the failure of the state subsidies to keep pace with inflation, counties did not fare very well financially under the program.[9]

The National Advisory Commission on Criminal Justice Standards and Goals has said of community correction and public protection:

> The managerial goals are of special importance because of the sharp contrast between the per capita costs of custody and any kind of

community program. Any shift from custodial control will save money. But the criterion of correctional success is not fiscal. A major object of correctional programs is to protect the public. Therefore, any savings of public funds must not be accompanied by a loss of public protection. When offenders can be shifted from custodial control to community-based programming without loss of public protection, the managerial criteria require that such a shift be made. Otherwise public funds will have been spent without satisfying a public objective.[10]

In sum, the findings are inconclusive. Few, if any, have alleged that community correction is more expensive than traditional correctional dispositions—and, given the fact that traditional incarceration has, in the opinion of many, failed, it is argued that at least community correction offers some hope for a more effective criminal justice system and is therefore worthy of stronger consideration by policy makers. As Commissioner Schoen noted, fiscal consequences may be considerable in developmental stages because two systems—community correction and the existing traditional correctional system—are being supported. But long-range community correction goals involve reduction in the growth and the eventual phasing out of certain components of the traditional correctional system. If these objectives are realized, correctional costs, as Schoen asserts, would be decreased, or at least stabilized.

## Incapacitation and Rehabilitation

There can be little argument that the placement of an offender in a secure institution (i.e., state prison or county jail) is, at least during the term of such imprisonment, a better incapacitator than a community residential facility. The National Advisory Commission, however, has emphasized that the effectiveness of community correction's noninstitutional control should not be minimized: "Indeed, the deterrent effect of proper control within the community, coupled with realistic opportunities for the offender to make an adjustment there, may be expected to be considerable."[11]

In terms of recidivism rates, the results of evaluative studies are inconsistent. There are indications that recidivism rates of offenders released from secure institutional settings differ very little from those of offenders who have participated in alternative programs.[12] It must be emphasized that *recidivism rates* can mean many different things, and an almost endless number of variables can be included in or excluded from recidivism studies, with considerable shaping of the results reported.[13]

A study of California's Probation Subsidy Program has noted that the expanded probation effort in California did result in some increase in crime and recidivism rates attributable to the program. Nevertheless, the study concluded,

> Unless some significant accomplishment can be shown, however, it is difficult to argue the case for prison. It is unlikely that prison performance will improve, while it is possible that community performance—which is still in its infancy—could become better. Even if one adopts the emerging view of a punishment-oriented sentencing system, there is little to be said for extended prison terms unless they produce some appreciable payoff in lessened crime. . . . While it is true that correctional agencies everywhere have had difficulty in developing either institutional or noninstitutional programs capable of reducing recidivism, only a handful of the many possible approaches have been systematically tried and evaluated. If the choice now is to give up the attempt to develop programs that will be effective in reducing recidivism or to continue to try to develop such programs, it seems clear that the choice should be to continue to try. The potential benefits are great and the alternatives totally unpromising.[14]

It is generally accepted that extended terms of imprisonment in traditional prison settings have had no effect on crime rates. Indeed, the findings of the National Advisory Commission on Criminal Justice Standards and Goals include the following:

> Current measurements hardly support the contention that incarceration deters. . . . The deterrence of potential offenders has not been supported by evidence. . . no one has ever proved that the threat of severe punishment actually deters crime.

> Similarly, studies of confinement length do not establish that lengthier prison terms result in decreased recidivism.

> We can conclude that, at the least, there is no established statistical base relating crime rates to the severity of dispositions imposed. . . .[15]

An official recidivism rate may be viewed as an index of rehabilitation and reintegration. Community correction has its critics and defenders on this broader ground too. Greenberg has stated, ''Despite manifestly high hopes for corrections in the community, evaluations suggest that most such programs are no more effective than those conducted in prison.''[16] Equally discouraging is the Minnesota report that half the offenders placed in a community residential program eventually wound up in prison.[17] Some thought-provoking points raised by Greenberg concerning the rehabilitation issue include—

1. An offender's community of residence is where he is already known as a criminal—and this could pose more barriers to the abandonment of criminal activities than would placement in a new residential location.

2. "One might ask why, if the community is so therapeutic, the offender got into trouble in the first place?"

3. "To the extent that criminal activity represents a rational response to the absence of opportunities realistically available, community corrections may be largely irrelevant because it is in a position to generate few new opportunities." High levels of unemployment and lack of access to nonmenial jobs, for example, hinder the success of the exoffender in the community.

4. A community ". . . may have little desire to be reintegrated with its criminals."

5. Many community correction programs have emphasized counseling or group therapy programs, as opposed to the acquisition of vocational or academic skills. "The relevance of these psychologically oriented programs to criminal activity is not particularly clear. . . ." Greenberg suggests that this may be why such programs have had little success in reducing recidivism.

6. Even when such "psychologically oriented programs" are relevant, their effectiveness may be undermined when attendance is compulsory and the programs are administered by those responsible for some custodial or surveillance activities. "The antagonism between correctional staff and prison inmates is not necessarily eliminated when coercive programs are relocated from the total institution to the community."[18]

Responses to these points are difficult given the absence of a comprehensive community correction effort that has been operating long enough to permit meaningful analysis in terms of long-range successes or failures. One counterargument, noted by the California Probation Subsidy Study, is that community correction is still in its infancy and could improve, while there is little indication that prison performance will improve. Another is that only a handful of many possible community correction approaches have been systematically tried; and there is the cost-effectiveness argument (subject to the caveats noted above): "Policy-makers must resolve whether society derives sufficient benefit in terms of reduced criminal activity to justify the additional costs of . . . increased control."[19] Finally, there is the realization that the offender must live in the community, and the community must live with the offender—

1. "The social malfunctions of unemployment, discrimination, economic inequity . . . affect most citizens. The offender, like other citizens, must find a way to live with his deficits and with the disorder around him."[20] That is, the offender must be taught to cope and survive within his community without turning to criminal

activity. While it is not clear whether this task is possible, it is clear that it has not been or cannot be accomplished in a traditional prison setting.

2. All too often the convicted are transferred to the custody of the "state" for x number of years and forgotten by the community. But, as Schoen has pointed out,

> We know that the forces that lead to it [crime] occur in the community. . . . So if we are going to do something about it it's not going to be at some remote prison setting. . . . Let's involve the community in dealing with crime and delinquency, rather than its being a state responsibility. Now that shouldn't strike people as being strange, since most of our criminal justice system is already community based — our police, courts, prosecutors, defense. . . . It shouldn't strike people as being strange at all, or even highly innovative, to have corrections there too.[21]

3. The National Advisory Commission on Criminal Justice Standards and Goals stresses the need to mesh community correction with

> a whole range of social support services as needed. . . . To a much larger extent than has been realized, social support services must be given outside the official correctional apparatus and inside the community. Schools must accept and help reintegrate the delinquent instead of exiling him to reform schools. Unions and employers must open doors to adult offenders instead of restricting their employment to the most menial and insecure labor. . . . [The correctional system must begin to develop a] brokerage service in which the agency, i.e., corrections, opens up to the offender community services where such services exist, or helps create new services for the entire community where none existed before.[22]

## Humanitarianism

The following statement of the National Advisory Commission on Criminal Justice Standards and Goals perhaps best represents the humanitarian position on community correction:

> The humanitarian aspects of community-based corrections is obvious. To subject anyone to custodial coercion is to place him in physical jeopardy, to narrow drastically his access to sources of personal satisfaction, and to reduce his self-esteem. That all these unfavorable consequences are the outcome of his own criminal actions does not change their reality. To the extent that the offender can be relieved of the burden of custody, a humanitarian objective is realized. The proposition that no one should be subjected to custodial control unnecessarily is a humanitarian assertion.[23]

Greenberg, however, raises some cautionary points: "The substitution of a halfway house or a group home for a prison or reformatory is not 'deinstitutionalization' but the replacement of one institution by another.'' Some of the prisoner resentment found in traditional prisons often is also found in community correction settings. While community correction is probably more humane than the current prison system, this would not necessarily be the case if prison sentences were shorter or prison conditions improved.[24]

Also tending to controvert the argument that community correction involves less restrictive control and is therefore more humane is the report that

> there appears to be a strong tendency among dispositional decisionmakers to utilize . . . community residential projects as alternatives to probation rather than as alternatives to institutionalization. As a result, an unintended consequence of these projects has been to increase the level of social control in the correctional system.[25]

This potentially disastrous outcome may be avoided by directing educational and lobbying efforts, with respect to the objectives of community correction, toward judges, probation officers, and other components of law enforcement.

## Subsidies for Community Correction

### Overview

A common and effective way to promote and encourage the development of community correction has been state support through direct dollar subsidies to local governments. Such subsidies represent a philosophy of shifting correctional responsibilities from the state to local governments. In addition, there are some practical concerns which make such subsidies necessary, if not vital.[26] These include —

1.  A need in many jurisdictions at least to stabilize the spiraling number of prisoners being sentenced to state institutions. When this factor is at issue, the availability and amount of state subsidy monies often are tied to a reduction in the number of prisoners which the county or other political subdivision is committing to the state system. By encouraging local governments to retain offenders in the community, the need for costly expansion of state correctional systems has been avoided.

2.  The fact that many local governments are in the midst of fiscal crises and are unable properly to fund and support a wide range of county responsibilities and interests.

3.  For two centuries, correction has been a low budgetary priority of local governments. This tradition, coupled with a host of pressing

local fiscal issues, makes the appropriation of sufficient local funds for correction unlikely.

4. In recent years, the availability of LEAA program funds has been decreasing, making the survival of existing programs, not to mention the institution of new programs, much more difficult.

Many types of correctional services have been subsidized by various states. Subsidy programs have included both residential and nonresidential community correction operations, improvements in existing secure detention facilities (e.g., county jails and penitentiaries and pre- and postadjudicative detention programs). Subsidies have generally been made available for operating and maintenance costs of personnel services and related expenses, but they seldom are used for the acquisition or construction of local correctional facilities (i.e., capital improvements).[27]

A number of methods have been used for allocating state subsidy funds.[28] It should be noted that in the majority of subsidy programs participation by local governments is voluntary. Allocation techniques have included—

1. State reimbursement for a certain percentage of actual local cost (e.g., New York State's Probation Reimbursement Program).

2. Use of a demographic-type formula (e.g., subsidy amount determined by amount of reduction in commitments to state institutions).

3. Awarding by the state to local governments of funds similar to grants. These awards involve an application by a local government to the state, review by the state, and the awarding of usually limited funds on an annual basis.

4. Awarding of funds on the basis of implementation of and compliance with state standards.

### Minnesota and California Reimbursement Formulas

The most commonly used methods for allocating state subsidy funds are—

1. A flat award amount based upon a local government's reduction in the number of individuals committed to the state correctional system or a flat percentage of the expenditures attendant to a local correctional program.

2. An equalization formula designed to reflect a county's correctional needs and ability to generate enough funds to meet its correctional needs.

The Minnesota Community Corrections Act[29] exemplifies the second method. The Minnesota equalization formula takes four factors into consideration: (1) the per capita correction expenditures of a participating county, (2) the total risk population (set in Minnesota as individuals between the ages of six and thirty) of a participating county, (3) the per capita income in a participating county, and (4) the per capita taxable value in a participating county. For each participating county, each factor is computed and is then compared with the statewide average of that factor. This comparison results in a "score" for each factor, and annual monies are allotted on the basis of these scores.

It is important for any subsidy allocation process to take inflation into account. A problem with the California Subsidy Program was that subsidy allocations did not keep pace with inflation. As a result, with each passing year, the allocation amount was less and less a true reflection of the amount of funds needed by local governments to meet their correctional needs. The Minnesota formula does include an inflation factor.

The four factors used by Minnesota have generally been an adequate basis for the allocation of state funds. The only one that has been criticized is the so-called per capita correction expenditures factor (the correctional need factor). In Minnesota, this factor includes only expenditures for probation services.[30] Obviously, this does not include all the correctional expenditures of a participating county. Minnesota's justification for this approach is "since the purpose of the formula, in the Department's view, was to provide an equitable allocation system for both large and small counties, the criteria for the selection of correctional need factors was their commonality among counties."[31]

Serious criticism of this approach has been raised by more urbanized counties in Minnesota. These counties have contended that the correctional need indicators used by Minnesota fail to take into account the often high levels of services already provided in many urban counties and the high crime rates of urban as opposed to more rural jurisdictions. Urban counties argue that the equalization formula exists for ". . . counties that least need State assistance for corrections and that contribute only a marginal number of offenders to state institutions."[32] Minnesota has established a task force to study measures which may better address these contentions of urban counties without discriminating against smaller rural jurisdictions.

California's Probation Subsidy is based upon only one criterion: the success of a participating county in reducing the number of individuals committed to state detention facilities. A participating county which fails to reduce state commitments receives no subsidy. A "base commitment rate" is established for a county on the basis of the county's commitment rate in prior years.[33] A participating county receives subsidy funds if its total commitment for any given year is less than its expected number of commitments, that is, less than its "base commitment rate." The amount of subsidy monies a county receives for reducing commitments is based on a formula which provides for amount from $2,080 to $4,000 per case. The subsidy amount per case increases as each county increases its percentage of reduction. For example, if a participating county's base commitment rate were between 40 and 49 persons per 100,000 of total population, it would be entitled to a $2,285 subsidy award per case for a 1 percent decrease in commitments. If its reduction in commitments were 7 percent or more, the county would be entitled to $4,000 per case.[34] In general, counties with comparatively low base commitment rates need to reduce their commitment rates by much lower percentages than are required of counties with comparatively high base commitment rates to reach the maximum $4,000 per case subsidy.

The California Subsidy Program did not include a factor designed to address inflation. It was found that ". . . the monies received by counties have not only not increased but have shrunk by inflation. By 1975, the purchasing power of the $4,000 state payment to counties was worth only $2,230, a drop of nearly 50%."[35]

It should be noted that California is in the process of redesigning its probation subsidy program. It appears that the redesigned program will include many of the features of the Minnesota act, for example, county advisory boards, a comprehensive correction plan, expansion of the programs for which subsidy funds will be used, and an increase in subsidy monies to keep pace with inflation.[36]

## New York's Probation Subsidy

New York State has had a probation subsidy program in operation since 1955. The program is designed to assist local governments (counties and New York City) in providing probation services. Under this program, each county and New York City are eligible to be reimbursed for up to 50 percent of salaries and other operational costs attendant on the delivery of probation services.[37] Reimbursement is based upon county compliance with standards as promulgated by the New York State Division of Probation. These standards cover (1) space standards and design guidelines for local probation offices, (2) rules for staff development, (3) probation management, (4) case record management, (5) supervision of persons sentenced to or placed on probation, and (6) procedures with respect to probation violations.[38]

According to a 1973 audit of the New York State Division of Probation, the supervision costs attendant on probation are much less than the expenses of traditional incarceration. The audit report found that probation services costs about $550 a year per client. This compares favorably with the per client costs of county jail incarceration (approximately $8,000 to $9,000 a year) and incarceration in a Department of Correctional Services facility (estimates are as high as $19,000 a year).[39]

Reimbursement under New York State's program does not include criteria other than those noted above; that is, reduction of state commitments is not considered. (However, local correctional facilities housing state prisoners are reimbursed at the rate of $15 per day per prisoner from nonprobation state funds.)

## Reduction of Commitments to State Prisons through Fiscal Disincentives

Both the California Probation Subsidy and the Minnesota Community Corrections Act are aimed primarily at reducing the number of persons committed to state correctional facilities. In Minnesota, participating counties are fiscally penalized for individuals sentenced from their jurisdictions to terms of imprisonment of five years or less in a state correctional facility: Minnesota deducts $25 from the amount of subsidy funds a county is eligible to receive for each day such a prisoner spends in state custody.[40] In California, as noted above, counties that do not reduce state commitments do not receive subsidy monies.

Both Minnesota and California have seen a reduction in the number of prisoners committed to their state correctional systems after implementation of these community correction programs, and it has been suggested that New York should consider using the reduction of state commitments as a basis for reimbursing counties for probation services in lieu of its current criteria.

Obviously, the reduction of commitments to a state correctional system has direct benefits for that system. However, without proper planning and preparation, the repercussions at the local level could be disastrous. For example, under such a program, sentencing judges might begin using county jails much more frequently. The resulting overcrowding and additional pressure on county jail services could cause a serious breakdown in local secure facilities. In New York State, many jails are now operating near capacity, making such a breakdown likely. It is probable that New York is not atypical in this regard. While California claims that jail overcrowding has not occurred as a result of the California Probation Subsidy, Minnesota has indicated that substandard jails and jail overcrowding are now a serious concern.

Other problems implicit in using fiscal disincentives to reduce state commitments are—

1. Is a county still to be penalized fiscally for not reducing state commitments if its crime rates, arrest rates, or conviction rates increase?

2. Could such a policy improperly influence sentencing judges?
3. Is the offering of additional funds to local governments in order to improve the state correctional system in the best interests of all concerned?

The reduction of unnecessary state commitments is a widely supported objective, but it is critical to ensure that sufficient funds and adequate local correctional options exist. If counties enter such a program without sufficient resources to address the increased demands which will almost assuredly fall upon their county correctional systems, the potentially dangerous repercussions which will face local governments may far outweigh any gains to the state.

## Recommended Features

### Community Advisory Boards

The establishment of a local constituency for local correction is crucial to the success, or at least the proper promotion, of any community correction effort. To address this need, Minnesota employs a "corrections advisory board."[41] Minnesota's advisory board format has been adopted with little modification by other jurisdictions implementing community correction.

There are generally four issues involved in the establishment of a community advisory board: (1) the size and makeup of the committee, (2) the length of the terms to be served by committee members, (3) the appointment or selection of committee members, and (4) the committee's responsibilities.

Minnesota's committee consists of eighteen to twenty members. A community correction program being developed in Kansas uses committees of twelve members. Each committee includes a cross-section of the criminal justice community (police, judges, prosecutors, public defenders, probation and parole officers, and sheriffs), representatives of the general public and county agencies (social services, mental hygiene, and health), and offenders. Certain officeholders are permanent members of the committee (e.g., sheriff and county attorney); other appointments are generally made by the person chairing a county's legislature for a term of two years with the advice and consent of the county legislature.[42]

In Minnesota, the advisory board's responsibilities are to ". . . actively participate in the formulation of the comprehensive plan for the development, implementation and operation of the correctional services program and service. . ." and to ". . . make formal recommendations at least annually . . ." to the county board.[43]

Problems that Minnesota has had with its advisory board structure include the following—

1. Lay members (individuals not directly concerned with criminal justice) generally have made few contributions and have frequently become inactive in committee activities.

2. Confusion exists among members as to the role or objectives of the community advisory board.

3. There is no mechanism to ensure committee accountability.

4. The size of the committee has been, at times, unwieldy. (There is, however, no consensus as to which members should be eliminated.)

5. Many committee members have a vested interest in the existing criminal justice system. This may include a direct economic interest in programs recommended for implementation or elimination by the committee.

6. Sentencing judges who are also committee members realize that the amount of money available to a local government under the Minnesota Community Corrections Act is a direct result of their sentencing practices. Therefore, the sentencing practices of judges may be improperly influenced in the interest of obtaining more funds for community correction. As a result, charges of conflict of interest have been raised.[44]

Despite these criticisms, most community correction efforts continue to endorse the community advisory committee concept. The problems have not been fatal to committee operations in other jurisdictions, and one can surmise that, through proper implementation and guidance, such committees can be a valuable asset in the criminal justice process.

## Statewide Master Plans

Any extensive community correction effort must be part of a statewide criminal justice plan. Some states, notably Minnesota, have developed what could be termed a master plan for the implementation of community correction.[45] The Minnesota plan encompasses virtually all aspects of criminal and juvenile justice and evidences a genuine commitment at all levels to the placement of major responsibilities for correction with local governments. In Minnesota, the state primarily provides local governments with fiscal incentive, some monitoring of programs, and technical assistance.

Many states have correctional systems much larger than Minnesota's (e.g., New York). In such states, establishing and coordinating an inclusive statewide plan may present difficulties not encountered in Minnesota.

## Pilot Projects

It is possible, and perhaps advisable, for a state to initiate a few pilot community correction projects. This approach would enable policy makers to explore various community correction concepts with a view to a long-term, more comprehensive commitment. Such "testing" would —

1.  Give the state and counties a chance to experience some of the more fundamental community correction objectives in a limited fashion.
2.  Afford an opportunity to observe the success or failure of different kinds of programs and the problems that arise in each (which can seldom be anticipated before the actual implementation of programs).
3.  Lay the foundation for state-locality cooperation.

# Pretrial Services

## Pretrial Release

Pretrial detention is expensive for the taxpayers (it cost New York State counties, exclusive of New York City, more than $26 million in 1976) and accounts for a significant percentage of the population of county jails (conservative estimates in New York State are that between 60 to 70 percent of all persons incarcerated in county jails are pretrial detainees).[46] Furthermore, it subjects the prisoner to human hardship; it can cost him his job; and it can adversely affect the outcome of his criminal proceeding.

Pretrial detention can be reduced by means of pretrial services — a system or procedure designed to ensure that the appropriate local court promptly receives all relevant information necessary for the issuance of an informed determination of the suitability of a defendant for pretrial release.[47] Pretrial services can also include measures designed to divert certain cases from criminal adjudication.

The objectives of pretrial release and/or diversion include (1) a decrease in the number of days spent in pretrial detention by individuals who could, with proper evaluation, be released before trial, (2) reduction of jail overcrowding, (3) development of more effective procedures to ensure timely court appearances by defendants, (4) issuance of more informed decisions by the courts, and (5) fiscal savings through the reduction in jail population. Pretrial services are intended to, and can, effect these objectives while maintaining the safety of the community.

A number of innovative pretrial services programs have been

implemented or experimented with across the nation.[48] A proposed pretrial release program for counties which currently have none should include two primary components. They are—

1. Release on recognizance (hereinafter referred to as ROR). In this component, a person charged with a crime who meets specific criteria could be released without bail on his own recognizance or in the custody of a third party. Pretrial services would include screening to determine release eligibility, a recommendation to the appropriate court concerning ROR, and follow-up contacts to ensure the individual's reappearance in court at the proper time and place.

2. Release under supervision (hereinafter referred to a RUS). This component would afford a pretrial services program with a mechanism designed to meet the needs of individuals who do not qualify for release on their own recognizance. For example, a condition of the release of such a person by a court might be a requirement that he be contacted on a regular basis or appear at certain times and places both to ensure reappearance in court and to provide additional elements of control.

ROR and RUS could also include, on a voluntary basis, counseling or other services offered within the community or by governmental agencies (e.g., social services, psychotherapy).[49]

*Release on Recognizance.*   Any pretrial services ROR program should include the following steps—

1. Preinterview procedures. An important part of any pretrial services program is the early identification of the detainee population. Procedures should be set up to ensure that program staff are immediately made aware of all arrests and possible commitments. Arrangements should be made to notify potential detainees, arresting authorities, and courts of the program's existence and purpose.[50] Preinterview procedures would include daily examination of appropriate police or court records (e.g., police blotters, court calendar, county jail or lockup rosters). From these records the following information should be extracted: accused's name, address, and age, nature of the charge, employment, criminal history, and any other pertinent information available in such records. Additional information that is readily available from other sources should also be obtained at the preinterview stage. It is possible that many persons may be found to be ineligible for ROR at this stage, for example, individuals subject to outstanding warrants or "holds" from parole or probation authorities or those who have been arrested on bench warrants for nonappearance for court proceedings.

2. Interview procedures. Contacting and interviewing of detainees awaiting court appearance should be accomplished as soon as possible after booking. The interviewer could use a standard eligibility instrument similar to the one developed by the Vera Manhattan Bail Reform Project. This instrument is designed primarily to evaluate the suitability of an individual for ROR on the basis of family and community ties and prior criminal history. The Vera interview process assesses five basic variables tapping the likelihood that a person will appear in court as scheduled. The variables are length of residence in the local community, nature and extent of local family ties, time in the local area, stability of employment, and nature and extent of prior criminal record.

3. Postinterview procedures. These include contacting references and other sources to verify information obtained during the interview, completing the ROR recommendation, and noting other relevant information concerning the interview. This report and the recommendation resulting from it should then be submitted to the appropriate court.[51]

*Release under Supervision.* RUS programs attempt to serve that segment of a detainee population that does not qualify for ROR but may be eligible for varying levels of supervised release. RUS candidates would be those detainees who do not have ties in the community, who have relatively extensive prior criminal records, or who are alcohol or drug abusers.[52] These programs often include a counseling or assistance component designed to do far more than ensure the individual's reappearance in court; the Des Moines program, for example, includes diagnostic testing, counseling, therapy, and job development and placement.[53]

Decisions concerning eligibility for RUS are much more subjective than the ROR determinations. The process may involve interviewing and review by a number of experienced staff persons, who attempt subjectively to probe the likelihood that the detainee (1) will appear in court if released, (2) will avoid criminal activity during the pretrial period, and (3) will cooperate with the program.[54]

RUS programs also provide information which may help in identifying correctional needs, should the individual eventually be convicted.

### Diversion

The pretrial release system can also be used to screen for diversion. Individuals who may be eligible for some type of pretrial release may very well be excellent candidates for accelerated or other alternative methods of disposing of the underlying pending criminal proceeding.

**Alternative Dispute Resolution**

There are a variety of third-party dispute resolution techniques other than traditional criminal adjudication, including arbitration, mediation, conciliation, and fact finding. Diverting cases from the criminal court to these alternative processes could alleviate the following problems facing our criminal court system:

> (1) *problems of delay* . . . (2) *limited access to the courts* due to the high costs resulting from legal fees, lost wages while attending court sessions, court fees, etc., (3) *inefficiency due to high dismissal rates* (e.g., over 40% of cases involving felony charges were dismissed in the New York courts in 1971). This inefficiency results in high costs to society for the partial processing of cases, and (4) *logical limitations in the use of adjudication* due to the fact that many matters involve reciprocal offenses between the parties, or complex issues requiring compromises not readily achieved by the winner takes all approach of adjudication.[55]

The fact that in New York City 56 percent of all felony arrests for crimes against persons involve individuals who had a prior relationship with the defendant and 87 percent of such cases result in dismissal because of complainant noncooperation indicates that some type of third-party resolution technique may often be far more efficient, effective, and appropriate than the traditional criminal justice adjudication process.[56] As a Vera study noted,

> Because our society has not found adequate alternatives to arrest and adjudication for coping with inter-personal anger publicly expressed, we pay a price. The price includes large court caseloads, long delays in processing and, ultimately, high dismissal rates. These impose high financial costs on taxpayers and high personal costs on defendants and their families. The public pays in another way, too. The congestion and drain on resources caused by an excessive number of such cases in the courts weakens the ability of the criminal justice system to deal quickly and decisively with the "real" felons, who may be getting lost in the shuffle. The risk that they will be returned to the street increases, as does the danger to law-abiding citizens on whom they prey.[57]

# Recommendations

Both community correction and pretrial release and alternative resolution programs should be under a central administration which monitors the programs and serves as a conduit for state funds to local governments developing or operating such programs. It may be advisable to use the services of existing state agencies to develop the community correction system, provide technical assistance, ensure that proper operational standards for community correction programs are maintained, and disburse subsidy funds.

Clearly, all programs must have the input and cooperation of prosecutors, defense attorneys, public defenders, the courts, police, and the general public. As was noted earlier, community advisory boards help establish this cooperation.

It is also important to offer local governments maximum flexibility in expending any state funds made available. For example, if a particular county has an adequate and properly funded ROR program, it should be given the option of using state-provided ROR monies in another pretrial diversion area (or even in another area of correction, e.g., postconviction alternatives).

The states should give serious consideration to appropriating sufficient funds to pay for a major portion of such programs. Since many counties are near fiscal disaster now, the allocation of additional monies by county governments sufficient to meet their correctional needs is unlikely. It is clear that the states may have to carry the primary fiscal responsibility for such efforts. Certainly, the potential direct benefits to local governments and possible secondary benefits to the state correctional system make such a fiscal investment worthwhile.

States should also shoulder part of the burden of bringing county jails up to minimal correctional standards. Ensuring that such facilities are operated and maintained as acceptable and humane environments is an objective which must be met before serious consideration of large-scale community correction.

## Conclusion

If the rehabilitation and successful reintegration of offenders are to remain objectives of the correctional system, we must continue to promote and emphasize alternative approaches to traditional incarceration. Community correction at present has serious drawbacks, which should not be glossed over, but it has the potential for great improvement. Imprisonment does not.

### Notes

[1] For a thorough discussion of this introductory concept, see National Advisory Commission on Criminal Justice Standards and Goals, *Corrections* (Washington, DC: Government Printing Office, 1973), pp. 73-90.

[2] Minnesota Department of Corrections, Research and Information Systems, *The Effect of the Availability of Community Residential Alternatives to State Incarceration on Sentencing Practices: The Social Control Issue* (St. Paul, MN: Department of Corrections, 1977), p. 1.

3 D. F. Greenberg, "Problems in Community Corrections," *Issues in Criminology*, Spring 1975, p. 6.

4 Ibid.

5 John Blackmore, "Minnesota Community Corrections Act Takes Hold," *Corrections Magazine*, March 1978, p. 53.

6 Indiana Correctional Economics Center of the American Bar Association, *Cost Analysis of Community Corrections Centers — a Case Study* (Washington, D.C., 1975), pp. 21-22.

7 Minnesota Department of Corrections, *Effect of the Availability of Community Residential Alternatives*, p. 30.

8 Ibid.

9 See Center on Administration of Criminal Justice, "An Evaluation of the California Probation Subsidy Program: A Summary" (Davis: University of California, 1977), pp. 12-20. Also see Institute of Public Policy Alternatives, *Final Report on Community Alternatives to Maximum Security Institutionalization for Selected Offenders* (Albany, NY: State University of New York at Albany, 1975), pp. 274-500.

10 National Advisory Commission, *Corrections*, p. 222. A caveat concerning the public protection issue raised by the Advisory Commission was: "It is necessary here to note that public protection is not always the sole objective of correctional programming. Some kinds of offenders, especially the most notorious, often could perfectly well be released without jeopardizing public safety. But their release will not be countenanced because public demands for retribution have not been satisfied. Offenders in custody should be there predominantly because public protection seems to require it. Decision-makers must disentangle these objectives to assure that use of community-based correctional programs is not denied for irrelevant reasons" (p. 222).

11 Ibid., p. 224.

12 See Governor's Commission on Crime Prevention and Control, "Residential Community Corrections Programs in Minnesota: An Evaluation Report" (November 1976). This report indicates that residential projects do not increase the rate of recidivism, compared with state incarceration. Also see Floyd Feeney and Travis Hirschi, "Impact of Commitment Reduction on the Recidivism of Offenders," vol. 5, "Evaluation of the California Probation Subsidy Program," Center on Administration of Criminal Justice. This study suggests that there is little difference in the recidivism rates: ". . . local treatment programs . . . have not proved noticeably better than regular probation or parole following state incarceration. In addition, there has probably been some increase in crime and recidivism attributable to the program" (p. 36). This article is an excellent example of just how difficult it is to properly analyze and assess recidivism rates. Also see Greenberg, "Problems in Community Corrections," p. 3. Greenberg notes some shortcomings of studies which have touted community correction as reducing recidivism rates, including the fact that lower recidivism risks are usually assigned to community correction or other alternative-type programs.

13 Center on Administration of Criminal Justice, "Evaluation of the California Probation Subsidy Program," pp. 20-44.

14 Ibid., pp. 36-37. Also see Blackmore, "Minnesota Community Corrections Act Takes Hold," p. 47. This article notes that community correction is in its decline in many jurisdictions. The decline is attributable at least in part to the fact that in many jurisdictions ". . . the community effort amounted to little more than an expansion of probation and the operation of a few Federally funded halfway houses and the other programs that had no impact on the traditional corrections system."

15 National Advisory Commission, *Corrections*, p. 225.

16 See Greenberg, "Problems in Community Corrections," p. 4.

[17] Minnesota Department of Corrections, *Effect of the Availability of Community Residential Alternatives.*

[18] See Greenberg, "Problems in Community Corrections," pp. 4-6.

[19] Minnesota Department of Corrections, *Effect of the Availability of Community Residential Alternatives,* p. 31.

[20] National Advisory Commission, *Corrections,* pp. 223-24.

[21] Blackmore, "Minnesota Community Corrections Act Takes Hold," p. 47.

[22] National Advisory Commission, *Corrections,* pp. 223-24.

[23] Ibid., p. 222. Also see pp. 223-36.

[24] Greenberg, "Problems in Community Corrections," pp. 8-9.

[25] Minnesota Department of Corrections, *Effect of the Availability of Community Residential Alternatives,* p. 31.

[26] Council of State Governments, "State Subsidies to Local Corrections: A Summary of Programs, 1977." This document contains a thorough listing of state subsidy programs in effect as of 1977. A listing of additional objectives sought by state subsidy programs appears on p. 3.

[27] Ibid., p. 4.

[28] Ibid.

[29] Community Corrections, *Minnesota Statutes,* sec. 401.10.

[30] Generally, the factor is based upon the number of adults under probation supervision, the number of presentence investigations completed, police officers' salaries, and overhead.

[31] Council of State Governments, "A State-Supported Local Corrections System: The Minnesota Experience" (1977), p. 10.

[32] Ibid.

[33] State Aid for Probation Services, *California Statutes* (1965), ch. 1029, Art. 7.

[34] Ibid., sec. 1825, subdivision (d). This subdivision contains a table entitled "Per Capita Subsidy in Relation to Percentage Decrease Base Commitment Rates/100,000."

[35] Center on Administration of Criminal Justice, "Evaluation of the California Probation Subsidy Program," p. 17.

[36] Blackmore, "Minnesota Community Corrections Act Takes Hold," p. 55.

[37] It should be noted that while *Executive Law,* sec. 246, authorizes reimbursement up to 50 percent, current fiscal restraints in New York State have resulted in the actual reimbursement's being as low as approximately 42 percent. The reimbursement scheme for New York generally includes personnel and operations and maintenance costs but excludes any local costs incurred for capital expenditures, debt service, fringe benefits, rentals, and indirect costs. (For a detailed statement of reimbursable costs, see *New York State Codes, Rules, and Regulations,* vol. 9, Part 360).

[38] See *New York State Codes, Rules, and Regulations,* vol. 9, Subtitle H.

[39] Institute for Public Policy Alternatives, *Final Report of Project on Community Alternatives,* p. 20.

[40] *Minnesota Statutes,* sec. 401.13. In addition, participating counties in Minnesota are not permitted to reduce their current local budget appropriations for correction. This prohibition prevents counties from using subsidy funds as replacement, as opposed to a supplement, for local correctional efforts.

[41] Ibid., sec. 401.08.

[42] Ibid.

[43] Ibid.

[44] Council of State Governments, "A State-Supported Local Corrections System," pp. 6-7.

[45] Ibid.

46 In New York State in 1976, approximately 84,604 individuals were confined in county jails (excluding institutions under the jurisdiction of the New York City Department of Correction) as unsentenced detainees. These individuals accounted for approximately 1,142,154 detention days, an average of 13.5 detention days per detainee. At an approximate average cost of $23 per day to house an individual in a county jail, some $26,269,542 was spent by counties for pretrial detention (outside of New York City) in 1976. These figures are based upon data compiled by the New York State Commission of Correction.

47 In New York, the only accepted statutory basis for the court's exercising "control" over a defendant at this stage of criminal proceeding is that which is necessary to ensure the defendant's appearance before the court. See *Criminal Procedure Law*, sec. 510.30, which provides in pertinent part that the court is to decide ". . . the kind and degree of control or restriction that is necessary to ensure his [the defendant's] court attendance. . . ." This decision is to be based on the following: (1) character, reputation, rehabilitation, and mental condition; (2) employment and financial resources; (3) family ties and length of residence in the community; (4) criminal record; (5) any history of juvenile delinquency or being a youthful offender; (6) previous record of court appearances when required; (7) probability of conviction; and, (8) if defendant is convicted, the length of sentence which may be imposed. See *Criminal Procedure Law*, sec. 510.30(2)(a).

48 In New York City, these are provided by the quasi-governmental New York City Criminal Justice Agency. This agency issues quarterly reports which include a detailed analysis of their operations during each quarter of the year. This agency is an excellent resource for anyone who is involved or concerned with pretrial services issues.

49 Under current New York law, there may be some question as to whether an individual can be required to participate in treatment programs at the pretrial stage of a criminal proceeding.

50 See David Borkman et al., *An Exemplary Project: Community Based Corrections in Des Moines* (Washington, DC: National Institute of Law Enforcement and Criminal Justice, 1976), pp. 15-16 for discussion of techniques used in Des Moines to identify the detainee population.

51 Discussion of Des Moines' experience with the Vera assessment form and the information its prerelease program forwarded to the courts can be found ibid., pp. 16-17. Des Moines has modified the original Vera instrument (e.g., decreased the length of residency necessary in the community, forwarded only the recommendation for ROR eligibility to the court without details or supporting information, and instituted some novel ROR and postrelease procedures).

52 Ibid., p. 21.

53 Ibid., pp. 21-26.

54 Ibid., p. 21.

55 National Institute of Law Enforcement and Criminal Justice, *Neighborhood Justice Centers: An Analysis of Potential Models*, p. 2.

56 Vera Institute of Justice, *Felony Arrests: Their Prosecution and Disposition in New York City's Courts* (New York: Vera Institute, 1977), p. 135.

57 Ibid., p. xv. There are a number of excellent publications and evaluations concerning alternative dispute resolution techniques. See, for example, National Institute of Law Enforcement and Criminal Justice, *Neighborhood Justice Centers*; report of IMCR Dispute Center, New York; and that of the Community Board Program, 149 Ninth Street, San Francisco.

# Part II

## Investigation and Offender Supervision

The field of community corrections has undergone considerable change in the last fifteen years due to the increased public acceptance of incarceration as a form of punishment for criminal offenders. While much attention has been drawn to prisons (overcrowding, poor conditions, cost of construction, violence, gangs, and so on), this change in attitude has also had a profound effect on correctional agencies in the community as well. The effects of changes in policy, in the laws governing community correctional agencies, and in public attitudes is explored in "Have Community Supervision Officers Changed Their Attitudes Toward Their Work?" Updating earlier research on the attitudes of workers, authors Patricia Harris, Todd Clear, and Christopher Baird report that community supervision officers have, in fact, changed their attitudes toward their work. The history of probation and parole is rooted in offender reintegration, yet these authors suggest that staff members have begun to shift their attitudes away from rehabilitation and treatment and toward enforcement and surveillance. The implications resulting from this shift are discussed.

Within the probation and parole profession, considerable attention has been given to issues associated with offender supervision. It is estimated that three-quarters of an officer's time is spent in supervision-related activities. These include personal offender contact, home visits, employment verifications and job searches, and drug and alcohol screening, as well as monitoring court and parole board ordered condition of release. Less attention is given in the literature to the balance of the officer's work activity—investigation, particularly the presentence investigation.

In "A Typology of Presentence Probation Investigators," John Rosecrance draws on his probation experiences as well as interviews with court personnel to describe how probation investigators use the presentence report to advance their careers and to support their personal viewpoints. Through his research, Rosecrance has developed a typology of presentence investigators, *team player, mossback, hardliner, bleeding heart liberal,* and *maverick.* Each aspect of the typology views the purpose of sentencing within a different context. For example, the "team player" views sentencing as a reflection of the values of society, while a "hardliner" maintains that the purpose of sentencing is to deter others from committing crimes.

Large caseloads have plagued probation and parole systems for some time, but have taken on added significance in recent years with larger numbers of felony offenders being released under community supervision. The size and complexity of these caseloads have altered the job routine of probation and parole officers—specifically, they have elevated the importance of offender classification and case supervision. The situation has gotten to the point where some argue that probation supervision has become ineffective in either rehabilitating the offender or protecting the community. In "Difficult Clients, Large Caseloads Plague Probation, Parole Agencies," Randall Guynes of the National Institute of Justice reports on an in-depth survey of 49 state probation and parole directors and 339 local offices. He describes the organization of probation services in the United States and ranks the most serious problems in the system as perceived by probation and parole administrators. Among the highest rated problems are prison overcrowding, staff shortages, and a lack of public understanding. Data submitted indicates that the expansion of the domain of probation and parole agencies must stop because of the system's inability to absorb more offenders.

"Screening Devices in Probation and Parole," by Todd Clear and Kenneth Gallagher, identifies the importance of utilizing an offender classification system in conjunction with an agency's stated mission, its available resources, and its environment. They argue that arbitrarily establishing risk/needs cutoff scores and developing supervision standards without considering these factors will doom the classification system to failure. Each system should be flexible and adapted to local needs and demands.

John Rosecrance offers a solution to the problem of offender supervision in "Probation Supervision: Mission Impossible." Simply stated, the supervision function should be eliminated, with service needs provided by agencies outside of the criminal justice system. According to Rosecrance, enforcement and surveillance activities would be handled by the police. Probation staff would assume complete duties as officers of the court, responsible for the "unambiguous function" of compiling and presenting court evaluations.

# 5

# Have Community Supervision Officers Changed Their Attitudes Toward Their Work?

## Patricia M. Harris, Todd R. Clear, S. Christopher Baird

*Studies of probation and parole officers' attitudes conducted in the 1960s and 1970s indicated respondents' preference for assistance over authority as the most important goal of community supervision. The present research compares results obtained from the 1970s and 1980s applications of the Authority/Assistance Questionnaire and the Correctional Policy Inventory. The findings point not only to increased concern for authority but also to the diminished meaningfulness of the assistance objective. The authors suggest that a new emphasis on surveillance, in which delivery on service is largely a means for monitoring client risk, has "crowded" the rehabilitative ideal.*

Descriptions of probation and parole practice draw frequent attention to the importance of officers' attitudes. Typologies of community supervision officers generated from the study of attitudes (Glaser 1964;

Source: Patricia M. Harris, Todd R. Clear, and S. Christopher Baird (1989). "Have Community Supervision Officers Changed Their Attitudes Toward Their Work?" *Justice Quarterly* 6 (2): 233-46. Reprinted with permission of the Academy of Criminal Justice Sciences.

Klockars 1972; Rosecrance 1987; Tomaino 1975) commonly contrast officers who emphasize law enforcement objectives of supervision with those who emphasize treatment and assistance objectives. Goal discordance is believed to have important consequences and has been linked to variation in the severity of presentence recommendations (Katz 1982; Rosecrance 1987), officers' acceptance of agency directives on weapon use by staff (Sigler and McGraw 1984), and officers' response to violations by probationers (Baird, Clear, and Harris 1985).

Although some researchers have expressed concern over officers' failure to agree on the objectives of community supervision (e.g., Czajkoski 1969), much previous work in this area portrayed treatment as the most beneficial or most prevalent of correctional attitudes. In descriptive studies, relinquishment of rigid control techniques was identified as an essential ingredient of effective officer-client relationships (Klockars 1972; Tomaino 1975). Among studies measuring support for various correctional philosophies, results revealed that the majority of officers accepted treatment or assistance as the most important of community supervision objectives. The earliest of these studies, undertaken by Miles (1965) on a sample of 48 probation and parole officers, suggested that the majority of officers placed facilitating "the client's opportunity for self-help" above other supervision activities (p. 21). Only nine percent of the 486 federal probation officers studied by Glaser (1964) could be considered "punitive" types; the vast majority expressed preferences for high-assistance supervision styles. In a slightly later study, Van Laningham, Taber, and Dimants (1966) reported the attitudes of several hundred probation officers toward the relevance of a large number of tasks to their work; they found that officers expressed wide consensus about the appropriateness of "referral" and "advice and guidance" activities, but displayed little agreement regarding the relevance of law enforcement tasks. Support for the earlier findings is provided in Donnellan and Moore's (1979) survey of 146 probation and parole officers. In this study, officers ranked "assisting clients with their problems" and "changing clients' behavior" respectively as the first and second goals of community supervision, but ranked "protection of society" only third.

More recent research suggests that probation and parole officers may be turning away from treatment and assistance as primary philosophies of community supervision. In a survey that required 133 probation and parole officers to place themselves along a continuum bounded by treatment philosophy on one end and law enforcement philosophy on the other, the distribution was skewed slightly in favor of the latter (Sigler and McGraw 1984). Rosecrance's (1987) typology of a smaller sample of 60 presentence probation investigators in three states also points to the likelihood of increased ambivalence among officers. According to this research, the largest proportions of officers fell into what Rosecrance labeled the "team player" and the "mossback" categories, consisting of individuals who regarded "society's values" and "whatever value resolved the matter fastest" respectively as the primary purposes of probation. Smaller proportions of officers held their own firm beliefs about the aim of community supervision; among these were "hardliners," for whom deterrence was the overarching purpose of supervision, and "bleeding hearts," for whom rehabilitation was primary. Of much interest was Rosecrance's finding that hardliners outnumbered bleeding hearts by two to one. The current study evaluates the relative importance of law enforcement and treatment concerns to community supervision officers in the 1980s. This research contributes to the literature on probation and parole officers' attitudes because it compares results obtained from the application of the same instruments at periods at least 10 years apart. Employed in these comparisons are the Authority/Assistance Questionnaire, developed by Daniel Glaser (1964), and the Correctional Policy Inventory, developed by Vincent O'Leary (1972).

## The Authority/Assistance Questionnaire

The Authority/Assistance Questionnaire was used first by Glaser in 1962 in a survey of 486 federal probation officers. Drawing upon his observations of officers' styles and building on earlier work by Ohlin, Piven, and Pappenfort (1956), Glaser argued that the parole officer's job included two dimensions of responsibility: *assistance*, or the provision of services to the offender; and *authority*, or the exertion of control over the offender's behavior. To classify the officers in his sample, Glaser devised a questionnaire from which he extracted two Guttman scales, one each for authority and assistance. Originally Glaser's questionnaire included 70 questions, from which two scales of five questions each were established.[1] The authority scale produced a coefficient of reproducibility (R) of .92 and a coefficient of scalability of .72.[2] The assistance scale produced an R of .92 and a coefficient of scalability of .70. Interestingly, the two scale values were not related significantly.[3]

Using 1974 data, Clear (1977) updated Glaser's questionnaire to reflect changes in social values (e.g., one of Glaser's items probes officers' response to parolees who live with women out of wedlock) and to incorporate the concept of reintegration, which in 1964 was still an undeveloped idea. He also adapted the questionnaire for use by probation officers. His sample included probation officers from the Tremont section of the South Bronx, New York City (N = 21) and officers from Middlesex County, an urban county in Massachusetts (N = 21). Using the updated instrument, Clear produced two valid Guttman scales of five items each, with an R of .93 and a coefficient of scalability of .63 for the assistance dimension and with an R of .94 and a coefficient of scalability of .65 for the control dimension. These new scales, like Glaser's, were independent.[4]

## The Correctional Policy Inventory

The Correctional Policy Inventory was designed by Vincent O'Leary to measure the attitudes of corrections personnel toward their work. The questionnaire, which is adapted from Herbert Kelman's (1958) categorization of strategies of change, measures respondents' affinity for each of the following four correctional philosophies: *reform*, a community-centered attitude which emphasizes offenders' compliance with rules, regulations, and community standards; *rehabilitation*, an offender-centered attitude which emphasizes the diagnosis and treatment of the offender; *restraint*, an organization-centered attitude which reflects minimal concern for either the community or the offender; and *reintegration*, a hybrid position which observes the needs of both the community and the offender.

The instrument contains 10 questions. Respondents rate four possible responses, corresponding to each of the four policy models, by placing each of the choices somewhere along a 10-point scale. Because every item response corresponds to one strategy for change, it is possible to compute the emphasis that each respondent gives to each policy.[5]

The questionnaire was administered between 1968 and 1970 to a nationwide sample of corrections managers who attended a series of training seminars conducted by the National Council on Crime and Delinquency. O'Leary found that respondents placed greater emphasis upon policies reflecting rehabilitation and reintegration than on those reflecting restraint and reform.

## Methods

Both the updated Authority/Assistance Questionnaire and the Correctional Policy Inventory were administered to a total of 223 probation officers from Travis County (Austin), Texas (N = 30), Hennepin County (Minneapolis), Minnesota (N = 44), and Milwaukee and Dane (Madison) Counties, Wisconsin (N = 140) during May and June 1983.

The earlier and the later applications of the Authority/Assistance Questionnaire lend themselves to two comparisons. First, variation in cutoff points between the 1974 and the 1983 scales suggests changes in officers' willingness to initiate assisting or controlling behaviors. Second, diminished or enhanced scalability of the assistance and authority items indicates the changing relevance of assistance or authority objectives in community supervision.

The 1970 and the 1983 applications of the Correctional Policy Inventory permit us to compare the relative ranks of the rehabilitation, reform, restraint, and reintegration positions. This contrast addresses two questions: whether attitude change has occurred and what the extent of change has been, if change has taken place.

## Results

Using Clear's version of the Authority/Assistance Questionnaire, we produced two scales of five questions each from our survey (authority, R = .93 and coefficient of scalability = .57; assistance, R = .92 and coefficient of scalability = .53).[6]

Several changes were necessary before we could create the most recent scales. For both scales, some changes in cutoff points were required. Control items for which cutoff points changed from the 1974 to the 1983 survey included the following three questions: "How often should a probation officer make unannounced home visits?" (from "occasionally" to "very frequently"); "How often is it necessary for a probation officer to keep close checks on the associations of his probationers?" (from "occasionally" to "often"); and "How often should probation revocation be recommended for juvenile probationers who are persistently truant from school?" (from "occasionally" to "often"). For three of the items in the assistance sales, no cutoff changes were necessary. In an item that measured the probation officer's response to a probationer who was having difficulty paying a court-imposed fine, the cutoff was shifted from "discuss the financial problems with the probationer, exploring ways in which he may handle his finances differently in order to pay his fine" to "keep a record of his payments and tell him that he is expected to fully pay his fine."

Table 1 summarizes results of the application of Clear's 1974 cutoff points and items to the responses yielded by the most recent group of respondents. Coefficients of reproducibility and scalability for the assistance dimension are .95 and .58 respectively, but the distribution of the scale is sufficiently skewed that the utility of this scale as a variable is limited.

Coefficients of reproducibility and scalability for the control dimension were .95 and .35 respectively; these values showed that the original cutoffs no longer produced a valid scale. The main reason for low scalability was that on the control items, respondents exhibited a greater

Table 1

**Comparison of 1974 and 1983 Responses to Authority/Assistance Questionnaire, Using Original (1973) Scale Items and Cutoffs***

| | Authority | | Scale Concern | | | | Assistance | |
| | Middlesex and Tremont Samples | | Madison, Hennepin, Milwaukee, Travis Samples | | Middlesex and Tremont Samples | | Madison, Hennepin, Milwaukee, Travis Samples | |
| Scale Position | % | (N) | % | (N) | % | (N) | % | (N) |
|---|---|---|---|---|---|---|---|---|
| 0 (lowest) | 5.0 | (2) | 0.0 | (0) | 5.0 | (2) | 2.7 | (6) |
| 1 | 0.0 | (0) | 0.5 | (1) | 5.0 | (2) | 15.0 | (22) |
| 2 | 42.0 | (16) | 11.0 | (24) | 32.0 | (12) | 58.2 | (128) |
| 3 | 34.0 | (13) | 65.1 | (142) | 41.0 | (15) | 22.7 | (50) |
| 4 | 18.0 | (7) | 21.1 | (46) | 14.0 | (5) | 1.4 | (3) |
| 5 | 0.0 | (0) | 2.3 | (5) | 3.0 | (1) | 0.0 | (0) |
| Total N | | (38) | | (218) | | (37) | | (220) |
| Coefficient of reproducibility | .94 | | .95 | | .94 | | .95 | |
| Coefficient of scalability | .64 | | .38 | | .61 | | .58 | |

*The Pearson's product-moment correlation for the control and assistance scores in Clear's study is $r = .0618$ ($p = .337$); in the present study it is $r = .0710$ ($p = .148$).

willingness to select more controlling answers; thus their responses reflected much greater agreement in 1983. This situation made it more difficult to improve the scalability statistic in any of the extractable scales. As shown by the frequencies in Table 1, it made our sample considerably more supportive of "control" concerns than did the 1974 samples.

Table 2 presents a comparison of O'Leary's Correctional Policy scores (N = 440) and those produced by our sample. Results show that O'Leary's respondents placed greater emphasis upon rehabilitation and reintegration than did the more recent group of respondents. Whereas highest scores were obtained for reintegration in the earlier sample, highest scores in our study were attached to the reform dimension. The greatest change took place with respect to reform, where the median score increased 24 percent. It is important to note that the median scores of both controlling postures (reform and restraint) increased and that those of both assistance postures (rehabilitation and reintegration) decreased. In addition, the magnitude of change across complementary philosophies is similar.

Table 2

**Comparison of Median Correctional Policy Scores for O'Leary's (1972) and Our (1983) Sample**

|               | **Median Score** | | **Percentage of Change from 1970** |
| **Policy**    | **1970** | **1983** | |
|---------------|------|------|------------|
| Reintegration | 70   | 57   | − 18.6     |
| Rehabilitation| 67   | 55   | − 17.9     |
| Reform        | 50   | 62   | + 24.0     |
| Restraint     | 37   | 44   | + 18.9     |

Table 3 displays product-moment correlations for the six correctional policies for each of the two sets of respondents. In this case, Correctional Policy Inventory scores reflect responses of the 1974 sample studied by Clear (1977). As Table 3 shows, notable differences distinguish the two samples. For example, the relation between like dimensions is similar for the two studies (i.e., significant correlations between logical combinations of policies, such as rehabilitation and assistance or reform and authority, maintain the same direction), but the strength of the association between the dimensions across the two instruments changes. Although significant positive associations emerge between authority and

Table 3

**Correlation Matrix of Questionnaire Results for 1974 (N = 42) and 1983 (N = 214) Samples**

| Probation Questionnaire | Probation Questionnaire | | | | Correctional Policy Inventory | | | | | | | |
| --- | --- | --- | --- | --- | --- | --- | --- | --- | --- | --- | --- | --- |
| | Authority | | Assistance | | Reintegration | | Rehabilitation | | Reform | | Restraint | |
| | 74 | 83 | 74 | 83 | 74 | 83 | 74 | 83 | 74 | 83 | 74 | 83 |
| Authority | 1.0 | 1.0 | .21 | .07 | −.32* | −.16* | −.25 | .03 | .04* | .27* | .27 | .24* |
| Assistance | | | 1.0 | 1.0 | .27 | .06 | .28 | .10 | −.30 | .02 | −.22 | .13* |
| **Correctional Policy** | | | | | | | | | | | | |
| Reintegration | | | | | 1.00 | 1.00 | | | | | | |
| Rehabilitation | | | | | .25 | .31* | 1.00 | 1.00 | | | | |
| Reform | | | | | .60 | −.16* | −.11 | .04 | 1.00 | 1.00 | | |
| Restraint | | | | | −.65* | −.25* | −.19 | −.06 | .57* | .32* | 1.00 | 1.00 |

*p < .05

reform and between authority and restraint, assistance in 1983 produces only a meager correlation with restraint, and this relation is unexpectedly positive ($r = .13$, $p < .05$). Of further interest is the finding that reintegration, an assistance-related policy minus the "medical model" dressing, is correlated positively with rehabilitation ($r = .31$, $p < .05$) but bears no significant relation to the assistance scale for the most recent applications. The correlation between reintegration and authority continues to be negative in the 1983 application, as it was in 1974 ($r = -.32$ and $-.16$ respectively, $p < .05$), but the strength of this association is halved. Associations between reintegration and restraint across the two samples change in a similar fashion (from $-.65$ to $-.25$, $p < .05$). Taken together, these findings raise the possibility that assistance is no longer as distinct an objective of community supervision as it once was, and as authority continues to be.

Because the Guttman scales produced by our sample were so weak, we attempted to compute additive scales by summing response frequencies from "least" to "most" characteristic of the values for all of the items associated with each scale in both applications of the Authority/Assistance Questionnaire. Table 4 presents the relation between these new variables and the results produced by the earlier applications of the Authority/Assistance Questionnaire and the Correctional Policy Inventory. In comparison to the findings shown in Table 3, the association between the new authority variable and restraint is stronger and more consistent, but the recalculated assistance variable bears no significant associations whatever with any of the Correctional Policy Inventory variables.

## Discussion

The preceding analysis raises the possibility of substantial attitude change among probation officers. The data suggest that concern for authority among community supervision officers has increased, and that authority is now a more meaningful concept in supervision than either assistance or treatment.

Several findings in this study support a conclusion that concern for authority has grown among probation officers. Reapplication of nine-year-old Guttman scale cutoffs on questionnaire items produced a set of responses with a greater emphasis upon authority. Control items from Glaser's 1964 survey indicated less control-oriented concern among his respondents than was found among the present subjects. A most dramatic shift surfaced when we compared O'Leary's 1969-1970 Correctional Policy norms with the norms displayed by the more recent subjects.

Concern for authority has become a more meaningful philosophy

Table 4

**Correlation Matrix of Questionnaire Results for the 1983 Sample (N = 214), Using Recalculated Authority and Assistance Values**

| Probation Questionnaire | Recalculated | Values |
|---|---|---|
| | Authority | Assistance |
| Authority | .69** | .13** |
| Assistance | .07 | .80** |
| Correctional Policy Inventory | | |
| Reintegration | − .27** | .14 |
| Rehabilitation | − .24** | .14 |
| Reform | .27 | 0.00 |
| Restraint | .34** | .05 |
| **p < .05 | | |

than either assistance or treatment, as demonstrated primarily by the difficulty associated with scaling the assistance variable for the data produced by the most recent survey. In Clear's scale, cut-offs and items could be selected to allow for a six-point scale with almost 60 percent of the cases falling at one point on the scale and 95 percent falling at three adjacent points. Our own "best" scale is itself not very discriminating — despite a slight improvement over Clear's scale — and the Guttman scale statistics produced here are slightly below values which are regarded as sufficient qualification for a "true scale." Further, neither our assistance scale nor the rehabilitation score produced by our application of the O'Leary instrument was correlated with the other.

How can these findings be explained? Because of the scales' proved utility as measures of the assistance/treatment constructs in prior research, it would be difficult to accept a suggestion that the instruments discussed here fail to capture the attitudes in question (i.e., that the activities depicted in the questionnaire items have lost their relevance to contemporary supervision). To the contrary, assistance items in both instruments reflect issues — e.g., the quality of family relationships, educational achievement, living arrangements, and employment and financial status — with which probation officers continue to be concerned. As a matter of fact, these very concerns are embodied firmly in such classification systems as the Wisconsin Risk-Needs System, which are fast becoming standard in probation departments nationwide.

What *has* changed is the significance of service provision. Service delivery no longer carries the connotations of rehabilitation and reintegration, but is now a more rigid enterprise that is tied to the task of monitoring client risk. Consequently, assistance is a less distinct concept than authority.

Alternatively, one might attribute the findings to the study's methodological weaknesses. The sample sizes are substantially diverse, and neither of the groups of respondents to which this paper refers reflects a national random sample of opinion. This study did not control for differences among subgroups. Therefore, the present research, standing alone, is insufficient indication that attitudes among community supervision officers have undergone substantial transformation.

Yet there are many reasons to believe that the trend noted here is genuine, for the findings are consistent with other changes that have occurred in the corrections field over the last decade. As a result of prison crowding, felons now constitute larger proportions of probation populations and present greater public risks than in the past (Petersilia 1985). Thus probationers as a whole now require more control by community supervision officers than in earlier times. Intensive supervision probation, which carries an explicit commitment to the philosophies of authority and restraint, has become a component of probation services in many states, often by the choice of constituents external to the probation agency (Friel, Vaughn, and del Carmen 1987). Through civil actions, greater numbers of officers are being held accountable for harmful behavior by persons entrusted to their supervision (del Carmen 1986; del Carmen and Trook-White 1986). The observed differences also correspond to a marked decline in the public's confidence in the rehabilitative potential of correctional institutions, as evidenced by changes in responses to nationwide public opinion polls over a 15-year period (Flanagan and Caulfield 1984). Additional support is found in other recent studies of the attitudes of community supervision officers, which demonstrate officers' increasing endorsement of control philosophies (Rosecrance 1987; Sigler and McGraw 1984).

Thus it would appear that attitude change among probation and parole officers is a likely phenomenon, in view of a nationwide shift toward conservatism in correctional policy generally. Rising caseloads, increased public awareness of crime (and concern about public protection), concern over prison crowding, and the demise of treatment as an officially mandated objective of probation provide strong incentives for generalizing from the present findings that community supervision officers are more concerned with control than in the past.

Certainly, measurement of community supervision officers' attitudes will continue to be a focus of research on probation and parole. The analyses reported here, which indicate the elasticity of officers' attitudes, illustrate the utility of repeating application of the same instruments at different times. Because the present research incorporated analyses from previous studies, the possibility of matching samples on size and characteristics was far beyond our reach. In future research, researchers can take care to overcome the methodological limitations of the current study in order to confirm or disprove the speculations raised here.

## Notes

[1] To evaluate whether the items of a questionnaire constitute a valid Guttman scale, we used two statistical criteria. The values of these criteria depend partially upon the cutting point chosen for each item. Cutting points separate passing responses from failing responses to each of the questions in a scale. The following example is reproduced from Glaser's control scale:

How often do you check upon your parolees for drinking:

> Always (95-100% of the time)
> Very frequently (70-94% of the time)
> Often (30-69% of the time)
> Occasionally (5-29% of the time)
> Never (0-4% of the time)

The selection of "often" as a cutting point means that only those persons who respond with "often," "very frequently," or "always" can pass this item. Thus cutting points represent thresholds of tolerance toward the attitude being measured. The choice of particular cutting points determines the number of respondents who pass and fail each item.

[2] The coefficient of reproducibility is an indication of the extent to which a cumulative response pattern — or ordinality — is reflected in the subjects' scale scores. The coefficient of reproducibility is represented by R, where R equals the number of errors divided by the total number of responses. Some sources state that to be acceptable, the value of R must equal at least .90 (see Guttman 1950; Torgerson 1958). High values of R, however, occur whenever the items in question elicit a high rate of ordinality due to agreement in the response pattern for any particular category. When this happens, it is the marginal values which inflate the level of R. One way of assessing to what extent R is affected by marginal values is to take into consideration a second statistic known as the minimum marginal reproducibility (MMR), where MMR equals the number of responses in modal categories divided by the total number of responses. A comparison of these two statistics shows the degree to which R is merely the byproduct of the relative frequencies of item response. The difference between R and MMR is known as the "percent improvement." There is little guidance concerning the desired size of the percent improvement, although one source recommends that "only when R greatly exceeds MMR . . . is there an advantage in using the Guttman scale" (Fishbein and Ajzen 1975:68). A more accurate evaluation of the utility of the Guttman scale is the coefficient of scalability, where scalability equals the percent improvement divided by the difference obtained by subtracting MMR from 1. The coefficient of scalability should be greater than .6 (Menzel 1953).

[3] Glaser reports a Goodman-Kruskal gamma of .079 between responses to authority items and responses to assistance items.

[4] Pearson's product-moment correlation computed for Clear's data equaled .0618, significant at .337.

⁵ The following is a sample question (we added the policies in parentheses): The chief obstacle for correctional systems to overcome in assisting most offenders to avoid further criminal behavior is:

    a. The existence of poor attitudes and values on their part which must be replaced by more positive ones. (Reform)

    b. The availability of practical alternatives which the community is willing to provide and the offender's perception of those alternatives. (Reintegration)

    c. The maintenance of the correctional system's program from which the offender can benefit if he desires. (Restraint)

    d. The presence of emotional problems within offenders which can usually be traced back to early defective relationships with parents. (Rehabilitation)

Completely............................................................Completely
Characteristic........................................................Uncharacteristic

⁶ When extracting Guttman scales from a questionnaire, the researcher tries to address a variety of conditions. Minimum levels of MMR and high coefficients of scalability are not the only concerns because usually one intends to use the scales as dependent or independent variables in subsequent analyses. As a consequence, one looks for a combination of items and cutoffs that meet minimum statistical requirements while also producing enough variability in the scale values to make the scale results useful in later analyses. A typical approach is to test a number of combinations of items and cutoff points until a "best" result is achieved in this regard. It is noteworthy that each of our "best" scales is somewhat weaker than the earlier scales of either Glaser or Clear. Much of the low scalability in the more recent scales is due to high minimum marginal reproducibility, which reflects substantially reduced distributions of values in comparison to the earlier surveys.

## Bibliography

Baird, S. C., T. R. Clear, and P. M. Harris (1985) "The Use and Effectiveness of the Behavior Control Tools of Probation Officers." Unpublished report to National Institute of Justice.

Clear, T. R. (1977) "The Specification of Behavioral Objectives in Probation and Parole." Unpublished Ph.D. dissertation, State University of New York at Albany.

Czajkoski, E. H. (1969) "Functional Specialization in Probation and Parole." *Crime and Delinquency* 15:238-46.

del Carmen, R. V. (1986) *Potential Liabilities of Probation and Parole Officers.* Cincinnati: Anderson.

del Carmen, R. V. and E. Trook-White (1986) *Liability Issues in Community Service Sanctions.* Washington, DC: National Institute of Corrections.

Donnellan, M. C. and H. A. Moore (1979) "Rehabilitation and Protection: The Goals and Orientations of Probation and Parole Officers." *Offender Rehabilitation* 3:207-18.

Duffee, D. (1975) *Correctional Policy and Prison Organization.* New York: Halsted.

Fishbein, M. and Ajzen, I. (1975) *Belief, Attitude, Intention and Behavior.* Reading, MA: Addison-Wesley.

Flanagan, Timothy J. and Susan L. Caulfield (1984) "Public Opinion and Prison Policy: A Review." *Prison Journal* 64:31-46.

Friel, C. M., J. B. Vaughn, and R. del Carmen (1987) *Electronic Monitoring and Correctional Policy: The Technology and Its Application.* Washington, DC: National Institute of Justice.

Glaser, D. (1964) *The Effectiveness of a Prison and Parole System.* New York: Bobbs-Merrill.

Guttman, L. L. (1950) "The Basis for Scalogram Analysis." In S. Stoufer et al. (eds.), *Studies in Social Psychology in World War II.* IV. Princeton: Princeton University Press, pp. 60-90.

Katz, J. (1982) "The Attitudes and Decisions of Probation Officers." *Criminal Justice and Behavior* 9:455-75.

Kelman, H. (1958) "Compliance, Identification and Internalization: Three Processes of Attitude Change." *Journal of Conflict Resolution* 2: 51-60.

Klockars, C. (1972) "A Theory of Probation Supervision." *Journal of Criminal Law, Criminology and Police Science* 63:550-57.

Menzel, H. (1953) "A New Coefficient for Scalogram Analysis." *Public Opinion Quarterly* 1953:268-80.

Miles, A. P. (1965) "The Reality of the Probation Officer's Dilemma." *Federal Probation* 29:18-23.

Ohlin, L. E., H. Piven, and D. M. Pappenfort (1956) "Major Dilemmas of the Social Worker in Probation and Parole." *National Probation and Parole Association Journal* 2:211-25.

O'Leary, V. (1972) *Correctional Policy Inventory.* Hackensack, NJ: National Council on Crime and Delinquency.

Petersilia, Joan (1985) *Probation and Felony Offenders.* Washington, DC: National Institute of Justice.

Rosecrance, J. (1987) "A Typology of Presentence Probation Investigators." *International Journal of Offender Therapy and Comparative Criminology* 31:163-77.

Sigler, R. T. and B. McGraw (1984) "Adult Probation and Parole Officers: Influence of Their Weapons, Role Perceptions and Role Conflict." *Criminal Justice Review* 9:28-32.

Tomaino, Louis (1975) "The Five Faces of Probation." *Federal Probation* 39: 42-45.

Torgerson, W. S. (1958) *Theory and Methods of Scaling.* New York: Wiley.

Van Laningham, Dale E., Merlin Taber, and Ruta Dimants (1966) "How Adult Probation Officers View Their Job Responsibilities." *Crime and Delinquency* 12:97-108.

# 6

# A Typology of Presentence Probation Investigators

## John Rosecrance

### Abstract

*There is a lack of knowledge concerning the most basic of probation services — the presentence investigation. In order to develop an understanding of this service, a typology of probation officers who conduct these investigations is presented. An analysis of data, drawn from fifteen years of probation experience and qualitative interviewing of court personnel, revealed that officers use presentence reports to advance personal careers and individual perspectives. The usefulness of presentence investigations is questioned, as well as the willingness of the probation bureaucracy to provide an environment conducive to objective reporting.*

## Introduction

The editor (Petersilia, 1985) of a recent *Crime and Delinquency* issue featuring articles on community supervision warned that efforts to establish viable alternatives to imprisonment were problematic since

Source: *International Journal of Offender Therapy and Comparative Criminology*, Vol. 31, No. 2. Copyright © 1987 The Oregon Health Sciences University. Reprinted with permission of the Guilford Press.

social scientists and correctional planners "know so little about probation and parole services as they are now administered." The purpose of this article is to add to the body of knowledge concerning probation services. In order to develop an accurate description of probation services, it is essential to understand the presentence investigation process (Keve, 1962, 1967; Carter, 1967, 1978; Curry 1975; Allen et al., 1979; and Blumstein et al., 1983). The initial investigation of adult criminal defendants is the most basic of probation responsibilities — leading (Cromwell et al., 1985) authors of a contemporary criminal justice textbook to conclude, "the ultimate merit of probation as a correctional tool is dependent to a very great extent upon the nature and quality of the presentence report." Additionally, the functions and objectives of the presentence investigation report have been delineated clearly in a government probation manual (Administrative Office, 1974).

> (1) To aid the court in determining the appropriate sentence; (2) to aid the probation officer in his rehabilitative efforts during probation and parole supervision; (3) to assist Bureau of Prisons institutions in their classification and treatment programs and also in their release planning; (4) to furnish the Board of Parole with information pertinent to its consideration of parole; and (5) to serve as a source of information for systematic research.

> The objectives of the presentence report are to focus information on the character and personality of the defendant, to offer insight into his problems and needs, to help understand the world in which he lives, to learn about his relationships with people and to discover those salient factors that underlie his specific offense and his conduct in general and to suggest alternatives in the rehabilitation process.

While researchers generally agree concerning the purposes of presentence reports, there is a lack of understanding how probation officers actually go about compiling their reports. In particular there is a critical void in our knowledge of the methods utilized by probation officers in arriving at particular sentence recommendations (Carter, 1967; Petersilia et al., 1985). Even though plea bargaining (Hagan et al., 1979; Kingsworth and Rizzo, 1979), determinate sentencing (Brewer et al., 1981), and informal guidelines (Neubauer, 1974; Rosecrance, 1985) limit probation officer decision-making — there is sufficient opportunity for individual discretion in many presentence investigations. Although it is commonly acknowledged that the probation officers' perspectives of the correctional system and their role in that system vary considerably (Reed and King, 1966:121; Carter and Wilkins, 1970:153; Shover, 1979:208), the process whereby these differing perspectives influence presentence investigations and subsequent court recommendations remains unidentified. The specific goal of this article is to clarify that process.

The method chosen for achieving this goal is to present a typology of presentence probation investigators. The typology, based upon 15 years' experience as a probation officer and qualitative interviewing of court personnel, was developed by identifying the types that probation workers recognize and by exploring the criteria they use in placing themselves and other officers into various categories. The concept of role in this study is defined as ". . . an unique combination of certain customary ways of responding to recurrent situations—this unique combination being known and expected by others who deal with persons in this role, as well as by persons who occupy the role" (Van Landingham et al., 1966:98). In constructing the present typology the present author retained the actual terms used by probation officers themselves in the typing process. Thus, the resulting schema is a community rather than a researcher designated typology (Spradley, 1970; Emerson, 1983).

Previous researchers have identified several typologies of parole and probation officers (Ohlin et al., 1956; Glaser, 1964; Takagi, 1967; Klockars, 1972; Blake et al., 1979). These classification systems involved supervision officers and not investigation officers. Since the priorities and responsibilities of probation investigators are often different from those of supervision personnel (Glaser, 1985), the extant typologies are not directly applicable to presentence writers. Typologies of supervising officers are oriented around the continuing dilemma of whether to emphasize control or assistance in relationships with defendants (Glaser, 1964:430-40). These schemas invariably depict one type of officer as a problematic figure whose vacillation "leads to very inconsistent behavior—helping an offender one day and issuing a technical violation the next. It is this officer who wraps his client in a warm hug, brushing him with his gun butt as he does so" (Duffee, 1984:187).

The dichotomy of control and assistance is not a central issue for probation investigation officers. Their contacts with defendants are brief, usually consisting of one face-to-face interview. Most investigators are interested in presenting plausible reports to the court and rarely concern themselves with the extent or nature of their relationships with probationers. Typically, their overarching goal is to "shepherd the case through court" and they prefer to leave the job of "salvaging offenders" to supervision officers. While there are similarities between the concerns of supervision and investigation officers, e.g., protecting the community, avoiding controversies, and advancing careers—sufficient differences exist to warrant developing separate typologies.

The presentation of a probation investigator typology is an appropriate first stage in the development of a comprehensive understanding of probation practices. These categorizations, by providing systematic guidelines, will allow researchers to examine objectively the actions of presentence investigators. An analysis of these types and the reasons for their continuance suggest that, with regard to court reporting, many probation departments will be unable to implement meaningful change — even in the face of escalating case loads and financial striction. Although one type of probation officer (not previously identified by prior research) could serve as an exemplar for significantly improving the investigation process, bureaucratic imperatives (Tepperman, 1973) work against such an eventuality. The existing organizational dynamics of modern day probation departments may preclude the possibility of significantly improving the quality of probation services.

## Method

The data for the present study were developed from 15 years of work experience as a probation officer and one year of qualitative interviewing of court personnel. For a major part of my probation career I was assigned to the presentence investigation unit of a county probation department in California. While working as an investigator I maintained personal case notes on my assignments and activities. These notes were a valuable source of ethnographic data concerning probation work in general, and presentence investigations in particular. Several researchers have emphasized the importance of an ethnographic perspective in collecting criminal justice data (Sudnow, 1965; Cicourel, 1968; Shover, 1974; McCleary et al., 1982; Spencer, 1983).

While conducting the present study, I interviewed over sixty active and former probation officers. The respondents were drawn from probation departments in California, Louisiana, and Nevada.[1] The fact that as a former probation officer I could relate to the occupational experiences of my respondents, greatly facilitated the interview process. The probation officers generally were cooperative and candid. I was able to collect qualitative data that might have been unavailable to other researchers. Typically, the officers were supportive of my research and were not reluctant to talk with me. Several of them had experience doing research for graduate courses and tended to be rather helpful.

During the interviews I sought to discover how probation investigation officers view themselves and their co-workers, and to relate these viewpoints to specific kinds of work performance. I questioned their sentencing philosophies, their occupational goals, their relationships with probation supervisors, the techniques they used in gathering information for the court, the methods they had developed for determining presentence recommendations, their perceptions of the criminal justice system and their role in that system, as well as their opinions of other presentence investigators. I interviewed other court

Figure 1

**Typology of Presentence Probation Investigators**

| Type and % of Investigators | Assumed Role | Purpose of Sentencing | Presentence Recommendation |
|---|---|---|---|
| team player 30% | facilitating department policies | to reflect society's values | non controversial |
| mossback 30% | following the rules | to resolve the matter | middle of the road |
| hardliner 20% | upholding traditional values | to deter others | strict |
| bleeding heart liberal 10% | sticking up for the underdog | to rehabilitate the defendant | lenient |
| maverick 10% | weighing the case's individual merits | to see that justice is done | varied |

personnel: judges, attorneys, bailiffs, police officers, and probation supervisors to ascertain their views concerning the purpose of presentence investigations, the quality of work done by presentence writers, and the factors that influence probation recommendations.

The method I used to analyze the accumulated data closely followed the grounded theory approach (Glaser and Strauss, 1967). This approach seeks to develop analyses that are generated from the data themselves (Blumer, 1979). In the early stages of the investigation I attempted to maintain a flexible and open approach. As the study progressed and theoretical propositions emerged, they were modified, compared, and in turn formed the basis for further data collection.[2]

## Findings

Probation investigators typically belong to identifiable sub groups that usually fit one of five general types. Individual officers within the types manifest similar orientations toward presentence report writing. These similarities in job behavior can effectively be placed into categories. This regular patterning led to the development of a presentence investigator typology. A description of each type will clarify the typological framework. These descriptions will consider three factors (1) thematic characteristics (including role orientation), (2) sentencing philosophies, and (3) reporting techniques.

## Team Player

The *leit motif* of this category is adherence to department policies, acquiescence to supervisors, and avoidance of controversy. This type of officer closely follows guidelines contained in department manuals. The statement of a "team player" reflects this orientation:

> When I'm doing a report I usually go by the book—by that I mean the department manual. A lot of p.o.s don't even know we have a manual. But I figure there's a good reason for it being here and I might as well use it. I found it helps me. Having those guidelines keeps me from getting too far off base and maybe looking stupid in court. I work for the probation department and my reports should reflect its policies. Some of these jokers see themselves as free lance report writers. I work closely with my supervisor; it makes the job easier and looks good on my progress reports.

Some officers in this category view their willingness to follow policies of the department and supervisorial suggestions as avenues for advancing their careers. Other "team players," less occupationally mobile, related they simply felt comfortable with this role. One such officer indicated, "I guess I'm a conformist but it's better than knocking myself out trying to beat the system." The sentencing philosophies of this type of officer are reflexive in nature, rather than espousing any particular concept they believe that "sentencing should follow the dictates of society." Such a pragmatic perspective maintains if societal priorities change, judicial sentencing should reflect those changes. Thus "team players" found no conflict in recommending lenient sentences for certain drug offenses when public sentiment dictated. On the other hand, they willingly increased their prison recommendations when imprisonment became a more popular option. A veteran "team player" commented about her prison recommendation for a young offender:

> If this person had come in here a year ago I would have recommended probation with some minor county jail time. But today, it's a 'joint' recommendation without a second thought. Times have changed— the public wants us to get tough these days.

In compiling and presenting presentence investigations "team players" are constrained to avoid any semblance of controversy. This methodology is reflected by: (1) mode of expression; (2) inclusion of data; and (3) sentence recommendations. "Team players" invariably use bland, innocuous, and prosaic syntax in their reports. They have learned that this style is approved by probation supervisors and helps ensure their reports will not "cause waves." "Team players" usually include an excess of social data which they know to be superfluous. One member of this type related, "I always include a lot of social history like family background and educational information—stuff that no one ever reads. But it looks like I am really on top of things."

In cases where recommendations are not easily determined by reference to plea bargaining agreements, determinate sentencing, or informal judicial policies—presentence investigators suggest a wide range of sentencing options for judicial consideration. In this manner they obfuscate their own recommendations and avoid taking a controversial stand. A probation supervisor marveled at the expertise with which a team player handled cases for which sentencing recommendations were open to question and therefore possibly harmful to the department.

> _____ really knows how to handle those dicey cases. Reading his summary you aren't sure whether the defendant should go to prison or be sent home with a medal. He disguises his recommendations so well the department comes out okay no matter what the judge does.

## Mossback

The sine qua non of this type is a passive, routine job performance. "Mossbacks" demonstrate a superficial commitment to their jobs by fulfilling minimum requirements and following departmental regulations. However, they rarely do more than is necessary and can be characterized as "time servers" (Klockars, 1972:551). Members of this type include older workers who are putting in their time until retirement. A long-time probation officer stated:

> I don't get worked up over this job anymore. I know what's expected and give the department its worth; but I'm not going out of my way. I don't need the hassle. I've paid my dues. In a few years I'll be gone so there's no sense in bust'n my ass.

Not all probation officers in this category are nearing retirement. There are those who definitely qualify as "young mossbacks." These relatively young officers have varied reasons for their lack of occupational commitment, e.g., blocked career opportunities, job disillusionment, or burnout. One probation officer who had been passed over for promotion stated, "I'll give them [the department] eight hours per day, but no more." A particularly cynical investigator related, "These pre-sentence reports don't really matter. Who cares what we say? It's easier to just give them what they want." An officer, who was attending law school, snapped, "I don't give a shit about this crummy job. This is just a waystation for me. As soon as I pass the bar, it's on to better things. Meanwhile I'm just following their silly rules and going through the motions."

"Mossbacks" rarely demonstrate a unified sentencing philosophy. When questioned concerning approaches to sentencing—typical replies were: "It's up to the judge;" "Whatever the court wants;" or "Whatever will fly." "Mossbacks" tend to view sentencing as a final resolution rather than a search for justice. The actual sentence brings closure to an unpleasant situation. They approach sentencing with the attitude "Let's get it done with a minimum of effort."

"Mossbacks'" presentence reports are routine communications compiled with a modicum of effort. These officers know the requirements of a court report and include essential information. A "mossback" indicated: "I know what should be in a report. I give the court what it needs. No more, no less. That's all that is called for. There's no overtime in this job." Their reports are usually brief and free of personal observation. A municipal court judge described this style: "I can always recognize _____'s reports. They never tell you much about the defendant but at least they aren't riddled with psychiatric or sociological jargon." The "mossback's" approach to supplying court recommendations is characteristic; they seek to minimize difficulty. They do not routinely seek supervisor approval, as does the "team player," preferring to find their own solutions. A veteran "mossback" explained:

> I don't run to my supervisor for every recommendation. I know how to work out these things. I don't sweat these sentence recommenda-tions anymore. I haven't got the wisdom of Solomon. How do I know what's just or fair? I gave up such thoughts a long time ago. I try to steer a middle course—that way neither side gets pissed at you. I've found the curve of justice usually falls somewhere in the middle. No sense fighting it.

## Hardliner

The overarching goal of the "hardliner" is to protect society from its miscreants. These officers see themselves as bastions of order in an overly permissive world. They believe that laws must be enforced with continual vigilance. When offenders flaunt laws with impunity, the very fabric of society is threatened, they believe. Members of this type do not shrink from labeling themselves "hardliners"; "I'm proud to consider myself a hardnose p.o. Sure I'm a hardliner and I don't care who knows it." "Hardliners" frequently see other probation officer types as negligent in their duties. The following is a typical perspective:

> A lot of the other p.o.s are too lenient. Even the supervisors aren't tough enough in every case. Some of these p.o.s encourage the criminals by giving them one break after another. Those bleeding hearts aren't doing anyone any good. But things are changing, and there is more sentiment for punishment today than ever before.

Although acknowledging they are punitive, "hardliners" see themselves as eminently fair. They firmly believe that strict adherence to legal codes and stern punishment should be applied to all segments of society. "Hardliners" frequently contend that they treat all defendants with equanimity. One "hardliner" proudly indicated, "I am just as tough with middle-class snivelers as I am with lower-class punks."

The "hardliners'" maintain that lenient sentences will actually encourage criminality. They believe offenders to be rational individuals who know what they are doing. A favorite expression is "you did the crime, now you gott'a do the time." They often view judges as liberal and inconsistent in their sentencing. On one occasion, upon returning from court, a "hardliner" announced: "I lost my case! The chickenshit judge wouldn't bite the bullet and send the guy off to the joint where he belongs. Probation, my ass; that was a miscarriage of justice."

The evaluations submitted by "hardliners" are predictable in their punitive orientation. One such officer was candid about his investigation approach: "I look for things to justify a strict recommendation. Other "hardliners" admitted they were "selective" in what they included in their reports since they were unwilling "to make the defendant out to be some sort of saint." Members of this type often believe that defense attorneys have undue influence at sentencing and see their reports counterbalancing this advantage.

"Hardliners," like other investigators, sanction all pre plea agreements. In order to maintain credibility with the court they must keep their recommendations within certain limits, even though leaning toward the punitive end of the sentencing spectrum. Thus, only in certain cases are they free to recommend strict sentences. A "hardliner" explained this strategy:

> I don't shoot my wad in every case. I know that in many cases the deal's all set and my function is to rubber stamp it. In other cases, I can't really be too tough or the judge would disregard my recommendation. I would get a reputation as a right-wing fanatic. But in certain cases, where there is no deal and no particular judicial

concern, I really lower the boom and go for the max. My supervisors know this and when they want a joint recommendation I get assigned the case.

## Bleeding Heart Liberal

The unifying characteristic of this type is a common perspective that the criminal justice system is unfair. Liberals contend that the system is so weighted against the defendant that it is incumbent upon them to "even up the odds." They frequently view those charged with crimes as "unwitting pawns" in an inequitable social system, and see themselves as champions of the underdog. The following comment of a liberal probation officer reflects such a perspective:

> A lot of these defendants are really victims of an unfair system. Selective arrest, selective prosecution and the end result is that some poor bastard gets caught up in something over his head. I'm not naive that these people are all innocent or noble characters — just that they deserve a fair shake. I see myself as a kind of equalizer. I try to bring some equity to what we call the criminal justice system.

"Bleeding heart" liberals are often cynical about the role of a probation officer. One such officer commented to me: "We are really purveyors of middle-class bullshit." They often feel isolated from other probation officers, especially in today's punitive atmosphere. "Bleeding hearts" feel that some investigators are morally bankrupt for expeditiously embracing the current punishment philosophy. One "bleeding heart" probation officer mused, "What happened to all the liberals. Guess they're blowing in the wind, or they have found out who's buttering their bread. Well, I'm still here but I really feel more like a spy for the public defender's office than a p.o."

"Bleeding heart" liberals embrace the positivist philosophy that sentencing should serve to rehabilitate the offender. Members of this type oppose both the just deserts and deterrence models of sentencing. They hold that society is best served if defendants are improved and changed through their court experiences. For example, one investigator observed: "These criminals are going to be released from custody some day. Everyone will be better off if we try to help them change their lives."

Liberals, like "hardliners," tend to slant their reports; however, in this situation it is done to picture the defendant in a favorable light. I was told by a "bleeding heart": "Soon as I get the court referral sheet my mind is racing. How do I get this person the best deal possible? How far can I go?" This type of investigator emphasizes the defendant's social history and includes sociological information to help explain the offender's behavior. One judge told me that a particular report (done by a liberal) was ". . . more of a sociology term paper than a probation report."

The "bleeding heart" liberals cannot give free rein to their liberal tendencies (in much the same manner that "hardliners" cannot be consistently punitive)—instead have to "call their shots." They go along with plea bargaining deals and keep the majority of their recommendations "in the ball park" to maintain a reputation with the court and their supervisors. "Bleeding hearts" believe that court recommendations deemed excessively lenient by probation supervisors will result in their being censured, demoted, or transferred to another unit. One such investigator indicated that she had a "harder time getting recommendations out of my own office than getting them accepted by the court." She added that her supervisor keeps saying, "but how will this look to the D.A., the police, or God forbid the newspapers?" When discretion is feasible "bleeding hearts" go "out on a limb" to recommend lenient sentences; "Most of the time I look just like all the rest of the assholes. But when I get a real chance to help someone, I really give it a shot," reported one such p.o.

## Maverick

The thematic characteristic of this type is a search for individual justice. These officers try to consider, independently, each case and to recommend an appropriate course of action. They attempt to evaluate every case on its own merits. Mavericks conceive of themselves as objective judicial advisors and not advocates of a particular point of view. They do not consider themselves active participants in an adversary proceeding and try not to favor either the prosecution or the defense. A maverick offered this observation of his role in the probation department:

> It's not that complicated. I'm charged with the responsibility of investigating a case and giving an informed opinion as to what brought the defendant to this point. Granted, it's not always easy to be objective, but we should try.

The sentencing philosophy of mavericks can be considered a search for justice. They believe that while sentencing should be fair, each case deserves to be evaluated individually. Mavericks maintain that individual penalties must not only fit the criminal but also the crime. This type of orientation is not always popular with judges or district attorneys—who need to clear crowded court calendars.

Mavericks typically conduct a thorough investigation and present their reports in a straightforward manner. Their concern for objectivity precludes the slanting of reports to reflect a personal bias. Mavericks attempt to offer recommendations that are both fair and consistent. They cannot be categorized as liberal or conservative nor as lenient or punitive. One such officer indicated that she never knew what the recommendation would be on a particular case until her investigation was complete. This approach interjects an element of uncertainty into the investigation process. A probation supervisor complained to me about a maverick: "I never know what _____ is going to do. His recommendations are unpredictable. Sometimes his reports are too good and all kinds of issues come up—like a can of worms. Makes my job tougher."

## Summary and Analysis

In this article I have presented a community designated typology of probation investigators. Prior classification schemes have been researcher designated—and were developed from studies of supervision officers. The present typology has identified a type of probation officer—the maverick—not prominently acknowledged by prior researchers. Mavericks seem bent upon fulfilling the idealized prescription (Carter et al., 1984) of what a presentence investigator should be. The data also revealed that "mossbacks" are not always older officers with only a few years of service to fulfill; instead they are often comparatively younger officers with several years of unenthusiastic probation work ahead of them. Other researchers (Glaser, 1964; Takagi, 1967; Klockars, 1972) have characterized such passive officers as invariably nearing retirement. Although the present typology is directly related to presentence investigators, preliminary indications are that it may be applicable— with modification—to other criminal justice agencies. People working in this area have indicated they can recognize a similar personnel patterning in their own agencies.

The typological framework presented in this article is not a static conceptualization. There is movement within and between the types. A common movement is from "team player" to "mossback." On occasion those officers who have closely followed department policies and supervisorial suggestions, upon finding their career aspirations blocked (often for what they deem unfair reasons), decide to drop out and become "mossbacks." In another situation "bleeding heart" liberals, in order to render themselves promotable, abandon their lenient tendencies and become "team players."

An analysis of the data indicated that belonging to a particular type is not necessarily a permanent condition—rather it is a consequential designation for probation officers. Their assumed roles within both the probation department and the criminal justice system are directly affected by typological orientations which in turn impact upon their work behavior and result in distinct kinds of sentencing recommendations. These dynamics need further clarification and discussion.

Perhaps the most striking aspect of the probation officers' job behavior, revealed in this article, is their use of elaborate strategies to advance personal careers or individual points of view. "Team players" use the investigation report to demonstrate departmental loyalty; "mossbacks" use the report to justify their jobs; while "hardliners" and "bleeding heart" liberals use the report to advance their concepts of criminal justice. In order to implement these strategies, investigators engage in maneuvering and reputation-building. The reputations cultivated by investigation officers allow them to promote their particular position at opportune times. This type of posturing is similar to that reported by McCleary (1978:209) in his study of a parole office, who wrote, "...p.o.s maximize their freedom within the organization by manipulating their reputations."

Considering the widespread use of personal strategies by investigation officers, the objectivity and usefulness of court reports can be seriously questioned. The extent of actual investigation is often minimal as officers quickly decide what they hope to achieve and then gather information that justifies their position. In many cases presentence recommendations are framed more by the pragmatism of the investigating officer than by a consideration of the facts and circumstances. Contrary to other research (Carter, 1967; Gross, 1967; Spencer, 1983) this author did not find (except in cases of open hostility) that defendant attitudes played a significant part in the presentence recommendations of most officers. In many cases the investigator's personal strategy outweighed the import of the defendant's attitude. Interviews with offenders were perfunctory routines which served to legitimate the already-arrived-at decision. On the other hand, the maverick type does seek to compile and present objective investigation reports. However, there are organizational restrictions within the probation department which are unfavorable to this type of probation officer.

The adult investigation unit is the most visible of probation services (Rosecrance, 1985). Presentence reports are open to inspection by district attorneys, private attorneys, police officials, judges, defendants, and other interested parties including newspaper reporters. Notorious and sensational court cases ordinarily require a presentence investigation. This visibility has caused probation administrators to scrutinize carefully presentence writers. Supervisors in this unit review each investigation and must approve the report before it can be filed with the court. The presentence recommendation—usually considered the most important part of the report—is a departmental recommendation. In cases of serious disagreement between supervisor and investigator, it is the supervisor's recommendation that appears on the presentence report in the court record.

The probation administration's rationale for such scrutiny is a desire to avoid controversy. Those who supervise presentence writers are charged with the task of avoiding any hint of notoriety. In order to achieve a noncontroversial status, supervisors seek officers who are predictable, willing to follow orders, and in tune with current sentencing policies. The types of investigators who are compatible with these requirements are "team players," "mossbacks," and "hardliners." Through bureaucratic winnowing, presentence units retain these three types while rejecting the other two types. "Team players" easily adapt their reports to fit the organizational goal of noncontroversy; "mossbacks" can be relied upon not to rock the boat, and since probation departments are ideologically aligned with the prosecution (McHugh, 1973) there is always room for "hardliners." "Bleeding heart" liberals, in light of the current emphasis upon punishment, find themselves in frequent conflict with supervisors. These "running battles" (Shover, 1974:357) leave this type of officer at risk for burn out, transfer, dismissal, or weakening of resolve.

Mavericks cause problems for probation supervisors since their reports do not follow a routine, predictable pattern. In the process of conducting investigations, these officers often reveal information that while germane to the case, raise questions concerning the efficacy of plea bargaining arrangements. Their recommendations, sometimes at odds with current sentencing policies, cause judicial questioning. Mavericks are usually unwilling to "play ball" by favoring the prosecution and are subject to criticism from the district attorney's office. In summary the maverick is considered a "pain in the ass" by probation supervisors and administrators. Such disapproval translates into lack of promotional opportunities, transfers to less sensitive assignments, and frequent case reviews. Mavericks generally find such actions untenable, and eventually leave the probation department for other employment. Several prior researchers have observed that highly qualified officers often do not remain in probation or parole work (Shover, 1974; Wallace, 1974; Imlay and Reid, 1975; McCleary, 1978).

It is ironic that the maverick's policy of weighing each case on its individual merits should jeopardize his or her probation career. This finding and other data developed in the present article suggest that independent judgement—the linchpin of objective probation services—may be antithetical to the organizational realities of contemporary probation departments.

**Notes**

[1] The probation departments in the three areas were organized differently. In California, probation was a separate department of county government; in Nevada, probation was part of a state-wide system; in Louisiana, probation officers worked for a parish court. Although I did not conduct a random sample of probation officers, I attempted to interview a wide range of officers with varied backgrounds. In California, I interviewed 35 probation officers (10 women, 25 men, whose probation experience ranged from one year to twenty-five years); In Louisiana, 13 officers (five women, eight men, whose probation experience ranged from six months to fifteen years); In Nevada, 12 officers (six women, six men, whose probation experience ranged from 18 months to twenty years). After analyzing the interview data, it was apparent that factors such as the organizational differences between the three locales or individual differences among probation officers (age, sex, education, number of years experience) could not, in themselves, explain probation officers' perceptions of presentence investigations.

[2] Personal experience and interviews with probation officers were used as a basis for constructing the typology, while interviews with other criminal justice personnel were used to validate the merging types.

**References**

Administrative Office of the United States Courts. (1974) "The Selective Presentence Investigation Report." *Federal Probation* 38:47-54.

Allen, H., Carlson, E. and Parks, E. (1979) *Critical Issues in Adult Probation*. Washington, DC: National Institute of Law Enforcement and Criminal Justice.

Blake, R., Mouton, J., Touraino, L., and Guitierrez, G. (1979) *The Social Worker Grid*. Springfield, IL: Charles Thomas.

Blumer, M. (1979) "Concepts in the Analysis of Qualitative Data." *Sociological Review* 27:651-77.

Blumstein, A., Martin, S., and Tonry, M. (1983) *Research on Sentencing The Search for Reform*. Washington, DC: National Academy Press.

Brewer, D., Beckett, G., and Holt, H. (1981) "Determinate Sentencing in California: The First Year's Experience." *Journal of Research in Crime and Delinquency* 18:200-31.

Carter, R. (1967) "The Presentence Report and the Decision-Making Process." *Journal of Research in Crime and Delinquency* 4:203-11.

Carter, R. (1978) *Presentence Report Handbook*. Washington, DC: U.S. Government Printing Office.

Carter, R., Glaser, D. and Wilkins, L. (1984) *Probation, Parole and Community Corrections*. New York: John Wiley.

Carter, R. and Wilkins, L. (1970) "Some Factors in Sentencing Policy." In *Probation and Parole*, R. Carter and L. Wilkins, eds. New York: Wiley.

Cicourel, A. (1968) *The Social Organization of Juvenile Justice*. New York: Wiley.

Cromwell, P., Killinger, G., Kerper, H. and Walker, C. (1985) *Probation and Parole in the Criminal Justice System*. St. Paul: West.

Curry, P. (1975) "Probation and Individualized Disposition: A Study of Factors Associated with the Presentence Recommendation." *American Journal of Criminal Law* 4:31-81.

Duffee, D. (1984) "Models of Probation Supervision." In *Probation and Justice: Reconsideration of Mission*, P. McAnany, D. Thomson, and D. Fogel, eds. Cambridge: Oelgeschlager, Gunn, and Hain Publishing.

Emerson, R. (1983) "Ethnography and Understanding Members' Worlds," In *Contemporary Field Research*, R. Emerson, ed. Boston: Little Brown.

Glaser, B. and Strauss, A. (1967) *The Discovery of Grounded Theory*. Chicago: Aldine.

Glaser, D. (1964) *The Effectiveness of a Prison and Parole System*. Indianapolis: Bobbs Merrill.

———. (1985) "Who Gets Probation and Parole: Case Study Versus Actuarial Decision Making." *Crime and Delinquency*, 31:367-78.

Gross, S. (1967) "The Prehearing Juvenile Report: Probation Officers' Conceptions." *Journal of Research in Crime and Delinquency*, 4:212-17.

Hagan, J., Hewitt, J. and Alevin, D. (1979) "Ceremonial Justice: Crime and Punishment in a Loosely Coupled System." *Social Forces* 58:506-27.

Imlay, C. and Reid, E. (1975) "The Probation Officer, Sentencing and the Winds of Change." *Federal Probation* 39:9-18.

Keve, P. (1962) "The Professional Character of The Presentence Report." *Federal Probation*, 26:51-56.

Keve, P. (1967) *Imaginative Programming in Probation and Parole*. Minneapolis: Univ. of Minnesota Press.

Kingsnorth, R. and Rizzo, L. (1979) "Decision-Making in the Criminal Courts: Continuities and Discontinuities." *Criminology* (May):3-14.

Klockars, C. (1972) "A Theory of Probation Supervision." *Journal of Criminal Law, Criminology and Police Science*, 63:550-57.

McCleary, R. (1975) "How Structural Variables Constrain the Parole Officers' Use of Discretionary Powers." *Social Problems*, 23:209-25.

———. (1978) *Dangerous Men*. Beverly Hills: Sage.

McCleary. R., Nienstedt, B. and Erven, J. (1982) "Uniform Crime Reports As Organizational Outcomes: Three Time Series Experiments." *Social Problems*, 29:361-73.

McHugh, J. (1973) "Some Comments on Natural Conflict Between Counsel and Probation Officer." *American Journal of Corrections*, 35 (November-December): 34-36.

Neubauer, D. (1974) *Criminal Justice in Middle America*. Morristown, NJ: General Learning Press.

Ohlin, L., Piven, H. and Pappenfort, D. (1956) "Major Dilemmas of the Social Worker in Probation and Parole." *National Probation and Parole Association*, 11:211-25.

Petersilia, J. (1985) "Community Supervision: Trends and Critical Issues." *Crime and Delinquency*, 31:339-47.

Petersilia, J., Turner, S., Kahun, J. and Peterson, J. (1985) "Executive Summary of Rand's Study, Granting Felons Probation: Public Risks and Alternatives." *Crime and Delinquency*, 31:379-92.

Reed, J. and King, C. (1966) "Factors in the Decision-Making of North Carolina Probation Officers." *Journal of Research in Crime and Delinquency*, 3:120-28.

Rosecrance, J. (1985) "The Probation Officers' Search for Credibility: Ball Park Recommendations." *Crime and Delinquency*, 31:539-54.

Shover, N. (1974) "Experts and Diagnosis in Correctional Agencies." *Crime and Delinquency*, 20:347-59.

_____. (1979) *A Sociology of American Corrections.* Homewood, IL: Dorsey.

Spencer, J. (1983) "Accounts, Attitudes, and Solutions: Probation Officer-Defendant Negotiations of Subjective Orientations." *Social Problems*, 30:570-81.

Spradley, J. (1970) *You Owe Yourself A Drunk: An Ethnography of Urban Nomads.* Boston: Little Brown.

Sudnow, D. (1965) "Normal Crimes: Sociological Features of the Penal Code." *Social Problems*, 12:255-76.

Takagi, P. (1967) "Evaluation and Adaptations in a Formal Organization." Unpublished dissertation in Sociology, Stanford University.

Tepperman, L. (1973) "The Effect of Court Size on Organization and Procedure." *Canadian Review of Sociology and Anthropology*, 10:346-65.

Van Landingham, D., Taber, M. and Dimants, R. (1966) "How Adult Probation Officers View Their Job Responsibilities." *Crime and Delinquency*, 12:98-108.

Wallace, J. (1974) "Probation Administration." In *Handbook of Criminology*, D. Glaser, ed. Chicago: Rand McNally.

# 7

# Difficult Clients, Large Caseloads Plague Probation, Parole Agencies

## Randall Guynes

American probation and parole systems now face an increasingly difficult clientele despite less adequate resources. Despite greater financial resources, personnel increases are not keeping pace with rising caseloads of clients with serious problems. These are some of the major findings of a survey of State and local probation and parole officers conducted as part of the National Assessment Program (NAP) sponsored by the National Institute of Justice.

This *Research in Action* describes survey results from 49 State probation and parole directors and 339 local offices. Of the local offices, 43 percent provide probation services only, and 21 percent are parole field offices. The remaining 36 percent are responsible for both probation and parole and are referred to as "combined" agencies throughout this publication.

The primary aim of the National Assessment Program is to identify key needs and problems of local and State criminal justice practitioners. To accomplish this, the National Institute of Justice (NIJ) contracted with the Institute for Law and Justice, Inc., to conduct a national survey of approximately 2,500 practitioners from a sample of 375 counties across the Nation. Included were all 175 counties with populations greater than

Source: National Institute of Justice, *Research in Action*, U.S. Department of Justice, August 1988. 1-8.

250,000 and a sample of 200 counties having less than that number.[1] Persons receiving surveys in each sampled county included the police chief of the largest city, sheriff, jail administrator, prosecutor, chief judge, trial court administrator (where applicable), and probation and parole agency heads. In addition, surveys were also sent to State probation and parole agencies to obtain their viewpoints.

The survey covered five general areas: agency background, criminal justice problems, caseload, staffing, and operations. The results for each of these areas are discussed in detail in the following sections.

## Background

*Organizational Units*.    Using political subdivisions to sample probation and parole agencies obviously results in a diverse set of respondents including directors of county probation departments, heads of branch offices for State agencies, and agencies responsible for several counties. Yet this reflects the diversity of organizational arrangements in probation and parole generally (see Exhibit 1).

In about 25 percent of the States, probation is primarily a local responsibility, with the State accountable only for functions such as providing financial support, setting standards, and arranging training courses. This locally based approach accounts for about two-thirds of all persons under probation supervision in the United States.[2]

The governmental branch responsible also varies. A State or local department may be in the judicial or the executive branch of government, and supervision of probationers may cross branches or levels within branches. Despite these variations, agency functions are similar: supervising and monitoring persons; collecting and analyzing information for decisionmakers; and performing other duties such as collecting fees, fines, restitution, and child support payments.

*Staffing and budgets*.    For the agencies responding, the median numbers of employees are 32 for combined agencies, 47 for probation, and 62 for parole. The respective medians of cases monthly are 934, 1,225, and 885. Probation directors indicate a median of 129 presentence, revocation, diversion, or other investigations monthly, compared to 75 for parole and 94 for combined agencies.

As expected, parole cases are generally classified at higher supervision levels than cases handled by either probation or combined agencies. Parole reports the highest proportion of intensive (11 percent) and maximum (35 percent) cases and the lowest median caseload (65 cases per officer). The other two groups indicated from 22 to less than 4 percent in intensive and maximum supervision categories and had correspondingly higher median caseloads (probation 109, combined 99). However,

Exhibit 1

**Probation structures, National Assessment Project**

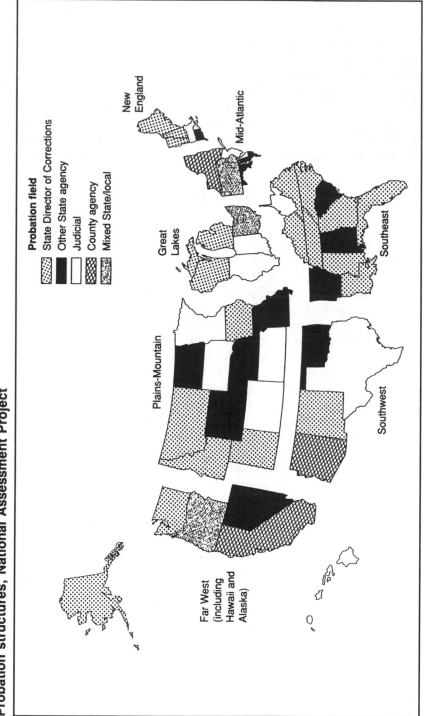

27 percent of the parole caseload is classified as "unsupervised."

A larger proportion of parole agencies (29 percent) report budget increases in excess of 30 percent over the last 3 years than did probation (22 percent) and combined agencies (16 percent). More than two-thirds of the directors of combined offices rate their financial resources as inadequate, while 55 percent of probation respondents and 48 percent of parole respondents rate their resources as inadequate.

## Criminal Justice Problems

Based on the previous National Assessment Survey in 1983,[3] the current survey asked respondents to rank the severity of seven criminal justice problems within their systems: lack of staff skills, prison crowding, agency management, staff shortages, jail crowding, coordination among agencies, and the public's lack of understanding of criminal justice agencies. Respondents ranked these items from most serious (1) to least serious (7). Exhibit 2 shows the average ranking for each issue by type of agency. The percentage of "number 1" responses appears in parentheses.

Staff shortage is clearly the dominant problem for all agencies. It has the highest average rank for probation and combined agencies and second highest for parole. Prison crowding also rates high among parole agencies and combined agencies. Similarly, State probation and parole directors (not shown in Exhibit 2) rank prison crowding and staff shortages as the most significant issues.

After staff shortage, probation respondents see the criminal justice system as being troubled almost equally by coordination problems, a lack of understanding by the public, and both jail and prison crowding. Coordination is significant to probation officers because the regular performance of their duties requires them to work with judges, law enforcement personnel, jail managers, and sometimes prison officials. As for crowding, probation officers are affected by both jail crowding, as local governments attempt to control jail populations with probation supervision, and prison crowding, as courts and legislatures attempt to control prison populations through increased probation.

In most of the remainder of the survey, respondents were asked to rate problems and needs on a scale of 1 to 4 with a rating of 1 representing "Not at all" and 4 representing "Major" problem or need. In the discussion that follows, the ratings of 3 and 4 combine to indicate a significant problem or need.

Agencies were asked to rate the degree to which eight factors had contributed to increased caseloads over the past 3 years (see Exhibit 3). All respondent groups identified increased supervision needs of

Exhibit 2

## Most serious criminal justice problem (average ranking by type of agency)

| Average rank | Probation only agencies | Probation and parole agencies | Parole only agencies |
|---|---|---|---|
| 1.0 | | | |
| 2.3 | | | |
| 2.4 | | | Prison crowding (41%) |
| 2.5 | | | |
| 2.6 | | | |
| 2.7 | Staff shortage (48%) | | |
| 2.8 | | Staff shortage (38%) | |
| 2.9 | | | |
| 3.0 | | | Staff shortage (30%) |
| 3.1 | | Prison crowding (25%) | |
| 3.2 | | | |
| 3.3 | | | |
| 3.4 | | | |
| 3.5 | Coordination (9%) | | Jail crowding (6%) |
| 3.6 | Jail crowding (16%) | Jail crowding (10%) | |
| 3.7 | Lack of public understanding (13%) | | |
| 3.8 | Prison crowding (11%) | Lack of public understanding (11%) | |
| 3.9 | | | |
| 4.0 | | | |
| 4.1 | | | |
| 4.2 | | Lack coordination (10%) | |
| 4.3 | | | Lack of public understanding (10%) |
| 4.4 | | | Lack coordination (1%) |
| 4.5 | | | |
| 4.6 | | | |
| 4.7 | | | |
| 4.8 | | Management (8%) | Management (10%) |
| 4.9 | | | |
| 5.0 | | | |
| 5.1 | | | |
| 5.2 | Lack staff skills (4%) | | |
| 5.3 | | | |
| 5.4 | Management (1%) | Lack staff skills (3%) | |
| 5.5 | | | Lack staff skills (3%) |
| 5.6 | | | |
| 7.0 | | | |

Note: the number in parentheses is the percentage of persons assigning rank of 1 to the problem.

For example, among probation and parole agencies, "staff shortages" was given an average seriousness of 2.8 on a scale of 1 down to 7, but 38 percent ranked it as a number 1 problem.

Exhibit 3

**Caseload contributors**

|  | | Type of Agency | | |
|  | State | Probation | Parole | Combined |
|---|---|---|---|---|
| Increased supervision needs | 75% | 82% | 80% | 79% |
| Staff increases not keeping pace | 73 | 79 | 74 | 73 |
| Prison crowding | 79 | 68 | 86 | 79 |
| Local jail crowding | 63 | 62 | 61 | 63 |
| Time for reports and investigations | 60 | 59 | 57 | 64 |
| Early parole release | 55 | 28 | 63 | 61 |
| Residential options not keeping pace | 53 | 57 | 64 | 52 |
| Increased supervision terms | 42 | 37 | 51 | 35 |

offenders as the first or second greatest reason for caseload increases. Other significant contributors to caseloads were jail and prison crowding, slow growth in residential options, and time required for investigations and reporting. Increased supervision terms were rated low by all groups. In general, directors of parole field offices rated all contributing factors higher than did directors of other agencies. Parole and combined agencies reported prison crowding and early parole release as important contributors to caseloads—a result in agreement with their views on significant criminal justice problems.

Reflecting their different perspectives, 63 percent of parole directors, but only 28 percent of probation directors, gave a high rating to the related issue of early parole release. State agency directors considered slow growth in community residential beds as less significant than did directors of local offices. However, State directors gave more emphasis than other respondents to investigation and reporting time as a contributor to caseloads.

There were significant regional variations in how much crowding, early parole release, and increased supervision terms affect caseload. From 80 to 100 percent of probation or parole directors in the Southeast and Plains-Mountain regions considered prison crowding an important factor in increasing caseloads. They were joined by parole agencies from New England and probation agencies from the Southwest. The greatest concern with early parole release was expressed by Southeast (93 percent) and Southwest (78 percent) parole directors.

As shown in Exhibit 3, increased supervision terms is rated lowest as a contributor by all groups of respondents. However, an interesting regional variation is that respondents from the Southeast and Southwest consider longer supervision terms as a very significant contributor to caseload increases (93 and 100 percent respectively). Generally, respondents from the Southeast and Southwest express greater concern on more items affecting caseloads than those from other regions.

## Responses to Caseload Management Problems

Respondents were asked to list projects in their jurisdictions that have improved personnel and operational problems. Projects listed to improve caseload management speak to changing times in probation and parole. Responding agencies exhibited creativity in managing increased and more difficult caseloads with little or no increases in human resources. Almost one-third of the projects mentioned involve differential supervision, including intensive, minimum, and unsupervised. Another third were examining their workloads or developing liaisons with other key criminal justice system actors (usually court officers) as precursors to reducing supervision levels.

About 10 percent of the respondents who listed projects used early terminations and about 25 percent relied on alternative program assignments (e.g., pretrial diversion and drug treatment programs). Other approaches included streamlining paperwork assignments while acknowledging that presentence investigations consumed considerable time. Interestingly, only one respondent cited reduction in service levels as a solution.

The two major reasons for increased caseloads were disproportionate growth in increased supervision needs of offenders and staffing levels. These reasons imply that personnel and case management issues will continue to be major operational concerns for probation and parole agencies.

## Operations and Procedures

Agencies were asked questions about their needs to improve operations and procedures in five general categories: classification, community resources, scheduling, management information systems, and private sector contracting. As explained in the sections that follow, the last three are the most salient concerns for the respondents.

*Classification.*   When asked to list projects that have improved classification, almost half the respondents stated that they had developed an evaluative technique incorporating risk. Less than 40 percent of each respondent group indicated a need to improve initial and subsequent classification of offenders' risks or needs.

***Scheduling***.    Since field services organizations are dependent on others to complete many of their tasks, it was hypothesized that scheduling with other criminal justice agencies might be a problem. Respondents were asked to rate the degree to which scheduling is a problem for each of the following groups or activities:

- Court hearings (sentence and revocation hearings).
- Prison officials (investigations).
- Timing for sentence investigations.
- Clerk of court (fines and fees).

From this list, only scheduling problems with regard to sentencing and revocation hearings were rated high. More than 50 percent of local directors and 47 percent of State directors noted this as a problem. Combined agencies indicated this was a more severe problem (68 percent) than the other agencies.

***Management information systems***.    The analysis of the questions on management information systems suggests that the use of these systems is limited. Only about 15 percent of the agencies have automated systems to support classification. The overwhelming majority of respondents either (1) did not have a system in place, (2) were just in the process of developing such a capability, or (3) limited the use of their system to minor applications such as word processing.

Respondents generally wanted historical data, such as criminal record and substance abuse information on their clients, to be computerized. The computerized system would further enhance the classification procedures and make the client information readily available for other uses. A need was also expressed for information on referrals for service to be used in the ongoing management of cases. Greater concern for referral information was reported by probation offices in the New England, Mid-Atlantic, and Far West areas. Interestingly, most groups did not place a priority on improving information on management supervision assignments and levels.

The needs expressed for management information reflected different collection strategies. Historical data on criminal records and substance abuse generally depended on information from other criminal agencies and the clients, supplemented by information from families and friends. In contrast, referrals for service and associated dates could generally be found within the agency — at least during the supervision period — and were easier to maintain within a system.

*Community resources.* Probation and parole rely on public and private resources outside their agencies to supply many services to offenders. Directors were asked to rate the degree to which they see the need to improve or create nine types of community services (Exhibit 4). In general, parole agencies rated the items as more significant needs than the other groups.

One-half or more of the directors reported that the number of residential options were not keeping pace with offenders' needs, and at least three out of four believed increased supervision requirements were contributing to caseload management problems. Given the higher levels of supervision now required, one respondent from the Northeast argued that halfway houses and other options were needed to "restore probation and parole as legitimate sanctions." In addition to current needs for residential programs, one director noted that the challenge of the next 3 years will be "development of new programs to divert those currently in jails awaiting transfer to prison custody—to the extent that the community is not jeopardized."

Other differences appeared to reflect the stage of the criminal justice process at which offenders were referred. For example, 80 percent of parole agencies reported a need for housing referral services, compared to about 62 percent of other field offices. In contrast, there were few differences among agencies regarding the need for job readiness training, which was cited by 65 to 73 percent of the field offices. Vocational education services were reported as a need by 74 percent of parole and 61 percent of probation agencies, and 56 percent of combined agencies.

Exhibit 4

**Need for new or improved community resources**

| Community resources | State | Type of Agency | | |
| | | Probation | Parole | Combined |
| --- | --- | --- | --- | --- |
| Residential programs | 80% | 72% | 83% | 73% |
| Housing referral sevices | 57 | 63 | 80 | 62 |
| Job readiness training | 65 | 68 | 73 | 69 |
| Mental health services | 72 | 60 | 71 | 67 |
| Drug programs | 81 | 63 | 79 | 62 |
| Employment referral services | 50 | 70 | 66 | 61 |
| Alcohol programs | 62 | 50 | 73 | 54 |
| Vocational education | 62 | 61 | 74 | 56 |
| Adult basic education | 31 | 33 | 60 | 33 |

There were several regional variations in perceived need for improved or expanded community resources. Although adult basic education was the lowest priority for everyone, directors in the Great Lakes, Mid-Atlantic, and Southwest rated the problem considerably higher than their colleagues. Drug programs were of more concern to parole directors in the Mid-Atlantic, Southwest, and Far West than in other parts of the country. Probation offices in New England (83 percent) and the Far West (91 percent) reported a greater need for mental health services than probation offices overall (60 percent).

*Contracted services.* Residential, drug, job readiness, and mental health programs can be provided internally or through arrangements with public or private service providers. Recent attention given to contracting in corrections and the reduction in government-supported social service programs suggests that the demand for privately sponsored arrangements may increase. Probation and parole officials were asked to indicate whether they currently purchase none, some, most, or all of eight specific services.

The most prevalent service currently provided under contract is staff training. At least four-fifths of the respondents contract for some or all of their staff training. In contrast, emergency food is provided under contract to fewer than one-third of parole agencies and in less than 15 percent of other field offices.

The private sector is used less overall in the Southeast than in other regions. All local directors in the Southeast report fewer purchases of drug testing and medical services. Single-function agencies contract for staff training less frequently than combined agencies. Only 7 percent of local parole offices and a lower percentage of combined agencies use the private sector for residential centers or emergency housing.

Fewer than 35 percent of Great Lakes parole directors contract for any staff training, urinalysis, mental health services, emergency food, or housing. Approximately the same percentage of probation agencies in the Great Lakes, Mid-Atlantic, and Plains-Mountain regions contract for medical services. Only about two-fifths of the Far West offices responsible for both probation and parole purchase any medical or halfway house services.

## Staff Recruitment and Retention

As reflected in Exhibit 2, staff shortages were rated high as a problem by all three groups of agencies. The results from the recruitment and retention sections of the survey provided insights into this problem.

*Recruitment.* Among the most significant recruitment problems are low salaries, locating qualified professional staff, shortages of qualified minority applicants, hiring freezes, and poor image of corrections work.

In general, State directors saw fewer recruitment problems than did local officers and considered a shortage of minority applicants the most important recruitment issue (Exhibit 5). In contrast, 50 percent of the local probation directors, 53 percent of the parole directors, and 68 percent of the combined agency directors considered low salaries an important recruitment problem. Approximately 45 percent of local agencies reported problems recruiting minorities.

Restrictions on hiring significantly affect recruitment for more than 47 percent of local probation directors, but only 38 percent of their counterparts in parole. In contrast, the poor image of corrections work was a significant problem for 43 percent of local parole agencies.

*Retention.* Agency directors were asked to rate the degree to which seven items contribute to staff turnover: salary increases, burnout, inability to use leave time, poor image of corrections work, substance abuse, inadequate career incentives, and excessive overtime. Career incentives were considered the number one staff retention issue by State directors (58 percent), local parole (70 percent), probation (60 percent), and combined agencies (71 percent). Salary increases and burnout were cited as serious by 40 percent or more of all four groups, with the remaining problems receiving substantially lower ratings. The salary problem was considered a major issue by 68 percent of the combined agencies.

Forty-seven percent of the probation offices and 67 percent of both parole field offices and combined agency directors rated burnout as a serious retention problem. ''Burnout'' is used to encompass a variety

Exhibit 5

**Recruitment problems**

| Issue | State | Type of Agency | | |
| | | Probation | Parole | Combined |
| --- | --- | --- | --- | --- |
| Low salaries | 33% | 50% | 53% | 68% |
| Shortage of minority applicants | 48 | 44 | 41 | 50 |
| Locating qualified staff | 31 | 46 | 52 | 49 |
| Hiring freeze | 29 | 47 | 38 | 40 |
| Poor image of corrections | 21 | 27 | 43 | 37 |
| Entrance requirements too high | 17 | 22 | 28 | 19 |

of situations, from personal crises unrelated to occupation, through systemic dysfunctions in organizations, to uncertain environmental conditions. Its causes may be personal, organizational, environmental, or (more frequently) a combination. Within the limits of this survey, it was not possible to determine the specific causes of burnout at the local level. Interestingly, from other survey responses, burnout is apparently not being caused by excessive overtime (rated as a problem by only one respondent in five) or employee substance abuse (rated as a problem by less than 2 percent of all respondents).

*Responses.* It is clear that compensation, including "career incentives," is perceived as essential for both attracting and holding probation and parole staff. What is unclear is whether salaries are considered inadequate relative to similar occupations and other public service jobs in terms of skill levels required and risks involved. Addressing these staffing issues tests the ingenuity of agencies facing increased demands with constrained resources. Few agencies, for example, cite new funding as the way they are trying to solve their personnel problems. Instead, evaluation and reorganization of workload are used as the major way of alleviating staffing burdens. Frequently cited recruitment methods (reported by over one-half of all those responding) included special minority recruiters and outreach in the community and at colleges.

*Training.* Respondents were asked to rate their agencies' interest in several training topics (Exhibit 6). Consistent with the finding that "increased supervision needs" increased caseload problems, at least 76 percent of all groups reported they need to upgrade staff skills to handle

Exhibit 6

**Training needs**

| Training area | | Type of Agency | | |
| --- | --- | --- | --- | --- |
| | State | Probation | Parole | Combined |
| Handling special problem offenders | 79% | 80% | 86% | 76% |
| Caseload management | 49 | 63 | 71 | 61 |
| Offender monitoring | 57 | 57 | 58 | 58 |
| Liability issues | 53 | 57 | 67 | 55 |
| Report writing | 41 | 54 | 63 | 53 |
| Stress management | 54 | 52 | 68 | 69 |
| Counseling techniques | 61 | 52 | 56 | 57 |

special problem offenders. Six other topics interested at least half of all local agencies: offender monitoring techniques, counseling, stress management, legal liability, report writing, and caseload management.

While overall training needs were high (with parole reporting the highest overall), responses varied substantially by agency function. Consistent with high burnout, stress management training was a greater need in parole and combined agencies, with almost 70 percent of agencies significantly interested. Probation agencies rank handling special offenders highest (80 percent), followed by case management (63 percent), offender monitoring (57 percent), and liability (57 percent).

There were also interesting differences between State and local perceptions of training needs. State directors reported a somewhat greater degree of interest in training in counseling techniques (61 percent) than did local offices (about 50 percent). Forty-one percent of State directors favored training in report writing, compared to 53 percent of local directors. Caseload management skills were among the most wanted training for local respondents, but among the least significant for State directors. If training policy and resource allocation were influenced primarily by State officials, these results suggested a need to reconcile local and State perspectives.

There are also some notable regional variations. Report writing was considered significant by parole in the Mid-Atlantic region and by parole and combined agencies in the Plains-Mountain States. Sixty-seven percent of directors responsible for both probation and parole in the Great Lakes region considered training in investigative techniques a significant need.

Legal liability training was deemed more serious by both probation and parole in the Plains-Mountain, Southwest, and Far West, where from 83 to 100 percent of agency directors considered this an important training topic.

What makes these results more striking is that monitoring, counseling, and report writing are fundamental to probation and parole functions. Along with investigations (a high priority only for parole respondents), there are the set of activities generally labeled "case management." Yet, probation and parole officials generally reported a significant need for training in these basic skills areas.

When acute basic skills deficiencies are considered along with workload, recruitment, and retention problems, they make a gloomy scenario for probation and parole. Staffing levels are not keeping pace with a growing caseload. At the same time, supervision needs are increasing. Recruitment is made difficult by low salaries that will not attract enough qualified applicants, and, once hired, employees are discouraged by poor career incentives, small salary increases, and burnout.

## Conclusion

In broad strokes, the NAP survey painted a picture of America's probation and parole systems as facing unprecedented challenges. Despite recent budget increases of more than 20 percent for many agencies and major improvements in risk management, more than 75 percent of all agencies said staff increases are not keeping pace with the number of offenders.

Compounding this increase in staff-to-client ratio is the fact that at least three-fourths of the respondents believe offenders' supervision needs are greater now than in the past. Thus, not only are the numbers larger, the offenders are also a more difficult group to manage.

Fifty to sixty-eight percent of all local probation and parole offices report that salaries are too low to attract qualified applicants. Once hired, personnel did not find financial and other incentives sufficient to stay in positions where burnout is a major problem.

Employees in general have extremely high training needs, even in such basic skills as counseling, report writing, offender monitoring, and caseload management. Fifty-five to seventy-five percent of all local directors rate one or more of these as a significant need. In addition to training in basic skills, training in handling special problem offenders, stress management, and legal liabilities are also needed by the majority of respondents.

Unlike institutions, probation and parole agencies depend on a supply of community resources to carry out their core responsibilities. Today, over half the local offices report a need to expand or improve all types of community resource efforts, including drug programs, residential programs, housing referral services, vocational education, job readiness training, and mental health services.

Over the last 15 years, probation and parole agencies have expanded their domain from primarily presentence investigations and offender supervision to pretrial diversion, halfway houses, alleviating institutional crowding, and a host of other activities. "Dealing with an increased number and variety of alternative programs in an effective manner" was cited by one director as the most serious management problem over the next few years.

Data submitted by these 388 professionals suggested that not only must this type of growth stop or slow dramatically, but also that serious questions must be raised about the system's present capacity to absorb additional offenders. Large and difficult caseloads coupled with a lack of staff and a shortage of community resources reflect a criminal justice subsystem strained to its limits.

## Notes

¹ The random sample was drawn from counties with populations greater than 50,000 and less than 200,000.

² *Juvenile and Adult Correctional Departments, Institutions, Agencies, and Paroling Authorities,* College Park, Maryland, American Correctional Association, 1987.

³ The 1983 National Assessment Survey was conducted for the National Institute of Justice by Abt Associates, Inc., Cambridge, Massachusetts.

# 8

# Screening Devices in Probation and Parole
## Management Problems

## Todd R. Clear
## Kenneth W. Gallagher

Risk screening is increasingly common in correctional field services. Typically, screening involves the assessment of a client's potential for "risk" behavior (usually, rearrest prior to termination of supervision) through the application of a standardized, more-or-less objective instrument that evaluates the client's background and current situation. The instrument normally contains a series of items with established "point" values, the sum of which constitutes a "risk score" representing the client's overall potential for failure. A typical item on a risk-assessment instrument might read:

> Number of prior felony convictions:   None = 0 points
> One = 2 points
> Two = 4 points
> Three or more = 6 points

Source: *Evaluation Review*, Vol. 7, No. 2 (April 1983), 217-34. Copyright © 1983 Sage Publications, Inc. Reprinted by permission of Sage Publications, Inc.

Because the items taken as a whole are correlated to risk, the sum of the scores on the items yields an assessment of the client's risk. Normally, risk-assessment instruments contain 4 to 12 items determined through a statistical analysis of closed cases and score ranges of up to 50 points or more.

The risk-assessment score is often misinterpreted, perhaps because risk-screening devices are frequently called prediction instruments. In fact, the result of a risk assessment is not a true prediction of a client's behavior. Instead, the risk score corresponds to a probability statement similar to the logic underlying the actuarial calculations of insurance premiums—clients are placed, by virtue of their numerical score, into a group of persons with a similar combination of characteristics (as determined by the assessment instrument). This combination of characteristics is associated with a given rate (frequency per 100) of "accidents" or failures. The more the points (characteristics associated with failure), the greater the rate of failure. We can illustrate this by a mythical instrument of, say, five items, yielding a potential range of between 0 points (no failure-associated characteristics) and 11 points (all characteristics failure associated). Table 1 shows the results that might occur from a study of a random sample of 800 closed cases (a validation study of the instrument). Thus those clients scoring 4 points on the instrument have exhibited in the past a rearrest rate of 10%, while those with 10 points have failed at a rate of 50%.

It is not really appropriate to conclude that a given client with 4 points on our mythical instrument has a 10% chance of failure, though it is appropriate to say that clients with that score are about one-fifth as likely to commit an offense as those with 10 points. The more accurate interpretation recognizes first that the score represents averages for outcomes of persons falling in certain scoring groups, and, second, that the averages are merely estimated rates. Clearly, however, they are not predictions, since each client in each scoring category will either fail or succeed.

If the instrument is valid, however (as our hypothetical case proves to be), there will be a virtually linear relationship between the person's score on the risk instrument and the rate of failure. This is true in our example, indicating what is perhaps the best way to interpret scores on these instruments: they are a *ranking* of clients in terms of potential for failure. This is an important distinction—we are dealing with ranked potentials rather than pure predictions.

By focusing on behavior potentials, we are able to place clients into aggregates having substantially different rates of potential failure. In our example, clients scoring 0-3 have an expected rearrest rate of 6%, those with a score of 4-6 have an expected rate of 14%, while those scoring 7 and above are expected to fail at a rate of 34%.

Table 1

**Hypothetical Results of a Validation Study of a
Risk-Assessment Instrument**

| Risk Score | N of Clients | Percentage Failing |
|:---:|:---:|:---:|
| 0 | 20 | 0 (N = 0) |
| 1 | 40 | 5 (N = 2) |
| 2 | 60 | 10 (N = 6) |
| 3 | 80 | 5 (N = 4) |
| 4 | 100 | 10 (N = 10) |
| 5 | 100 | 12 (N = 12) |
| 6 | 100 | 20 (N = 20) |
| 7 | 100 | 30 (N = 30) |
| 8 | 80 | 20 (N = 16) |
| 9 | 60 | 40 (N = 24) |
| 10 | 40 | 50 (N = 20) |
| 11 | 20 | 60 (N = 12) |

Such statistics are of crucial importance to those who must manage community supervision agencies: If it is known that about one-third of a subgroup of clients will offend, while about one-twentieth of another group will do so, it is reasonable to expect closer supervision to be given to the former group. The use of a risk-screening device places management in a position of accountability for the manner in which it uses its agency's resources to handle clients.

This point is illustrated by simple mathematics. Making the assumption, supported by some literature (Baird, 1979), that more intensive casework can reduce the degree of criminal behavior committed by probationers and parolees, and that those who are less likely to offend are more likely to be influenced by extensive casework, the problem of resource allocation becomes clear. For example, if one-fourth of low-risk cases can be prevented from new crimes by intensive casework, while only one-seventh of moderate risk cases can be prevented from committing crimes, the expected impact of providing intensive casework to each group is shown in Table 2.

Thus even if supervision is generally more effective with lower risk clients, by focusing attention on higher risk clients, it is possible that the total crime-control impact is greater (assuming casework has any influence at all on rearrest rates).

Table 2

**Impact of Intensive Casework Under Assumptions of
Decreasing Impact of Casework on Clients of Higher Risk**

| Risk Group | N | Assumed Preventive Impact of Casework (Percentages) | Total Decrease in Crimes per 100/Client | Crimes Prevented |
|---|---|---|---|---|
| 0-3 | 200 | 25 of crimes | 1.5 | 3 |
| 4-6 | 300 | 15 of crimes | 2.1 | 6.3 |
| 7-11 | 300 | 8 of crimes | 2.7 | 8 |

Consequently, most agencies that have adopted risk-screening devices have moved toward a linear, differential supervision policy, with lower risk cases receiving the least attention and higher risk cases receiving the most. The general strategy is to scale supervision—in our illustration, supervision standards might be established as follows:

| Category | Cut-Off Score | Supervision Frequency |
|---|---|---|
| High Risk | 7-11 | 1 contact per week |
| Medium Risk | 1-6 | 2 contacts per month |
| Low Risk | 0-3 | 1 contact per month |

Those familiar with most contemporary field services classification standards recognize this example as a typical, if perhaps ambitious, differential supervision standard. If more intense casework does reduce the failure level of clients (what other assumption can the administrators of field services realistically allow to guide their efforts?), then this general model is logical, insofar as it goes.

The intention of this article is to criticize the general model, logical as it may seem, in terms of its administrative applications. Particularly, the simple, increasingly frequent linear supervision approach to screening obscures a number of critical management issues facing field services. Even assuming it is true that (1) more intensive casework reduces rates of failures, and (2) greater impact in crime-control results from concentrating field services resources on higher risk clients, it is our position that a number of central management issues remain unresolved by simple, linear supervision standards. Indeed, while screening may appear to be a relatively simple procedure in practice, we believe that the availability of a risk score may complicate the requirement that management establish rational supervision policies. Our feeling is that many field services agencies, in adopting a screening approach, have either ignored or failed to comprehend subtle complexities that a risk-based supervision model involves.

We should make it clear that our remarks are not directed toward the legitimacy of risk screening. Others have commented on the technical problems of the risk-screening approach to field services: errors in prediction (Monahan, 1977); ethics of prediction (von Hirsch, 1979); statistical comparability of risk-assessment techniques (Gottfredson and Gottfredson, 1981); varieties in risk-assessment models (Bohnstedt, 1979); need for more widespread adoption of risk screening (GAO, 1976); and the sensitivity of instruments to changes in the target populations (Wright et al., 1981; Ford, 1977). We expect that statisticians and philosophers will continue to debate these issues of science and morality. Our remarks are directed toward a more pragmatic aim: rational administration of field services. We hope to illustrate the complex, yet essentially unobtrusive problems in managing field services raised by a risk-screening system.

We will use a currently popular model—the so-called Wisconsin Model—now being disseminated on a national scale by the National Institute of Corrections as the model system for probation and parole.[1] The Wisconsin Model uses two client-assessment scales: a risk scale that is similar to that described above, and a needs scale that assesses client functioning in several areas (with the result that a higher objective score suggests greater overall needs for services).[2] These two scales form the basis for a supervision classification system that requires closer supervision for those clients scoring higher on the scales.

We believe that risk/needs screening as represented by the Wisconsin Model is an important contribution to the field of community supervision. However, we also believe that the unthinking application of this innovation, represented by simplistic standards of ascending supervision intensity, misuses the tool and fails to take advantage of the many management applications made possible by such screening devices. Our position is that, by being able to rank clients according to their relative risk and needs, managers make visible a series of fundamental issues regarding the administration of correctional field services.

## The Management Supervision Policy

### Determining the Cutoff Scores
### for Supervising Based on Risk and Needs

The use of a two-scale classification instrument highlights the traditional dilemma of the community supervision function: service delivery versus surveillance. The needs instrument normally provides a gross indication of the client's overall relative need for services. The risk instrument provides an assessment of the client's relative appropriateness for surveillance. Community supervision agencies are continually balancing the concerns they give to these two functions.

However, agencies vary in the emphasis they give to these two functions for a variety of reasons, including resources, type of staff, type of clients, and community environment (Clear, 1981). Because a supervision classification system is the agency's primary mechanism for organizing staff and other agency resources, it is the central tool for implementing supervision policy—and making the agency mission operational. Since the client-assessment cutoff scores are typically used to determine supervision levels, it follows that the selection of cutoff scores is a decision that closely relates to the agency's broad supervision policies and mission.

Yet the importance of selecting the cutoff scores is very often underestimated, partly because the supervision standards that flow from the scores are frequently so simple: a trilevel system of supervision intensity with ascending levels of contact. But the significance of cutoff scores can be illustrated by the results of a classification system used in the New York City Department of Probation. Largely as a result of heavy workloads, the New York City Probation Department emphasizes supervision directed toward crime-control aims by focusing efforts on clients most likely to commit offenses (Jacobs, 1979). The classification system also provides for cases with many needs to be seen intensively, and the classification system is exemplified by the cutoffs below, with the supervision level determined by either instrument, whichever is the highest:

|  | Risk Score | Need Score |
|---|---|---|
| High Supervision | over 14 | over 19 |
| Moderate Supervision | 7-14 | 10-19 |
| Low Supervision | under 7 | under 10 |

Of interest in this classification system is which scale ultimately classifies the case. In New York, because of the purpose of the classification sytem, cut-off scores should maximize supervision based on risk rather than needs. Other, more service-delivery-oriented agencies, might prefer that the needs scale heavily influence supervision. Thus, given the same clientele, different agencies would be able to use cut-off scores to create supervision classifications that represent different orientations toward the mission of supervision. Because the scale scores represent relative client characteristics of risk and need (not absolute characteristics), the managerial decision is to determine how to establish supervision priorities in accordance with overall mission by selecting appropriate cutoffs. The question in New York is whether these cutoffs produce supervision practices consistent with the mission of risk control.

Table 3 shows the results of these cutoffs for the probationers classified in the Bronx (the initial implementation site for the classification system). As can be seen, the New York City assessment cutoffs are generally consistent with the agency's stated mission. When risk assessment determines supervision level, almost three-fourths of the time it places the case into intensive supervision. On the other hand, when needs classify the case, more than half the time the client will receive moderate supervision. Almost half of the most intensively supervised cases are in that category solely because of their risk, while less than one-fifth are there due to needs. Thus the general supervision a client will receive in New York will be heavily based on the client's risk, even though service needs are represented in some classifications.

The point of this illustration is that there are underlying policy considerations of the most fundamental sort inherent in the agency's determination of the supervision cut-off scores. By not giving these issues careful consideration in selecting scale cutoffs, agencies can create a situation in which they may unwittingly implement a supervision approach contrary to the intended agency mission due to the impact of cut-off scores. For example, by altering cutoffs in New York, it would

Table 3

**Results of NYC Probation Classification of Risk and Needs (N = 2518)**

| Final Supervision Level | Risk and Needs Agree | Risk Score Determined Level | Needs Score Determined Level | Total |
|---|---|---|---|---|
| High | 316 (37.8)* (19.2)** | 372 (44.4) (72.4) | 149 (17.8) (42.1) | 837 (33.2) |
| Moderate | 290 (45.5) (17.6) | 142 (22.3) (27.6) | 205 (32.2) (57.9) | 637 (25.3) |
| Low | 1044 (100.0) (63.3) | — | — | 1044 (41.5) |
| Total | 1650 (65.5) | 514 (20.4) | 354 (14.1) | 2518 (100.0) |

*Row percentage.
**Column percentage.

be possible to create the situation where most cases seen intensively are placed in that category by virtue of their need scores. This would be accomplished by lowering the needs cutoffs to a level below those now used.

As a consequence, what is often felt to be a fairly arbitrary decision — selection of cutoffs — is in fact a central managerial concern relating directly to the organization's mission. Insufficient attention to this decision can result in illogical policies or inappropriate supervision. Moreover, the problem is not merely one of workload. That is, various cutoffs can create equivalent workload levels for differing emphases on risk and needs. The community supervision manager must be closely attentive to the selection of cutoffs so that the nature of the workload is consistent with the agency's mission in addition to controlling the level of workload.

## Establishing Supervision Standards

### Creating a Linkage Between Knowledge and Mission

The supervision standards (as implemented by the cutoffs) perform several functions. Most directly, the supervision standards organize line officer resources around the case load. That is, the specification of supervision requirements in a classification system acts as a constraint in line officers' use of time and energy on cases and therefore is an essential resource-management policy of the agency.

Obviously, the supervision standards must meet several managerial needs. They must be realistic, not calling for more time or effort than staff can actually provide (otherwise, they will be uniformly ignored by staff). They must be simple enough to be manageable by the line officers who must implement them and supervisors who must hold staff accountable for them. This is probably why the most frequent approach to supervision standards is to create three levels of supervision similar to those described earlier (sometimes a fourth — administrative — level is established requiring no contact).

The use of ascending supervision levels meets needs for administrative simplicity, but may not reflect contemporary knowledge about how to supervise clients. Unfortunately, very little is known about supervision appropriateness for different types of clients, except that most experts agree on the need to vary supervision quality and intensity to reflect the problems in the case. Because lower scoring cases (low risk and needs) provide very few intervention points for services and have a low base-expectancy for failures, they seem to call appropriately for limited supervision. And even though high risk or need clients appear to benefit from more intense supervision, it is unclear whether this results from greater surveillance or more adequate services (Stanley, 1976; von Hirsch and Hanrahan, 1979). For those offenders falling in the middle ranges of risk and need, the problem is even more complicated. The existence of increased need, as measured by a need scale, does not automatically translate into a requisite need for greater intensity of supervision. In fact, the opposite may be true for some cases. A common item such as "mental health" may lead to a professional referral with the requirement that community supervision contact with the client be minimized in order to prevent contamination of the treatment process. Finally, cases with various combinations of item scores resulting in the same aggregated supervision score may actually call for very selective intervention, while others require constantly reinforced limit-setting supervision, even though their assessment scores sometimes call for identical levels of supervision intensity (Arling and Lerner, 1980).

The point is that supervision standards are a two-sided coin. While they provide for greater accountability and structured differentiation of supervision via an easily administered system of classification, a set of standards may fail to distinguish sufficiently some actual differences among clients. While most existing classification systems seem to take this into account by allowing for an officer override of the instrument classification, it is arguable whether this override sufficiently allows for the needed flexibility.

In addition, the supervision standards necessarily reflect unobtrusive policy issues. We have argued that the selection of cut-off scores is a managerial decision relating to mission, and this is also true for the construction of supervision standards. For purposes of illustrating this point, let us adopt the standard approach in which the two scales are treated as if they are independent. Three levels of supervision intensity (I = highest, III = lowest) are then assigned to the client groups based on risk and needs. Table 4 displays different approaches that might be used to assign supervision standards, each approach based on different assumptions and knowledge about supervision effectiveness.[3]

Part A is the traditional approach for establishing supervision standards. The major assumption underlying this model, which is perhaps the most commonly used in establishing standards, is that either risk or need issues in a case may require adjustment of supervision intensity, and that the nature of the adjustment required is essentially equivalent for each scale. This is a conservative administrative policy, and we have already examined some of the issues inherent in its operation.

Parts B and C depict policy-oriented supervision standards. In Part B, for example, the supervision standards for three cells have been reduced in order to reflect a greater interest in risk control. This is not

Table 4

**Approaches to Supervision Standards**

|  | Risk High | Moderate | Low |
|---|---|---|---|
| **Part A** | | | |
| Need: | | | |
| High | I | I | I |
| Moderate | I | II | II |
| Low | I | I | III |
| **Part B** | | | |
| Need: | | | |
| High | I | II | II |
| Moderate | I | II | III |
| Low | I | II | III |
| **Part C** | | | |
| Need: | | | |
| High | I | I | Discretion (I or II) |
| Moderate | I | II | Discretion (II or III) |
| Low | Discretion (I or II) | Discretion (II or III) | III |
| **Part D*** | | | |
| Need: | | | |
| High | Surveillance | I | II |
| Moderate | I | I | I |
| Low | II | I | III |

*Modified from Clear (1980).

a minor change, since the additional time made available from these cases can be redistributed among the higher risk cases to provide even greater supervision intensity for the latter.

Part C reflects a change from the traditional model in four cells in which officer discretion to classify is increased. Here, on cases scoring low on one dimension, but high or moderate on the other, the officer is required to make a judgment as to the supervision intensity required by the case. This can be thought of as a service-delivery model, since it allows the nature of the service required by the case to determine supervision intensity: For example, high risk/low needs cases often may need to be seen only intermittently due to the limited potential of services; high need/low risk cases sometimes will be handled by referral with little direct contact, and other times will be seen intensively for direct services. Under this model, the officer would review each case in order to make an assessment that is more qualitative in content, and then assign cases falling in the four discretionary cells to one of the two supervision levels based on nature of needs. The assumption underlying this model is that services can influence supervision needs of clients.

Part D is a modified version of the supervision standard adopted by one county in the New Jersey Case Management Project (Clear, 1981). The county was very resource poor (caseloads averaged about 140 clients), and this was seen as an impact-maximizing approach under limited resources. High risk/high needs cases were felt to be normally intractable (with a rate of rearrest on probation exceeding 50%), and the decision was to have them report to the office on a five-minute sign-in basis once a week, with a once-monthly surprise home visit. For them, no direct services would be provided. Intensive services are provided to those clients of moderate risk or needs. The assumption underlying this model is that the impact of supervision is greatest for clients not already committed to a criminal lifestyle nor heavily handicapped by multiple needs.

These examples illustrate how the development of supervision standards is also a managerial policy decision. While the simple approach is to establish three levels of sequentially increasing intensity, standards can also be very creative, reflecting the agency's mission as well as the limited knowledge that now exists regarding supervision effectiveness. Pragmatically, the development of supervision standards must also be consistent with available officer resources of time and expertise — it must not be based on an erroneous estimate of officer expertise or skill. The central requirement is to approach the development of supervision standards as another formula by which officer resources available to the agency will be distributed among clients. Hand in hand with the development of cut-off scores, the determination of standards can directly translate the agency's mission into policy. Standards also reflect reasonable knowledge about supervision effectiveness, since they are a mechanism for redistribution of a fixed amount of officer time among cases in order to improve agency impact.

## Managing the Supervision System

### The Implications of Workload Measures

The use of an objective classification system leads directly toward the development of *workload* measures instead of caseload measures of supervision. This enables the manager to overcome a number of the weaknesses in simple caseload arithmetic (Carter and Wilkins, 1979), while still measuring the work required of cases. The typical approach is to use a time study to measure the amount of work required by cases of different supervision classes, and then establish weights for each case. Again, however, the existence of a workload measure highlights several management dilemmas that remain obscured by a caseload system.

*Equalizing officer workload.*   For a variety of reasons, officers are able to hide behind their caseload figures. Sometimes they will keep cases active that should have been discharged; sometimes cases requiring low contact are included in the figures. The point is that caseload counts do not measure actual workload; often, the former are inflated. In addition, the focus on caseloads is often a source of much officer dissatisfaction, since these figures can make the officer feel called upon to do an inordinate amount of work.

Conceptually, workload enables the case-distribution system to equalize the amount of work required of each staff member. However, conversion to a workload system also makes visible inequities that are difficult to revise. Table 5 shows the results of a supervision unit's current workload after conversion to an objective-classification system. Under the previous case-distribution system, caseload sizes had been kept roughly equal at 120 cases per officer, so this figure is used to calculate required contacts in the workload.

Clearly, this unit faces a number of inequities in workload;[4] in fact, two of the officers are being required to make more than twice as many contacts as one of their colleagues. Most of the differences in workload

Table 5

**Distribution of Workload in Unit: Illustration***

| Officer | Percentage of Cases by Supervision Level | | | Contacts per Month Required |
|:---:|:---:|:---:|:---:|:---:|
| | Level I | Level II | Level III | |
| A | 16.4 | 31.5 | 52.1 | 77 |
| B | 26.3 | 38.4 | 35.3 | 109 |
| C | 54.1 | 35.3 | 10.6 | 172 |
| D | 38.1 | 38.1 | 23.8 | 127 |
| E | 43.9 | 40.9 | 15.2 | 154 |
| F | 21.9 | 40.6 | 37.5 | 101 |
| G | 45.3 | 31.4 | 23.3 | 146 |
| Total | 35.2 | 36.2 | 28.5 | 128 per officer |

*Source: New York City Department of Probation (1981).

appear to be a product of variations in proportions of Level I and III cases among officers. How can this be resolved? One method might be to transfer cases to restore workload equity, although this would require adjusting absolute caseload sizes of officers to make them different within the unit, as well as disrupting services for those clients being seen intensively. Another approach would be to put a "cap" on the high workload officers, giving new cases to the underworked officers. However, new cases can be expected to distribute in the classifications roughly according to the unit totals; consequently, it will take some time before workloads are equalized through a cap system.

From a managerial standpoint, any change in the case-distribution method will result in questions by staff as to the rationality of the change. Thus staff will need to be trained in the workload method in order for them to understand the changes affecting their work.

The administrator must also ask the question: Why are these current differences so dramatic? Perhaps the officers are scoring the clients differently on the instruments due to a lack of understanding of the items or the system. In this case, the solution is more training, not redistributions of cases. In any event, either choice of training or case redistribution is likely to be a complicated process, since the target is to adjust both workloads and supervision practices. The existence of visible evidence of inequities forces the manager of this unit to confront these staff issues that had heretofore not been a formal problem for the unit.

*Regionalization of workload.* In the same way that risk-screening devices are used to equalize workload among officers, these instruments provide a basis for assessing staffing requirements of different regions served by a large agency. For instance, a nonurban area may have large numbers of low risk cases in comparison to an urban center, and the workload of the former might be manageable despite a larger client/staff ratio.

There is a danger in this approach, however, that the desire to carefully equalize workload will not allow regions to develop suitable policies for managing workload differences. This is an especially important problem for agencies that wish to maintain a reasonable level of autonomy for regionalized services. An illustration is provided by comparison of case-management policies developed in three counties in the New Jersey Case Management Project.

Table 6 shows the distribution of risk scores for intake cohorts in three counties in New Jersey, based on identical risk-screening devices. Rural County (A) has a slightly higher set of risk scores, rural (B) is slightly lower, but the differences between the counties are not extreme. Yet the supervision policies devised by the counties, based on the instrument, are quite different, as shown in Table 7.

Table 6

**Cumulative Frequencies of Risk Scores by County**

| Score | Urban County (N = 101) | Rural County A (N = 150) | Rural County B (N = 396) |
|-------|------------------------|--------------------------|--------------------------|
| 0-5 | 9.9 | 11.2 | 8.6 |
| 6-10 | 34.6 | 30.0 | 38.9 |
| 11-15 | 68.3 | 52.0 | 69.2 |
| 16-20 | 84.2 | 74.0 | 93.2 |
| 21-25 | 93.1 | 92.0 | 99.5 |
| 26-over | 100.0 | 100.0 | 100.0 |

The interesting fact is that the cutoffs are not the major source of differences between the counties. Instead, very different supervision standards are imposed. For example, rural (B) requires weekly contacts with a very high risk group representing about 10% of the population. Urban allows these contacts to vary, depending upon the case (both counties also allow the results of an objective needs instrument to influence contacts).

One obvious reason for the differences lies in workload—the cases-per-officer ratio in rural (A), for example, is twice that of rural (B). Perhaps if the resources were equalized, using workload, the standards that resulted would be less variable.

But this would obscure several administrative subtleties. Most obvious is the fact that, despite an understandable desire to intensify contacts with as many cases as possible, there is no single formula for appropriate supervision standards. No particular argument for any of these models can be advanced as empirically superior. A related point is that contact intensity is at least somewhat a function of external resources—when the latter are available, there is less of a need for direct supervision of cases. In addition, staff morale, experience, and mobility may well influence the workability of these standards.

The point is that the mere existence of comparable risk-related data does not require, nor even advance, the automatic idea of equal workload. While there are costs to be borne in maintaining workload inequities, there are also costs in failing to consider regional differences in local environment and operations that might suggest variable supervision standards in different regions of the same agency. Of course, the use of risk data can make it easier to establish the applicable standards, compare regional performance, and allocate resources, but all this does not necessarily connote the idea of uniform policies for all

**Table 7**

**Use of Risk Information by County**

| County | Average Cases per Officer | Level | Classification Policy Risk Scores | Percentage of Cases | Reporting Frequency |
|---|---|---|---|---|---|
| Urban | 104 | Low | 0-10 | 34.6 | Quarterly personal contact with monthly letter to monthly personal contacts* |
| | | Medium | 11-20 | 49.6 | Monthly to biweekly personal contacts* |
| | | High | 21 + | 15.8 | Biweekly to semiweekly personal contacts* |
| Rural (A) | 183 | Low | 0-10 | 30.0 | Nonreporting (those with fines & rest.— monthly reporting form) |
| | | Regular | 11-20 | 44.0 | Bimonthly personal contacts |
| | | High | 21 + | 26.0 | Monthly personal contact and monthly telephone contact (with high needs— weekly sign in) |
| Rural (B) | 85 | Minimum | 0-9 | 33.3 | Nonreporting or monthly personal contact* |
| | | Medium | 10-19 | 56.3 | Monthly to weekly personal contacts* |
| | | Maximum | 20 + | 10.4 | Weekly personal contacts |

*Decision based on needs score and risk score.

areas served by, say, a state agency. There may be good administrative reasons for maintaining variety, the variety that uniform risk data may help to eradicate.

## Discussion

Our general point has been that the practice of risk screening, which has recently become a popular element of classification systems (often compiled together with needs-screening devices), raises a number of management issues, from selection of cut-off and supervision policy to reorganization of staff and workload. Just as this innovation proves to be a potential administrative tool, the availability of risk information makes probation and parole administration vulnerable to rational, external assessment in a way not previously existent. Not only are data available that estimate client risk levels prior to supervision (and therefore presumably lead to post hoc accountability of supervision decision), but also a firm, visible set of criteria become available by which managerial decisions may be made, evaluated, and criticized.

The question, of course, is whether the general quality of management in probation and parole is sufficient to meet the challenge of these new devices, which are, after all, administrative tools even more than they are casework aids. As for any tool, the utility of risk screening will be only as great as the skills of those who apply the tool.

Too often, agency administrators who are anxious for risk-screening devices, yet are not capable of using them skillfully, will adopt standard cutoffs and override policies almost as if they were nonnegotiable. This kind of practice will inhibit innovation and lead to the implementation of supervision policies that do not fit the agency's mission, resources, and environment. Unfortunately, there are indications that many organizations are doing just this—adopting the so-called Wisconsin Model without reassessing any of its specifics, and without considering the implications of transferring it in unaltered form to a different setting. Attempts by administrations to borrow so unquestioningly (instead of managing changes toward a new system) are probably doomed to fail. The lack of organizational fit alone will be a problem. In addition, the refusal to modify the Wisconsin approach will mean that administrators fail to learn from the change process that which can be used to resolve administrative problems. We hope this kind of mindless dissemination will be limited.

The alternative, in which administrators would become familiar with the method of screening as well as the practice, is more attractive. In so doing, they will learn how to operate screening systems as managerial tools; they will anticipate the problems these devices will raise; they will elaborate on skeletal, existing practices to find total systems that suit agency needs.

## Notes

[1] The principal author is currently a staff member on this national project and a consultant to perhaps a dozen agencies now implementing adaptations of this approach.

[2] The needs scale was developed by a team of probation and parole officers. It involves an assessment of a number of problem areas (such as mental stability or employment), and is related to the general, overall amount of time that will be required to deal with the client, due to his or her needs.

[3] Obviously, each of these matrices makes no assumption about distribution of cases in the cells, since this is a result of the cutoff scores. Selection of supervision standards are used to articulate policy and supervision effectiveness assumptions.

[4] Ordinarily, workload is measured in units based on time required for cases of different supervision levels. In this illustration, we are using "contacts required" as an estimate of workload. Workload units would be a simple mathematical transformation of contact counts.

## References

Administrative Office of the Courts, State of New Jersey (1977). *An Evaluation of Supervision in Essex County Probation Department.* Trenton, NJ: Administrative Office of the Courts.

Arling, G. and K. Lerner (1980). *Client Management Classification.* Washington, DC: National Institute of Corrections.

Baird, S. C. et al. (1979). *The Wisconsin Case Classification Staff Development Project: A Two-Year Follow-Up.* Madison: Wisconsin Bureau of Community Corrections.

Bohnstedt, R. (1979). *Screening for Risk: Classification Instruments for Criminal Justice Decisions.* Washington, DC: National Institute of Corrections.

Carter, R. and L. T. Wilkins (1979). *Probation, Parole and Community Corrections.* Philadelphia: J. B. Lippincott.

Clear, T. R. et al. (1981). "Objectives-based case management." *Criminal Justice J.* 5, 1:69

_____. (1980). *New Jersey Case Management Project.* School of Criminal Justice, Rutgers University.

Ford, C. and R. Johnson (1977). *Probation Prediction Models and Recidivism.* Correctional Manpower Services and Project. Springfield: Illinois Department of Correction.

General Accounting Office (1976). *Probation and Parole Activities Need to be Better Managed.* Report to Congress, Washington, DC: Government Printing Office.

Gottfredson, D. et al. (1981). *Final Report of The Intensive Correctional Field Services Project.* School of Criminal Justice, Rutgers University.

Gottfredson, S. and D. Gottfredson. (1981). "Risk screening: a comparison of methods." *Criminal J. and Behavior 8,* 1: 35-49.

Gray, C. M. (ed.). (1979). *The Costs of Crime.* Beverly Hills, CA: Sage. Pub. Co.

Jacobs, T. (1979). *New York City Differential Supervision Project.* New York: New York City Department of Probation.

Monahan, J. (1977). "The prediction of violent behavior," in *Report of the Panel on Deterrent and Incapacitative Effects*. Washington, DC: National Academy of Sciences.

New York City Department of Probation (1981). *Differential Supervision Implementation Project*. New York: New York City Department of Probation.

Stanley, D. T. (1976). *Doing Justice*. New York: Hill & Wang.

Stanley, D. T. and K. Hanrahan (1979). *The Question of Parole*. Cambridge, MA: Ballinger.

Wright, K. et al. (1981). "A critique of the universal applicability of the Wisconsin probation risk assessment instrument." Presented to the American Society of Criminology, Washington, DC, November.

# 9

# Probation Supervision: Mission Impossible

## John Rosecrance

Probation is in serious trouble! Unfortunately this statement is not particularly shocking or even controversial. This litany of accusations against probation departments runs the gamut from depicting them as do-nothing bureaucracies (Blackmore, 1980:13) to accusing them of being harmful intervention agencies (Forer, 1980:210). Judicial support for probation services has eroded (Krajick, 1980:9; Johnson, 1985:206), public support has diminished (Fogel, 1984:67; Duffee, 1984:295), legislative funding has been reduced (Petersilia, 1985:339), and academic backing has wavered (Rothman, 1980; Wilson, 1983). Probation officers themselves question the efficacy and purposefulness of their actions (Lide, 1980; Cushman, 1985:327), while probationers seriously doubt that any good will come from their contacts with probation officials (Gilsinan, 1982:183). After examining the current probation situation, a leading researcher and consultant on correctional issues commented: "In the present circumstances the survival of the idea of probation as a service is in jeopardy. Little wonder that in most agencies the vitality of conventional practices is hardly seen." (Conrad, 1985:421).

There is consensus among academic researchers that probation departments will not be revitalized until they develop a clear-cut mission

---

Source: *Federal Probation*, Vol. 50, No. 1 (March 1986), 25-31.

(Breed, 1984; Harris, 1984; McAnany, 1984; Thomson et al., 1984; Petersilia, 1985). Upon completing an extensive study of probation practices in California, a group of Rand researchers recommended: "The mission of probation and the responsibilities of probation agencies should be redefined, limited, and explicitly stated, by statute if necessary." (Petersilia et al., 1985:388-89). In an attempt to establish a viable mission, probation practitioners and academicians have put forth several proposals that address the dilemma of whether probation services should stress assistance or control. Such proposals generally fall into three broad categories: (1) service orientation, (2) differential supervision, and (3) intensive supervision. These categories can be placed on an assistance-control continuum with service orientation at the assistance end, differential supervision occupying a center position, and intensive supervision at the control end.

Those espousing a service orientation (Fogel, 1978; Bottom and McWilliams, 1979; Conrad, 1982, 1984) would uncouple surveillance from probation responsibilities, leaving the officer free to provide help and assistance to the offender. Eschewing a law enforcement role, probation officers would counsel offenders and refer them to appropriate community services. Dutch probation officers have assumed such a mission and in some cases have refused to give the police information concerning possible criminal activity on the part of their probationers (Harris, 1984:34).

Supportors of the differential supervision approach (Wright et al., 1984; Clear and Gallagher, 1985; Glaser, 1985; O'Leary, 1985) advocate the implementation of risk assessments for offenders. The type of supervision given to probationers would be related to their risk potential. Classification is generally considered a tool for improving an existing probation system rather than a radical solution. The centrist position of proponents of differential supervision is reflected in the statement of the chief probation officer of Orange County, California:

> The goal of probation supervision should not singularly emphasize either rehabilitation or punishment. The focus should be on assessment and management of the offender in terms of risks and needs. The return on that investment will be a high level of community protection from those individuals who present the greatest risk of committing further law violations, good supervision and resocialization programs, and the ability to use resources wisely (Schumacher, 1985:445).

Intensive supervision programs would establish reduced caseloads in an effort to provide a punitive community-based alternative to prison (Petersilia, 1985:389). An integral feature of the intensive supervision approach is the inclusion of a strict surveillance component. The Georgia plan (generally considered an exemplar of intensive supervision programs) requires participants to abide by the following rules:

(1) five face-to-face contacts with the IPS team every week, one in the office, one on the job, three at home including one on the weekend;

(2) weekly verification of employment;

(3) nightly curfew, ordinarily at 8:00 p.m. unless the probationer has a job with hours that conflict with this limit;

(4) coordinated record check with law enforcement every week (Conrad, 1985:414).

The efficacy and appropriateness of the three prevailing approaches will be judged ultimately by their ability to reduce the criminal activity of those on probation. Although it has been argued that recidivism rates are not an accurate gauge of success (Reid, 1981:275), this single criterion continues to be the standard by which probation programs are evaluated (Walker, 1985:177). After analyzing the three prevalent motifs for revitalizing probation's mission, I suggest that, if implemented, these approaches will fail to reduce recidivism and that such failures will engender disillusionment and further weaken support for probation services. This position is informed by 15 years of probation experience wherein I was involved with supervision programs that incorporated these approaches. While probation planners have called for radical measures (Conrad, 1985), the prevailing approaches are not qualitatively different from past and current programs that have proven ineffective. There is ample research to justify this finding. I further contend that the three prevailing approaches will be ineffective for two basic reasons: (1) the emergence of organizational dynamics antithetical to program goals and (2) the conflicting nature of relationships between probation officer and defendant. My research is in agreement with Shover (1979:222) who contends that many correctional problems originate "in the structurally given conflict of interest between correctors and offenders, an inherent conflict that cannot be entirely eliminated — even by good intentions and human-relations training."

Following my critique of the current approaches I present a preliminary plan to redirect probation's mission. My proposal calls for the elimination of supervision by probation officers. Such an action would relieve probation officers of the control-assistance dilemma and free them to concentrate upon supplying objective and accurate information to the court. Probation departments would be charged with the responsibility of compiling and presenting court evaluations. If probation is recommended and counseling or treatment is needed, they would be provided by agencies outside of the criminal justice system. Monitoring those placed on probation would become a computerized function performed by clerical employees of the court. With this type of reorganization probation would have a parsimonious and achievable mission—providing in-depth court investigation services.

## Service Orientation

A basic assumption of service orientation maintains that probation and parole officers are unable to effectively combine service and surveillance responsibilities. The strain inherent in these conflicting roles culminates in an unsatisfactory level of supervision, leaving the client floundering and the community at risk. Advocates of a mission emphasizing service would invest the police with surveillance duties, allowing the probation or parole officer to adopt a helping or advocacy role. The legendary Zebulon Brockway (1912:324) sanctioned such an approach: "The most satisfactory person for supervision of paroled men is the chief of police; not the average policemen in the great cities, nor indeed a religious or philanthropic organization or private individual." The observation of David Fogel (1978:15) about the appropriateness of parole supervision reflects a basic tenet of the service orientation: "set parole officers to the task of helping the parolee find a job and set the police to the task of keeping an eye on the parolee."

The most well developed plan for structuring a probation organization around a service orientation has been devised by Conrad (1984:264-65). Under his plan

> All persons placed on probation will be required to accept surveillance by police. To manage this function the police will establish a bureau of supervision that will receive reports from probationers on terms and at intervals prescribed by the court.

A special probation unit designated as the division of service and liaison would be established to

> . . . carry out all contact services with probationers with the aim of helping them toward a satisfactory completion of probation. Personnel assigned to the division will be qualified as counselors. They must be prepared to assume an advocate role to assure that probationers needing special services will receive them.

Probation departments in the United States have not implemented service orientation on a system-wide basis, and Conrad (1985:420) himself admitted that such a reorganization was "an idea whose time had not yet come." On the other hand small supervision units have attempted to develop a service orientation. In California a few special supervision units defined their responsibility as service to the client rather than protection of the community. This was frequently done on an ad hoc basis with the tacit approval of probation administration. I myself worked in such a unit for over a year. Stressing a service approach placed the unit in direct conflict with the police and district attorney's office and decreased the unit's credibility in the criminal justice system. Those on probation were suspicious about the sincerity of their probation officer "advocates." When several of the unit's probationers became involved in additional illegal activities, the unit was reorganized and traditional surveillance practices were reinstated. In today's "get tough climate" it is unlikely that a service orientation would receive support from either the community or other criminal justice agencies (Bartollas, 1981).

## Differential Supervision Schemes

Differential supervision schemes are based upon the assumption that offenders should be supervised to an extent commensurate with their needs and the risk of recidivism. Probationers deemed unlikely to reoffend would receive minimal supervision, while those evaluated as likely to continue their illegal behavior would need close supervision. This approach seeks to ensure that supervision is applied according to objective criteria and not to question the efficacy of probation supervision. The use of classification scales lends an aura of rationality to the putative concept of differential supervision. Those familiar with probation caseloads generally acknowledge that some offenders need minimal attention while others require frequent contact. Classification systems are seen by probation administrators as providing scientific management practices which, if properly implemented, can lead to a reduction in recidivism rates.

All too often differential supervision, in reality, is a sham which serves to maintain the status quo (McCleary, 1978). Although researchers (Clear and Gallagher, 1985; Schumacher, 1985) have recommended the involvement of line staff in the planning of classification systems, in practice, probation officers are generally ordered to employ supervision scales with little or no input as to the construction of those scales. Based upon personal experience and reports from other researchers (Takagi and Robinson, 1969; Shover, 1974; McCleary, 1975, 1977; Lipsky, 1980) there is an uncertain relationship between classification standards and what actually occurs during the supervision of probationers. Rather than adhering to recommended standards (Bemus et al., 1983), individual probation officers do not accept the appropriateness of classification categories and allocate their time as they see fit. Line staff often rationalize their ad hoc style by claiming (not unrealistically) that large caseloads and classification inconsistencies make it impractical to follow strictly departmental guidelines. The idiosyncratic styles of supervision officers (Glaser, 1964) are antithetical to the goal of uniform classification and often culminate in a situation where the "paper system (classification) bears little relationship to the actual practice of staff" (Clear and Gallagher, 1985:431). In many instances, although a classification system exists, it is not being implemented.

The adoption of differential supervision will do little to resolve the assistance-control dilemma faced by probation officers. The assumption that better utilization of the probation officers' time will improve supervision capabilities and result in lower recidivism rates has not been empirically demonstrated (Empey, 1982). The implementation of classification scales will allow probation departments to claim they are updating their practices without coming to grips with fundamental issues. More of the same, even if done scientifically, will not revitalize probation's mission.

## Intensive Supervision

Recent intensive probation supervision (IPS) programs are being hailed as "promising alternatives to prison" (Petersilia et al., 1985:387), "what probation is supposed to be" (Gettinger, 1985:213), and as "wide-ranging renovations of American penology" (Conrad, 1985:410). Such fulsome praise is directed toward programs that began barely 3 years ago. The factor that generally has been credited for generating these sanguine opinions is the inclusion of a strict surveillance component in a supervision regimen. Strict surveillance is acknowledged as the element that sets current programs apart from traditional IPS efforts (Pearson, 1985). Probation officers report that assignments to IPS units have given them a more positive outlook on their jobs. The head of New York's probation service indicated: "People burned out because of a high caseload went out into the field with a whole new spirit, full of enthusiasm," while a Georgia IPS worker stated: "You don't notice the hours. You can really get into people's problems and try to help. We're so involved it's enjoyable" (Gettinger, 1985:218).

These glowing reports should be considered in light of prior experience with IPS. Typically, initial enthusiasm for such programs disintegrates when, upon closer scrutiny, it cannot be demonstrated that intensive supervision produces lower recidivism rates. An observation by McCleary et al. (1979:651) seems particularly germane when considering the effectiveness of current IPS efforts: "when social scientists tell you that your program has a miraculous effect, be skeptical."

The San Francisco Project, involving the use of IPS in Federal probation during the 1960s, clearly revealed that probationers randomly assigned to reduced caseloads were no more law abiding than their counterparts assigned to regular caseloads (Banks et al., 1977). California's extensive experiments with various IPS type programs in the 1960s and 1970s generally demonstrated that intensive supervision tactics failed to reduce recidivism (Shover, 1979). Some of these programs also included strict surveillance procedures. I was involved in a program that required offenders to report several times per week. It was clear that the probation officer's primary role in this unit was surveillance. Unfortunately such a watchdog approach was no more effective than an advocacy role in weaning probationers away from criminal activity, and the unit was eventually abandoned. In the middle 1970s the Unified Delinquency Intervention Services operated by the Illinois Department of Corrections claimed spectacular success in reducing delinquency among juveniles by using a package of intensive supervision methods (Walker, 1985:178). Subsequent research revealed that lower recidivism claims were more the product of a mathematical regression than an actual success rate (McCleary et al., 1978; McDowall et al., 1981).

While it is probably too early to ascertain accurately the effectiveness of current IPS programs, it can be questioned whether criteria for inclusion in such programs, generally only nonviolent offenders are accepted (Conrad, 1985), and the tendency for statistics producers to include information favorable to organization expectations (McCleary, 1975; Shover, 1979) are perhaps more significant factors in the "success" of IPS efforts than supervision measures—however intensive. The statement of a Georgia Institute of Technology researcher regarding IPS programs should be noted:

> Can they divert? Yes, they can. Are they cost-effective, compared to prison? Yes, they are. But if you ask me if they can rehabilitate people from a life of crime, that's another matter (Banks, quoted in Gettinger, 1985:218).

## Barriers to Effective Supervision

Fifteen years of probation experience and scores of empirical studies have convinced me that traditional practices of probation officials cannot appreciably change the behavior patterns of criminal offenders. Supervision efforts by probation officers—no matter how dedicated or rationally based—will not reduce recidivism rates. The relationships between officer and client, and those between officer and probation bureaucracy, are structured in such a way that effective supervision is restricted.

### Bureaucratic Relationships

The significance of bureaucratic dynamics in influencing supervision outcomes has been reported by several researchers (Takagi, 1967; Takagi and Robinson, 1969; Shover, 1974, 1979; McCleary, 1975, 1978; Prus and Stratton, 1976; Rosecrance, 1985). The very structure of probation organizations promotes distortions in the supervision process and many decisions are made according to bureaucratic imperatives, rather than case-specific goals. Often the "failure" or "success" of probationers is determined as much by organizational dynamics as by the offenders' behavior. Probation departments are organized in such a way that case decisions by line staff frequently are considered in light of anticipated responses by either their supervisors or probation administration. These considerations lead to anticipatory supervision and to actions ensuring that administration-approved programs will be evaluated positively.

Although individual supervision styles vary considerably, decisions of direct concern to probationers such as violations or revocations of probation generally are made with an eye to how the officer's supervisor will react. Perception of supervisor reaction is an important aspect of the case process. Takagi and Robinson (1969:85-6) found a

> ... high degree of correspondence between district supervisors and their subordinates on the case-recommendation task. This finding suggests that the selective enforcement of some rules is as much characteristic of the officials as selective adherence is a characteristic of the violator.

Traditionally, staff supervisors are concerned with uniform decisions that facilitate a smooth work flow rather than either rehabilitation of the offender or protection of the community (Blumberg, 1967). Since probation officers anticipate supervisorial responses, their decisions are in turn influenced by organizational considerations not directly related to the offender's behavior.

When new programs are actively supported by administration there is a tendency for probation officers to adjust their actions to ensure favorable evaluations of those programs. In many instances significant behavior changes occur among probation officers, not among offenders. While working as a probation officer I was aware of situations similar to the following incident reported by McCleary (1975:224). When preliminary estimates of an intensive supervision program showed no appreciable change in recidivism, administrators indicated that thereafter officers assigned to small caseloads

> ... would be promoted strictly on their caseload recidivism rates, the lower the rate the better the chance of promotion. A subsequent

re-evaluation of the program found that the smaller caseloads were more effective than the larger caseloads in reducing recidivism. . . . What happened, of course, is that the researchers did observe a statistical difference but they incorrectly attributed this difference to the effectiveness of the treatment. In fact, the change was due entirely to a shift in the structural dynamic of the parole agency.

## Client Relationships

In my probation experience I observed that interactions between probation officers and their clients were characterized by patent mendacity. Neither of the participants in this relationship trusted the other: Probation officers were afraid of being manipulated or "conned" (Dawson, 1969), while probationers assumed that if they "stepped out of line" the officers (no matter how friendly or treatment oriented) would take coercive action. Studt (1973:89) noted a similar pattern, i.e., a "context of suspicion" that permeated relationships between parole officer and parolee.

The difficulties experienced by probation officers when they attempt to combine surveillance and service duties has been well reported (Krajick, 1980). The probationer's problem in accepting the officer at face value has received less consideration. Gilsinan (1982:184) described the offender's dilemma:

> The relationship between the p.o. and his client forms a fulcrum for balancing the competing demands of treatment and control. The agent perceives himself as attempting to strike a balance that will be in the client's best interest. The client, however, is part of a different social world. For him, the distinction between treatment and control is a subtle one at best. More often he sees no distinction at all. Thus, control often becomes the dominant motif in the client's perspective of the relationship. Clients, then, must themselves learn how to do probation.

Inherent distrust was succinctly described by a dope addict on probation who told me: "When push comes to shove you dudes will give us up — everytime." David Rothman (1980:10) reported that progressive reformers (circa 1910-1930) had failed to link treatment and protection and that "when conscience and convenience met, convenience won. When treatment and coercion met, coercion won."

Inability to develop an honest relationship between probation officers and their offender clients is further exacerbated by the different social worlds they inhabit. Their perspectives of reality and purpose are often divergent. Ex-convicts who have described their probation and parole experiences (Irwin, 1970; Bunker, 1973; Braly, 1976) have emphasized that lack of common understanding rendered relationships with supervision officers shallow and unproductive. Irwin (1970:157) observed a phenomenon that can be applied to probation relationships:

> . . . the parole social system has brought into close contact, in an agent-client relationship, two people who represent different social worlds — one, the parole agency, which is unduly influenced at the formal level by conservative segments of society; and the other, a deviant subsociety.

## A New Probation Mission

The following is a preliminary outline of a plan for restructuring probation's mission. The basic direction of the reorganization will be put forth. The first step would involve the complete elimination of probation supervision. I would stress the word *complete*. If probation departments retain any vestige of supervision duties, they inevitably will seek to expand their responsibilities in that area (Thompson, 1984:107), and as long as probation departments are involved with supervision, other social agencies will be reluctant to provide similar services, out of respect for the territory of a powerful organization (Conrad, 1979). Even though researchers have called for scaling down the scope of probation (Von Hirsch, 1976; Wilks and Martinson, 1976; Wilson, 1983; Petersilia et al., 1985), they have stopped short of advocating an elimination of supervision. It seems appropriate to take the logical final step and discontinue probation supervision.

This plan does not espouse the abolition of probation. I would support increasing the use of summary and unsupervised probation. These forms of probation already are well-established in some jurisdictions (National Council on Crime and Delinquency, 1973). Those probationers actually in need of assistance in rehabilitation efforts could receive help from other community agencies. Some of the dollar savings that result from discontinuing probation supervision could be channeled to local agencies to improve services. Under the present system, probation personnel are expected to offer counseling and advice in areas where, as court officers, they have no particular training or skill. The comments of Wilks and Martinson (1976:5) illustrate this point:

> The criminal justice system has no special expertise in the field of education, mental health, vocational training or job development. In fact the provision of these services by the criminal justice system leads to costly duplication, unnecessary segregation of offenders from nonoffenders, and perhaps destructive competition between offenders and nonoffenders for scarce resources.

A branch of the court should be established to monitor adherence to court ordered probation conditions, e.g., restitution, fines, community service, or attendance at treatment programs. Such a branch would make extensive use of computers to track probationers. This type of monitoring essentially would be a clerical function, and employees would not require advanced educational training or social science backgrounds. When defendants fail to abide by the conditions of probation or are arrested on a new charge the monitor would schedule a violation hearing. At that hearing defendants would have an opportunity to explain their behavior. If the court found the defendant's explanation unsatisfactory, a revocation hearing would be scheduled. This two-step procedure would comply with *Morrissey v. Brewer* rulings. While this method of surveillance may be considered impersonal and overly structured, it would effectively eliminate the individual discretion that characterizes contemporary supervision.

Under this planned reorganization, probation would be left with an unambiguous mission — providing court investigation services. These services would include traditional presentence recommendations as well as investigations of violation reports, revocation hearings, or early termination requests. In some situations the judge might request follow-up investigations at periodic intervals. These would be considered progress reports rather than supervision regimens and would be done by probation investigators. In summary, the reorganized probation department would handle all probation matters that come before the court. Reporting to the courts generally has been acknowledged as the most professional aspect of probation work (Blackmore, 1980). Hopefully, concentrating exclusively on court reporting would improve the quality and objectivity of those reports.

## Summary and Conclusion

In order to revitalize probation's mission, it is essential to give it a task that is doable. Presently probation departments are overextended in trying to provide supervision that is neither wanted nor productive. Numerous empirical studies are unable to substantiate the claims of probation officials and their apologists who contend that if caseloads were smaller, better classification procedures were implemented, and more dedicated officers were hired, supervision could be improved significantly. There are structural components in present probation systems that virtually rule out meaningful improvement (Shover, 1979). Bureaucratic dynamics that operate contrary to overall program goals and the conflicting nature of officer-client relationships make it unlikely that probation supervision can ever reduce recidivism rates. Since supervision has proved an unachievable task, it seems counterproductive to continue the effort. Futile efforts to improve supervision capabilities detract from probation's central mission—court investigation services.

My reorganization proposal would definitely not do away with probation. For whatever reasons, probation has proven successful, in that three-quarters of those put on probation do not reoffend (Empey, 1982:379). On the other hand, supervision is frequently irrelevant to this process: "In all probability the offender would do just as well without any of that alleged treatment—that is to say would do just as well with a suspended sentence which is simply probation without the supervision" (Walker, 1985:177). The restructuring of probation does not signal an end to rehabilitation nor affirmation that "nothing works." It is merely an admission that probation supervision does not work. Other social agencies can and should take up the mantle of services that probation puts aside. While a variety of problems may be involved in discontinuing probation's supervision role, even more would accrue if we continue to shore up an ineffective system.

Leading researchers in the field of corrections have called for sweeping changes in probation services. The responses generally have recommended incremental and superficial modifications rather than radical reorientations. Although classification procedures and intensive supervision programs may have limited or regional success, they are not going to revitalize probation. An awareness that prior supervision programs have failed to reduce recidivism should be a caveat that continuation of the present probation system is extremely problematic.

A group of Rand researchers, after clearly demonstrating the failure of felony probation supervision in California, stated: "We certainly do not recommend that they abandon their counseling or rehabilitation goals" (Petersilia et al., 1985:389). On the contrary, it would seem that this is an opportune time to do precisely that—abandon an unworkable supervision system. Borrowing an investment analogy—it's time to cut our losses. While it is difficult to give up the dream of combining assistance and control, it must be recognized that probation supervision is an impossible mission.

## References

Banks, J., Porter, A. L., Rardin, R. L., Silver, T. R., and Unger, V. E. Evaluation of Intensive Special Probation Projects. Washington, DC: U.S. Government Printing Office, 1977.

Bartollas, C. Introduction to Corrections. New York: Harper and Row, 1981.

Bemus, B., Arling, G., and Quigly, P. Workload Measures for Probation and Parole. Washington, DC: National Institute of Corrections, 1983.

Blackmore, J. "Big City Probation: Treatment? There's No Treatment Going On Here," Corrections Magazine, 1980, 6, pp. 13-15.

Blumberg, A. Criminal Justice. Chicago: Quadrangle, 1967.

Bottoms, A. E. and McWilliams, W. "A Non-Treatment Paradigm for Probation Practice," in P. McAnany, D. Thomson, and D. Fogel (eds.), *Probation and Justice: Reconsideration of Mission*. Cambridge, MA: Oelgeschlager, Gunn and Hain, 1984, pp. 203-50.

Braly, M. *False Starts*. Boston: Little Brown, 1976.

Breed, A. "Foreword" in P. McAnany, D. Thomson, and D. Fogel (eds.), *Probation and Justice: Reconsideration of Mission*. Cambridge, MA: Oelgeschlager, Gunn and Hain, 1984, pp. ix-xi.

Brockway, Z. *Fifty Years of Prison Service*. New York: Charities Publication Committee, 1912.

Bunker, F. *No Beast So Fierce*. New York: Norton, 1973.

Clear, T. and Gallagher, K. "Probation and Parole Supervision: A Review of Current Classification," *Crime and Delinquency*, 1985, 31, pp. 423-43.

Conrad, J. P. "Who Needs a Doorbell Pusher?," *Prison Journal*, 1979, 59, pp. 17-26.

_____. "The Quandry of Dangerousness," *British Journal of Criminology*, 1982, 22, pp. 225-67.

_____. "The Redefinition of Probation: Drastic Proposals to Solve an Urgent Problem," in P. McAnany, D. Thomson, and D. Fogel (eds.), *Probation and Justice: Reconsideration of Mission*. Cambridge, MA: Oelgeschlager, Gunn and Hain, 1984, pp. 251-73.

_____. "The Penal Dilemma and Its Emerging Solution," *Crime and Delinquency*, 1985, 31, pp. 411-22.

Cushman, R. C. "Probation in the 1980's: A Public Administration Viewpoint," in P. McAnany, D. Thomson, and D. Fogel (eds.), *Probation and Justice: Reconsideration of Mission*. Cambridge, MA: Oelgeschlager, Gunn and Hain, 1984, pp. 327-46.

Dawson, R. O. *Sentencing*. Boston: Little Brown, 1969.

Duffee, D. "Client Biography and Probation Organization," in P. McAnany, D. Thomson, and D. Fogel (eds.), *Probation and Justice: Reconsideration of Mission*. Cambridge, MA: Oelgeschlager, Gunn and Hain, 1984. pp. 295-326.

Empey, L. T. *American Delinquency*. Homewood, IL: Dorsey, 1982.

Fogel, D. "Foreword," in R. McCleary, *Dangerous Men: The Sociology of Parole*. Beverly Hills: Sage, 1978.

_____. "The Emergence of Probation as Profession," in P. McAnany, D. Thomson, and D. Fogel (eds.), *Probation and Justice: Reconsideration of Mission*. Cambridge, MA: Oelgeschlager, Gunn and Hain, 1984, pp. 65-100.

Forer, L. G. *Criminals and Victims*. New York: W.W. Norton, 1980.

Gettinger, S. "Intensive Supervision: Can it Rehabilitate Probation," in J. Sullivan and J .L. Victor (eds.), *Annual Editions: Criminal Justice*. Guilford, CT: Dushkin Publishing, 1985, pp. 212-18.

Gilsinan, J. F. *Doing Justice*. Englewood Cliffs, NJ: Prentice-Hall, 1982.

Glaser, D. *The Effectiveness of a Prison and Parole System*. Indianapolis: Bobbs Merrill, 1964.

_____. "Who Gets Probation and Parole: Case Study Versus Actuarial Decision Making," *Crime and Delinquency*, 1985, 31, pp. 367-78.

Harris, M. K. "Rethinking Probation in the Context of the Justice Model," in P. McAnany, D. Thomson, and D. Fogel (eds.), *Probation and Justice: Reconsideration of Mission*. Cambridge, MA: Oelgeschlager, Gunn and Hain, 1984, pp. 15-38.

Irwin, J. *The Felon*. Englewood Cliffs, NJ: Prentice-Hall, 1970.

Johnson, L. "Frustration: The Mold of Judicial Philosophy," in J. Sullivan and J. L. Victor (eds.), *Annual Editions: Criminal Justice*. Guilford, CT: Dushkin Publishing, 1985, pp. 206-11.

Krajick, K. "Probation: The Original Community Program," *Corrections Magazine*, 1980, 6, pp. 6-12.

Lide, W. "A Victim of Probation's Burnout Blues," *Corrections Magazine*, 1980, 6, pp. 16-18.

Lipsky, M. *Street-Level Bureaucracy: Dilemmas of the Individual in Public Services*. New York: Sage, 1980.

McAnany, P. "Mission and Justice: Clarifying Probation's Legal Context," in P. McAnany, D. Thomson, and D. Fogel (eds.), *Probation and Justice: Reconsideration of Mission*. Cambridge, MA: Oelgeschlager, Gunn and Hain, 1984, pp. 39-64.

McCleary, R. "How Structural Variables Constrain the Parole Officer's Use of Discretionary Power," *Social Problems*, 1975, 23, pp. 361-73.

_____. "How Parole Officers Use Records," *Social Problems*, 1977, 24, pp. 576-89.

_____. *Dangerous Men: The Sociology of Parole*. Beverly Hills: Sage, 1978.

McCleary, R., Gordon, A. C., McDowall, D., and Maltz, D. *A Reanalysis of UDIS*. Chicago: Center for Research in Criminal Justice, University of Illinois, 1978.

_____. "How a Regression Artifact Can Make Any Delinquency Program Look Effective," in L. Sechrest (ed.), *Evaluation Studies Review Annual* (vol. 4). Beverly Hills: Sage, 1979, pp. 626-52.

McDowall, D., McCleary, R., Gordon, A. C. and Maltz, M. "Regression Artifacts in Correctional Program Evaluations," in S. E. Zimmerman and H. D. Miller (eds.), *Corrections at the Crossroads: Designing Policy*. Beverly Hills: Sage, 1981, pp. 27-47.

National Council on Crime and Delinquency. "The Nondangerous Offender Should Not Be Imprisoned: A Policy Statement," *Crime and Delinquency*, 1973, 19, pp. 449-56.

O'Leary, V. "Reshaping Community Corrections," *Crime and Delinquency*, 1985, 31, pp. 349-66.

Pearson, F. S. "New Jersey's Intensive Supervision Program: A Progress Report," *Crime and Delinquency*, 1985, 31, pp. 393-410.

Petersilia, J. "Community Supervision: Trends and Critical Issues," *Crime and Delinquency*, 1985, 31, pp. 339-47.

Petersilia, J., Turner, S., Kahan, J., and Peterson, J. "Executive Summary of Rand's Study, Granting Felons Probation: Public Risks and Alternatives," *Crime and Delinquency*, 1985, 31, pp. 379-92.

Prus, R. and Stratton, J. "Parole Revocation and Decision-Making: Private Typings and Official Designations," *Federal Probation*, 1976, 40, 48-54.

Reid, S. T. *The Correctional System*. New York: Holt, Rinehart and Winston, 1981.

Rosecrance, J. "The Probation Officers' Search For Credibility: Ball Park Recommendations," *Crime and Delinquency*, 1985, 31, pp. 539-54.

Rothman, D. *Conscience and Convenience: the Asylum and its Alternatives in Progressive America*. Boston: Little Brown, 1980.

Schumacher, M. A. "Implementation of a Client Classification and Case Management System: A Practitioner's View," *Crime and Delinquency*, 1985, 31, 445-55.

Shover, N. "Experts' and Diagnosis in Correctional Agencies," *Crime and Delinquency*, 1974, 20, pp.347-59.

_____. *A Sociology of American Corrections*. Homewood, IL: Dorsey, 1979.

Studt, E. *Surveillance and Service in Parole*. Washington, DC: National Institute of Corrections, 1973.

Takagi, P. "Evaluation Systems in a Parole Agency," unpublished dissertation, Stanford University.

Takagi, P. and Robinson, J. O. "The Parole Violator: An Organizational Reject," *Journal of Research in Crime and Delinquency*, 1969, 5, 78-86.

Thomson, D. "Prospects for Justice Model Probation," in P. McAnany, D. Thomson, and D. Fogel (eds.), *Probation and Justice: Reconsideration of Mission*. Cambridge, MA: Oelgeschlager, Gunn and Hain, 1984, pp. 101-36.

Thomson, D., McAnany, P., and Fogel, D., "Introduction," in P. McAnany, D. Thomson, and D. Fogel (eds.), *Probation and Justice: Reconsideration of Mission*. Cambridge, MA: Oelgeschlager, Gunn and Hain, 1984, pp. 1-14.

Von Hirsch, A. *Doing Justice*. New York: Hill and Wang, 1976.

Walker, S. *Sense and Nonsense About Crime*. Monterey, CA: Brooks Cole, 1985.

Wilks, J. and Martinson, R. "Is the Treatment of Criminal Offenders Really Necessary?" *Federal Probation*, 1976, 40, pp.3-9.

Wilson, J. Q. *Thinking About Crime*. New York: Basic, 1983.

Wright, K., Clear, T., and Dickson, P. "Universal Applicability of Probation Risk Assessment Instruments," *Criminology*, 1984, 22, pp. 113-34.

# Part III

## Alternative Sanctions

Since the early 1980s, when the community corrections system began to understand the public's desire to punish the offender, dozens of excellent articles and reports have been published that present both the philosophical arguments and the practical aspects of using alternative sanctions. While many would argue that the use of alternative sanctions may have a rehabilitative effect, it has become clear that control and punishment are its primary focus. Scholars and practitioners have argued that there should be a range of punishments available to the criminal justice system which are more stringent than regular probation, yet at the same time less severe than incarceration. The use of alternative sanctions has expanded significantly in virtually all jurisdictions. The availability and use of intensive supervision, electronic monitoring, house arrest, and community service appear to have focused interest on community correctional programs, if for no other reason than the fact that prison overcrowding has forced policymakers to rethink their use of incarceration as a sanction.

In the first selection, James Byrne presents an excellent overview of intensive probation supervision programs in the United States in "The Control Controversy." He reports that there exists little agreement as to the primary purpose of these programs and that the term "intensive supervision" is used to describe "a wide range of programs at distinct points in the criminal justice process." The author's presentation of an interstate comparison of intensive probation supervision programs will help readers better understand the unique features and status of programs in existence or under development. Next, Michael Tonry presents a hard-hitting critique of intensive probation supervision programs in the United States in "Stated and Latent Functions of ISP." Here, Tonry provides evidence that ISP programs do not achieve their stated goal of reducing prison overcrowding, saving money, and reducing recidivism. Instead, Tonry argues, ISP programs have latent goals which serve both bureaucratic and organizational needs, while at the same time allowing administrators to express the same intolerance for crime as that expressed by the public.

"The Future of Intensive Probation Supervision and the New Intermediate Sanctions," also authored by Byrne, proposes that such sanctions as probation, community service, intensive probation supervision, and house arrest must be used to accomplish proportionate sanctioning. Traditional models of sentencing, Byrne argues, have simply "stacked" these sanctions together and have treated them as part of a single intermediate sanction. Instead, consideration should be given to ranking these alternatives based on severity.

Joan Petersilia and Elizabeth Deschenes' article, "What Punishes? Inmates Rank the Severity of Prison vs. Intermediate Sanctions" contributes to our understanding of punishment in the context of community corrections. Many would argue that community correctional alternatives are "soft" on the subject of crime, failing to adequately punish offenders for their wrongdoing. The severity of punishment in our society is placed within the context of the prison or jail in which those who are incapacitated are unable to move freely in society and conduct their affairs privately. The authors examine the equivalency and severity of criminal sanction through the eyes of offenders who were asked to rank order both criminal sanctions in general and their individual perceptions of the difficulty of probation conditions. The results provide support for noninstitutional alternatives, such as intensive probation supervision, and their ability to provide a degree of punishment which inmates feel is greater than that provided in prison.

Can rehabilitation exist in the 1990s, especially within the context of a community correctional program whose original purpose was to reduce the risk of offender recidivism? Authors Paul Gendreau, Francis Cullen, and James Bonta present within "Intensive Rehabilitation Supervision: The Next Generation in Community Corrections" a review of the literature on offender treatment, including the principles of both effective and ineffective treatment programs. This approach to community supervision is refreshing in light of the often punitive nature of programs such as intensive supervision which frequently have proven ineffective in reducing offender recidivism. This work also lends support for the professional staff who offer services to offenders within the context of a punishment-oriented program such as intensive supervision. Incorporating a therapeutic role for those staff who have a traditional "enforcement" orientation may bring about conflict and confusion, an issue acknowledged as a problem by the authors, but not a problem which is insurmountable.

When "Community Service: A Review of the Basic Issues" was published in 1987, the use of community service as an intermediate sanction was not well defined. Authors Robert Carter, Jack Cocks, and Daniel Glaser discuss several issues that should be considered prior to the decision to utilize community service as a sentence or an alternative to a sentence. What criteria should be used to determine offender eligibility? How are offenders supervised and programs evaluated? This article is a fine contribution to the limited but growing body of knowledge in this area.

The final selection describes electronic monitoring as a rapidly expanding technology used to control and maintain close surveillance of offenders. The two primary types of electronic devices are described, the continuous signal and the programmed contact. Electronic monitoring use may generate controversy among some who argue that it is an inappropriate substitute for the personal contact between the offender and the supervising agency or officer, a relationship which has been at the heart of the community corrections movement for generations. In "Electronic Monitors: Realistically, What Can Be Expected," Annesley Schmidt, apparently borrowing from experience and contacts with professionals, cautions program planners to clearly identify program expectations at the outset. There is a frequent tendency for planners to develop unreasonable expectations when acquiring electronic monitoring equipment. For example, equipment purchases are recommended for the purpose of reducing jail or prison overcrowding, a justification which can become problematic if prison and jails continue to be overcrowded due to circumstances beyond the control of the supervising department. Ironically, while the number of offenders under electronic monitoring is growing, they represent a very small proportion of the total number of offenders supervised in the community. This form of "supervision" will continue as different forms of telecommunication equipment come into existence.

# 10

## The Control Controversy: A Preliminary Examination of Intensive Probation Supervision Programs in the United States

James M. Byrne

### I. Introduction: The Control Controversy

As policy makers throughout the country revise their criminal and juvenile codes, it is clear that community protection rather than offender rehabilitation is now their primary concern.[1] One consequence of this new crime control agenda is that both the philosophy and practice of probation have come under scrutiny. Invariably, the question is raised: Can probation officers effectively control the illegal behavior of the convicted offenders placed under their supervision? It should be apparent that the answer to this question hinges on the answers to a series of related questions such as: (1) *What* level of recidivism is acceptable to you: 20 percent, 30, 50? (2) *Who* do you want to be placed on probation: felons (violent, property), misdemeanors, drunk drivers,

Source: *Federal Probation*, Vol. 50, No. 2 (June 1986), 4-16.

delinquents? (3) *How long* do you want the probation department to supervise these offenders: 6 months, 1 year, 5 years? And (4) *how much* time, energy (and, therefore, money) are you willing to spend on probation services to achieve an "acceptable" level of control? Clearly, issues of offender control in community supervision are central to the restructuring of correctional priorities (and probation in particular) which is now under way in many states.

For years, we have relied on a sentencing policy—for both felonies and misdemeanors—which has been based on the assumption that most offenders can be allowed to return to the community without posing a major risk to the person or property of other residents. Despite recent changes in criminal (and juvenile) codes in many parts of the country, this basic assumption is still embedded in our sentencing policy. A recent Bureau of Justice Statistics report indicates that probation is the most common form of correctional placement: over 60 percent (1,502,247) of all adults under correctional supervision in 1983 were on probation, a 38 percent increase over the 1979 levels. Overall, this includes about an equal number of felony and misdemeanor probationers, although there is much interstate variation in the crime mix of probationers.[2]

Are these offenders effectively "controlled," or do they commit new crimes against person or property while under supervision? Data from 1983 available from 20 states (see Table 1) reveal that the percent of adult probationers who successfully complete their term is apparently high, ranging from 66 percent in Mississippi to 95 percent in Vermont.[3] Moreover, the percent incarcerated for a new offense (or a probation condition violation) varied from a low of 5 percent in Vermont to 23 percent in Mississippi.[4] While some would cite these statistics as indicators of the general appropriateness and success of probation supervision with the majority of offenders, others take a more jaundiced view. They point out that if we examine the percentage of rearrests/rearraignments, we would not appear nearly as successful. Moreover, if we separated administrative cases (such as drunk driving and collections) from regular, or risk/needs, cases, even higher failure rates would be identified for cases under risk/needs supervision. Finally, states which utilize a case classification system often allow the differentiation of success/failure rates for offenders receiving low, medium, and high (and in a few states intensive) supervision. In these states, failure rates are much higher for high risk than low risk offenders.

An examination of probation in Massachusetts underscores these three points concerning the illusion of success when examining total probation caseloads. In Massachusetts, only about one in five cases is placed on risk/needs supervision; the majority of a probation officer's caseload includes administrative cases. A 1984 study revealed that 35 percent

Table 1

## Probation Exits by Type for Selected Jurisdictions, 1983

| Jurisdiction | Number of exits | Percent of exits who were discharged from probation due to: | | |
|---|---|---|---|---|
| | | Completion of term | Incarceration on current or new term | All other reasons* |
| Total | 322,717 | 254,214 | 41,817 | 26,686 |
| Percent | 100% | 79% | 13% | 8% |
| Connecticut | 25,715 | 82 | 16 | 2 |
| Iowa | 9,187 | 79 | 10 | 11 |
| Kentucky | 3,172 | 83 | 15 | 2 |
| Louisiana | 9,164 | 80 | 14 | 6 |
| Maryland | 33,947 | 78 | 11 | 11 |
| Michigan | 9,361 | 73 | 19 | 8 |
| Minnesota | 25,375 | 92 | 8 | 0 |
| Mississippi | 2,357 | 66 | 23 | 11 |
| Missouri | 11,597 | 80 | 8 | 12 |
| Montana | 1,089 | 85 | 10 | 5 |
| New Jersey | 20,428 | 79 | 13 | 8 |
| New York | 27,900 | 84 | 16 | 0 |
| North Dakota | 662 | 77 | 17 | 6 |
| Oklahoma | 5,903 | 83 | 16 | 1 |
| Rhode Island | 3,277 | 92 | 8 | 0 |
| South Carolina | 8,791 | 84 | 12 | 4 |
| Texas | 110,197 | 73 | 12 | 15 |
| Vermont | 3,921 | 95 | 5 | 0 |
| West Virginia | 2,015 | 89 | 8 | 3 |
| Wisconsin | 8,659 | 77 | 20 | 3 |

* Includes absconders, deaths, discharges to custody, detainer or warrant and other miscellaneous discharges.

Source: Table 6, Bureau of Justice Statistics Bulletin, *Probation and Parole 1983*, NCJ-94776 (September 1984:4).

of all probationers under risk/needs supervision were arraigned on new charges. However, recidivism varied markedly by classification/supervision level: only about 15 percent of the minimum supervision cases were rearraigned as compared to 50 percent of the maximum supervision cases.[5] From this perspective, it appears that—in Massachusetts at least—a clearly identifiable subgroup (approximately 15 percent) of probationers "inflate" the overall failure rate. It is this group that poses a threat to community safety, not the majority of offenders under supervision.

In California, similar distinctions have been offered between the supervision of adult felons and misdemeanor cases. Joan Petersilia and her colleagues recently completed an evaluation of felony probation in California which offers a graphic portrait of a probation system without adequate control over certain offenders. They concluded that:

> In our opinion, felons granted probation present a serious threat to public safety. During the 40-month follow-up period of our study, 65 percent of the probationers in our subsample were rearrested, 51 percent were reconvicted, 18 percent were reconvicted of serious violent crimes (homicide, rape, weapons offenses, assault, and robbery), and 34 percent were reincarcerated. Moreover, 75 percent of the official charges filed against our subsample involved burglary/theft, robbery, and other violent crimes — the crimes most threatening to public safety. (Petersilia et al., 1984, vii)

Faced with findings such as these, legislators, judges, and probation administrators are currently reconsidering the basic mission of probation. Attempts to redefine probation are made more difficult by the reality of fiscal constraints (Harlow and Nelson, 1982), overcrowded prisons (Gottfredson and Taylor, 1983), and the public's recent "mood swing"; i.e., emphasis on community protection — rather than rehabilitation — as the purpose of corrections (Harris, 1982). To quote Conrad (1981) — albeit out of context — our current response to this problem ". . . may well be submerged in an attempt to navigate between Scylla and Charybdis" (1981:554). On one hand, the crime control advocates call for a "get tough" policy with traditional probationers as a method of legitimizing probation.[6] Concomitantly, community supervision advocates see probation as a viable alternative to incarceration for many "high risk" offenders who would otherwise go to prison.[7]

Nowhere are these conflicting views more apparent than in the current debate over the purpose and design of intensive probation supervision (IPS) programs. In the following article, I present the results of a preliminary examination of the use of these programs across the United States.[8] Before presenting these findings, I will briefly outline the conceptual framework for three "ideal" models of community supervision: (1) the Justice Model, (2) the Limited Risk Control Model, and (3) a Traditional Treatment-Oriented Paradigm. By examining the rationale underlying the development of intensive supervision programs in light of these alternative models, interstate variation in the form and substance of these programs can be explained.

## II. Three Conceptual Models of Intensive Supervision

The function (and design) of intensive probation supervision programs is a by-product of the dominant sentencing philosophy of a particular state. Consequently, we can expect these programs to be serving different "clients" across states. For example, Massachusetts has the highest percentage of violent offenders in prison (72 percent in 1981), while South Dakota has the lowest percentage (18 percent in 1981) of violent offenders in prison.[9] Sentencing alternatives with very different target populations would likely be developed in both states, reflecting the unique correctional philosophies which exist. Of course, during times of severe prison and jail crowding it is quite difficult to consistently adhere to a sentencing philosophy which requires incarceration. This is one reason that the concept of "intensive supervision" is so attractive to policy makers: It offers an *immediate* solution to the prison crowding problem which is not inconsistent with the "get tough" attitude of the public.

Recently, a number of authors have attempted to describe the broad parameters of a "rational" sentencing policy, including very specific models of the potential utilization of intensive supervision by probation departments. We highlight three such attempts below: a justice model, a limited risk control model, and a traditional, treatment-oriented model.

### A. The Justice Model

The justice model of probation supervision emphasizes punishment but within the bounds of fairness. According to Harris (1984), "Proponents of a just deserts or justice model have emphasized that the penalty imposed should be based on the crime committed. Since their function is punishment, penalties should not be selected for utilitarian reasons" (p. 24). Based on a "just deserts" rationale (see von Hirsch, 1976; Fogel, 1984; Singer, 1979), a program of probation supervision would focus on the following punitive conditions:

(1) Daily contact between probation officer and offender for certain crimes;

(2) Community service orders;

(3) Restitution and/or probation fees, fines, etc.

In the justice model, there is no required participation in specific treatment, counseling, etc. Objective risk assessment, which provides a prediction of *future* behavior, is not employed. Examples of a justice model sentencing schedule are presented in Table 2 (adapted from Thomson, 1984, Table 4:3). Commenting on the justice model of probation, Thomson (1984) has observed that:

Probation can fit well with other elements of the system when it is
recognized that the goals of the system are justice and retribution.
In such a system, probation is part of a set of sanctions ranging from
arrest, conviction and conditional discharge, at one extreme, through
fines, straight probation, monetary restitution, community service
orders, home confinement, and split sentences to incarceration as
the most severe measure. (1984:105)

Within a justice model, the primary responsibility for identifying the
appropriate sanctions for specific offense categories rests with the
legislature and/or a guidelines commission. Interestingly, no IPS
program currently in operation meets the criteria for a justice model.
However, many states do emphasize that one of the goals of their program
is justice/retribution. Indeed, the use of probation fees, fines, community
service, and (at least to some extent) house arrest as part of intensive
supervision suggests that many states do embrace certain features of the
justice model.

## B. The Limited Risk Control Model

Because it is not "forward-looking," the justice model of probation
has been criticized for placing a high priority on the fairness/uniformity
of punishment, at the expense of an assessment of offender risk. In its
place, O'Leary and Clear (1984) offer a "Limited Risk Control"
sentencing model[10] which attempts to balance offender risk with
concerns for fair punishment.

Under limited risk control, the seriousness of the offense establishes
a range of penalties that is just, with the lower range establishing
the minimally acceptable punishment, and the upper range
establishing the most severe punishment that may be imposed.
Within those limits, specific decisions about the amount and
character of state intervention are determined by the individual's
potential for new criminal behavior. (1984:3)

The prediction of future criminal behavior, within the confines of a
presumptive sentencing scheme, is the critical component of limited risk
control. The authors recognize that any attempts to predict the future
behavior of offenders will result in two types of error—false positives
and false negatives. Therefore, they argue, it is important to provide
decisionmakers with accurate information on the relative costs of both
false positives (i.e., offenders we think are bad risks but who do not
recidivate) and false negatives (i.e., offenders we think are good risks
but who recidivate). How have we balanced these errors in the past?
O'Leary and Clear's assessment bears repeating here: "It is a small
wonder that prisons are so crowded—they are full of the false positives
held to try to reduce the false negatives." (1984:9)

Table 2

**A Justice Model Sentencing Schedule: Some Examples**

| Offense | Sentence |
|---|---|
| Murder | 4,000 to 18,000 days incarceration |
| Rape, kidnapping for ransom | 750 to 3,000 days incarceration |
| Involuntary manslaughter | Probation Type A or 60 to 750 days incarceration |
| Indecent liberties with a child | Probation Type B or A or 10 to 200 days incarceration |
| Armed robbery | Probation Type B or A or 1 to 120 days incarceration |
| Residential burglary | Probation Type C or B or 1 to 100 days incarceration |
| Aggravated assault, battery, reckless conduct | Probation Type C or B or 1 to 30 days incarceration |
| Unlawful possession of weapons | Probation Type C or 1 to 5 days incarceration |

Note: Probation types are defined as follows:

A = weekly reporting for 24-36 months plus up to 800 hours of community service.

B = monthly to weekly reporting for 12-24 months plus up to 200 hours of community service.

C = quarterly to monthly reporting for 6-12 months plus up to 50 hours of community service.

Restitution or victim services could also be imposed as additional penalties in conjunction with those listed above.

Source: Adapted by author from Doug Thomson, "Prospects for Justice Model Probation" (Table 4.3, pp. 128-129), in McAnany, Thomson, and Fogel (eds.) *Probation and Justice* (Cambridge, MA: (Oelgeschlager, Gunn, and Hain, 1984).

In the O'Leary and Clear sentencing scheme, the initial assignment in an institutional or community program would be determined by the judge, while the length of stay could be established using a presumptive sentencing format, with longer and shorter stays determined by objective risk assessment. At sentencing, judges would select one of the three levels of control listed below. These assignments would be routinely reviewed, and as risk levels decrease, so too would the level of control.

| Control Level | Programs |
|---|---|
| I: | Maximum security prison |
| | Medium security prison |
| | Minimum security prison |
| II: | Local correctional facility |
| | Halfway house |
| | Home detention |
| III: | Intensive surveillance in community |
| | Community supervision in probation or parole |
| | Community service/restitution |

Intensive supervision is viewed as an important component of Control Level III of the limited risk control model. The authors view intensive supervision in the following terms: (1) very small caseloads (e.g., 10 to 1 client-officer ratio); (2) weekly contacts; (3) field visits; (4) the use of preventive conditions in recognized, high-need areas, such as alcohol, drugs, and education; and (5) swift and certain administrative review and revocation procedures for violation of conditions (O'Leary and Clear, 1984:19). The characteristics of offenders to be placed on intensive supervision in a limited risk control model can be compared to minimum and regular supervision offenders by examining Table 3. Unfortunately, a delineation of the probable offense types under intensive supervision is not offered.

Perhaps the most compelling feature of the O'Leary and Clear model is the use of preventive conditions, linked directly to each offender's immediate ability to reside safely in the community. These conditions are not designed with the general aim of rehabilitation in mind, for as the authors note: ". . . Any assistance rendered an offender must be reasonably related to a crime reduction goal. *A supervision agency is not a welfare agency*, and an extension of its activities beyond a crime control focus is both inappropriate and dangerous" (1984:18; emphasis added). Two states have based their programs on this model of intensive probation supervision: Oregon and Massachusetts. In Massachusetts, the elements of IPS are fairly consistent with a limited risk control model, but the state's overall sentencing philosophy is somewhat different. The Oregon model of IPS is an even closer approximation of the limited risk control philosophy. (Editor's note: Not coincidentally, Todd Clear has been involved in the development of the Oregon program. See the article by Clear and Shapiro, this issue, on the Oregon Model of IPS.)

Table 3

**Classification System Using Risk- and Nonrisk-Control Elements**

| Program Indicated by<br>Level of Risk | Client<br>Characteristics |
|---|---|
| Level 1: Minimum community supervision | Client does not now pose a significant threat to the public, no requirements of the court call for close supervision, and client has no important problems that are specifically related to potential serious violations of the law and that the probation service can reasonably expect to affect substantially. |
| Level 2: Regular community supervision | Client does not pose a significant threat to the public, and no close supervision is mandated by the court, but client is currently coping with a significant set of problems related to potential violations of the law. Client has some expectation of overcoming these problems with the assistance of the probation service. |
| Level 3: Intensive community supervision | Client has been recently assigned to probation and has a history of violent behavior toward others or is likely to commit a fairly serious violation of the law, or the requirements imposed by the court can be enforced only by close and persistent supervision. |

Source: Todd Clear and Vince O'Leary, *Controlling the Offender in the Community* (Lexington, MA: Lexington Books, 1984: 79).

## C. A Traditional, Treatment-Oriented Paradigm

Despite the "crime control" focus of recent legislative sentencing reforms, an examination of correctional policies in these reform states reveals a continued reliance on rehabilitation. This is particularly true in the area of "intensive" probation, as many states still rely on treatment-oriented probation conditions. Since these conditions are often mandatory, it is clear that their purpose is broader than immediate crime control. In fact, long-term change in offender behavior is the aim of these conditions.

A traditional, treatment-oriented model of intensive supervision may include punitive components which are identical to the above two strategies. Unlike the justice and limited risk control models, however, "treatment" is required (in addition to such conditions as fines, fees, and community service). Specifically, once individual "self-help" plans are developed, failure to make progress toward performance objectives may result in the institution of revocation proceedings. Thus treatment plans — once developed — place the primary responsibility for continued participation in the program on the offender. A good example of this approach is found in New Jersey's intensive supervision program, which is described elsewhere in this issue by Pearson and Bibel.[11]

Special features of this model include:

(1)  Development of individual plans for life in the community (work, study, community service, etc.);

(2)  A requirement of full-time employment or vocational training and community service by each participant;

(3)  The use of a community sponsor and other support persons who will provide extensive assistance and direction to each participant.

As the review of intensive probation supervision programs in the following section reveals, almost all states with IPS programs use this type of mandatory treatment condition, presumably based on a link between compliance and subsequent rehabilitation. This underscores a resistance to changing the treatment orientation of probation, even with the most serious offenders under supervision.

## III. A Preliminary Examination of Intensive Probation Supervision Programs in the United States

It should be clear from the brief overview of the various theoretical rationales underlying intensive supervision that there is no consensus concerning the purpose of IPS. But to what extent does this "competition over purpose" translate into variations in the actual design and practice of intensive supervision? To answer this question, the Center for Criminal Justice Research at the University of Lowell conducted an initial nationwide telephone survey of key probation administrators in each state during the spring of 1985. We extended (and updated) this survey in the spring of 1986. In total, the preliminary findings reported here are based on a survey of 48 states, plus Washington, D.C.[12] In many states, we were also supplied written program documents; and in a small number of states, preliminary evaluation data were also reviewed. The following review is based on these materials and the interviews with key administrators. We have focused here on an examination of adult probation supervision practices, although intensive probation supervision programs have also been developed exclusively for juvenile offenders.[13]

It is quite apparent from our preliminary survey that the term "intensive supervision" is a "catch-all" phrase which includes a wide range of programs at distinct decision points in the criminal justice process. It has been used alternately to describe programs which function as 1) a front-end alternative to incarceration (both in the form of a discretionary sentencing decision controlled by a judge and as an established presumptive term for a particular offense); (2) as a form of probation case management, once offenders are placed on general probation caseloads; and (3) as a "back-door," early-release mechanism from prison/jail.

The location of the IPS program at any one of these major decision points is a function of the relative (discretionary) power of legislators, judges, and correctional administrators. Briefly, legislators control the target population of IPS programs in states which have mandatory (or determinate) sentencing models. In addition, they are often the primary decisionmaker in states which use a presumptive sentencing model. In both instances, the legislators set the basic eligibility requirements but allow judges and administrators some flexibility based on the existence of aggravating and mitigating circumstances. (In the proposed Massachusetts Presumptive Sentencing Bill, for example, legislators would limit the use of intensive probation as a sanction for violent offenders to those individuals who were convicted of E and F felonies only. These are the least serious crimes against the person.)

In a judicial model, the legislature usually establishes the broad mandate for IPS by statute but allows the judge the discretion to select offenders for the program. The judge may or may not have access to an objective risk assessment (e.g., the Wisconsin Risk Assessment Model) when he or she makes this determination. These decisions are made either at sentencing (e.g., Georgia) or as a postsentencing alternative, utilizing some form of shock probation (e.g., Arizona), sentence modification (New Jersey), split sentence, or intermittent incarceration.[14]

Finally, an administrative model would give the primary decisionmaking power on the specific IPS target population to the probation department. The legislature often has approved an indeterminate sentencing model in these states. Once the judge places an offender on probation, the classification/supervision of probationers becomes an administrative responsibility. Many states have developed objective risk/needs assessment to help state and local administrators structure this (discretionary) decision. The current experiment in intensive probation supervision described by Cochran, Corbett, and Byrne (this issue) falls into this category.

Not only do the location and decisionmaking authority of IPS programs vary in the programs which we studied, but there was interstate variation in the content of these programs. This can be linked (in turn) to the philosophy of sentencing/correction which the program embodies.[15] Table 4 includes an interstate comparison of the development of IPS programs in the United States. These programs are now operating in 29 states, while 8 additional states (plus Washington, D.C.) expect to have an operational intensive probation supervision program by the end of this year. However, in many states these programs often exist in only a handful of "pilot" probation program sites. According to our review, eight states—Connecticut, Florida, Georgia, New Jersey, Oklahoma, Texas, Utah, and Vermont—have implemented statewide programs which include some form of intensive supervision. Review of the "comments" column in Table 4 reveals that the Georgia model of IPS is the most replicated program in the country (i.e., in six states), followed by the New Jersey program. (Editor's note: Both of these models are the subject of articles in this issue).

In addition, most states which have intensive probation supervision also have implemented the Wisconsin Probation Risk Assessment Instrument (or some variation of this model), in large part due to the training efforts of the National Institute of Corrections. However, these "objective" risk assessment instruments have two distinct limitations: (1) they are usually not validated (Wright, et al., 1984), and/or (2) in a number of states, they are not explicitly used to classify probationers as eligible for intensive supervision. In these states, function and purpose of objective risk assessment should be reassessed in light of the following: Should "risk assessment" results be presented to judges as a part of the presentence investigation? Or should these instruments only be used as a case management tool after a decision has been made on the appropriateness of a probation sanction? Answers to these questions are based on a determination of exactly who should control the target population and intake process for the IPS program. There is, of course, no single standard which can be established, since the philosophy (e.g., just deserts, limited risk control, rehabilitation) and the purpose (sentencing alternative, case management, release valve, etc.) of these programs vary from state to state (and within some states as well).[16]

Nonetheless, the importance of this issue can be highlighted by examining Georgia's intensive supervision program. Surprisingly, only 28.7 percent of the offenders placed on intensive supervision in Georgia were classified as maximum risk cases (7.9 percent were minimum risk cases, 28.9 percent were medium risks, and 34.5 percent were high risks). This finding suggests two general caveats: First, to speak generally about the "success" of Georgia's IPS without examining the impact of mixed risk levels would be misleading; further subgroup analyses are necessary. Secondly, others might legitimately question the allocation of scarce resources toward low risk cases. Little attention has been focused on the appropriateness of the state's selection criteria for offenders with low or medium risk levels. The assumption is that, in Georgia, these offenders would have been sent to prison if the IPS alternative were not available. Ironically, the Georgia program is being used as a model for other states around the country, despite the fact that the target population in these states may often be quite different. In this context, the suggestion we offer policy makers considering the Georgia model of IPS is deceptively simple: what "works" in Georgia may or may not work in your own state.

Our survey also revealed that there is considerable interstate variation in the target populations and intake criteria of IPS programs. For example, while many states do attempt to restrict offenders from consideration for intensive probation supervision who have committed crimes against the person, other states do allow these offenders to be considered for their program. Moreover, in some states it is not the nature of the offense per se, but the length/location of the sentence that is targeted. In Connecticut, offenders with sentences between 2 and 5 years in length are targeted (but only if crowding reaches a predetermined level). Louisiana also targets offenders with sentences of 5 years or less. Finally, our survey revealed intrastate variation in the target population of certain states (e.g., Pennsylvania, Ohio, Missouri).

Not only do the "target populations" of intensive supervision programs vary, but there are also basic differences in program design which can be highlighted. Table 5 focuses on interstate variations in (1) type of contracts, (2) use of curfew checks, and (3) minimum total monthly contacts. Small caseloads and multiple contacts are viewed by many as the cornerstone of intensive supervision (e.g., Clear and O'Leary, 1983). But caseload size varies greatly throughout the country, with an average caseload size of 25 intensive supervision probationers per officer. The intensity and range of contacts also varied greatly across the 37 states (plus Washington, D.C.) with current (or proposed) intensive probation supervision programs. For example, total minimum monthly contacts ranged from a low of 2 per month (in Texas) to 32 per month (in Idaho). Moreover, the number of face-to-face contacts ranged from two per month in Texas, Nevada, and Ohio to daily contacts in programs in California, Idaho, and Indiana. There were also wide variations in the use of curfew checks and the number/type of collateral contacts to be employed.

There are many other variations in program design which can be identified. Table 6 provides an overview of the extent of this design variation in the 31 states which currently have an IPS program in place as of June 1, 1986. Examination of this table reveals that there are certain features of IPS that are found in the majority of existing programs, including objective risk/needs assessment, the use of community service conditions, periodic record checks, mandatory referrals in high need

# Table 4

## Interstate Comparison of the Development of Intensive Probation Supervision Programs

| State | IPS Program(s) Exist | IPS Proposed | Comments on Program Model |
|---|---|---|---|
| Alabama | No | Yes (Fall 1986) | Contingent on funding. Modified Florida Model. |
| Alaska | — | — | — |
| Arizona | Yes (6/85; 10 counties 1st year, statewide 2nd year) | — | Georgia Model. Program will be extended to all 15 counties in 2nd year. |
| Arkansas | No | Yes (7/86) | Plan to begin development of IPS Program 7/86; contingent on funding. |
| California | Yes (selected sites only) | — | Contra Costa County House Arrest Program and Serious Offender Project (for juveniles). |
| Colorado | Yes (3 sites) | — | Georgia Model (modified). Legislation pending for funding to expand program statewide. |
| Connecticut | Yes (statewide; 7/1/84) | — | Targets sentenced offenders serving 2-5 years term in state prison system. |
| Delaware | No | No | Lack of funding cited, but IPS is under consideration. |
| Florida | Yes (statewide; 9/83) | — | Program is entitled the "Community Control House Arrest Program." |
| Georgia | Yes (statewide) | — | Mixed risk levels (H/M/L) included in IPS population. |
| Hawaii | — | — | — |
| Idaho | Yes (5 of 7 districts) | — | Includes both probationers and parolees. |
| Illinois | Yes (10 counties; 6/84) | — | Georgia Model (modified). |

| State | | | |
|---|---|---|---|
| Indiana | Yes (1 county) | — | Allen County Adult Probation Department programs; based on Georgia Model. |
| Iowa | Yes (4 sites; 7/85) | — | New Jersey Model. |
| Kansas | Yes (10 sites) | — | Part of Community Corrections Legislation, begun in 1982 (adult/juvenile). |
| Kentucky | Yes (25 of 120 counties; 1984) | — | Similar to New Jersey Model, limited to nonviolent offenders. |
| Louisiana | No | Yes (7/86) | Based on Georgia Model (parole eligible 1st offenders who receive sentences of 5 years or less). |
| Maine | No | Yes | Pending legislative approval. |
| Maryland | No | Yes (developing program) | Plan to test in Baltimore; targets offenders given 1-7 years sentence for nonviolent offenses. |
| Massachusetts | Yes (4/85) experimental program in 15 pilot courts | — | Pilot evaluation linked to proposed Presumptive Sentencing Package. |
| Michigan | No | No | No funding available. |
| Minnesota | No | No | Some courts do have ISP for drug offenders only; lack of funds. |
| Mississippi | Yes (3 sites) | — | Limited to severe drug and alcohol offenders; lack of funding for statewide program. |
| Missouri | Yes (3 pilot sites; 10/84) | — | Developed in conjunction with Community Sentencing Act, September 1983. |
| Montana | No | No | Developing a program for parolees only to be used as early release mechanism for nonviolent offenders. |
| Nebraska | No | No | Lack of funding. |

| State | | | |
|---|---|---|---|
| Nevada | Yes (2 sites; begun 7/73) | — | Focus on drug addicts and career criminals; 2 sites (Las Vegas and Reno); "team approach" different from Georgia Model. |
| New Hampshire | No | Yes (7/86) | IPS program now under legislative review. |
| New Jersey | Yes (statewide; as an alternative to prison) | Yes (Essex County; alternative to jail) | Cases based on NIC classification; currently being evaluated. |
| New Mexico | No | No | Reductions in probationer/officer ratio are being considered. |
| New York | Yes (begun 1978) | — | In addition to IPS, New York developed an Intensive Specialized Supervision Program which targets multiple recidivist drunk drivers. |
| North Carolina | Yes (3/84, selected counties) | — | Georgia Model (modified); legislation pending for statewide expansion. |
| North Dakota | No | No | Lack of funding. |
| Ohio | Yes (5 counties) | — | Modeled after Lucas County Incarceration Division Unit. |
| Oklahoma | Yes (statewide) | — | Limited to nonviolent offenders between ages 18 and 22. |
| Oregon | Yes (9/83, 1 county) | — | Viewed as an alternative to jail. |
| Pennsylvania | Yes (3 counties) | — | IPS in place in Chester, Schuykill, and York Counties. IPS proposal being considered in 1 other county. |
| Rhode Island | No | No | Severe understaffing. |
| South Carolina | Yes (September 1985) | — | Preferably no violent offenders included. |
| South Dakota | No | No | — |
| Tennessee | No | Yes (7/86) | Statewide program, focus on offenders from urban areas. |

| State | | | Comments |
|---|---|---|---|
| Texas | Yes (9/81, statewide) | — | Diversion occurs at time of sentencing. |
| Utah | Yes (statewide) | — | Program includes both probationers and parolees. |
| Vermont | Yes (statewide, 1981) | — | Split sentences frequently used; intake criteria include automatic (and discretionary) placement in ISP for specific offense types. |
| Virginia | Yes (1/85; 3 sites) | — | Probation officer has flexibility to establish supervision level within a specified range. |
| Washington | No | No | Intensive Parole Supervision begun in 1976 and designed as a prison alternative; multiple entry points. |
| Washington, DC | No | Yes (7/86) | Approved by Mayor, and a 7/86 start-up indicated. |
| West Virginia | No | No | — |
| Wisconsin | Yes (1984; selected sites only) | — | High Risk Offender Project (intensive parole supervision programs are also in place). |
| Wyoming | No | No (ISP proposal rejected) | Developed instead "intensified supervision" to increase the supervision levels of General Probationers. |
| TOTAL | 29 | 9 | — |

*Note:* — = No data available and/or not contacted as of 5/1/86.

*Note:* There were 2 states with no verifiable information. Thus, 37 of 48 states plus Washington, D.C. either have intensive probation supervision programs (29) or are about to implement them (9).

Table 5

**Interstate Variation in the Level and Type of Officer/Client Contacts Required in Intensive Supervision Programs**

| State | Type of Contact (#) Direct, Personal | Collateral | Curfew Checks | Monthly Total Contacts Only |
|---|---|---|---|---|
| Arizona | 4/week | 1/week (Employer) | — | 20 |
| California | 7/week | — | — | 30 |
| Colorado | 2/week | 1/week (Employer) | 1/month | 13 |
| Connecticut | 3/week | 1/week | — | 16 |
| Florida | 6/week | 1/week | 2/month | 28 |
| Georgia | 5/week | 2/week | 2/month | 28 |
| Idaho | 7/week | 1/week | (varies by offender) | 32 |
| Illinois | 5/week | 1/week | 1/week | 24 |
| Indiana | 7/week | — | — | 22 |
| Iowa | 5/week | — | 1 face-to-face 3 phone checks | 20 |
| Kansas | 3-5/week | — | — | 20 |
| Kentucky | 2-3/week | 2/week | random | 18 |
| Louisiana | 4/week | — | 2/week | 16 |
| Maryland | (min.) 2/week | — | random telephone calls | 10 |

| State | | | | |
|---|---|---|---|---|
| Massachusetts | 10/month | — | — | 10 |
| Missouri | 5/week | 2/week | — | 28 |
| Nevada | 2/month | 1/month (Employer) | — | 3 |
| New Jersey | 5/week | — | 5/month | 20 |
| New York | 1/week | 1/week | — | 8 |
| North Carolina | 5/week | 1/week | 3/week | 24 |
| Ohio | 2/month | 2/month | — | 4 |
| Oklahoma | 1/week | — | — | 4 |
| Oregon | 2/week | varies, non-specific | unannounced name visit | 8 |
| Pennsylvania | 2/week | 2/week | — | 16 |
| South Carolina | 1/week | 1/week (Employer) | — | 8 |
| Tennessee | 5/week | 1/week | 2/week | 24 |
| Texas | 2/month | varies, non-specific | — | 2 |
| Utah | 3/week | — | — | 12 |
| Vermont | 1/week | 6/month | — | 10 |
| Virginia | 1-5/week | Varies, non-specific | — | 4-24 |
| Washington | 1/week | 2/month | — | 6 |

*Notes:* A number of states do not break out categories of contacts, rendering comparisons difficult; direct contacts include face-to-face and telephone contacts.

This summary is preliminary and ignores possible intrastate variation.

areas (e.g., drugs, alcohol, education), curfews/house arrest, the use of "spot testing" for drug and alcohol abuse, specialized training for probation officers handling intensive supervision cases, and the use of shock incarceration or split sentences as part of intensive supervision. However, there are also many other dimensions in which these programs vary: organization (pooled vs. individual caseloads); role specialization (i.e., separation of surveillance and treatment functions); the use of electronic surveillance; the imposition of probation fees;[17] the designation of community sponsors; and, finally, the extent of restitution orders.

## IV. Conclusions

Does intensive supervision work? Ongoing evaluations in Georgia, New Jersey, and Massachusetts present favorable results (editor's note: see the articles by Erwin, Pearson and Bibel, and Cochran, Corbett, and Byrne, this issue, for a more detailed assessment of each program's impact). However, it should be apparent from this brief overview of IPS programs that any generalizations about the overall effectiveness of "intensive" supervision will be misleading because of the differences in program philosophy, target populations, and the basic elements of program design. Importantly, research which attempts to examine the relative impact of specific design features has not been conducted. Thus, policy makers are now faced with a smorgasbord of design options from which to choose, with inadequate information on the impact of these program components on different types of offenders.

More specifically, the current state of knowledge about the relationship between IPS inputs (target population, selection criteria), activities (elements of program design and degree of implementation), and outputs (recidivism, cost, displacement effects on traditional probationers, diversion, etc.) has been categorized as "inadequate" and "poor" by a number of reviewers (e.g., see the reviews by Banks, et al., 1979; Latessa, 1979; Fields, 1984). When we look at evaluations of programs across the country, we find that (1) many IPS programs have not been formally evaluated, and (2) few of the evaluations which have been conducted meet even the most basic methodological criteria. (Editor's note: This problem is discussed in detail by Burkhart, later in this issue.)

Eight years ago, an evaluation of 20 intensive supervision programs was completed by Banks (see Phase I Evaluation of Intensive Special Probation Projects, 1977). His assessment of IPS programs is still relevant today:

> In summary: Almost every element of information about IPS is knowable through direct empirical study yet almost nothing is

Table 6

# Key Features of Intensive Probation Supervision Programs in the United States[1,2]
The Control Controversy

| Program Components | AZ | CA | CO | CT | FL | GA | ID | IL | IN | IO | KS | KY | LO• | MA• | MD• | MO | NJ | NV | NY | NC | OH | OK | OR | PA | SC | TE | TX | UT | VA | VT | WI |
|---|---|---|---|---|---|---|---|---|---|---|---|---|---|---|---|---|---|---|---|---|---|---|---|---|---|---|---|---|---|---|---|
| *Objective Risk Assessment* | X | X | X | X | X | X | X | X | X | X | X | X | X | X | X | X | X | X | X | X | I | X | X | X | X | X | X | X | X | X | X |
| *Objective Needs Assessment* | X | X | X | X | X | X | X | X | X | X | X | X | X | X | X | I | X | X | X | X | I | X | X | X | X | X | X | X | X | X | X |
| *Periodic Record Checks* | X | I | X | I | X | X | X | X | X | O | X | X | X | X | X | I | X | I | X | X | I | X | X | I | X | X | I | I | X | X | X |
| *Mandatory Referrals* | I | X | X | X | X | X | I | X | X | X | X | X | I | I | I | X | X | X | X | X | I | I | X | U | X | X | I | I | X | X | I |
| *Probation Fees* | X | I | I | I | X | X | X | X | I | I | I | I | I | I | I | I | I | X | I | X | I | I | X | I | X | X | X | X | X | I | I |
| *Restitution* | X | I | I | I | X | X | X | X | X | X | O | X | X | O | O | O | X | O | I | I | I | I | X | I | O | X | X | X | O | O | I |
| *Community Service* | X | X | X | I | X | X | X | X | X | X | O | O | X | O | O | I | X | O | I | X | I | I | X | I | I | I | I | X | I | O | O |
| *Curfew/House Arrest* | X | I | O | O | O | X | X | X | X | X | X | X | X | X | X | X | X | I | O | X | I | X | X | I | O | I | X | X | O | O | O |
| *Test Substance Abuse* | X | X | X | X | X | X | X | X | X | X | X | I | X | X | X | X | X | X | X | X | O | X | X | X | X | X | I | X | X | X | X |
| *Test Alcohol Abuse* | X | X | X | X | X | X | X | X | X | X | X | I | X | X | X | X | X | X | X | X | O | X | X | X | X | X | I | X | X | X | X |
| *Training for PO's* | X | X | X | I | X | X | I | I | X | X | I | X | X | I | I | I | I | I | X | X | X | I | X | I | X | X | X | I | X | X | I |
| *Community Sponsors* | I | I | I | I | I | I | I | X | I | I | X | X | I | I | I | I | X | I | I | I | I | I | I | I | I | I | I | I | I | I | I |
| *Team Supervision* | O | X | X | I | O | X | X | X | X | X | I | I | I | X | X | I | X | X | X | X | X | X | X | I | X | I | I | I | X | I | X |
| *Shock Incarceration* | X | O | X | X | I | X | X | I | X | I | X | X | X | X | X | O | X | I | X | X | X | X | X | I | I | I | I | X | I | I | I |
| *Split Sentence* | I | I | I | I | I | I | I | X | I | I | X | X | I | I | I | O | X | I | I | I | I | I | I | I | X | I | I | I | I | X | I |
| *Electronic Surveillance* | X | I | I | I | X | I | I | I | I | I | I | I | I | X | I | I | X | I | I | I | I | O | I | I | I | I | I | X | I | I | I |

*Note:*

I = not a program component
O = optional program component
U = unclear from program description
X = component of program model
• = program in developmental stages, subject to change
1 = In the following states there was intercounty variation either in the use of IPS or in the specific program components adopted: Arizona, New York, Ohio, Pennsylvania, and Virginia.
2 = We have excluded states in which legislative approval and/or funding was still pending as of 5/15/86. (This includes Delaware, Washington, D.C., Maine, and New Hampshire).

scientifically known and little will ever be known until measurement techniques are improved.

Perhaps the outcome of the comprehensive IPS evaluations currently underway in Georgia, Massachusetts, and New Jersey will address this shortfall. In the interim, however, we must resist the temptations to assume that—in the name of intensive supervision—more control is always better control. As M. Kay Harris pointed out recently,[18] IPS programs seem to be continually adding new program features, with little concrete evidence that these new elements will increase community protection and/or result in a greater proportion of rehabilitated offenders. The only justifiable rationale for these controls is retribution, but is this the intended purpose of the programs? In this context, Harris suggests that the current "garbage can" mentality towards IPS is dangerous and a potential threat to individual rights and liberty.

The field is in need of research on the design, implementation, and effectiveness of intensive probation supervision programs. At minimum, decisionmakers need access to evaluation research on the relative effectiveness of IPS in each of the three conceptual models outlined here. It is only at this point that the IPS concept can be considered as one element in a comprehensive sentencing policy.

## Notes

[1] For a review of the shifts in sentencing policy which have occurred in this country over the past 15 years, see, for example: Todd R. Clear, "Correctional Policy, Neo-Retributionism, and the Determinate Sentence," in George F. Cole (ed.), *Criminal Justice: Law and Politics*, 4th ed., (Monterey, CA: Brooks Cole Publishing Company, 1984: 409-422); or Michael Sherman and Gordon Hawkins, *Imprisonment in America: Choosing the Future* (Chicago: University of Chicago Press, 1981).

[2] See Bureau of Justice Statistics Bulletin, *Probation and Parole 1983*, NCJ-94776 (September 1984:6).

[3] By "success," I am referring to a probationer completing the term of his/her probation without incarceration or discharge for special reasons, such as listed in Note 1, Table 6, Bureau of Justice Statistics Bulletin, *Probation and Parole 1983*, NCJ-94776 (September 1984:4).

[4] See Bureau of Justice Statistics Bulletin, *Probation and Parole 1983* (p. 4). Data were reported for 24 states.

[5] Brown, M. and D. Cochran, *Executive Summary: Massachusetts Risk/Needs Classification System* (Report No. 5, December 1984).

[6] For example, see Walter Barkdull, "Probation: Call It Control—And Mean It," in Travis, Schwartz, and Clear (eds.), *Corrections: An Issues Approach*, 2nd ed., (Anderson Publishing Company, 1983).

[7] For example, see John Ortiz Smykla, *Probation and Parole: Crime Control in the Community* (New York: MacMillan, 1984).

[8] A brief note on method of analysis is in order. We attempted to contact (via telephone) probation departments in every state between November 1984 and March 1985. We then updated this material in the spring of 1986. A listing of the key contact persons in each

state is available from the Center for Criminal Justice Research at the University of Lowell. We relied at the outset on a list of contacts identified in a report by Chris Baird, which we have updated and expanded. A number of states responded by sending us descriptive material about the operation of their probation system. We used these materials, together with the summaries of our telephone conversations, to complete the following preliminary analyses.

[9] One reason for Massachusetts' high ranking is that the county house of correction population is excluded from this state's figures. In Massachusetts, an offender can serve up to a 2-1/2-year sentence in the house of corrections. In many other states, offenders with sentences over 1 year in length are housed in the state prison.

[10] See, for example, V. O'Leary and T. Clear, *Directions for Community Corrections in the 1990's* (U.S. Department of Justice, National Institute of Corrections, 1984).

[11] The preliminary report on New Jersey's program was provided by Daniel Bibel, ISP, New Jersey Administrative Office of the Courts (Spring 1985). See the article by F. Pearson and D. Bible (this issue).

[12] We were unable to contact probation departments in Alaska and Hawaii.

[13] States have also experimented with intensive supervision for juvenile probationers. One such program was evaluated in Contra Costa County, California. For an overview and evaluation, see Jeffrey Fagan and Craig Reinarman, *Intensive Supervision for Violent Offenders — The Transition from Adolescence to Early Adulthood* (San Francisco, CA: The URSA Institute, 1985).

[14] See Bureau of Justice Statistics Bulletin, Probation and Parole, 1983, NCJ-94776 (Table 4).

[15] For a review of the justice model, see McAnany, Thomson, and Fogel (eds.), *Probation and Justice* (Cambridge, MA: Oelgeschlager, Gunn and Hain, 1984). For a review of the limited risk control model, see Clear and O'Leary, *Controlling the Offender in the Community* (Lexington, MA: D.C. Heath and Company, 1984). The traditional/treatment model is described in Smykla (1984).

[16] For example, the placement of low risk cases on intensive supervision may be unacceptable in Massachusetts, where 77 percent of the prison population are violent offenders and IPS is controlled administratively. However, in another state where "low risk" offenders are routinely placed in prison (e.g., South Dakota, Georgia), the program may be reasonable.

[17] An excellent review of current policies and practices regarding probation fees is found in Baird, et al. (1986).

[18] Author's summary of M. Kay Harris' remarks at a panel on intensive supervision at the November 1984 meeting of the American Society of Criminology in San Diego, California.

## Bibliography

Baird, Christopher, *Report on Intensive Supervision Programs in Probation and Parole*, Report to the Prison Overcrowding Project, July 1983.

Baird, Christopher, D. Holien, and A. Bakke, *Fees for Probation Services*, Madison, WI: National Council on Crime and Delinquency, 1986.

Banks, J., et al., Summary: *Phase I Evaluation of Intensive Special Probation Projects*, Washington, DC: National Institute of Law Enforcement and Criminal Justice, 1977.

Brown, M. and D. Cochran, *Executive Summary: Massachusetts Risk/Needs Classification System*, Report No. 5, December 1984.

Bureau of Justice Statistics Bulletin, *Probation and Parole 1983*, NCJ-94776, September 1984.

Clear, T. R. and V. O'Leary, *Controlling the Offender in the Community*, Lexington, MA: Lexington Books, D.C. Heath and Company, 1983.

Cole, G. F., *Criminal Justice: Law and Politics*, Brooks Cole Publishing Company, 1984.

Fields, D. C., *The Intensive Supervision Probation Program in Texas: A Two-Year Assessment*. Unpublished doctoral dissertation, Sam Houston University, 1984.

Fogel, D., "The Emergence of Probation as a Profession in the Service of Public Safety: The Next 10 Years," in P. D. McAnany, et al. (eds.), *Probation and Justice: Reconsideration of Mission*, Cambridge, MA: Oelgeschlager, Gunn, and Hain Publishers, Inc., 1984, pp. 65-99.

Fogel. D., *We Are the Living Proof: The Justice Model for Corrections*, 2nd ed., Cincinnati: Anderson Publishing Co., 1975.

Gottfredson, S. D. and R. B. Taylor, *The Correctional Crisis: Prison Regulations and Public Policy*, Washington, DC: U.S. Department of Justice, National Institute of Justice, 1983.

Harlow, N. and E. K. Nelson, *Management Strategies for Probation in an Era of Limits*, Washington, DC: National Institute of Corrections, U.S. Department of Justice, 1982.

Harris, L., *The Harris Survey*, New York: The Chicago Tribune, New York News Syndicate, May 24, 1982.

Harris, M. K., "Rethinking Probation in the Context of a Justice Model," in P. D. McAnany, et al. (eds.), *Probation and Justice: Reconsideration of Mission*, Cambridge, MA: Oelgeschlager, Gunn, and Hain Publishers, Inc., 1984, pp. 15-37.

Latessa, G. J., *Intensive Probation: An Evaluation of the Effectiveness of an Intensive Diversion Unit*. Unpublished doctoral dissertation, Ohio State University, 1979.

Logan, C. H., "Evaluating Research in Crime and Delinquency." *Journal of Criminal Law, Criminology and Police Science*, September 1972 (63):378-90.

McAnany, P. D., D. Thomson, and D. Fogel, *Probation and Justice: Reconsideration of Mission*, Cambridge, MA: Oelgeschlager, Gunn, and Hain Publishers, Inc., 1984.

O'Leary, V. and T. Clear, *Directions for Community Corrections in the 1990's*, Washington, DC: U.S. Department of Justice, National Institute of Corrections, 1984.

Sherman, M. and G. Hawkins, *Imprisonment in America, Choosing the Future*, University of Chicago Press, 1981.

Singer. R. G., *Just Deserts: Sentencing Based on Equality Deserts*, Cambridge, MA: Ballinger, 1979.

Smykla, J. O., *Probation and Parole: Crime Control in the Community*, New York: MacMillan, 1984.

Thomson, D., "Prospects for Justice Model Probation," in P. D. McAnany, et al., (eds.), *Probation and Justice: Reconsideration of Mission*, Cambridge, MA: Oelgeschlager, Gunn, and Hain Publishers, Inc., 1984. pp. 101-35.

Travis, Schwartz, and Clear, *Corrections: An Issues Approach*, 2nd ed., Anderson Publishing Co., 1983.

von Hirsch, A., *Doing Justice: The Report of the Committee for the Study of Incarceration*, New York: Hill and Wang, 1976.

# 11

# Stated and Latent Functions of ISP

## Michael Tonry

## Abstract

*The available evidence suggests that intensive supervision probation (ISP) programs do not achieve their stated goals of substantially reducing prison crowding, saving public monies, or reducing recidivism. Many probation officers and departments support ISP enthusiastically, however, and its more punitive features are strictly enforced in many jurisdictions. The proliferation of ISP in the United States in the last decade appears to have had less to do with its stated goals than with its effectiveness at achieving latent bureaucratic, organizational, political, professional, and psychological goals of probation departments and officers.*

There is good, albeit preliminary, reason to doubt that intensive supervision probation (ISP) programs substantially reduce prison crowding, save public funds, or increase public safety. Yet over the last half dozen years they have spread across the United States, and they

Source: Michael Tonry, *Crime and Delinquency* (Vol. 36, No. 1), 174-91. Copyright © 1990 Sage Publications, Inc. Reprinted by permission of Sage Publications, Inc.

continue today to proliferate. This essay examines the question of why these new programs are thriving.

The answer appears to be that ISP programs, despite their apparent failure to achieve their primary stated purposes, admirably serve a variety of other, latent, purposes. They serve bureaucratic and organizational goals by enabling probation administrators to be "tough on crime" and thereby increase the institutional and political credibility of probation. This brings more staff, more money, and new programs to probation. Bigger budgets and increased responsibilities are the traditional measures of bureaucratic success, and ISP programs are means to those legitimate organizational ends.

They serve administrators' normative goals. By being purposely more punitive than traditional probation, ISP programs permit administrators to express a reduced tolerance of crime and disorder that they share with the general public and political leaders.

They serve professional and psychological goals. By attracting new resources and new visibility, ISP programs put probation on the front lines of crime control and thereby enhance the esteem accorded probation and, vicariously, the professional and personal self-esteem of probation officers.

This is not a cynical point. Every serious person wants to believe that his work is important and socially useful. If smaller caseloads managed by collaborating probation and surveillance officers promise both enhanced public safety and more effective service delivery, probation officers can quite reasonably believe that theirs is a socially important role. Probation administrators who attract additional resources to their departments by means of new ISP programs can similarly believe that they have thereby augmented their department's ability to carry out its mission.

Thus, the argument to be made in this essay is that the spread of ISP can be understood better in terms of its latent functions, which it can accomplish, than in terms of its patent functions which, in most places, it apparently cannot. Section I summarizes the current state of research on ISP's effectiveness at performing its stated functions of reducing prison populations, saving money, and protecting public safety. Section II turns to ISP's latent functions and demonstrates how existing programs achieve the organizational, normative, psychological and professional goals mentioned earlier. Section III considers the desirability of social or governmental institutions that can be justified only in terms of their latent functions.

## I. The Stated Goals of ISP

Most people seem to agree that the primary formal goals of ISP programs are to reduce prison crowding, to save money, to protect public safety, and to provide a punishment that is more punitive and intrusive than ordinary probation. Here is how Frank Pearson, the evaluator of New Jersey's program, describes its goals:

> (a) To *improve the use of scarce prison resources* by releasing selected offenders from incarceration into the community after they serve three or four months of their prison term, thus saving prison space in which to confine the more serious offenders.
>
> (b) To have the program be *monetarily cost-beneficial and cost-effective* compared to ordinary incarceration.
>
> (c) To *prevent criminal behavior* by those selected offenders while they are in the community. . . .
>
> (d) To *deliver appropriate, intermediate punishment* in the community [Pearson, 1988, p.438, emphasis in the original].

A statement similar to Pearson's could be made about most ISP programs. As I read the evidence from evaluation research, only Pearson's last goal, delivering "appropriate, intermediate punishment in the community," is being realized. Many evaluations, including Erwin's (1987) for Georgia, Pearson's (1987) for New Jersey, and Thomson's (1987) for Illinois show that punitive, intrusive policies — frequent urinalysis, unannounced visits, astonishingly high levels of contacts, official intolerance of violations of technical conditions — were implemented vigorously. Whatever else it may or may not be, in many places ISP *is* punitive. By contrast, the evidence to support realization of the other goals is exceedingly weak. Before discussing the evidence, however, it may be appropriate to devote a few paragraphs to its nature.

Probation research has not traditionally been known for its methodological or analytical rigor. Evaluation experiments involving random allocation of subjects between experimental and control conditions have, until recently, not been carried out (Petersilia, in this issue, discusses a few of those now underway). When ISP evaluations have used control groups in an effort to learn what difference the new program has made, the matched comparison groups are generally patently noncomparable.

There is a substantial, though mostly fugitive, evaluation literature on differential caseload and ISP projects. Banks et al. (1977) discuss the research from the 1950s and 1960s on the recidivism-reducing effects of differential caseload projects and summarize evaluations of ISP projects funded by the Law Enforcement Assistance Administration in the 1970s. Dissertations by Latessa (1979) and Fields (1984) review ISP evaluations to their respective dates. More recently, Petersilia (1987) and Tonry and Will (1988) provide overviews of more recent ISP research.

There have been a handful of major recent evaluations. Three different

kinds of ISP projects have been examined. Some are caseload management efforts; they are created and controlled by probation managers and
by definition claim neither to serve as "alternatives to incarceration"
nor as a direct means to reduce prison crowding or save public monies.[1]
The most substantial recent evaluation of a case management project
is Byrne and Kelly's (1988) evaluation of Massachusetts's much-
publicized program. Some of the Ohio ISP projects evaluated by Latessa
(e.g., Latessa, 1987; Noonan and Latessa, 1987) involved major case
management components. The Association of the Bar of the City of New
York (1986) evaluated New York State's case management program in
the Bronx.

The other two types of ISP projects have been inelegantly described
as front-door and back-door programs. The doors are prison doors.
Programs of the former type operate as diversions from prison and
thereby notionally keep offenders from entering the prison's front door.
Programs of the latter type offer early release from prison, on condition
of the intense supervision of ISP, and thereby notionally hasten
prisoners' exit through the prison's back door. Both types of programs
seek their justification in claims that they reduce prison crowding and
save public funds by replacing expensive imprisonment with less
expensive ISP, all the while protecting public safety by means of
unrelenting and unforgiving surveillance.

Georgia's ISP program, the best known front-door project, has been
emulated in many states (Byrne, 1986), including Illinois (Thomson,
1987; Lurigio, 1987), Arizona (Duffie, 1987), and New York (Association
of the Bar of the City of New York, 1986). In Georgia, ISP operates as
a sentencing option. Ideally, ISP probationers are first sentenced to
imprisonment and then diverted to probation; in practice, many judges
sentence directly to ISP. A sizable number of documents report on a
series of in-house evaluations (Erwin, 1986; Erwin and Bennett, 1987).

New Jersey's is the best known back-door project. Offenders apply to
admission from within the prison. Eligibility standards eliminate those
who pose significant threats of public relations embarrassment or serious
new offending; several stages of subjective screening eliminate many
more (Pearson, 1987, pp. 93-98). Other back-door projects have been
evaluated in Washington (Fallen et al., 1981) and described in the federal
system (Hofer and Meierhoefer, 1987). There has been one major
evaluation of the New Jersey project (Pearson, 1987,1988).

## Reduced Jail and Prison Crowding[2]

There is little reason to believe that most ISP programs, by diverting
offenders from prison, do much to reduce crowding. The argument is
different for each type of ISP program, so I address them one by one.

Front-door ISP programs like Georgia's face two problems that easily could interact to increase prison use. First, in states that lack presumptive sentencing guidelines, it is exceedingly difficult to be sure that a purportedly prison-bound ISP offender really would otherwise have gone to prison. Of offenders receiving ISP in Georgia in 1983, half got there by amended sentence and half by direct sentence. In the latter case, judges were asked to sign a certificate that the offender would have been imprisoned had he not been sentenced to ISP; Billie Erwin, the primary Georgia evaluator, notes that "this was a formality that could hardly be considered proof" (Erwin, 1987, p. 11). Even in the former case, it would shock few observers of courts if judges, who wished to justify sentencing a probation-bound offender to ISP, would first announce some other sentence and then "amend" it to specify ISP. Erwin and Bennett note that judges "had been vocal in requesting stricter supervision standards" (1987, p.6). Evaluators of a New York front-door ISP program, who concluded that New York judges were not using ISP as an alternative to incarceration, noted "the frequently heard remark that ISP is 'only doing what probation ought to be doing'" (Association of the Bar of the City of New York, 1986, p.16). Thomson, in a preliminary report on an evaluation of Illinois's front-door program, which requires judges to certify that offenders sentenced to ISP would otherwise have been imprisoned, notes the possibility that ISP in that state would be used principally for those who would otherwise be sentenced to ordinary probation (Thomson, 1987, pp. 6, 21-22).

Circumstantial evidence suggests that Georgia judges are disingenuous in their "imprisonment certifications." During the pilot phase of Georgia's program, only 8% of the 542 people sentenced to ISP received "minimum scores" on a risk assessment instrument (Erwin, 1987, table 1). However, of the first 2,322 people sentenced to ISP from 1982 to 1985, 28% had minimum-risk scores (Erwin, 1987, table 3), and that is probably an underestimate.[3]

The second complexity that undercuts the effectiveness of front-door ISP programs at reducing prison populations is that they, like many ISP programs, have high revocation rates. Partly this results from the intensity of programs that involve 20 to 30 contacts per month compared with programs involving one or two contacts per month; inevitably the case officers know more about their clients. Partly also it stems from the avowedly punitive, intrusive nature of ISP programs; they are claimed to be tough, and low tolerance of violation of conditions is the best way to show probationers, prosecutors, and judges that they are tough.

In Georgia, 40% of ISP offenders in an evaluation of people sentenced to ISP in 1983 were rearrested (Erwin, 1987, table 11). As of September 1986, 18% of ISP clients to that date had absconded or had their status revoked.[4] By one calculation, only half of Georgia's ISP offenders successfully complete the program.[5] ISP programs of other types discussed below also report high revocation rates.

When these two problems of front-end ISP—use for offenders who were not prison-bound, high revocation rates—are combined, it becomes apparent that the net effect of a front-door ISP program may be to increase prison populations. Depending on the proportion of an ISP program's caseload diverted from prison, and the proportion imprisoned following revocation, it is possible that some ISP programs fill more prison beds than they empty.

On first impression, back-door ISP programs should not suffer from the same problems as the front-door variety. After all, if the aim of the program is to release people from prison early and it is available only to offenders who apply for admission from prison, it must reduce prison crowding. However, it is not so simple. Clear, Flynn, and Shapiro (1987) suggest that "there is a growing concern that some judges are 'backdooring' cases into ISP by sentencing borderline offenders to prison while announcing they will 'welcome an application for intensive supervision.'" This is not as far fetched as it may appear; a reasonable judge might well decide to create ad hoc "shock probation" sentences by imprisoning marginal offenders on the rationales that ordinary probation is a slap on the wrist, a short stay in prison will get the offender's attention, and the offender's marginal nature will assure early release to ISP. The problem, however, is that the eligibility screening is very rigorous and at the last of seven stages entirely subjective. Less than one-sixth of the prisoners who apply for New Jersey ISP are selected (Pearson, 1987, p. 94). Thus the creative judge may miscalculate: The prisoner whom he sentenced on the assumption of early ISP release may not be released. Clear (1988) has calculated that if 1.2% of the 20,000 felons sentenced in New Jersey each year receive short prison sentences because the judge predicts they will be admitted to ISP, the resulting increase in the prison population would exceed the ISP caseload and more than counterbalance any savings in cash or prison beds.

No one has hard evidence that many judges are attempting to second-guess New Jersey's ISP program; Clear's argument shows, however, that a small amount of second-guessing could undermine much of what New Jersey's ISP purports to accomplish. If there is any significant amount of judicial second-guessing going on, the impact would be substantial, because roughly 40% of the ISP clients are returned to prison after revocation (Pearson, 1988, p. 440); nearly half of the violations appear to be for technical violations of conditions.[6]

Pearson has carried out an admirably complete cost- and prison-use analysis of New Jersey's program. It makes a number of doubtful assumptions (including that no judges are sentencing people to prison in order to place them on ISP, and that a patently noncomparable comparison group is comparable to the ISP offenders) which, for the purposes of this paragraph, I accept. Pearson concludes that New Jersey's ISP program saved 186 "prisoner-years" of prison use (Pearson, 1987, p.182). Compared with the 15,500 state prisoners in New Jersey in 1987 (Bureau of Justice Statistics, 1989), saving 186 prison beds is unlikely to have significantly reduced prison crowding. And if Pearson's assumptions are wrong and tend to overestimate savings of prison beds, the prison-crowding effects will be even less.

It will vary from case to case but, in some jurisdictions, either front or back-door ISP may increase prison crowding. By definition this will happen with case management ISP, like that in Massachusetts. The heightened surveillance experienced by the high-risk offenders assigned to the ISP program should, in the nature of things, uncover more technical violations and new crimes which in turn, should send more people to prison. Most people would presumably regard this as a desirable result of the more efficient use of probation resources.

## Cost Savings

If the case for ISP as a prison population reducer is weak, the case for cost savings must also fail. Before demonstrating why this is so, a few general words about cost-benefit analyses of ISP programs may be in order.

Many analyses that purport to show that a new program billed as a "sentencing option" or an "alternative to incarceration" will save the state money do not withstand scrutiny. The biggest problem is that evaluators nearly always compare average per-capita costs for prisoners and, for example, ISP probationers, factor in the number of days the average offender would have been imprisoned and the number of days on ISP, do some multiplying and comparing, and conclude that the ISP project will save the state a substantial sum. A fundamental problem with this kind of analysis is its use of average costs. The reality is that one more prisoner costs the state only marginal costs—a bit of food, some disposable supplies, some record keeping. Only when the numbers of people diverted from prison by a new program permit the closing of all or a major part of an institution or the cancellation of construction plans will there be substantial savings.

Table 1 summarizes an analysis showing that Georgia's ISP saves substantial sums. To illustrate why ISP cost-savings estimates are often suspect, I use Table 1 as an illustration. For the sake of argument, I accept as given all the estimates of days on ISP and regular probation, days that would have been served in prison, and amounts per day for each treatment.[7]

Table 1

**Georgia ISP—Comparison of 1986 Costs per Offender, Incarceration versus ISP**

| | | |
|---|---|---|
| Incarcerated Group (255 days at $30.43) | | $7,759.65 |
| ISP Group | | |
| 196 days ISP at $4.37 | $856.52 | |
| 169 days Regular Probation at $.76 | 128.44 | |
| | | 984.96 |
| Cost avoidance per ISP Offender | | $6,774.69 |

Source: Erwin, 1987, p. 64.

Consider these problems. First, some percentage of the ISP offenders have been diverted not from prison but from ordinary probation. Erwin's best guess (1988) is that 80% are diverted from prison; I would guess half. For those not diverted from prison, ISP costs per day are six times higher than the cost of ordinary probation, the sanction from which they were diverted, not less, and that has to be taken into account.

Second, whatever sentences they were diverted from, many ISP offenders will commit new crimes or technical violations, have their ISP revoked, and be sent to prison. As noted above, New Jersey's revocation rate was nearly 40%. In Georgia, 40% of the 1983 ISP offenders were arrested for new crimes, and roughly half of those terminated from the program by December 1985 suffered revocations. This seems to suggest that 40 to 50% of ISP offenders will be returned to prison; that additional time incarcerated must be included in any cost estimates.

Last, the use of average per capita prison costs is, as it usually is, misleading. In September 1986, Georgia ISP had 1,914 active cases (Erwin, 1987, p. 44), which would by the assumptions of Table 1 be active for an average of 196 days. In other words, ISP's annualized caseload was then 1,004 clients (1,914 x 196/365). And, as noted, 20 to 50% of those were diverted not from prison but from something else, and 40 to 50% of them will have their ISP revoked. On the assumptions most favorable to Georgia ISP, 80% diversion from prison and 40% revocation, ISP saved roughly 400 prisoner-years of prison use. On the least favorable assumptions, 50% diversion and 50% revocation, no prison space was saved and the ISP program was a substantial net drain on the financial resources of Georgia's corrections system. Georgia's prison population at the end of 1988 was 18,787 (Bureau of Justice Statistics, 1989). Even on the favorable assumptions that lead to a savings of 400 prison beds in 1986, a 2% reduction in Georgia's prison population is not likely to result in the closing of an existing institution or the cancellation of plans to build a new one. Per capita costs simply don't seem applicable.

In contrast to these skeptical calculations of cost savings associated with reduced prison use ranging from little to none, Georgia Corrections Commissioner David Evans claimed after the first 542 offenders were sentenced to ISP, "That is one twenty million dollar prison we did not build" (Erwin, 1986, p. 24). By 1987, Georgia evaluators were claiming that "if these [2,322] offenders had been incarcerated, the threshold would have been crossed requiring the construction of at least two prisons" (Erwin, 1987, p. 63).

The New Jersey cost savings estimates hold up little better. Table 2 sets out Pearson's (1987) lower cost-savings estimates, which show that each ISP case saves the state $7,303. Pearson does take account of the probability that a large percentage of ISP offenders will be reimprisoned following revocation; that is the basis of the "next prison time" estimates. If Clear's (1988) apprehension is warranted that judges are sending offenders to prison only because they are expected to be released to ISP, the savings would be reduced or wiped out. But there are other problems. Pearson uses average per capita imprisonment costs when, for a savings of 186 prison beds in 1986 (compared with 15,500 prison inmates in 1987 [Bureau of Justice Statistics, 1989] and 6,000 jail inmates in 1983 [Bureau of Justice Statistics, 1984, table 3]), there is no plausible reason to believe that the savings were other than marginal costs. If the marginal cost of one additional state or jail prisoner per day is $5.00,

Table 2

**New Jersey ISP—Lower Bound Estimates Using $50 Daily Per Capita for Incarceration Cost and Excluding Indirect Administrative Costs**

|  | ISP Group | Incarcerated Group |  |
|---|---|---|---|
| Instant Prison Time | 109 days at $50 = $5,450 | 308 days at $50 = $15,400 |  |
| Supervision in the Community | 449 days ISP at $13 = $5,837 | 896 days Parole at $2.50 = $2,240 |  |
| Next Prison Time | 120 days at $50 = $6,000 | 139 days at $50 = $6,950 |  |
| TOTAL | $17,287 | $24,590 | $7,303 |

Source: Pearson, 1987, Table 8.1.

ISP at Pearson's estimate of $13 per day probably costs New Jersey $8.00 more per prisoner per day than just locking them up.

By definition, case management ISP costs the state more than not having it would. Closer scrutiny inevitably turns up otherwise unobserved violations of probation conditions and new crimes. The punitive philosophy of many ISP programs presumably results in reduced tolerance of those additional technical violations that are discovered. Although at the time of writing the pertinent chapter of Byrne and Kelly's (1988) Massachusetts evaluation is unavailable, both the Georgia (Erwin, 1987, tables 6 and 11) and New Jersey (Pearson, 1987, p. 106) experiences show high rates of revocations for reasons other than new crimes. In Washington, Fallen et al. found that an ISP sample suffered three times the rate of technical violations experienced by a comparison group whose members on average presented higher risks of future offending (1981, p. 17). All of these additional violations and revocations must be processed and, in some proportion of cases, offenders are imprisoned who otherwise would not have been. All of this costs money.

### Crime Prevention and Recidivism Reduction

Two conclusions stand out about the crime-reduction properties of ISP. First, if ISP programs really divert offenders from prison, it is inevitably at the cost of increased crime in the community. Study after study (e.g., Petersilia and Turner, 1986; Wallerstedt, 1984) demonstrates that released prisoners have nontrivial recidivism rates. In the nature of things, diverting offenders from prison or releasing them earlier results in crimes and victims in the community that would not exist if those offenders had not been diverted or released. Most of the research compares the recidivism rates of ISP clients with those of comparison groups of offenders released from prison; this is, however, like comparing apples and oranges. The truest crime reduction analysis would compare crimes in the community that would have occurred if the offenders had not been diverted or released (none) with those that did occur. By that measure, all ISP programs that divert offenders from prison should increase crime victimization.

Second, insofar as the ISP evaluation research is reliable,[8] it has consistently failed to show any crime reduction effects. Pearson, after noting that his New Jersey comparison group may not have been comparable to his sample of ISP offenders, asserts "in any event, we can be confident that ISP at least did not increase recidivism rates" (1988, pp. 443-44). Forty percent of Erwin's exceedingly nonthreatening ISP sample in Georgia were rearrested within 18 months, and the rate was about the same whether the offenders were rated as low medium, high, or maximum risk (1987, p. 54). In a recidivism analysis comparing Ohio ISP cases with a comparison group, Noonan and Latessa found "no significant differences between the samples" (1987, p. 16). In Washington, Fallen et al. found no evidence that ISP offenders had lower recidivism rates than did a comparison group (1981, p. 40).

Thus it now appears that those ISP programs that have been evaluated do not reduce recidivism rates, significantly reduce prison crowding, or save much (if any) money, though they do seem often to deliver the punitive, intrusive sanctioning experience that their proponents promise. My guess is that completion of ongoing ISP evaluations, including those with experimental designs, will yield findings similar to those reported above.

## II. ISP's Latent Functions

If ISP programs do not accomplish their stated goals, and yet continue to proliferate, they must be serving some other purposes of value to someone. My hypothesis is that a combination of latent institutional, professional, and political aims are being well-served by ISP programs, and that their proliferation is attributable to their effective achievement of those aims. These different aims interact, but for purposes of analysis the following sections discuss them one by one. Because Georgia's program has generated the most extensive literature, I draw principally on it for illustrations.

### Institutional Aims

ISP has served to increase the institutional credibility of probation, and therein lies much of its allure. Under the pressures in many places of staggering caseloads, and everywhere of disillusionment with probation's ability to achieve its traditional rehabilitative goals, probation was a demoralized institution. Many people saw probationary sentences as token punishments. One veteran probation executive observed that most people see probation "as a slap on the wrist" (Duffie, 1987, p. 125). A veteran prosecutor has observed that probation has become "just something you slap on people when you don't know what else to do with them. We waste a lot of resources on probation, which means absolutely nothing in most places" (Prosecuting Attorneys' Research Council, 1988, p. 3).

The "slap on the wrist" rap may be a bad rap, but it was and is commonly believed. ISP has given probation administrators a chance to rebuild probation's credibility, influence, and, not incidentally, material resources. In Georgia, beset by massive prison crowding, one of ISP's original goals was to demonstrate that probation can be tough and thereby to increase the willingness of judges to sentence offenders to probation. ISP was tough and, evaluators suggest, judges began to take probation generally more seriously; compared with a base year of 1982 when 63% of felons were sentenced to probation, by 1985 73% received probation. ISP's spokesmen claim much of the credit for that change (Erwin, 1986, p. 18). In 1987, Georgia probation received more than 61,000 new cases (Bureau of Justice Statistics, 1988), and the prisons then held 18,575 people (Bureau of Justice Statistics, 1989). If ISP's toughness did give judges more confidence in probation and thereby cause (or significantly contribute to) the change in sentencing patterns, the accomplishment was considerable: In 1987 alone the incremental 10% of probationers would have been nearly 9,000 people and ISP by itself could have received no more than 1,000.

If ISP increased the credibility of probation, from an institutional perspective it doesn't really matter whether it actually achieved its formal goals so long as people believe it did. If Georgia judges and other public officials believed in 1986, as Commissioner Evans claimed, that ISP spared a need for a $20,000,000 prison (or as Erwin [1987] later suggested, avoided the need to build "at least two prisons"), then probation is likely to have achieved for itself institutionally, and for its staff professionally, greatly increased stature. This translates into more resources, more staff, a larger agency.

The Georgia institutional accomplishment is even more impressive because the ISP program was paid for entirely from newly instituted probation fees that were initiated at the same time ISP was implemented (Erwin and Bennett, 1987, p. 6). The fees were collected from all probationers who could afford to pay them, and the money collected in the first four years "exceeded ISP costs and was used for numerous additional special probation needs" (Erwin and Bennett, 1987, p. 6).

Assuming the story summarized here is substantially true, Georgia probation officials have created the opposite of a zero-sum game: everyone wins. Offenders are spared imprisonment. Judges have to hand a new, believable intermediate punishment. Prison crowding is reduced. The state saves money. The probation department is seen to have achieved all these things and, at the same time, increased the department's size and funding. From an organizational perspective, these are remarkable accomplishments for a department of government theretofore in most places accorded little esteem. From a bureaucratic perspective, the probation officials in charge are little short of wizards and can feel that they have served their institution well.

## Professional Aims

Everyone wants to feel useful and important. For probation officials and officers in Georgia, ISP must have made them feel both more useful and more important. Their agency was seen to be in the middle of things and performing crucial public services. Personally and politically, probation officials were probably accorded more visibility, acknowledgment, and respect than before ISP became part of Georgia's criminal justice system. The substantial national attention, the media coverage, the invitations to discuss Georgia's program at national meetings must all have been flattering and reinforced probation officials' self-esteem. It would not be astonishing to learn that more Georgians chose careers as probation officers and that recruitment became easier.

There is considerable evidence that line probation officers value new ISP programs. In Georgia, staff "were spotlighted as emissaries of the new intense supervision and responded with remarkable energy and dedication to the success of the program" (Erwin, 1987, p.31). In New Jersey, it was not increased pay that kept probation officers working at ISP but the opportunity "to do probation work the way it ought to be done" and "to work closely with just a few people so you can make a difference in their lives" (Pearson, 1987, p. 105). In Illinois, Thomson found "an impressive degree of commitment and enthusiasm on the part of ISP officers and managers. . . . For some there is almost an atmosphere of a conversion experience, with observations about how the program has rejuvenated their commitment to the profession" (1987, pp. 13-14).

The matters speculated about above are not trivial and they are not unimportant. And besides their obvious benefits to Georgia probation institutionally and to many probation professionals personally, the new resources permitted Georgia probation officers to do their jobs better. People choose the roles they play, and there is no reason for probation professionals to be different. Most of them presumably believe in the good that probation can provide to probationers and to society at large. More resources and enhanced esteem translates into the ability to do more of the work they believe in and to do it better.

## Political Aims

One last, more speculative, benefit deserves mention, though I realize I am stumbling ever deeper into the realm of pop psychology. Winds of reduced public and political tolerance of crime and criminals have been blowing across the United States for at least fifteen years. There is no reason to suspect that probation professionals have been unaffected by those social and cultural trends. ISP, especially in its hybrid helping and hurting form symbolized by paired probation and surveillance officers, permits probation simultaneously to reflect tougher attitudes toward crime and to carry out probation's traditional commitment to provision of social services and humane support to the disadvantaged who have committed crimes.

Insofar as probation officers believe, and no doubt many do, that much ordinary probation has been deprived of its meaning as a criminal punishment by high caseloads and by judges whose own caseloads make them loathe to take most condition violations seriously, ISP can serve as a meaningful punishment for offenders who deserve a meaningful punishment. High revocation rates are in one sense evidence that probation and its conditions must be taken seriously. Playing a role in making this new, stricter probation a reality may allow probation officers to carry into their work toughened law-and-order sentiments that they share with many fellow citizens.

There is another political advantage to ISP. Many public figures feel torn between a wish to be tough on crime and a wish to be fiscally responsible. In the face of overcrowded prisons and heavy construction costs for new prisons, the official cost-saving, crime-reducing, punitive characterization of ISP allows officials to assure constituents that crime is being dealt with seriously and that state financial constraints are being acknowledged.

In any case, in the current political climate, it cannot hurt the professional and institutional interests of probation to have launched programs that are politically salable because they accord with public and political calls for severe punishment of criminals.

## III. Latent Goals and Just Institutions

Suppose that my analysis is substantially correct and that ISP excellently serves latent organizational, professional, and political goals of probation professionals but fails to achieve its stated goals of diversion from prison, cost savings, and crime prevention. Should ISP be dropped?

One answer, which derives from the principles we all learned in Civics 101, is that ISP should survive only if it achieves its stated goals. By that test, ISP fails. In the world as we find it, however, that rationalistic approach seldom guides governmental decisions. If it did, we would build prisons and mental health institutions near their catchment areas irrespective of not-in-my-backyard politics, and we would make military procurement and base closing decisions on the military merits irrespective of their economic ramifications for affected communities.

A more complicated answer, which derives from the utilitarian principle of the greatest good for the greatest number, would consider the overall package of stated and latent goals and their varying states of realization, and be guided by the best estimate of whether retention or abandonment better serves the public good. The problem with that answer is that we are not very good at the calculations it requires. If, for example, thousands of people in Georgia are diverted from imprisonment each year because ISP has vicariously heightened judges' respect for ordinary probation, a utilitarian analysis would support the ISP program even if it is all smoke and mirrors and the people sentenced to it, many of whom will later be imprisoned for failure to meet technical conditions, are diverted not from prison but from probation.

A complication is that while there is reason to suspect that many ISP offenders were not prison-bound, there is also reason to doubt that Georgia judges impose more probationary sentences because ISP has enhanced their respect for probation. During the period when Georgia ISP was implemented and evaluated, lots of other things were happening that might have influenced judicial sentencing patterns. Georgia was subject to federal court orders limiting prison population. In 1983, the Georgia legislature authorized the parole board to control prison populations by releasing offenders according to criteria independent of sentence length; this change might well restrain judges' decisions to imprison low-risk offenders when the effect might be to force the release of a current higher-risk prisoner. Also during this period, Georgia established or greatly expanded a community service program, a community restitution center program, and a shock incarceration program (Erwin, 1987, pp. 56, 72). It is entirely possible that the political and economic forces that produced all of those changes would have resulted in substantially increased use of probationary sentences had Georgia not decided to establish ISP and that ISP in Georgia is an epiphenomenal distraction rather than a causal factor.

A final answer to the question "whether ISP?" derives from principles relating to retributive punishment philosophies. This view would consider it unjust to sentence probation-bound offenders to ISP, knowing that they will experience conditions more intrusive than those of ordinary probation and a substantial probability of imprisonment for failure to meet conditions, even though ISP does result in the diversion of much larger numbers of people from imprisonment to less intrusive sentences. This is the traditional moralist's response to utilitarian claims; the individual's right to just treatment acts as a trump over state action. My sympathies lie in that direction, but I am willing to concede that, as a political matter, achievement of important latent goals is often likely to result in survival of government practices and institutions that fail to achieve their stated goals.

Whatever the justification of the existence of ISP in particular states today on the basis of the existing evidence, there is a place for ISP and other intermediate punishments in the future. Most states lack meaningful punishments that are more severe than ordinary probation or less severe than imprisonment. A moment's reflection should teach that some offenders deserve punishments that are more than nominal but less than all-encompassing. ISP is one of these. But until the time comes, as it will, when sentencing guidelines or other approaches to structuring judicial discretion are implemented in most states, including within their scope a full range of punishments of graded severity, it is unlikely that these mid-range punishments will be preponderantly used for the mid-range offenders for whom in principle they are designed. Until that day, judges who are frustrated by the lack of rigor of ordinary probation are likely to use newer intermediate punishments for the more villainous among the probation-bound rather than for the less villainous among the prison-bound for whom, in public declaration, they are designed.

## Notes

1. Case management projects might arguably pursue these goals indirectly by preventing crimes through close surveillance and thereby reducing future needs for prison beds. Recent research does not suggest that case management projects reduce crime by probationers (Byrne and Kelly, 1988). Contrariwise, evidence from a variety of types of ISP projects shows that their heightened surveillance intensity produces higher rates of technical and other revocations than under regular probation and thereby creates needs for more prison space and more correctional dollars.

2. ISP programs often aim to divert offenders from both jail and prison. To avoid repetition of the clumsy phrase "jail and prison crowding," I refer throughout to prison crowding to indicate both forms of incarceration.

3. When 343 cases for which data are missing (many of these were probably minimum-risk) are deleted from that analysis, the 643 minimum-risk cases make up 33% of those for which data are available. When the first year's data (35 minimum-risk cases of 443 for which data are available) are dropped from the calculation, 608, nearly 40%, of the 1,536 post-1983 cases for which data are available are minimum-risk cases. This analysis suggests both that ISP in Georgia is used for many nonserious cases and that the proportion of nonserious cases has grown substantially since the program began.

4. This is a considerable underestimate because the percentages are calculated against the number of all persons ever sentenced to ISP. By December 1985, 14.9% of persons ever sentenced to ISP had had their status successfully terminated, and 14.2% had been revoked either for technical violations (6.5%) or for new crimes (7.7%) (Erwin 1987, table 6). By this calculation, nearly half of Georgia's ISP caseload results in revocation.

5. See revocation calculations in note 4.

6. Pearson's report does not give revocation details but does indicate that 24.7% of an evaluation sample of ISP cases were arrested within 24 months of release on ISP (Pearson 1987, table 7.2).

7. Actually though, some of the figures are facially implausible. Average incarceration costs of $30.43 provided by the Georgia Department of Corrections seem reasonable, but an average daily cost of $4.37 for ISP offenders (Erwin, 1987, pp. 64-65) is unreasonable. The caseload norm is two officers for every 25 offenders. Personnel

costs alone must exceed $4.37 a day. If salary and fringe-benefit costs per officer per year average $35,000, and each officer annually handles 12.5 person-years of supervision, the daily cost per offender is $7.67, and that does not include overhead, mileage, equipment, drug testing, and treatment services. Turned around, the daily ISP costs of $4.37 each for a single officer's 12.5 clients would yield $19,938 per year, which is probably not enough to pay one officer's salary, much less all the other costs of operation.

8 Its reliability is generally in doubt because all the published research relies on the use of comparison groups of released prisoners that are patently noncomparable. These groups include people who present higher recidivism risks than do ISP offenders, who are usually carefully screened to eliminate people who present any serious public safety risk. (For detailed analyses that support these generalizations, see Tonry and Will [1988, chapter 3]). Joan Petersilia (in this issue) describes evaluations in progress that rely on randomized assignment and may shed brighter light on the comparative recidivism rates analysis.

## References

Association of the Bar of the City of New York. 1986. *New York State Probation's Intensive Supervision Program: A Reform in Need of Reform.* Unpublished manuscript.

Banks, J., A. L. Porter, R. L. Rardin, T. R. Siler, and V. E. Unger. 1977. *Phase 1 Evaluation of Intensive Special Probation Projects.* Washington, DC: Government Printing Office.

Bureau of Justice Statistics. 1984. *The 1983 Jail Census.* Washington, DC: Bureau of Justice Statistics.

_____. 1988. *Probation and Parole.* Washington, DC: Bureau of Justice Statistics.

_____. 1989. *Prisoners in 1988.* Washington, DC: Bureau of Justice Statistics.

Byrne, J. M. 1986. "The Control Controversy: A Preliminary Examination of Intensive Probation Supervision Programs in the United States." *Federal Probation* 50:4-16.

Byrne, J. M. and L. Kelly. 1988. *Restructuring Probation as an Intermediate Sanction.* Report to the National Institute of Justice. Lowell, MA: University of Lowell, Department of Criminal Justice.

Clear, T. 1988. Personal communication with author.

Clear, T., S. Flynn, and C. Shapiro. 1987. "Intensive Supervision in Probation: A Comparison of Three Projects." In *Intermediate Punishments: Intensive Supervision, Home Confinement and Electronic Surveillance,* edited by B. R. McCarthy. Monsey, NY: Willow Tree Press.

Duffie, H. C. 1987. "Probation: The Best-Kept Secret Around." *Corrections Today* (August):122-26.

Erwin, B. S. 1986. "Turning Up the Heat on Probationers in Georgia." *Federal Probation* 50:17-24.

_____. 1987. *Final Evaluation Report: Intensive Probation Supervision in Georgia.* Atlanta, GA: Georgia Department of Corrections.

_____. 1988. Personal communication with author.

Erwin, B. S. and L. A. Bennett. (January) 1987. "New Dimensions in Probation: Georgia's Experience with Intensive Probation Supervision (IPS)." *Research* in Brief. Washington, DC: National Institute of Justice, U.S. Department of Justice.

Fallen, D. L., C. Apperson, J. Hall-Milligan, and S. Aos. 1981. *Intensive Parole Supervision*. Olympia, WA: Department of Social and Health Services, Analysis and Information Services Division, Office of Research.

Fields, C. B. 1984. *The Intensive Supervision Probation Program in Texas: A Two-year Assessment*. Doctoral dissertation. Huntsville, TX: Sam Houston State University, College of Criminal Justice.

Hofer, P. S. and B. S. Meierhoefer. 1987. *Home Confinement: An Evolving Sanction in the Federal Criminal Justice System*. Washington, DC: Federal Judicial Center.

Latessa, E. J. 1979. *Intensive Probation: An Evaluation of the Effectiveness of an Intensive Diversion Unit*. Doctoral dissertation. Huntsville, TX: Sam Houston State University, College of Criminal Justice.

_____. 1987. "Intensive Supervision: An Eight Year Follow-up Evaluation." Paper presented at the annual meeting of the Academy of Criminal Justice Sciences, St. Louis, March.

Lurigio, A. 1987. "Evaluating Intensive Probation Supervision: The Cook County Experience." *Perspectives*:17-19.

Noonan, S. and E. J. Latessa. 1987. "An Evaluation of an Intensive Supervision Program." Paper presented at the annual meeting of the Academy of Criminal Justice Sciences, St. Louis, March.

Pearson, F. S. 1987. *Research on New Jersey's Intensive Supervision Program*. Washington, DC: National Institute of Justice, U.S. Department of Justice.

_____. 1988. "Evaluation of New Jersey's Intensive Supervision Probation Program." *Crime and Delinquency* 34:437-48.

Petersilia, J. 1987. *Expanding Options for Criminal Sentencing*. Santa Monica, CA: RAND.

Petersilia, J. and S. Turner. 1986. *Prison versus Probation in California: Implications for Crime and Offender Recidivism*. Santa Monica, CA: RAND.

Prosecuting Attorneys' Research Council. 1988. *The Prosecutor's Role in Sentencing Reforms*. New York: Author.

Thomson, D. R. 1987. *Intensive Probation Supervision in Illinois*. Unpublished manuscript.

Tonry, M. and R. Will. 1988. *Intermediate Sanctions*. Washington, DC: Preliminary report to the National Institute of Justice, U.S. Department of Justice.

Wallerstedt, J. F. 1984. *Returning to Prison*. Bureau of Justice Statistics Special Report. Washington, DC: Bureau of Justice Statistics.

# 12

# The Future of Intensive Probation Supervision and the New Intermediate Sanctions

## James M. Byrne

Intensive probation supervision (IPS) has been marketed in the United States as both a solution to our current prison crowding problem and the central component of a new ("get-tough") surveillance-oriented probation image. Unfortunately, a careful review of the development, implementation, and impact of IPS programs suggests that they run the risk of being quickly discarded as the latest, failed panacea. The author begins by discussing the politics of IPS evaluation and then focuses on four key policy issues: purpose, design, implementation, and impact. Based on a review of these issues, the author offers a basic framework for the continued development of intensive supervision and other intermediate sanctions, which combines the use of formal and informal deterrence mechanisms with traditional offender rehabilitation strategies.

Source: James M. Byrne, *Crime and Delinquency*, Vol. 36, No. 1 (January 1990), 6-41. Copyright © 1990 Sage Publications, Inc. Reprinted by permission of Sage Publications, Inc.

## Introduction and Overview

Intensive Probation Supervision (IPS) is the central component of a new wave of intermediate sanctions that has captured the attention of both liberal and conservative policymakers across the United States. To liberals, intensive supervision represents a strategy for diverting offenders from prison and jail without appearing "soft on crime." To conservatives, it provides an opportunity to "get tough" with—and increase control over—offenders without adding to the overall cost of corrections. One of the more interesting aspects of the development of intermediate sanctions generally, and intensive supervision in particular, has been the ability of program developers to integrate the primary concerns of both groups—diversion, punishment, control—into their program models. But by trying to "be all things to all people," program developers run the risk that IPS programs will be viewed as yet another in a long line of failed panaceas, which promise much more than they could ever possibly deliver.

Fortunately, we are still in the early stages of the design and development of a new wave of intermediate sanctions that includes such alternatives as intensive supervision, split sentencing (i.e., shock incarceration), and house arrest (with and without an electronic monitoring component). In 1987, less than 3% of the 3,460,960 offenders under correctional supervision were placed in IPS programs (Byrne, Lurigio, and Baird, 1989). Perhaps another 10,000 were placed under house arrest during this period (Petersilia, 1987), while only a few thousand offenders have been supervised using electronic monitoring devices since the mid-1980s (Schmidt, 1989). Before expanding these new sanctions further, we need to examine a number of critical issues about their purpose, design, implementation, and impact. This article draws on the results and commentary of the authors included in this special issue to provide a critical examination of these issues and to suggest a strategy for transforming the surveillance-oriented community corrections programs of the 1980s into the community control-oriented corrections programs of the 1990s. This strategy is based on a social ecologist's view of the appropriate focus of correctional policy: offender behavior must be viewed in the broader community context of both formal and informal social control systems (Gottfredson and Hirschi, 1988). When viewed from this perspective, the misplaced focus of current institutional and community control policies becomes apparent.

# Correctional Crowding and
# the Politics of IPS Evaluation Research

Between 1983 and 1987, the total correctional population in this country increased by 39.8%, from 2,475,100 to 3,460,960 offenders (Bureau of Justice Statistics, 1988a, 1988b). Because neither the institutional nor the community corrections systems expanded their facilities and resources adequately during this period, we currently have a serious correctional crowding problem.[1] While one solution to the institutional crowding problem is simply to build more prisons as quickly as possible, the cost of building these institutions has led many policymakers to ask: How can we develop programs/sanctions that provide incapacitation effects in community settings? Program developers have responded by implementing a range of community-based alternatives that focus on the surveillance and control of offenders. It is obvious that the development of intensive supervision and other intermediate sanctions has little to do with policymakers recognizing the limits of incapacitation as an effective crime control policy (Gibbons, 1988); rather, it reflects a preoccupation with another conservative notion—the need to limit governmental spending. As Petersilia (this issue) comments in her article on IPS implementation strategies, "the entire movement towards [intensive supervision] is economically driven. It is commonly acknowledged that if prison crowding disappeared tomorrow, thereby eliminating the need to create less expensive sanctions, so would the incentive to develop intensive supervision."

When viewed in this context, supporters of incapacitation appear to be in a no-lose situation. Regardless of the outcome of the current wave of evaluations of intensive supervision and other intermediate sanctions, empirical support will be provided for the policy of incapacitation. If the surveillance-oriented IPS strategies are deemed a success—as the evaluations by Pearson and Harper (this issue) and Erwin (this issue) suggest—then the underlying assumptions of incapacitation will be supported. If the results are negative—as the critical reviews by Tonry (this issue) and by Clear and Hardiman (this issue), and the results of the experiment by Petersilia and Turner (this issue) suggest—then these findings will be viewed as support both for the continued use of incapacitation and the development of even more intrusive, surveillance-oriented community control programs.

The implications of evaluation research for intermediate sanctions—and intensive supervision in particular—are somewhat different for liberal reformers. If one takes the view that even the most intrusive community control program is less harmful than prison, the stakes involved in the current round of IPS evaluations are high, because a series of negative evaluations could threaten the future of these alternative sanctions. There are two exceptions to this generalization. First, evidence that this new wave of intermediate sanctions actually widens the net of formal social control would be viewed as a step backward (see Baird, this issue, for evidence of such net widening in Florida's community control program). Second, evidence that suggests the need to expand the treatment components of IPS programs — rather than to simply increase surveillance (or improve surveillance technology) — would be viewed as a step forward (see Byrne and Kelly, 1989, for evidence of the importance of treatment).

I have outlined the stakes involved in the evaluation of this new wave of intermediate sanctions in order to highlight the decidedly political context in which both internal and external evaluation research is developed, funded, and ultimately disseminated. While it is generally recognized that external evaluations are more objective than internal evaluations,[2] there are a variety of factors that will affect both the quality and the policy significance of all evaluation research. As Rossi and Freeman (1982, p. 301) have observed,

> Evaluation . . . is not just a technical activity. It is research designed to aid in the processes of policy formulation, program design and implementation, and management. Hence, it is also a political activity. By that phrase, we mean that *evaluations always are conducted within contexts in which there are many interested parties with stakes in the outcomes of the efforts.* These stakeholders affect both the evaluators ability to carry out evaluations effectively and the ways in which evaluation results are employed by policy-makers, planners, funders and managers.

In the area of IPS, the "interested parties" to whom Rossi and Freeman (1982, p. 310) refer include (1) *policymakers and decision makers* at the federal, state, and local levels, who determine the purpose and design of IPS program initiatives, (2) *program sponsors* such as the Bureau of Justice Assistance (BJA), which funded the replications of the Georgia intensive supervision program,[3] (3) *evaluation sponsors* such as the National Institute of Justice (NIJ), which funded the Advisory Board that directed the evaluation of Georgia's IPS program, as well as the evaluations of intensive supervision in New Jersey, Massachusetts, and Florida highlighted in this special issue,[4] (4) *evaluators* from both private organizations (e.g., National Council on Crime and Delinquency [NCCD], the RAND Corporation, and university research centers, (5) *program management and staff,* who are responsible for the actual implementation of the programs, (6) *program competitors,* including both institutional corrections and (traditional) probation itself, who will obviously be affected by the development of this new wave of intermediate sanctions (in terms of resources and staff), (7) a variety of *contextual stakeholders*, such as local service providers (e.g. counseling, employment, substance abuse) and community groups affected by these programs, and (8) the *offenders* who are ultimately placed in these programs.

While I agree with Rossi and Freeman's contention (1982, p. 310) that "it is not completely clear how the interests of each [group] are engaged and acted upon by a given evaluation outcome," it seems safe to assert that political considerations have limited both the number and quality of evaluations that have been conducted in the community corrections field. In this regard, every major review of probation research in the past 50 years has decried the poor quality of the evaluations that have been conducted. For those who need proof of this assertion, consider the following: Lipton, Martinson, and Wilks (1975) underscored the poor quality of probation research in their comprehensive review of correctional research conducted between 1945 and 1967; Banks et al. (1977), Gottfredson, Finckenauer, and Rauh (1977), and Albanese et al. (1980) reached similar conclusions concerning the probation (and intensive supervision) research conducted in the 1960s and 1970s; and Tonry and Will (1988), Byrne et al. (1989), and Tonry (this issue) offer negative assessments of the latest wave of IPS program evaluations.

Focusing on this last group of IPS evaluation studies for a moment, I should point out that despite their apparently poor quality—or, as a skeptic would suggest, because of it—the results are generally very positive, supporting the current policy choices of key decision makers. This raises an important, but difficult, question: *Why is the research so consistently weak and uncritical in this area?* While there are a number of possible answers to this question, it appears that two key factors are at work. First, because decision makers often develop new program initiatives for a variety of reasons that have very little to do with the *stated* purpose of the program (e.g., reduce prison crowding, save money, protect the public), they are often reluctant—and with good reason—to allow an objective evaluation to proceed. Tonry (this issue) offers an excellent assessment of the *latent functions* of intensive supervision programs, in which he concludes that the current expansion of these programs can be linked to the realization of the following sets of unstated goals: (1) bureaucratic and organization goals, (2) administrators' normative goals, and (3) professional and psychological goals:

> . . . Despite their apparent failure to achieve their primary stated purposes, [IPS programs] admirably serve a variety of other, latent purposes. *They serve bureaucratic and organizational goals* by enabling probation administrators to be "tough on crime" and thereby increase the institutional and political credibility of probation. This brings more staff, more money, and new programs to probation. . . . *They serve administrators' normative goals.* By

being purposely more punitive than traditional probation, [IPS] programs permit administrators to express a reduced tolerance of crime and disorder that they share with the general public and political leaders. *They serve professional and psychological goals.* By attracting new resources and new visibility, [IPS] programs put probation on the front lines of crime control and thereby enhance the esteem accorded probation and, vicariously, the professional and personal self-esteem of probation officers [emphasis added].

Of course, the *evaluator* also has an impact on the quality of the research that is completed in this area. It is evaluators who are responsible for the development of the research design and the successful completion of the study. It would be naive to assume that external evaluators are not affected by such factors as (1) the need for current funding and the priorities of the funding agency, (2) the potential for future funding, and (3) the pressure to publish positive findings.[5] Far too often, evaluators are so eager to evaluate the latest "panacea" that they agree to conditions that make the actual assessment of program effects quite difficult, either because the program was poorly designed and/or implemented or because the evaluation design was weak. Etzioni (1989, p. 124) offers the following observation about such exercises in rational ritualism: "Usually most of those involved (or all of them) know the data is unreliable and the analysis unreal but dare not say that the emperor is naked. Instead, they make ritualistic projections — and know enough to ignore them." The advantage of this approach to evaluation is that it makes any subsequent "damage control" efforts by decision makers relatively simple. Paraphrasing Cressey (1958), it appears that by using a *vocabulary of adjustment*, decision makers "can discount or attack the results of research that show their favorite program to be ineffective" (Shover and Einstadter, 1988, p. 196). If the evaluation is negative, the decision maker can easily dismiss the results by blaming evaluators who are "out of touch with the real world" and/or pointing out how "probation has changed" since the evaluation was completed. The local decision makers often get the last word in these exchanges. The evaluator has, of course, already moved on to his or her next evaluation by this time.[6]

Despite this pessimistic view of the interaction between researchers and practitioners, there is evidence that collaborative relationships *can* be developed, resulting in the completion of sound, policy-relevant evaluation research in the community corrections area. The work of Petersilia (in press) and of Petersilia and Turner (this issue) offers perhaps the best recent example of such collaboration. Petersilia and her colleagues at the Rand Corporation are currently completing an evaluation of 11 separate intensive supervision demonstration programs that were initiated with support from BJA, an agency within the U.S.

Department of Justice. Petersilia (in press, p. 4) points out the financial incentive for participation: "Each project was funded for 18 to 24 months, at a level of $100,000 to $150,000 per site." All participating agencies had to agree to implement an intensive supervision model following the central tenets of Georgia's highly publicized program, while also allowing the *random assignment* of offenders to treatment and control groups.[7] To insure proper program design and implementation, BJA provided funding for a series of training sessions by Rutgers University's Program Resource Center (directed by Todd Clear and Carole Shapiro), as well as on-site technical assistance by the NCCD's Dough Holien and Audrey Bakke. The ongoing (11-site), randomized field experiment is being funded by both BJA and the National Institute of Justice. The preliminary results from the three California sites — Contra Costa, Ventura, and Los Angeles Counties — are included in this issue. Because the study represents "the largest randomized experiment ever conducted in the field of American corrections" (Petersilia, in press, p. 5), it is likely that the final evaluation results (due out sometime in 1990) will have a profound effect on the future direction of community corrections in this country. However, I should emphasize that just as there are both good and bad evaluations employing *quasi*-experimental designs,[8] there will be variations in quality across these 11 randomized field experiments (Petersilia, in press). Byrne and Kelly (1989, p.132) recently underscored the need for a critical review of these randomized field experiments:

> While the movement toward increased use of randomized field experiments is an important step forward, *there is reason to be cautious about its application to criminal justice policy development.* . . . At a recent conference on randomized field experiments in civil and criminal justice held at Northwestern University, three major problems found in randomized field experiments were discussed: (1) failure to achieve complete randomization, (2) threats to external validity, and (3) the difficulties inherent in the measurement of multi-dimensional treatment packages.

Petersilia (in press) reports that failure to achieve randomization was not a major problem in her evaluation, though a small number of cases were lost because of attrition or overrides by judges. However, the fact that offenders convicted of a violent offense were not included in the target population at *any* of the 11 sites obviously limits the external validity of the study's findings to *nonviolent* offenders.[9] In addition, the fact that these projects were federally funded demonstration projects begs the question of what will happen in the real world, given resource constraints and competing organizational interests. Finally, resource constraints placed on the evaluator by funding agencies ("RAND received about $25,000 per site to conduct the evaluation" [Petersilia, in press, p. 7]) made it difficult to fully assess level of program implementation. As Byrne and Kelly (1989, pp. 133-134) point out, "the danger here is that a promising strategy may be dismissed not because it was ineffective, but because it was poorly implemented."

The implications of the above review of the ongoing IPS field experiments are straightforward. First, we need to find new techniques for fostering collaborative efforts between researchers and practitioners that result in *quality* research. Federal support for *demonstration* projects (with a built-in evaluation commitment) is certainly one approach, but a strategy for evaluating existing, ongoing programs also has to be developed.[10] Second, we need to recognize that randomized field experiments represent only one of "a variety of possible impact evaluation strategies, to be employed only after issues related to program *purpose* and *integrity of implementation* have been resolved satisfactorily" (Byrne and Kelly, 1989, p. 134). And finally, we need to understand the importance of telling the public the truth about what we know (and don't know) in this policy area. By highlighting the limits of our knowledge, we emphasize the need for sound evaluation research to *inform* policy (Garner and Visher, 1988). The critical reviews of past and present IPS research by Clear and Hardiman (this issue) and by Tonry (this issue) are certainly one step in this direction. I recognize that some policymakers, decision makers, and local administrators—especially those who have a stake in the *public* perception of effectiveness—will react with hostility to these negative reviews, viewing any subsequent evaluation proposals with skepticism. However, I must agree with the recommendation of James K. Stewart, Director of the National Institute of Justice, that,

> The time has come . . . to move the criminal justice community from a *craft*—which bases its knowledge on tradition, "seat of the pants" technologies, and intuition—to a *profession* in which decisions are based on sound research, research involving testing and replication [Stewart, as quoted by Lempert and Visher, 1987, p. 14].

Open exchanges between practitioners and researchers about how to achieve this goal are needed, based on a shared realization that "state-of-the-art evaluation is one means of speeding up efforts to contribute to human and social progress" (Rossi and Freeman, 1982, p. 299). Nonetheless, there are limits to the utility of evaluation for decision making that must be recognized by both groups, even as they develop strategies to improve our knowledge about the implementation and impact of intensive supervision and other intermediate sanctions. For example, Etzioni (1989, p. 122) recently offered the following assessment of decision making in the 1990's: "Decision-making in the 1990s will be even more of an art and less of a science than it is today. Not only is the world growing more complex and uncertain at a faster pace, but the old [rational] decision-making models are failing, and we can expect their failure to accelerate as well.''

Etzioni (1989, p. 124) concludes that a new decision-making model, which he refers to as "humble decision making," is needed to cope with the coming decade of "data overload and pell-mell change." When applied to the field of adult sentencing and corrections, *humble decision making*, also referred to as "mixed scanning," would involve "two sets of judgments. The first are broad, fundamental choices about the organization's basic policy and direction; the second are incremental decisions that prepare the way for new, basic judgments and that implement and particularize them once they have been made" (Etzioni, 1989, p. 124). The following review of the current debate over the purpose, design, implementation, and impact of intensive supervision programs highlights the unique blend of philosophical and pragmatic concerns that must be addressed by such humble decision makers before they expand the intensive supervision movement any further.

## The Debate Over the Purpose of IPS Programs

Even a cursory review of IPS program models reveals that program developers typically identify multiple goals for their particular version of intensive supervision. The goals most often identified are punishment, diversion, cost effectiveness, and recidivism reduction. Clear, Flynn, and Shapiro (1987, pp. 10-11) take a dim view of such broad claims:

> Advocates of IPS programs are not humble in the claims they made for these programs. Commonly, IPS is expected to reduce prison crowding, increase public protection, rehabilitate the offender, demonstrate the potential of probation, and save money. Even a skeptic is bound to be impressed. [However] if IPS can do this, why has it been only in the 1980's that it became so popular? If IPS can achieve these goals, it must be the wonderchild of the criminal justice system.

Leaving aside the effectiveness issue for a moment, it is obvious that IPS program developers need to clearly articulate the *primary* purpose of these programs. Commenting on the initial development of IPS programs, Bennett (1987b, p.9) observed that "the intent [of IPS in most states] is to respond in a sensible way to the problem of *prison crowding*," rather than to the problems of either offenders or communities. But perhaps the most important aspect of our current "solution" to the prison crowding problem is that the *sensible* response, as viewed by many policy makers is a combination of *diversion* and *community control*. By transferring the technology of control from the institution to the community, it is assumed that we can continue our reliance on the philosophy of incapacitation even as we divert offenders from institutions. Of course, the acid test of this strategy is that improved surveillance strategies actually work, i.e., protect community residents from offenders at a lower cost than institutionalization. In other words, we can only justify the current policy of diversion into intensive surveillance programs by demonstrating to the public that they are not "at risk" as a result of this strategy. If the incapacitating effects of the surveillance-oriented IPS programs do not stop offenders from committing new crimes while under supervision, then the goals of crime control through incapacitation will not have been realized.[11]

While diversion and control appear to represent the "primary" goals of the majority of IPS programs currently in operation, there seems to be a growing recognition that we need to develop intermediate sanctions — including intensive supervision, regardless of the level of crowding in our correctional system — based on the notion of just deserts. The justification for expanding our sanctioning options in this way has been stated eloquently by Tonry and Will (1988, pp. 6-8,10):

1. *The need for alternatives.* "The prison or nothing psychology of American sentencing is unimaginative and underdeveloped and has impeded efforts to develop constructive non-incarcerative correctional programs." [p. 6]

2. *The need for just deserts.* "There has been little meaningful proportionality in punishment for those who are not bound for prison . . . Intermediate sanctions may provide the successive steps for a meaningful ladder of scaled punishments outside prison." [p. 6]

3. *The need for fairness and equity.* "The creation of meaningful intermediate sanctions removes the arbitrariness and unfairness that occur when prison and probation are the only choices available to the judge." [p. 7]

4. *The need for intermediate punishments.* While the possible *net-widening* effect of intermediate sanctions should be examined closely, "Not all intermediate sanctions . . . need to be designed to serve as *alternatives* to incarceration. Some may be designed as punishments for people whose crimes and criminal records make it inappropriate to do nothing to sanction their criminality and yet unduly harsh . . . to incarcerate them." [p. 8]

5. *The need to distinguish general and specific sentencing aims.* "Individualized efforts to fit the punishment to the offender and the applicable purposes of sentencing are, however, possible only when a range of punishment options is available, and that is part of what intermediate sanctions provide." [p. 10]

With a few notable exceptions (Thomson, 1984; Wasik and von Hirsch, 1988; von Hirsch, Wasik, and Green, 1989; Morris and Tonry, 1990) the debate over the purpose of intermediate sanctions has ignored the issue of commensurate punishments (or just deserts) almost completely. However, von Hirsch (this issue) argues that any assessment of the effectiveness of intermediate sanctions must take place in the broader context of both the *proportionality* of existing punishment alternatives and the *intrusiveness* of specific sanctions. As von Hirsch (this issue) observes,

> Innovative non-custodial penalties are only beginning to be explored in this country, so that little thought has yet been devoted to limits on their use. Such thinking is now urgently necessary. With adequate ethical limits, community-based sanctions may become a way to a less inhumane and unjust penal system. Without adequate limits, however, they could become just another menace — extending the network of state intrusion into citizens' lives. We should not, to paraphrase David Rothman, decarcerate the prisons to make a prison of our society.

Any discussion of "deserts" principles cannot ignore the potential negative effects of plea bargaining on legislative efforts to match "the proportionality of the sanction to the gravity of the crime of conviction" (von Hirsch, this issue). In this regard, Thomson's analysis (this issue) of the use of intensive probation supervision as a plea bargaining tool in Illinois courts will be troublesome to advocates of a just deserts philosophy of sentencing (see also Champion, 1988). According to Thomson, IPS programs are more likely to be used by local decision makers (judges, prosecutors) as a *net-widening* device, given current institutional arrangements. Thomson concludes that "if IPS programs are to function as an effective alternative to incarceration (ATI) resource, . . . defense counsel will probably have to play a more central and adversarial role in the decision-making process." Because the majority of IPS offenders in Illinois are represented by public defenders, Thomson's analysis suggests needed changes in the "commitment" of public defenders to this new wave of intermediate sanctions.

By this point, it should be obvious that a system of intermediate sanctions based on the need for *diversion* to programs that provide crime control through *incapacitation*, albeit in community settings, would look quite different than a system developed on the assumptions of a *just deserts* model. Of course, a *third*, more traditional goal for the new wave of intermediate sanctions can also be identified: recidivism reduction through a combination of rehabilitation and deterrence, both specific and general. After reviewing the results of the initial wave of research on intensive supervision — focusing specifically on the evaluation of

California's experimental Special Intensive Patrol Unit, highlighted by Martinson (1974) — Byrne and Kelly (1989, p. 217) concluded that there is evidence that this goal was realized in the SIPU project:

> . . . The threat of prison resulted in a higher level of compliance with the *rehabilitative* aspects of intensive supervision, which in turn led to lower recidivism. In other words, the deterrent component of intensive supervision may have had an indirect effect on recidivism through increased compliance with the treatment component of the program. Thus, the results of the early round of intensive supervision programs . . . suggest that probation and parole policy makers need to develop supervision programs that attempt both to rehabilitate and to deter. They certainly do not reveal any glaring flaw in the rehabilitative strategy that would justify the subsequent abandonment of this approach to community corrections.

In their evaluation of the Massachusetts IPS program, Byrne and Kelly (1989) argue that it is possible to distinguish the effects of rehabilitation strategies from the effects of such deterrence-oriented strategies as increased surveillance and the enforcement of probation conditions. Petersilia and Turner (this issue) offer similar distinctions between surveillance and treatment, which I discuss in more detail in my analysis of impact issues. Two points related to the goal of recidivism reduction through a combination of treatment and control strategies are in order at this point. First, to paraphrase both Clear (1987) and Morris (1987) we need to limit the use of the special conditions of probation to those activities directly linked to recidivism reduction.[12] Second, we must strictly enforce the conditions we do impose because to do otherwise undermines the stated goals of intermediate sanctions under this model (i.e., recidivism reduction).

But what should strict enforcement actually mean? In New Jersey's intensive supervision program, it apparently refers to monitoring the condition that offenders refrain from using drugs. Pearson (1987) reported that approximately 40% of the IPS offenders were returned to prison within one year of being placed in the program. The vast majority (75%) of these offenders were returned to prison for failing a urinalysis check for substance use. While such a strategy may indeed have a *short-term* recidivism reduction effect, it is also possible that this strict revocation policy for substance abuse violations may actually have a detrimental *long term* effect, due to the negative consequences of subsequent incarceration on offender recidivism (Petersilia, Turner, and Peterson, 1986). In recognition of the New Jersey program's high reincarceration rate, Pearson and Harper (this issue) suggest that what may be needed is a structured hierarchy of sanctions for offender noncompliance with probation conditions, including "increased community service, additional curfew restrictions, and home detention.'' The use of residential community corrections, or halfway houses, is also being considered in New Jersey as a halfway-back mechanism. These recommendations represent an important policy shift, because IPS program developers often have been laboring under the same ''all or nothing'' approach to probation violations that I discussed earlier regarding sentencing strategies.

One final issue pertinent to the appropriate purpose of intensive supervision programs can be identified: whose responsibility is it to locate the offender who *absconds*? In my view, the *location* of absconders is clearly a probation function, and this is true regardless of whether the primary purpose of the organization is viewed as (1) diversion and control, (2) punishment, or (3) recidivism reduction (through deterrence and rehabilitation). However, most programs around the country still view the location and apprehension of absconders as primarily a police function; very few agency resources are directed toward this problem. It will be interesting to see whether the current trend toward increased surveillance and control results in the expansion of probation's role in this area.

## IPS Design and Implementation Issues

There are a variety of issues related to the design and implementation of IPS programs that are raised in the articles included in this special issue. Focusing first on design issues, it is clear that the programs often vary in target population; intake decision-making procedures; and quantity, style, and duration of ''intensive supervision'' (Byrne, et al., 1989). Obviously, any discussion of the effectiveness of the new intensive supervision programs must begin with an important caveat: The key features of these programs are often quite different, including any combination of the following:

- Curfew/house arrest (without electronic monitoring)
- Curfew/house arrest (with electronic monitoring)
- Special conditions established by the Judge (i.e., employment, counseling)
- Team supervision
- Drug and/or alcohol monitoring
- Community service
- Probation fees
- Split sentences/shock incarceration
- Community sponsors

• Restitution

• Objective risk/need assessment

In addition, even programs that appear to be similar may emphasize different aspects of probation practice (e.g., surveillance versus treatment) and/or respond differently to offender noncompliance with particular features of the program. Petersilia and Turner (this issue) highlight this point in their description of intensive supervision at each of their three California sites. While such design diversity is perhaps inevitable in the early stages of the development of intermediate sanctions, it makes it quite difficult to accurately assess "what works, with whom, and why?" For this reason, evaluators of IPS programs should be encouraged to assess not only the *overall* impact of the IPS model under review but also the specific, comparative impact of key elements of the programs.[13]

If there is one *common* element in the current array of IPS programs, it is an emphasis on the surveillance and control of offenders rather than offender treatment. The longer a program has been in operation, the more likely program administrators are to become preoccupied with the "technology" of control (Byrne, Kelly, and Guarino-Ghezzi, 1988). An examination of the brief history of intensive supervision programs reveals that decision makers continue to expand the surveillance components of programs, while treatment components remain fairly constant. For example, both Pearson and Harper (this issue) and Erwin (this issue) point out that *electronic monitoring* has been added as an enhancement to their program model for at least some of the offenders placed under IPS supervision. The assumption of decision makers in these states appears to be that if surveillance was "good," then surveillance via electronic monitoring will be even "better." Unfortunately, Harris's warning that "IPS programs seem to be continually adding new program features, with little concrete evidence [of effectiveness]" has been ignored by most program developers (Harris, 1986; as quoted in Byrne, 1986, p. 14).

In many jurisdictions around the country, the development and implementation of IPS programs represented a drastic departure from traditional probation practice. A comparison of IPS development in New Jersey and Massachusetts highlights these differences. Program developers took two quite different paths to select the line staff needed to implement this shift in orientation: In New Jersey, they recruited and selected probation officers who adhered to this new philosophy; in Massachusetts, they attempted to "change" existing probation officers' attitudes towards the IPS program. In addition to differences in probation officer selection strategies, it is important to keep in mind that while the New Jersey program was established as a special program outside the existing county probation structure, no changes in the organization and administration of probation in Massachusetts were undertaken in order to implement the IPS program. Finally, the probation officers originally involved in the New Jersey program were not unionized, while those involved in the Massachusetts program were.

Given these basic differences, it is not surprising that the level of implementation reported by the New Jersey evaluator (see Pearson, 1987) was much higher than Byrne and Kelly (1989) found in Massachusetts. While it is certainly possible that these differences can be linked to the scope of the process evaluation that was completed at each site,[14] it is more likely that such "resistance to change" was inevitable in Massachusetts, given the philosophical shift involved and the existing organizational structure of the Massachusetts probation system (Cochran, Corbett, and Byrne, 1986). Program developers—who are attempting to (1) utilize existing staff and resources and (2) operate within the framework of existing union contracts and administrative procedures—should anticipate less than perfect implementation during the early stages of IPS development and act accordingly (Corbett, Cochran, Byrne, 1987).

What can program developers do? Petersilia (this issue) addresses this question directly. Based on her experiences as the evaluator of the 11-site IPS demonstration project described earlier, Petersilia has identified nine conditions for the successful implementation of IPS programs:

1. The project addresses a pressing local problem.
2. The project has clearly articulated goals that reflect the needs and desires of the "customer."
3. The project has a receptive environment in both the "parent" organization and the larger system.
4. The organization has a leader who is vitally committed to the objectives, values, and implications of the project and who can devise practical strategies to motivate and effect change.
5. The project has a director who shares the leader's ideas and values, and uses them to guide the implementation process and ongoing operation of the project.
6. Practitioners make the project their own, rather than being coerced into it—that is, they "buy into" it, participate in its development, and have incentives to maintain its integrity during the change process.
7. The project has clear lines of authority; there is not ambiguity about "who is in charge."
8. The change and its implementation are not complex and sweeping.
9. The organization has secure administrators, low staff turnovers, and plentiful resources.

While it is likely that new program initiatives would be more fully implemented if these "conditions for success" were met, it is not at all clear what would occur when one or more of these conditions are not in place. For example, is it impossible to successfully implement an IPS program with *limited resources* or when a fundamental *change in department philosophy* is required? Unfortunately, researchers have generally ignored these basic implementation issues in the current round of IPS evaluations.[15]

An examination of the implementation of state-mandated community corrections policy in Connecticut, Colorado, and Oregon by Michael Musheno and his colleagues represents one important exception. These authors concluded that "the conditions necessary to evoke policy changes that are more than cosmetic occur rarely (Musheno et al., 1989, p. 164). Their recommendations for successful policy change in the community corrections area involve the use of an implementation strategy that appears to be entirely consistent with Etzioni's "humble decision-making" model:

> We argue that getting community corrections to work as an operational program is a continuous process of organizational innovation driven by what we call *transformative rationality*—the sustaining over time of broad policy premises while, simultaneously, engaging in constructive adaptation of these policies to local contexts. It requires adaptive administration and participatory organizations . . . in which "change agents" emerge from various quarters to mobilize commitment to the policy, rank-and-file personnel participate in the decision-making process, and community as well as a broad array of institutional interests play a role in governance [Musheno et al., 1989, p. 137].

It should be fairly obvious from the descriptions of policy/program implementation strategies offered by Petersilia (this issue) and Musheno et al. (1989) that despite the rhetoric of the new intensive supervision movement, large-scale organizational change will be quite slow. Current IPS programs do represent a change in philosophy, but they operate on the margins and do not represent mainstream probation practice in the United States. This is an important point to keep in mind as you consider the following review of the available evidence of IPS program effectiveness.

## Punishment, Diversion, Cost Effectiveness, and Recidivism Reduction

The previous discussion of the debate over the purpose of IPS programs highlighted four important questions that policymakers need answered: (1) Does intensive supervision represent an appropriate *punishment* for offenders, given the availability of other alternatives (e.g., prison versus regular probation)? (2) Do intensive supervision programs *divert* offenders from prison or increase our control over a subgroup of regular probationers? (3) Do intensive supervision programs reduce the overall *cost* of corrections? (4) Does intensive supervision raise or lower the *recidivism* rate among offenders, when compared to other alternatives (e.g., prison versus regular probation)?

The articles included in this special issue provide an overview of the best available research evidence regarding each of these questions. Unfortunately, it is clear from the commentary and conclusions of these authors that, in this instance, "our best has not been good enough." After summarizing what we know now in each impact area, I will suggest a possible agenda for future research and program development efforts in the community corrections area.

**Punishment**

As Andrew von Hirsch (this issue) emphasizes in his analysis of the application of just deserts principles to the emerging intermediate sanctions field, we have simply not focused adequate attention on the question of how much punishment is actually involved in each of these sanctions. Moreover, we have tended to ignore the equally important issue of the proportionality of these "punishments" to the seriousness of the crime. According to von Hirsch (this issue),

> The disregard of proportionality has reinforced a tendency to assess community-based sanctions principally in terms of their effectiveness. If a program (say, an intensive supervision scheme) seems to "work" in the sense of its participants having a low rate of return to crime, then it is said to be a good program. Seldom considered are questions of the sanction's severity, and of the seriousness of the crimes of those recruited into the program.

Perhaps the best way to get a "fix" on questions concerning intermediate punishment severity and proportionality is to consider the response of both the *public* and the *offender* to these new intermediate sanctions. Byrne (1989, p. 482) has observed that "the public is ambivalent about current correctional strategies, but unsure of how to proceed." While there has been little good research published to date on how the public views these new intermediate sanctions,[16] it appears that policymakers vastly overrate the public's support for punishment as an appropriate sentencing goal in and of itself (Cullen, Cullen, and Wozniak, 1988; Gottfredson and Taylor, 1983). It is more likely that punishment is viewed by the public as a *means* to an end—safer communities—and that if this current round of sanctioning does not achieve this goal, the cycle of new reform will begin anew (Byrne, 1989). The public expects more out of intermediate sanctions than just deserts; like it or not, the use of punishment as a sanctioning strategy has been inexorably linked both by policymakers and the public to the goal of recidivism reduction. The task for just deserts advocates is to convince the public that the development of fair, proportionate punishments in no way compromises their legitimate desire for community protection from those offenders who we do catch and convict.

How do *offenders* view intensive probation supervision and other intermediate sanctions? The answer to this question is that "it depends." If the offender anticipated a traditional probation sentence, there is little doubt that he or she would view intensive supervision as a more punitive sanction. However, it is not entirely clear whether an IPS sanction is viewed by offenders as more or less punishment than a period of confinement (Pearson, 1987; Petersilia, 1989). Two factors appear to affect the offender's perception of the relative severity of IPS and incarceration: the length of the initial prison/jail term involved, and the certainty and severity of the system's response to offender noncompliance with probation conditions. Given the number and type of probation conditions that are established for IPS offenders (e.g., random drug/alcohol testing, mandatory treatment, community service, fines) and the practice in some courts of *punishing* offenders who violate these conditions by giving them longer incarceration sentences than they would have received originally (Clear, Flynn, and Shapiro, 1987), it is not surprising that *more than a few offenders would rather do the time and get it over with.* Petersilia (1989, p. 15) highlights this point in a recent discussion of the "lessons learned" from implementing random experiments at 11 separate sites. In one of these sites—Marion County, Oregon—convicted offenders were randomly assigned to either prison or intensive supervision. The group of offenders who were assigned to the IPS program ". . . were asked to sign a form "waiving" their prison term in lieu of the [IPS] program. Much to everyone's surprise, about 25% of the offenders chose prison over the [IPS] program!" It appears that some offenders would rather *interrupt* their lifestyle (via incarceration) than deal with attempts to *change* it (via compliance with probation conditions). While it would be a mistake to generalize to all potential IPS participants from a single study, it seems certain that the offender's view of the relative punitiveness of intensive supervision is contingent on a variety of factors: (1) The specific sentence the offender anticipated (e.g., prison versus probation). (2) The number and type of special conditions imposed. (3) The track record of the agency in detecting violations and imposing subsequent sanctions. As von Hirsch (this issue) and Clear (1987) have observed, the *fairness* of this new wave of intermediate sanctions will ultimately depend on how policymakers and program developers decide to address these issues.

### Diversion and Cost Effectiveness

It is one thing to develop IPS programs with the stated purpose of *diversion* from prison or jail, resulting in *cost savings* for taxpayers; it is quite another to implement programs that do, in fact, divert offenders and save money. A review of the available research on intensive supervision dramatically underscores this point, while also highlighting the dangers inherent in publicizing the results of preliminary evaluations. Tonry (this issue) provides a detailed critique of the initial claims of diversion and cost effectiveness espoused by both IPS program developers and evaluators. He concludes that "those [intensive supervision] programs that have been evaluated do not . . . significantly reduce prison crowding, or save much (if any) money, though they do seem often to deliver the punitive, intrusive sanctioning experience that their proponents promise." The irony is that we deliver an intermediate *punishment* to offenders who often pose less serious risks than those on traditional probation supervision (Clear, this issue). When the high revocation/return to prison rates of these (comparatively) "low risk," nonprison-bound offenders are considered, the accuracy of von Hirsch's assessment of this new wave of noncustodial sanctions becomes apparent: "It is precisely when we seem to ourselves to be 'doing good' for offenders that we need most to safeguard their rights" (von Hirsch, this issue).

Perhaps the fairest statement that can be made about the current wave of IPS programs is that until decision makers clarify their primary purpose, these programs will continue to divert some offenders from prison, while simultaneously widening the net of social control over others. Baird (this issue) argues that at least some net-widening is inevitable when diversionary programs are implemented. After evaluating the "front-end" diversionary impact[17] of the Florida Community Control Program (FCCP), Baird (1988, p.30) concluded that "Our most rigorous test of program impact indicated that over 50% of FCCP placements were diversions from prison. Given the rather grim record of alternative programs, a diversion rate that exceeds 50% constitutes an unqualified success."

Baird's findings highlight the dilemmas inherent in the development of a full range of intermediate sanctions. In order to justify a *policy* of diversion from prison and jail, we design programs that attempt to provide the incapacitation effects of these institutions in community settings (at a lower cost than institutionalization, of course). But in actual *practice*, we place into these programs a considerable number of non prison-bound offenders who neither deserve the punishment (von Hirsch, this issue) nor need the control these programs provide (Clear, this issue). It should be obvious that the further expansion of intensive supervision and other intermediate sanctions cannot be justified in terms of the cost effectiveness and diversionary impact of the *current* wave of IPS programs.

### Recidivism Reduction

Although the public is certainly interested in such issues as punishment proportionality, diversion versus net-widening, and the cost of corrections, it appears that community protection may be their overriding concern (Byrne, 1989). Because only a relatively small number of the offenders in any community are arrested, prosecuted, convicted, and sentenced, the public is likely to be more interested in the crime (and/or victimization) rate in their own community than in the results of any evaluation of correctional effectiveness. It should go without saying that it is possible for a community to have a serious crime problem *regardless* of the quality of its correctional system. Nonetheless, the conclusions of highly *publicized* studies do have an impact on the public in general and on legislators/legal decision makers in particular. The problem is that in some cases, these studies are "too flawed or limited to serve as a reliable guide to legal decision making" (Sherman and Cohn, 1989, p. 117). Unfortunately, no one seems to remember to point this out until policies have already been changed. Sherman and Cohn (1989, pp. 117-118) offer the following examples:

1. The Martinson (1974) and Lipton et al. (1975) research on the ineffectiveness of rehabilitation, for example, was widely cited by policy-making opponents of rehabilitative programs yet attacked by correctional researchers for concluding too much from too little evidence [see Sechrest, White, and Brown, 1979, p.34].

2. The Greenwood (1982) scale of predictive factors for selective incapacitation was apparently quite influential among criminal sentencing decision makers, but researchers criticized it as being too often inaccurate [Blumstein et al., 1986, p.180].

3. The Kansas City Preventive Patrol Experiment (Kelling et al., 1974) has been widely discussed in decisions about police staffing levels but criticized by researchers as being too weak a test of the deterrent value of patrol (Larson, 1975; Fienberg et al., 1976; Sherman, 1986a, pp. 362-364). All three studies received substantial press attention when they were released.

Even more recently, the publicity surrounding the release of the results of the Minneapolis Domestic Violence Experiment has resulted in changes in domestic violence arrest policies in a number of states that critics argue may have been premature. Garner and Visher (1988, p. 2) highlighted this issue in a recent issue of *NIJ Reports*: "The findings received considerable publicity and have been used to support adoption of a "pro-arrest" policy in misdemeanor spouse assault cases. In fact, there is some concern that this single experiment from one jurisdiction has been accepted too readily by too many agencies." The positive results of the initial evaluations (i.e., diversion, cost effectiveness, and low recidivism rates) of IPS in Georgia and New Jersey have also been highly publicized (e.g., Erwin and Bennett, 1987), resulting in these two "models" being utilized by state and local probation departments across the country (Byrne et al., 1989). In addition, both Georgia (see Erwin, this issue) and New Jersey (see Pearson and Harper, this issue) used these initial evaluation results to justify expansion of both program technology (e.g., electronic monitoring at both sites) and target populations (e.g., IPS for juvenile offenders).

My concern is that the initial claims of recidivism reduction are not supported either by a critical review of evaluation results (see Tonry, this issue; Tonry & Will, 1988; Byrne, et al., 1989) or the initial findings from the 11-site randomized field experiment by Petersilia and her colleagues (this issue). When taken together, the results point to only one conclusion: The current emphasis of IPS programs on *surveillance* cannot be justified based on a goal of recidivism reduction. An examination of the level of implementation of the original IPS model at each of the three California sites is revealing: While there were significant differences between treatment and control groups in the key *surveillance* components—average number of face-to-face contacts, collateral contacts, and drug tests—across all three sites, similar significant differences in the two treatment components—counseling and employment—were found at only one site (Contra Costa). And even there, only the percentage of offenders receiving counseling was significantly higher in the experimental group. Petersilia and Turner (this issue) also pointed out that "about 50% of the offenders were identified as needing drug treatment. Yet, very few received such treatment. It is thus not surprising that a significant portion of all new incidents [arrests] involved drugs." These results certainly challenge the notion that all we have to do is watch offenders more closely to reduce recidivism. According to Petersilia and Turner (this issue): "All that intensive supervision does is monitor offenders' success or failure in meeting the conditions [of IPS]. It has no apparent effect on recidivism. With minimal monitoring, regular probation has no worse recidivism rates [than IPS]. Given how much more expensive it is than probation, why do we need something that does nothing more than take its own pulse?"

It would be a mistake to infer too much from these preliminary results, which are based only on a six-month follow-up period at only three of the eleven study sites. However, it should be obvious that we appear to have once again underestimated the importance of treatment as a crime reduction strategy (Clear and O'Leary, 1983; Gendreau and Ross, 1987).

The results from the evaluation of the Massachusetts IPS program (Byrne and Kelly, 1989) underscore the need for surveillance (i.e., contacts), control (i.e., enforcement of probation conditions), and treatment (i.e., in the areas of substance abuse, employment, and/or marital/family relationships) if intensive supervision programs are to be effective in reducing offender recidivism. Based on their evaluation of the Massachusetts IPS program, the authors conclude that

> The profiles of successful and unsuccessful high risk offenders . . . certainly underscore the importance of treatment to successful probation practice. But the findings we presented also suggest that the deterrent aspects of probation—surveillance and control—are important to recidivism reduction, due in large part to their effects on an intermediate outcome—offender rehabilitation.

Byrne and Kelly (1989) have also analyzed the impact of split sentences and/or a recent period of incarceration (in the year prior to disposition) on IPS and non-IPS offenders. Their findings underscore the negative impact of incarceration on high-risk offenders (see also Petersilia, et al., 1986), while also challenging Tonry's (this issue) contention that "all [IPS] programs that divert offenders from prison should increase crime victimization." In fact, it appears that any estimates of the comparative effects of prison versus IPS are affected by two basic factors: the length of the prison/jail term to be served, and the length of the follow-up period used by evaluators (Petersilia, et al., 1986).

The findings reported by both Byrne and Kelly (1989) and by Petersilia and Turner (this issue) suggest that it is time to reconsider the respective roles of rehabilitation and surveillance in IPS programs.[18] However, we must emphasize the preliminary nature of these findings and the need for a comprehensive assessment of the rehabilitative and deterrent effects of IPS. Up to this point, our attention has been focused on evaluating the effectiveness of increased *surveillance* in community settings. It is time now to evaluate the effectiveness of increased offender *treatment* (e.g., substance abuse, employment, and family problems) in these same community settings, both alone and in combination with closer surveillance. Such evaluations must explicitly incorporate measures of community context into their designs, along with traditional measures of surveillance and treatment (Byrne, 1989).

## The Future of IPS and the New Intermediate Sanctions

The articles included in this special issue have highlighted three issues that policymakers will have to address in the 1990s: the proportionality of the new intermediate sanctions, the development of probation-based strategies to strengthen *informal* social control mechanisms, and the role of probation in community change efforts. The first issue policymakers must consider is whether we should continue to "muddle through" our correctional crowding crisis rather than attempt a broad reassessment of current sentencing policy. As Musheno et al. (1989, p. 136) recently observed,

> Most U.S. states are well into the second decade of massive reinvestment in prisons for incapacitating adult felons as the mainstay of their correctional policies. In these states, politicians and executives of the criminal justice system have institutionalized incapacitation as the sole, legitimate goal of corrections to harmonize their get-tough-on crime recitations, now embedded in the public ethos, with the formal intent of corrections.

The irony of Musheno and his colleagues' assessment of our current reliance on the *philosophy* of incapacitation will not be lost on anyone with even the most rudimentary knowledge of U.S. sentencing *practices*: Despite the increased use of incarceration, most convicted offenders are still placed on probation. A recent report on felony sentencing in 18 local jurisdictions by the Bureau of Justice Statistics (1985) revealed that for the most serious offense categories (homicide, rape, robbery) the majority of convicted offenders received a prison term. However, convicted felons in the remaining offense categories (aggravated assault, burglary, larceny, drug trafficking) were more likely to receive either a straight probation sentence or a split sentence, including a period of time in jail followed by probation supervision.[19] Because the bulk of offenders who pass through our courts are convicted of either these less serious felonies or a range of misdemeanors, it is not surprising that two-thirds of the offenders under correctional control in 1987 were on probation. But what we have failed to consider is that while we have *incarcerated* more "serious" offenders in recent years, we have also been increasing the use of formal *probation* for less serious offenders (Byrne et al., 1989). The result, as we mentioned earlier, is a community corrections system that is currently growing at a faster pace than the institutional corrections system (Byrne, 1989).

Our current correctional crowding crisis has forced policymakers to reassess their use of incarceration and to consider the development of such alternatives to incarceration as intensive supervision, house arrest (with and without electronic monitoring), split sentencing (or shock incarceration), and residential community corrections.[20] However, we have not given sufficient thought to the development of an equally creative set of alternatives to traditional probation supervision, including—but not limited to—the use of day fines, community service orders, and restitution (Wasik and von Hirsch, 1988; von Hirsch, Wasik, and Green, 1989; Byrne, 1989). Because our tendency at *both* ends of the sentencing scale has been to "mix and match" these various alternatives, any assessment of punishment severity is currently quite difficult, if not impossible. Before we can begin to move toward the system of "proportionate" sanctions that von Hirsch (this issue) proposes, we must attempt to (1) disentangle these sanctions and (2) rank their severity. Figure 1 offers one possible starting point for this effort, focusing on the need to distinguish, in terms of the level of punishment, between (and among) various alternative sanctions. A number of other observers have offered similar rank-ordered sanctions in recent years (e.g., Petersilia, 1987; O'Leary and Clear, 1984), only to find that judges, legislators, and guidelines commissions have generally ignored their recommendations (Tonry, 1987).

Figure 1

**A Range of Sentencing Options, Ranked by the Level of Punishment**

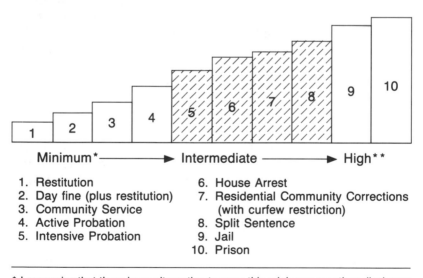

Minimum*————▶ Intermediate ————▶ High**

1. Restitution
2. Day fine (plus restitution)
3. Community Service
4. Active Probation
5. Intensive Probation
6. House Arrest
7. Residential Community Corrections (with curfew restriction)
8. Split Sentence
9. Jail
10. Prison

* I recognize that there is an alternative to even this minimum sanction: discharge (absolute and conditional).

** The distinction between prison and jail is based solely on sentence length (i.e., actual time to be served).

Figure 2 represents the typical *sanction stacking* that is associated with the current wave of intermediate sanctions. My point is simple: We need to treat each of these sanctions as unique rather than as elements of a single, comprehensive intermediate sanction. Unless we can agree on the level of punishment involved in each of these sanctions, any discussion of such related topics as punishment proportionality, exchange rates (e.g., 10 days in jail equals 3 months on intensive supervision), and/or sanctioning units would be an exercise in frustration (Morris and Tonry, 1990).

Given the track record of the current wave of intermediate sanctions, I agree with Tonry's conclusion that until new techniques for structured decision making (e.g., sentencing guidelines) are introduced, judges in many states will continue to use these intermediate sanctions as a net-widening device, while simultaneously expanding the use of regular probation. According to Tonry (this issue):

> . . . Until the time comes, as it will, when sentencing guidelines or other approaches to structuring judicial discretion are implemented in most states, including within their scope a full range of punishments of graded severity, it is unlikely that these mid-range punishments will be preponderantly used for the mid-range offenders for whom in principle they are designed. Until that day, judges who

## Figure 2

### Two Examples of Typical "Sanction Stacking" that Occurs Both with Regular Probation and the New Wave of Intermediate Sanctions

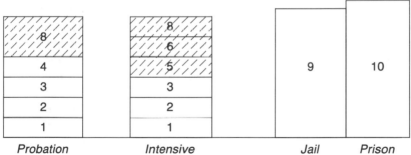

| Probation | Intensive Supervision | Jail | Prison |

1. Restitution
2. Day fine (plus restitution)
3. Community Service
4. Active Probation
5. Intensive Probation
6. House Arrest

7. Residential Community Corrections
   (with curfew restriction)
8. Split Sentence
9. Jail
10. Prison

are frustrated by the lack of rigor of ordinary probation are likely to use newer intermediate punishments for the more villainous among the probation-bound rather than for the less villainous among the prison-bound for whom, in public declaration they are designed.

There is an added advantage to the development of a range of distinct (rank-ordered) sanctions: these same sanctions can be used to respond quickly and decisively to evidence of offender noncompliance. As both Clear (1987) and Morris (1987) have emphasized, we not only need to *limit* the use of conditions, but also to *enforce* the conditions we impose. O'Leary and Clear's (1984) "limited risk control" model offers one possible strategy for establishing necessary probation conditions, based on objective risk/need classification. However, we need to improve our techniques for both risk (Clear, 1988) and need (Duffee and Clark, 1985) classification, while also developing a consistent sanctioning policy for noncompliance, before we can fully utilize this decision-making strategy.

A second issue emerges from a review of these articles: *How do we convince policymakers that it is useless to focus only on techniques for the formal social control of offenders?* The articles included in this special issue do not support the assumption that increased surveillance and control translates into increased community protection. However, it is likely that Petersilia and Turner echo the response of many program developers when they suggest that if the technical violation/return to prison rates had been *higher* for the intensive supervision cases at their three test sites, "then the arrest rates for [intensive supervision] would have been much lower than the rates for probation." The authors go on to point out the only real impediment to this strategy—the high cost of prison crowding. I suspect that at least some of the newer IPS programs will move quickly in this direction, while others will expand their surveillance capability even further (see Pearson and Harper, this issue).

It is my contention that both strategies—increased surveillance and/or increased control over offender noncompliance with technical conditions—are self-defeating because they ignore the underlying problems of offenders and communities. Moreover, while efforts to combine the rehabilitative and *formal* deterrent elements of IPS programs may represent a step in the right direction (Wilson, 1986; Byrne and Kelly, 1989), they also provide an inadequate framework for understanding the impact of the various aspects of community context— attitudes, tolerance, community structure/organization, and support (i.e., resource availability)—on offender behavior (Byrne, 1989). According to Gottfredson and Hirschi (1988, p. 209), we may have our greatest recidivism reduction effect by focusing limited correctional resources on improving informal social controls among young offenders:

> . . . Crime primarily occurs among youth (and it is there that it must
> be prevented), and . . . it occurs primarily in the absence of restraints.
> *The restraints traditionally come from a variety of sources, only one*
> *of which is the criminal justice system.* Deterrence research has erred
> in thinking that the state alone provides the restraints necessary to
> prevent law violation among children, and incapacitation research
> has erred in thinking that the state can reasonably consider control-
> ling crime by simply locking up its children. [emphasis added]

Of course, Gottfredson and Hirschi's discussion of the need to improve
informal social control mechanisms among *young* offenders begs the
question of appropriate *adult* offender control strategies in a manner
similar to the identification of the "30-year-old career criminal" by
selective incapacitation advocates. Nonetheless, it is difficult to argue
with their contention that we need to (1) recognize the limits of formal
control strategies and (2) be more creative in developing techniques for
strengthening informal restraints. The type of informal *controls* to which
Gottfredson and Hirschi refer are a consequence of interactions with
family, job, friends, and community. Not surprisingly, these are the
traditional areas for probation officer interventions, utilizing (1)
diagnostic skills, (2) brokerage skills, and (3) advocacy skills (Byrne,
1989). But since the 1980s, decision makers in many states have deem-
phasized this approach to high-risk offenders, preferring instead to focus
on increasing the level of offender surveillance and control.

By utilizing formal deterrence in this manner (see Smith and Gartin,
1989, for an overview), we may have undermined the potential of
another, even more powerful, deterrent strategy: the relationship
between the probation officer and the offender. Braswell (1989, p. 51)
has lamented the lost art of relationships: "More than any specific
systemic approach to treating offenders, it seems [that] the quality and
credibility of relationships offenders have with treatment staff and significant others may well have the greater correctional influence." IPS
programs may be important *not* for the surveillance and control afforded
offenders but for the relationships that develop as a result of closer
contact. In our rush to embrace this new wave of intermediate sanctions,
we have not adequately considered the implications of this basic change
in the probation officer-offender relationship for subsequent offender
recidivism. If Braswell is correct, closer contacts that lead to a strong
relationship between offenders and probation officers have a greater
deterrent effect than an equal number of surveillance contacts that do
not involve such close interaction. Stronger ties appear much more likely
when the probation officer views his or her role in terms of such outcomes as, for example, (1) improved marital/family relationships
(Edelman, 1987; Laub and Sampson, 1988) and (2) improved employment prospects (Orsagh and Marsden, 1984, 1985, 1987; McGahey,

1988). In many cases improvement in both these areas is related to the identification and treatment of the offender's substance abuse problem (Byrne and Kelly, 1989). Thus, a focus on individual offender treatment may result in increased community control through the strengthening of informal restraints. If this is correct, then the intermediate sanction programs of the 1990s need to focus on *informal* — rather than formal — deterrence mechanisms.

One final issue that needs to be addressed is *the extent of the advocacy role for probation officers involved in intensive supervision programs.* Erwin (this issue) highlights the need for advocacy in her discussion of the lack of treatment programs in Georgia for offenders with drug/alcohol problems:

> The development of treatment resources has simply not been commensurate with the need both in institutional drug treatment programming and in the area of community-based alternatives. . . . It was clear that the levels of need found in many cases were not matched by available treatment slots for specialized treatment either on an in-patient or out-patient basis. This problem was particularly acute in the metropolitan Atlanta area, where officers stated that out of 15 cases needing specialized treatment at any given time, there may be two available slots provided by the existing treatment resources. *Substance abusers provide us with a clear example of the false economy involved in focusing on surveillance and control without giving attention to underlying needs.* [author's emphasis]

Inadequate treatment resources were also cited by the evaluators of the Massachusetts IPS program. Byrne and Kelly (1989) cited a review conducted by Spangenberg Associates (1987, p. 110) of the rehabilitative services available to probation departments: ". . . only a patchwork system of social services within and outside the probation system has been developed in the Commonwealth." The result of this resource shortfall is that IPS offenders must comply with probation conditions while awaiting treatment for substance abuse, individual/family problems, and/or educational/employment problems. The longer the waiting period, the more difficult compliance becomes. When probation officers in Massachusetts were asked which types of programs were actually needed they identified (1) mental health services, (2) substance abuse counseling, (3) urinalysis programs, and (4) job counseling and placement (Spangenberg Associates, 1987, p. 111). Unfortunately, the current fiscal crisis in Massachusetts — and in many other states as well — has resulted in even more cuts in these programs, which translates into fewer treatment options for offenders.

The initial results of the randomized field experiments in California, in conjunction with the assessment of treatment availability in Georgia, and treatment *effects* in Massachusetts, suggest what many probation officers probably knew all along: (1) you cannot change these offenders' behavior unless you address their (usually long-standing) problems, and (2) individual offender problems must be addressed in the broader contexts of lifestyles and communities (Hagan and Palloni, 1988). In this regard, the research on both person-environment interactions (e.g., Gottfredson and Taylor, 1986) and the community context of crime (e.g., Reiss and Tonry, 1986; Stark, 1987; Bursik, 1988; Currie, 1989) has much to offer the field of community corrections, because it underscores the need for probation to become involved in efforts to change both offenders *and* communities (Reiss, 1986).

In my discussion of the results of the Massachusetts IPS evaluation, I have suggested a four-part strategy for reintegrating the concept of community into community-based corrections:

1.  The coordination and development of community resources to assist offenders with problems in the areas of substance abuse, employment/ education, and marital/family relations.
2.  The generation of support for the de-escalation of both community-based and institution-based sanctions.
3.  A focus on the problems and needs of communities as well as offenders.
4.  The direct placement of probation officer teams in neighborhoods, with responsibility for resource development (as well as offender control) within a specific geographic area. [Byrne, 1989:474-475]

Whether we move toward, — or further away from — the community-oriented offender "control" strategy advocated above will certainly be affected by the response of policymakers to the current wave of research on intensive supervision that is highlighted in this special issue. If federal, state, and local policymakers decide that a "humble decision-making" approach to sentencing and community corrections is appropriate, then the continued development of intermediate sanctions will be based on a comprehensive reassessment of the community context of current sanctioning policy. As part of this reassessment process, researchers and practitioners will have to work together to develop and implement a series of evaluations on a full range of *formal* sanctions and *informal* restraints (Gottfredson and Hirschi, 1988). The results of this evaluation effort, if developed correctly, should result in specific strategies not only for punishing and controlling *individual* offenders but also for changing the *communities* in which these offenders reside. Currie (1989, p. 11) offers his perspective on the task before us:

> I suggest that the approach we need toward crime in the coming decades might be called "social-environmental" — or, to resurrect an older term, "human-ecological." By that I mean a strategy which includes interventions on the level of individuals and families "at

risk,'' but also moves beyond that level to exert social control over those larger forces which are now increasingly undermining communities and placing families at risk in the first place. . . . Such an approach, moreover, should raise questions not simply about *what* forces in our society need controlling, but also *who* may decide and who is held responsible for the consequences of those decisions. *If we think of the era of liberal criminology as the first stage of recent criminological thinking and consider the conservative revolution as the second, such a social-environmental vision can serve as the bedrock for a third, more sophisticated stage which both builds upon and transcends the stages that came before* [emphasis in original].

If Currie is correct, the current wave of surveillance-oriented intermediate sanctions may very well disappear in the next few years. But if they do, they will still have served an important function: To provide a bridge between the focus of the 1980s on *incapacitation* and a focus of the 1990s on the problem of both offender and community control. The evaluation results included in this special issue provide ample evidence that it is now time to cross that bridge into a new decade of community-based program development efforts.

## Notes

[1] Byrne, Lurigio and Baird (1989) provide a detailed analysis of the causes of correctional crowding in this country. They point out that the probation and parole populations have increased at a slightly *faster* rate than the prison and jail populations during the 1980s. See also Skovron (1988), Tonry and Will (1988), and Byrne and Kelly (1989).

[2] Rossi and Freeman (1982) argue that "the political context" in which *any* research effort takes place can effect the objectivity. and thus the quality, of the resulting evaluation. They point out that the gap in quality between external and interval evaluations has narrowed considerably in recent years.

[3] Program "sponsors" obviously exist at the federal, state, and local levels. Focusing on federal-level sponsors, Petersilia (1989) offers an interesting analysis of the implementation of the 11 BJA-sponsored demonstration programs, which often varied from site to site in specific design features. See also the "program brief' on Intensive Supervision Programs (U.S. Department of Justice, 1987) for a description of both the Georgia and New Jersey models. Examples of IPS program initiatives sponsored at the *state* level include the New Jersey program, established by the Administrative Office of the Courts; and the Massachusetts IPS program, established as an 18-month "pilot project" by the Office of the Commissioner of Probation. A variety of local IPS programs have also been developed without state and/or federal support.

[4] Evaluations have also been sponsored by *other* federal agencies. For example, the U.S. General Accounting Office (GAO) is currently completing an assessment of the effectiveness of the new wave of intermediate sanctions, which is likely to include at least one GAO-sponsored evaluation. In addition, researchers have received support from private foundations with clear political agendas (e.g., the Edna McConnell Clark Foundation). But the typical evaluation in this area has been completed for a state agency by an *in-house* evaluation unit (e.g., Georgia's IPS evaluation was conducted by Billie Erwin, currently the Chief of Evaluation, Georgia Department of Corrections).

[5] In-house evaluators are affected by a somewhat different set of factors. See Twain (1983) and Rossi and Freeman (1982) for a complete discussion of the sociopolitical context of evaluation research.

[6] There are exceptions to this rule. For example, external evaluators who live and/or work in the particular state in which the evaluation was conducted have a different stake, in both the local media coverage and ongoing policy debate.

[7] Petersilia (1989) points out that "because each site was allowed to individualize the ISP model, no two projects are identical. In a very real sense, RAND is evaluating eleven different programs." Intersite variations were identified in (1) the target population, (2) design elements (e.g., electronic monitoring, drug testing, mandatory treatment), (3) length of intensive supervision phase, and (4) revocation policy.

[8] I do not agree with Petersilia and Turner's assertion (this issue) that because "there was never any random assignment to IPSs in the previous work . . . comparisons of IPS and probation or parole outcomes were irrelevant, if not invidious." A review of the controversy surrounding the last highly publicized field experiment—the Minneapolis Domestic Violence Experiment—should remind readers that there are "minefields" in both quasi-experimental and experimental research. See Sherman and Cohn (1989), Sherman and Berk (1984), Garner and Visher (1988), and Binder and Meeker (1988) for a good discussion of this issue. More generally, see Farrington (1983) and Visher (1988).

[9] External validity is further limited by the lack of actual replications. What we have are eleven small and different randomized field experiments. The most promising of these pilot projects will need to be replicated at a variety of sites across the country before we can assess external validity issues further.

[10] Both Patton (1978) and Twain (1983) offer recommendations involving techniques for improving the quality of in-house evaluation units, but the issue of randomized field experiments is not directly addressed. Garner and Visher (1988, p. 7) suggest that a "team approach" between external researchers and practitioners is crucial for the successful completion of an experimental evaluation of a criminal justice policy issue.

[11] I do not attempt to trace the changes in criminal justice policy during the last three decades that have culminated in our current preoccupation with an incapacitation philosophy, but see von Hirsch (1985) and Gottfredson and Hirschi (1988) for a more complete discussion. Tonry (this issue) highlights the futility of this "diversion plus control" approach in his assessment of the likely impact of IPS programs that divert the crime/victimization rates of communities.

[12] The unfortunate problem with this strategy is that because the evaluation research on probation effectiveness is so poor, we don't know which activities are related directly to recidivism reduction. However, an evaluation by Byrne and Kelly (1989) suggests that special conditions can be justified, based on the goal of recidivism reduction, in three areas: employment, substance abuse, and marital/family relationships.

[13] Due to resource and time constraints, detailed data on program implementation may not be collected on individual offenders. For example, Pearson's evaluation of the implementation of the New Jersey intensive supervision program was based on monthly summary reports of the number of offenders employed, in treatment, etc.; no individual-level implementation data were included in the evaluation, precluding any assessment of which specific elements of the program worked (i.e., reduced recidivism). See Pearson (1987,1988) and Pearson and Harper (this issue). In addition, detailed data on the treatment of offenders in control groups are also not collected, leaving the reader to surmise what actually occurred in the proverbial "black box."

[14] Byrne and Kelly (1989) have completed one of the most comprehensive implementation evaluations conducted to date, in which they compare changes in probation practices in experimental and control courts over time (pretest versus posttest). Unfortunately,

cost and time constraints appear to have limited the collection of similar data in other IPS evaluations.

[15] Focusing on the implementation of intensive supervision in Massachusetts, the issue of "resistance to change" is addressed by Cochran, Corbett, and Byrne (1986), while a general strategy for introducing and implementing major policy changes in organizations is offered by Corbett, Cochran, and Byrne (1987).

[16] A sampling of recent public opinion regarding (1) the use of imprisonment, (2) the role of probation and parole, and (3) possible solutions to the prison crowding problem can be found in the latest *Sourcebook of Criminal Justice Statistics* (e.g., Jamieson and Flannagan, 1989). Durham (1989, p. 75) recently presented results that "suggest question type may indeed have an effect on the character of the punishment identified as appropriate by respondents." Perhaps the best assessment of public opinion in the area of intermediate sanctions has been offered by Cullen, Clark, and Wozniak (1985, p. 22): "The public "will" . . . is much more complex and tolerant than politicians acknowledge."

[17] Baird's evaluation (see Baird, this issue; and Baird, 1988) focuses exclusively on the group of offenders in Florida's Community Control Program who were diverted to the program at sentencing, even though the program also serves as a *halfway-back* mechanism for probation violators. An assessment of possible *back-end* diversionary effects will be included in the next phase of the evaluation, along with an examination of subsequent recidivism (and return to prison) rates across three groups of offenders (prison, community control, probation). Until this second phase of the evaluation is completed, any discussion of the overall diversionary impact of the program would be misleading.

[18] The reader should bear in mind that these two studies have not received the same careful scrutiny afforded earlier evaluations in Georgia (Erwin, 1987) and New Jersey (Pearson, 1987, 1988).

[19] According to a *BJS Special Report* (1985, Table 1, p. 3), the proportion of convicted felons receiving prison terms was as follows: homicide (85%), rape (69%), robbery (65%), aggravated assault (39%), burglary (46%). larceny (29%), and drug trafficking (23%). The authors explain the low percentage of drug traffickers sent to prison by pointing out that "many of the drug cases involve small-time dealers" (*BJS Special Report*, p. 2).

[20] See the review of these alternatives by Byrne, Lurigio, and Baird (1989) and Tonry and Will (1988). Perhaps the best available research on shock probation has been conducted by Latessa and Vito (1988). See also the reviews by the U.S. General Accounting Office (1988) and Parent (1989). Lauen (1988) offers a comprehensive assessment of residential community corrections programs.

## References

Albanese, Jay S., Bernadette A. Fiore, Jerie H. Powell, and Janet R. Storti. 1980. *Is Probation Working?* Washington, DC: University of America Press.

Baird, Christopher. 1988. *Analysis of the Diversionary Impact of the Florida Community Control Program: Preliminary Report.* Madison, WI: National Council on Crime and Delinquency.

Banks, J., A. L. Porter, R. L. Rardin, T. R. Silver, and V. E. Unger. 1977. *Summary Phase I Evaluation of Intensive Special Probation Project*, Washington, DC: National Institute of Law Enforcement and Criminal Justice.

Bennett, Lawrence A. 1987a. "A Reassessment of Intensive Service Probation," In *Intermediate Punishments: Intensive Supervision, Home Confinement, and Electronic Surveillance*, edited by B. McCarthy. Monsey, NY: Criminal Justice Press.

Bennett, Lawrence A. 1987b. *Practice in Search of a Theory: The Case of Intensive Supervision — An Extension of an Old Practice or a New Approach?* Washington, DC: National Institute of Justice, U.S. Department of Justice.

Binder, Arnold and James M. Meeker. 1988. "Experiments as Reforms," *Journal of Criminal Justice* 16(4):347-58.

Blumstein, Alfred, Jacqueline Cohen, Jeffrey A. Roth, and Christy A. Visher, eds. 1986. *Criminal Careers and "Career Criminals".* Washington, DC: National Academy Press.

Braswell, Michael C. 1989. "Correctional Treatment and the Human Spirit: A Focus on Relationship." *Federal Probation* 53(2):49-60.

Bureau of Justice Statistics. 1985. *Felony Sentencing in 18 Local Jurisdictions,* Washington, DC: U.S. Department of Justice.

_____. 1988a. "Prisoners in 1987." *BJS Bulletin.* Washington, DC: U.S. Department of Justice.

_____. 1988b. "Probation and Parole 1987." *BJS Bulletin.* Washington, DC: U.S. Department of Justice.

Bursik, Robert J., Jr. 1988. "Social Disorganization and Theories of Crime and Delinquency: Problems and Prospects." *Criminology* 26(4):519-52.

Byrne, James M. 1986. "The Control Controversy: A Preliminary Examination of Intensive Probation Supervision Programs in the United States." *Federal Probation* 50:4-16.

_____. 1989. "Reintegrating the Concept of Community Into Community-Based Corrections." *Crime and Delinquency* 35:471-99.

Byrne, James M. and Linda Kelly. 1989. *Restructuring Probation as an Intermediate Sanction: An Evaluation of the Massachusetts Intensive Probation Supervision Program* (Final Report to the National Institute of Justice, U.S. Department of Justice, Research Program on the Punishment and Control of Offenders). Washington, DC.

Byrne, James M., Linda Kelly, and Susan Guarino-Ghezzi. 1988. "Understanding the Limits of Technology: An Examination of the Use of Electronic Monitoring in the Criminal Justice System." *Perspectives* Spring:30-36.

Byrne, James M., Arthur Lurigio, and Christopher Baird. 1989. "The Effectiveness of the 'New' Intensive Supervision Programs." *Research in Corrections* 5:1-70.

Champion, Dean J. 1988. "Felony Plea Bargaining and Probation: A Growing Judicial and Prosecutorial Dilemma." *Journal of Criminal Justice* 16(4):291-302.

Clear, Todd R. 1987. "Helping, Punishing and Controlling: The Use (and Misuse) of Conditions in Community Supervision." Paper presented to the American Society of Criminology, Montreal, Canada, November.

_____. 1988. "Statistical Prediction in Corrections." *Research in Corrections* 1(1):1-40.

Clear, Todd R., Suzanne Flynn. and Carol Shapiro. 1987. "Intensive Supervision in Probation: A Comparison of Three Projects." In *Intermediate Punishments: Intensive Supervision Home Confinement and Electronic Surveillance,* edited by B. McCarthy. Monsey, NY: Willow Tree Press.

Clear, Todd R. and Vincent O'Leary. 1983. *Controlling the Offender in the Community.* Lexington, MA: Lexington.

Cochran, Donald, Ronald B. Corbett, Jr., and James M. Byrne. 1986. "Intensive Probation Supervision in Massachusetts: A Case Study in Change." *Federal Probation* 50:32-41.

Corbett, Ronald P., Jr., Donald Cochran, and James M. Byrne. 1987. "Managing Change in Probation: Principles and Practice in the Implementation of an Intensive Probation Supervision Program." In *Intermediate Punishments: Intensive Supervision, Home Confinement and Electronic Surveillance*, edited by B. McCarthy. Monsey, NY: Willow Tree Press.

Cressey, Donald. 1958. "The Nature and Effectiveness of Correctional Techniques." *Law and Contemporary Problems* 23:754-72.

Cullen, Francis T., Gregory A. Clark, and John F. Wozniak. 1985. "Explaining the Get Tough Movement: Can the Public be Blamed?" *Federal Probation* 49:16-24.

Cullen, Francis T., John B. Cullen, and John F. Wozniak. 1988. "Is Rehabilitation Dead? The Myth of the Punitive Public." *Journal of Criminal Justice* 16:303-17.

Currie, Elliott. 1989. "Confronting Crime: Looking Toward the Twenty-First Century." *Justice Quarterly* 6:5-27.

Duffee, David E. and David Clark. 1985. "The Frequency and Classification of the Needs of Offenders in Community Settings." *Journal of Criminal Justice* 13:243-68.

Durham, Alexis M., III. 1989. "Judgements of Appropriate Punishment: The Effects of Question Type." *Journal of Criminal Justice* 17:75-85.

Edelman, Marian Whright. 1987. *Families in Peril: An Agenda for Social Change.* Cambridge, MA: Harvard University Press.

Erwin, Billie S. 1987. *Evaluation of Intensive Probation Supervision in Georgia.* Atlanta, Georgia: Department of Corrections.

Erwin, Billie S. and Lawrence A. Bennett. 1987. "New Dimensions in Probation: Georgia's Experience with Intensive Supervision Probation (ISP)." *Research in Brief* January. Washington, DC: National Institute of Justice. U.S. Department of Justice.

Etzioni, Amitai. 1989. "Humble Decision-Making." *Harvard Business Review* July-August:122-26.

Farrington, David P. 1983. "Randomized Experiments on Crime and Justice." Pp. 257-308 in *Crime and Justice: An Annual Review*, edited by Michael Tonry and Norval Morris. Chicago: University of Chicago Press.

Garner, Joel H. and Christy A. Visher. 1988. "Policy Experiments Come of Age." *NIJ Reports* 211:2-8.

Gendreau, Paul and Robert R. Ross. 1987. "Revivification of Rehabilitation: Evidence from the 1980s." *Justice Quarterly* 4(3): 349-408.

Gibbons, Don C. 1988. *The Limits of Punishments as Social Policy.* New York: Edna McConnel Clark Foundation.

Gottfredson, Don M., James O. Finckenauer, and Carol Rauh. 1977. *Probation on Trial.* Newark, NJ: School of Criminal Justice, Rutgers University.

Gottfredson, Michael and Travis Hirschi. 1988. "Career Criminals and Selective Incapacitation." Pp. 199-210 in *Controversial Issues in Crime and Justice*, edited by Joseph E. Scott and Travis Hirschi. Newbury Park, CA: Sage.

Gottfredson, Stephen D. and Ralph B. Taylor. 1983. *The Correctional Crisis: Prison Populations and Public Policy.* Washington, DC: National Institute of Justice, U.S. Department of Justice.

Gottfredson, Stephen D. and Ralph B. Taylor. 1986. "Person-Environment Interactions in the Prediction of Recidivism." In *The Social Ecology of Crime*, edited by J. M. Byrne and R. J. Sampson. New York: Springer-Verlag.

Hagan, John and Alberto Palloni. 1988. "Crimes as Social Events in the Life Course: Reconceiving a Criminological Controversy." *Criminology* 26(1):87-100.

Jamieson, Katherine M. and Timothy J. Flanagan, eds. 1989. *Sourcebook of Criminal Justice Statistics: 1988*. Washington, DC: Bureau of Justice Statistics.

Kelling, George L., Tony Pate, D. Dieckman, and C. Brown. 1974. *The Kansas City Preventive Patrol Experiment: A Summary Report*. Washington, DC: Police Foundation.

Latessa, Edward J. and Gennaro F. Vito. 1988. "The Effects of Intensive Supervision on Shock Probationers." *Journal of Criminal Justice* 16(4):319-30.

Laub, John H. and Robert J. Sampson. 1988. "Unraveling Families and Delinquency: A Reanalysis of the Gluecks' Data." *Criminology* 26(3):355-80.

Lauen, Roger L. 1988. *Community-managed Corrections*. Washington, DC: American Correctional Association.

Lempert, Richard O. and Christy A. Visher, eds. 1987. "Randomized Field Experiments in Criminal Justice Agencies: A Summary of Workshop Proceeding." National Research Council, Commission on Behavioral and Social Sciences, Committee on Research on Law Enforcement and the Administration of Justice (mimeo).

Lipton, Douglas, Robert Martinson, and Judith Wilks. 1975. *The Effectiveness of Correctional Treatment: A Survey of Treatment Evaluation Studies*. New York: Praeger.

Martinson, Robert. 1974. "What Works? Questions and Answers About Prison Reform." Reprinted in *Rehabilitation, Recidivism, and Research*, by R. Martinson, T. Palmer and S. Adams. Hackensack, NJ: National Council on Crime and Delinquency.

McGahey, Richard. 1988. "Jobs and Crime." *Study Guide for the Crime File Video Tape Series*. Washington, DC. National Institute of Justice, U.S. Department of Justice.

Morris, Norval. 1987. "Alternatives to Imprisonment: Failures and Prospects." *Criminal Justice Research Bulletin* 3(7): 1-6.

Morris, Norval and Michael Tonry. 1990. *Between Prison and Probation: Intermediate Punishments in a Rational Sentencing System*. Oxford, England: Oxford University Press.

Musheno, Michael C., Dennis J. Palumbo, Steven Maynard-Moody, and James P. Levine. 1989. "Community Corrections as an Organizational Innovation: What Works and Why." *Journal of Research in Crime and Delinquency* 26(2):116-35.

O'Leary, Vincent and Todd R. Clear. 1984. *Directions for Community Corrections in the 1990s*. Washington, DC: National Institute of Corrections, U.S. Department of Justice.

Orsagh, Thomas and Mary Ellen Marsden. 1984. *Rational Choice Theory and Offender Rehabilitation*. Draft final report submitted to National Institute of Justice, U.S. Department of Justice under Grant #81-IJ-CX-0061, Washington, DC.

Orsagh, Thomas and Mary Ellen Marsden. 1985. "What Works When: Rational-Choice Theory and Offender Rehabilitation." *Journal of Criminal Justice* 13(3):269-78.

_____. 1987. "Inmates and Appropriate Programs — Effective Rehabilitation." *Corrections Today* August:174-80.

Parent, Dale. 1989. *Shock Incarceration: An Overview of Existing Programs.* Washington, DC: National Institute of Justice.

Patton, Michael Q. 1978. *Utilization-Focused Evaluation.* Beverly Hills, CA: Sage.

Pearson, Frank S.1987. *Research on New Jersey's Intensive Supervision Program.* Final report submitted to National Institute of Justice, U.S. Department of Justice under Grant #83-IJ-CX-K027, Washington, DC.

_____. 1988. "Evaluation of New Jersey's Intensive Supervision Program." *Crime and Delinquency* 34(4):437-48.

Petersilia, Joan M. 1987. *Expanding Options for Criminal Sentencing.* Santa Monica, CA: RAND Corporation.

_____. 1989. "Implementing Randomized Experiments: Lessons From BJA's Intensive Supervision Project." *Evaluation Review* 13(5):435-459.

Petersilia, Joan M., Susan Turner, and Joyce Peterson. 1986. *Prison Versus Probation in California: Implications for Crime and Offender Recidivism.* Santa Monica, CA: RAND.

Reiss, Albert J. 1986. "Why are Communities Important in Understanding Crime?" In *Communities and Crime*, edited by A. J. Reiss and M. Tonry. Chicago: University of Chicago Press.

Reiss, Albert J., Jr. and Michael Tonry, eds. 1986. *Communities and Crime.* Chicago: University of Chicago Press.

Rossi, Peter H. and Howard E. Freeman. 1982. *Evaluation: A Systematic Approach.* Beverly Hills, CA: Sage.

Schmidt, Annesley K. 1989. "Electronic Monitoring of Offenders Increases." *NIJ Reports*, (2-5). Washington, DC: National Institute of Justice, U.S. Department of Justice.

Sechrest, Lee, Susan O. White, and Elizabeth D. Brown, eds. 1979. *The Rehabilitation of Criminal Offenders: Problems and Prospects.* Washington, DC: National Academy of Sciences.

Sherman, Lawrence W. and Richard A. Berk. 1984. "The Specific Deterrent Effects of Arrest for Domestic Assault." *American Sociological Review* 49:261-72.

Sherman, Lawrence W. and Ellen C. Cohn. 1989. "The Impact of Research on Legal Policy: The Minneapolis Domestic Violence Experiment." *Law and Society Review* 23(1):117-27.

Shover, Neal and Werner J. Einstadter. 1988. *Analyzing American Corrections.* Belmont, CA: Wadsworth.

Skovron, Sandra Evans. 1988. "Prison Crowding: The Dimensions of the Problem and Strategies of Population Control." In *Controversial Issues in Crime and Justice*, edited by Joseph E. Scott and Travis Hirschi, pp. 183-98. Newbury Park, CA: Sage.

Smith, Douglas A. and Patrick P. Gartin. 1989. "Specifying Specific Deterrence: The Influence of Arrest on Future Criminal Activity." *American Sociological Review* 54:94-105.

Spangenberg Associates. 1987. *Assessment of the Massachusetts Probation System*. Prepared for the Office of the Chief Administrative Justice of the Trial Court. Newton, MA: Spangenberg Group.

Stark, Rodney. 1987. "Deviant Places: A Theory of the Ecology of Crime." *Criminology* 25(4):893-910.

Thomson, Doug. 1984. "Prospects for Justice Model Probation." In *Probation and Justice: Reconsideration of Mission*, edited by Patrick D. McAnany, Doug Thomson, and David Fogel, pp. 101-35. Cambridge, MA: Oelgeschlager, Gunn and Hain.

Tonry, Michael H. 1987. *Sentencing Reform Impacts*. Washington, DC: National Institute of Justice, U.S. Department of Justice.

Tonry, Michael H. and Richard Will. 1988. *Intermediate Sanctions*. Preliminary report to the National Institute of Justice. Washington, DC.

Twain, David. 1983. *Creating Change in Social Settings*. New York: Praeger.

U.S. Department of Justice. 1987. *Intensive Supervision Probation and Parole (ISP)*. Program Brief prepared by the Bureau of Justice Assistance, Office of Justice Programs in conjunction with regulations implementing the Justice Assistance Act of 1984.

U.S. General Accounting Office. 1988. *Prison Boot Camps: Too Early to Measure Effectiveness*. Briefing report to the Honorable Lloyd Bentsen, U.S. Senate, September.

Visher, Christy. 1988. *Randomized Field Experiments in Criminal Justice Agencies: Summary of Conference Proceedings*. Washington, DC: National Institute of Justice, U.S. Department of Justice.

von Hirsch, Andrew. 1985. *Past or Future Crimes*. New Brunswick, NJ: Rutgers University Press.

von Hirsch, Andrew, Martin Wasik, and Judith Greene. 1989. "Punishments in the Community and the Principles of Desert." *Rutgers Law Journal* 20(3):595-618.

Wasik, Martin and Andrew von Hirsch. 1988. "Non-Custodial Penalties and the Principles of Desert." *Criminal Law Review* September:555-72.

Wilson, James Q. 1986. "What Works? Revisited: New Findings on Criminal Rehabilitations." In *The Dilemmas of Punishment: Readings in Contemporary Corrections*, edited by Kenneth C. Haas and Geoffrey P. Alpert, pp. 327-41. Prospect Heights, IL: Waveland Press.

# 13

# What Punishes? Inmates Rank the Severity of Prison vs. Intermediate Sanctions

## Joan Petersilia
## Elizabeth Piper Deschenes

### Introduction and Research Questions

The intermediate sanctions movement of the 1980s was predicated on the assumption that the two extremes of punishment—imprisonment and probation—are both used excessively, with a near vacuum of useful punishments in between. According to Morris and Tonry (1990), a more comprehensive sentencing strategy that relies on a range of "intermediate" punishments—including fines, community service, intensive probation, and electronic monitoring—would better meet the needs of the penal system, convicted offenders, and the community than the current polarized choice. The central thesis of the Morris and Tonry proposal is that there are "equivalencies" of punishment and that, at some level of intensity, community-based punishments are as severe as

Source: *Federal Probation*, Vol. 58, No. 1 (March 1994), 3-8.

prison terms (i.e., have roughly the same punitive "bite"). They encouraged states to identify these roughly equivalent punishments (or "exchange rates") and allow judges to choose among sentences of rough punitive equivalence. They predicted that in many instances judges would choose to substitute restrictive, intermediate punishments in lieu of a prison term.

Implementing intermediate sanction *programs* within states' broad-based sentencing structure (particularly in states with sentencing guidelines) has proven much easier than developing the comprehensive sentencing *system* that Morris and Tonry envisioned. A major stumbling block has been reaching consensus on the relative severity of different community-based punishments (e.g., house arrest versus community service) and, more importantly, on *which* intermediate sanctions, in what dosage, can be substituted for prison. When the choice was simply prison versus standard probation, most everyone agreed that prison was more severe. But with the emergence of highly restrictive community-based punishments—which often require drug testing, employment, and curfews—it is no longer obvious.

Most law-abiding citizens probably still believe that no matter what conditions probation or parole impose, remaining in the community is categorically preferable to imprisonment, but recent evidence suggests that offenders might not share this view. When Oregon implemented an intensive supervision probation (ISP) program in 1989 and offenders were given the choice of serving a prison term or participating in ISP (which incorporated drug testing, employment, and frequent home visits by the probation officer), about a third of the offenders chose prison instead of ISP (Petersilia, 1990).

It may also be that prison is losing some of its punitive sting. For example, Skolnick (1990) reported that, for certain California youth, having a prison record was no longer seen as stigmatizing, and the prison experience not particularly isolating, since they usually encountered family and friends there. If prison is not judged as severe as we presume it is, this may have important implications for sentencing policy. Since the major purposes of the criminal law are retribution and deterrence, this means that sanctions must be viewed as punitive to fulfill their goals. And, as Crouch (1993, p. 68) has noted, "Theoretically, for prison to have the punitive and deterrent effect on offenders that the public desires, a fundamental assumption must be met: that offenders generally share the state's punitiveness in the ranking of criminal sanctions."

The unanswered question is, "do they?" If they don't, and if community-based punishments can be designed so that they are seen as equally punitive by offenders, then perhaps policymakers—who say they are imprisoning such a large number of offenders because of the public's desire to get tough with crime—might be convinced that there are other means besides prison to exact punishment.

Despite the importance of the offender's perspective as noted by Crouch (1993), there have been only three prior attempts to survey the opinions of criminal offenders regarding the perceived severity of sanctions (McClelland & Alpert, 1985; Apospori & Alpert, 1993; Crouch, 1993), and none of these studies included the newer intermediate sanctions (e.g., intensive probation). In addition, most prior research on sanction severity has used either paired comparisons or magnitude estimation to measure judgments, and both techniques have methodological or analytical flaws.[1]

McClelland and Alpert (1985) surveyed 152 arrestees in a midsize western city, following the example of Erickson and Gibbs (1979) who used magnitude estimation techniques to survey policemen and adults in households. Respondents were given a list of penalties (randomly ordered), including different levels of fines, probation, jail, and prison, and instructed to assign a number to each penalty based on the standard of 100 for 1 year in jail. They found that persons who had more experience with the criminal justice system (e.g., more prior convictions) minimized the seriousness of prison in comparison to other punishments. And in later research, Apospori and Alpert (1993) suggested that as the threat of the legal sanction became realized, arrestees raised their perceptions of the severity of sanctions. In a survey of 1,027 incoming prisoners at a Texas institution who were asked if they would prefer probation or prison, Crouch (1993) found that the majority of inmates preferred prison to probation, believing probation was stricter. In addition, Crouch found that those who were married preferred probation to prison, yet minorities and older inmates preferred prison.

This article presents the results of an exploratory study undertaken in cooperation with the Minnesota Department of Corrections and the Minnesota Sentencing Guidelines Commission and funded by the National Institute of Justice to explore these issues. The study developed an instrument and methodology for measuring offender perceptions of sanction severity and, using that method, collected data on the following questions:

1) How do inmates rank the severity of criminal sanctions, and which sanctions are judged equivalent in punitiveness?

2) What background characteristics are associated with variations in the perception of sanction severity?

3) How do inmates rank the difficulty of probation/parole conditions, and how does this affect their ranking of sanctions?

Our research attempted to build upon prior research by adding the newer intermediate sanctions to the survey and including both magnitude estimation and rank ordering scaling techniques. The simpler technique of rank ordering is likely to give a more accurate model of the ratings of various punishments, since offenders may not have the mathematical skills necessary for the magnitude estimation judgment of severity. Besides increasing the simplicity of the task, the use of ordered logistic regression to model the underlying latent scale of sanction severity and test for differences between individuals allowed greater flexibility in the analysis (Agresti, 1990). The basic model being tested assumes that each individual has an underlying scale of the severity of different sanctions. Ordered logistic regression allows us to more easily test whether various sanctions are indeed equivalent with less rigid assumptions about the data.[2] For these reasons, the rank ordering analysis is preferred and this article focuses on those results.

## Study Design and Results

### Sample Selection

The sample selection criteria were designed to identify offenders who would likely be targeted for intermediate sanctions and therefore whose perceptions about the severity of such sanctions are particularly relevant. We used the same criteria to identify our sample that had been outlined by the Minnesota Legislature in deciding which inmates qualified for the state's Intensive Community Supervision (ICS) program. To be eligible for ICS, offenders must be either a probation violator or a new court commitment with less than a 27-month prison sentence to serve. Offenders with prior convictions for murder, manslaughter, or rape are ineligible. The sample was drawn from incoming inmates who met the ICS eligibility criteria at the two main receiving facilities in Minnesota, St. Cloud and Stillwater. Forty-eight male inmates were so identified during the months of April-July 1992, and all agreed to participate in the study.

The sample of inmates was 50 percent white, and the majority of nonwhites were Afro-American; the average age at the time of the current offense was 26. Inmates tended to be unemployed prior to prison, and about half had less than a high school education. Inmates were serving, on average, prison terms of 17 months, and most had been convicted of property offenses. Inmates averaged seven prior arrests and two prior felony convictions, and one-third had previously served time in prison.

### Data Collection

RAND staff coded various demographic and criminal history data from each inmate's official corrections file. Interviews were administered with those who agreed to participate in the study, and respondents received $20 for participating. The interview took about an hour to administer and was divided into four sections:

1) *The Magnitude Estimation Task.* Fifteen legal sanctions were selected for the study (see table 1). Each sanction description was printed separately on a 3x5-inch card and presented one by one to the respondent in a random order. Respondents were instructed to compare each of the sanctions to the standard of 1 year in jail, which was equivalent to 100 points.

2) *Offender Background Interview.* About 25 open-ended questions were asked offenders requesting information on employment, housing arrangements, family relationships, present prison experiences, and their perceptions of prison versus community-based sentencing.

3) *The Ranking of Probation Conditions.* Inmates were asked to estimate "the difficulty you would probably experience in trying to meet the (specified) condition." They were asked about 13 commonly imposed conditions and directed to place each "condition card" next to one of five responses (ranging from not difficult at all to very difficult).

4) *The Rank Ordering Task.* To rank order the sanctions, inmates were given a stack of 4x6-inch cards (randomly ordered). Each card had printed on it one of the 15 sanctions (see table 1). Inmates were instructed to simply place the cards on the table, from left to right, in order from least severe to most severe.

### Inmate Rankings and Equivalencies of the Severity of Criminal Sanctions

The means and standard deviations for the rank orders of the 15 sanctions presented in table 1 suggest that inmate consensus is greatest at the lowest and highest levels—i.e., $100 fine and 5 years in prison. The larger values for the standard deviations on other sanctions suggest there is some variation between individuals, particularly on the ratings of a $5,000 fine, 3 months in jail, and 1 year in prison. Nonetheless, the means and medians provide similar results in the overall rank ordering of the various sanctions. For example, there appear to be "clusters" of sanctions—5 years probation, 3 years intensive probation, and 1 year in jail all have a median rank of 10. To statistically test for significant differences in the rank ordering of various sanctions, further analysis was necessary.

The data were analyzed using ordered logistic regression to model the ordered categorical responses as a function of the type of sanction. In the simplest case the model is of the form:

Table 1

**Inmates' Rank Ordering of Criminal Sanctions**

| Criminal Sanction | Mean | Standard Deviation | Median Rank Order |
|---|---|---|---|
| *Fines* | | | |
| $100 | 1.3 | 1.1 | 1 |
| $1,000 | 4.5 | 3.4 | 3 |
| $5,000 | 7.6 | 3.6 | 7 |
| *Probation* | | | |
| 1 year | 4.2 | 2.0 | 4 |
| 3 years | 6.8 | 2.7 | 6 |
| 5 years | 9.8 | 2.8 | 10 |
| *Intensive Probation* | | | |
| 1 year | 7.1 | 2.2 | 7 |
| 3 years | 9.5 | 2.2 | 10 |
| 5 years | 11.4 | 2.6 | 11.5 |
| *Jail* | | | |
| 3 months | 4.6 | 3.1 | 3.5 |
| 6 months | 6.4 | 2.9 | 6 |
| 1 year | 9.6 | 2.8 | 10 |
| *Prison* | | | |
| 1 year | 9.7 | 3.2 | 11 |
| 3 years | 13.0 | 2.0 | 14 |
| 5 years | 14.5 | 1.5 | 15 |

$$\text{ranking} = f(\text{sum } \beta(i)*\text{sanction}(i))$$

The results of this type of analysis are a collection of parameter estimates or "betas," one for each sanction in the simplest case. The estimated coefficients in this model form a latent variable scale yielding an interval valued "score" for the various sanctions. The betas represent ranking of the sanctions and standard errors for the sanction's position on the latent scale. The statistical test of the difference between the ranking of the sanction and the ranking of the omitted category is a chi-square test with 1 degree of freedom.

The first model tested using ordered logistic regression compared all other sanctions to 1 year of intensive supervision. For this model, the parameter estimate for 1 year ISP was set to zero, and as shown in table 2, sanctions that are not statistically different from 1 year intensive

Table 2

**Inmates' Perceived Severity of Criminal Sanctions**

| Criminal Sanction | Parameter Estimate | Standard Error | Chi-Square |
|---|---|---|---|
| $100 fine | -7.42 | .68 | 118.3* |
| $1,000 fine | -2.14 | .38 | 32.4* |
| 3 months jail | -1.85 | .36 | 25.8* |
| 1 year probation | -1.80 | .35 | 26.5* |
| 6 months jail | -0.49 | .34 | 2.1 |
| 3 years probation | -0.15 | .34 | 0.2 |
| 1 year intensive probation | 0.00 | | |
| $5,000 fine | 0.24 | .36 | 0.4 |
| 3 years intensive probation | 1.25 | .33 | 14.2* |
| 1 year jail | 1.35 | .34 | 15.4* |
| 5 years probation | 1.45 | .35 | 17.4* |
| 1 year prison | 1.56 | .35 | 19.5* |
| 5 years intensive probation | 2.49 | .36 | 47.9* |
| 3 years prison | 4.17 | .39 | 113.1* |
| 5 years prison | 7.38 | .56 | 175.1* |

* Chi-square test of difference between this parameter estimate and the estimate for the omitted category (1 year ISP) is significantly different at $p < .05$.

probation include 6 months jail, 3 years probation, and a $500 fine. The parameter estimates for the other sanctions show results that are consistent with the simple comparison of the median rank orders.

To test for equivalencies in the ratings of the sanctions, the ordered logistic regression analysis was repeated, each time omitting a different sanction, and chi-square tests performed, comparing sanction to the omitted category. The results of this analysis can be used to devise formulas for the substitution of incarceration for community-based punishments as shown in table 2.

A number of things are worth noting. First, inmates judged 1 year spent in jail as equivalent to 1 year spent in prison. In fact, in the open-ended interviews, several inmates stated that prison time was easier to do because there were more activities to occupy their time and conditions were generally better. Inmates also ranked 5 years of intensive probation supervision as harsher than 1 year in prison but not as harsh as 3 years in prison. Five years in prison was judged more severe than any other sanction and had no equivalent in terms of the intermediate sanctions measured here. Similarly, a $100 fine was judged as significantly less severe than any other sanction measured here, having no other statistical equivalent.

## Differences Between Individuals

To test for differences between individuals, ordered logistic regression was used and various models compared by using the chi-square differences from likelihood ratio tests. Only two of the background variables were significantly related to the perceptions of sanction severity: (1) inmates who were married and/or had children tended to rank prison and jail confinement as more severe than those who were single; and (2) inmates who were single tended to rank financial penalties (e.g., fines, restitution) as more severe than inmates who were married. We found no differences in the rankings of sanction severity by race, prior prison experience, employment history, drug dependency, or how safe the inmate felt in prison. It is possible that the sample was too small to detect differences or the characteristics of our sample too homogeneous. On the other hand, it may be that the differences noted in earlier studies reflect the clearer distinctions in the offender's mind between prison and probation, which because of the inclusion of intermediate sanctions, was not as pronounced in our study as in earlier research.

## Rating the Difficulty of Complying
## with Various Probation Conditions

We were interested in learning how inmates varied in their perception of the difficulty of complying with various probation conditions and whether this perception affected their rankings of different sanctions. Figure 1 presents the results, with the responses averaged over all inmates.

Inmates generally felt they would have little difficulty in complying with various restrictions. The overall rating for the 13 probation conditions was 2.1, which is "relatively easy." They judged the easiest conditions to be payment of a $100 fine and 10 hours per week of community service and the most difficult conditions to be house arrest

Figure 1

**Inmate Perceptions of the Difficulty of Probation Conditions**

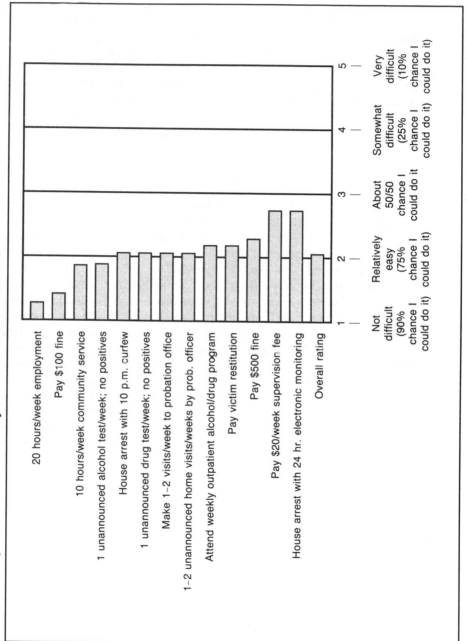

with 24-hour electronic monitoring and the payment of a $20-per-week probation/parole supervision fee.

It might seem contrary that inmates who judged certain intermediate sanctions as equivalent to prison in harshness would also judge the individual conditions making up those sanctions as rather easy to comply with. Information offered by inmates during the interviews suggests that while each individual condition might be easy to comply with, when conditions are stacked together—*particularly over longer time periods*—they become much more difficult. House arrest sentences are often for periods of 6 months to 1 year, and intensive probation is usually for 1-2 years.

We analyzed the relationship between background characteristics and inmate ratings of probation conditions and found only one significant difference: Those with no history of drug or alcohol use (as noted on their official prison records) reported finding it more difficult to attend a weekly outpatient treatment program than did the users. We also tested whether the inmates' overall rating score on probation conditions was related to the ranking of the severity of the overall criminal sanctions but found no significant differences between those who rated the probation conditions as easy to comply with and those who rated the conditions as more difficult.

## Discussion and Policy Implications

Our results provide empirical evidence to support what many have suggested: that it is no longer necessary to equate criminal punishment solely with prison. The balance of sanctions between probation and prison appears to have shifted, and at some level of intensity and length, intensive probation is the more dreaded penalty.

These findings have a number of research and policy implications. For one, the clusters of sanctions identified as "equivalent" in severity should be useful to sentencing commissions attempting to incorporate alternatives into sentencing guidelines and to devise formulas showing the equivalency of alternative sanctions to imprisonment.

Ideally, one wants to devise an intermediate sanction that includes enough conditions (but not more than necessary) to exact punishment and protect the public. But since little knowledge exists about how many conditions, or what type, are necessary to achieve those goals, jurisdictions continue to add conditions, thus negating one of the major purposes of intermediate sanctions, which is to provide suitable punishment at less cost than prison. Inmate judgments on punitive equivalence could be useful in setting some boundaries on what types of conditions, imposed for how long, are required to mete out "tough" probation sentences and to suggest some rough ordering that might be used to create a continuum of punishments—from fines through community service, standard probation, intensive probation and house arrest, then moving on to jail, and finally prison.

The study results also have implications for sentencing and deterrence research. Sentencing studies routinely build mathematical models of punishment that treat anything other than prison as "zero" and assign positive values only to increments of imprisonment. Similarly, deterrence studies assign numerical ranks reflecting sanction seriousness and then analyze whether there is a relationship between the severity rankings and some post-treatment outcome (e.g., usually recidivism). Both types of studies rely on scales of sanction severity, which our study suggests are in need of refinement. At a minimum, sentencing studies need to recognize different levels of probation supervision (i.e., not code all probation sentences identically) and that probation terms do not equate to "zero," which implies no sanction at all.

Our findings also have implications for sentencing policy more generally. It is argued by some that the United States has failed to develop a sufficient range of criminal sanctions because the dialogue is often cast as punishment (prison) or not, with other sanctions being seen as "letting off" or a "slap on the wrist." The results of this study show that certain community-based sanctions are not a "slap on the wrist" and are judged quite punitive. This should give justice officials pause, particularly those who state they are imprisoning such a large number of offenders to get "tough on crime." Our results suggest that, in the minds of offenders, community-based sanctions can be severe, and it can no longer be said that incarceration is preferred simply because, as Fogel (1975) stated, "we have not found another satisfactory severe punishment."

## Notes

[1] For example, one problem with magnitude estimation is that the validity depends on the adequacy of subjects' mathematical skill, since it requires subjects to rate various stimuli in comparison to the standard numerical value. Although used in numerous psychological experiments on subjects with varying skills, research has shown that the use of magnitude estimation techniques among naive or poorly educated subjects is questionable (Jones & Shorter, 1972).

[2] Ordered logistic regression does not depend on the use of an interval level of measurement, as do the magnitude estimation techniques.

## References

Agresti, A. (1990). *Categorical data analysis*. New York: John Wiley and Sons.

Apospori, E. & Alpert, G. (1993). Research note: The role of differential experience with the criminal justice system in changes in perceptions of severity of legal sanctions over time. *Crime and Delinquency, 39*(2), 184-94.

Crouch, B. M. (1993). Is incarceration really worse? Analysis of offenders' preferences for prison over probation. *Justice Quarterly, 10*(1), 67-88.

Erickson, M. L. & Gibbs, J. P. (1979). On the perceived severity of legal penalties. *Journal of Criminal Law & Criminology, 70*(1), 102-16.

Fogel, D. (1975). "*. . . We are the living proof . . ." The justice model for corrections.* Cincinnati: W. H. Anderson Co.

Jones, B. C. & Shorter, R. (1972). The ratio measurement of social status: Some cross-cultural comparisons. *Social Forces, 50,* 499-511.

McClelland, K. A. & Alpert, G. P. (1985). Factor analysis applied to magnitude estimates of punishment seriousness: Patterns of individual differences. *Journal of Quantitative Criminology, 1*(3), 307-18.

Morris, N. & Tonry, M. (1990). *Between prison and probation: Intermediate punishments in a rational sentencing system.* New York: Oxford University Press.

Petersilia, J. (1990). When probation becomes more dreaded than prison. *Federal Probation, 54*(1), 23-27.

Skolnick, J. H. (1990). Gangs and crime old as time: But drugs change gang culture. *Crime and Delinquency in California, 1980-1989.* Sacramento: Bureau of Criminal Justice Statistics, State of California, pp. 171-79.

# 14

# Intensive Rehabilitation Supervision
## The Next Generation in Community Corrections?

Paul Gendreau
Francis T. Cullen
James Bonta

Since their inception in the early 1980s, "intensive supervision programs" (ISPs), which emphasize the close monitoring of offenders in the community, have spread rapidly across the United States. Today, virtually every state has some form of ISP for the supervision of parolees and probationers (Camp & Camp, 1993; Petersilia & Turner, 1993). It is estimated that over 120,000 offenders are now placed in ISPs (Camp & Camp, 1993).

Although exceptions exist, the distinctive feature of ISPs is an abiding faith in the power of the threat of punishment to effect prosocial conformity. ISP programs emphasize supervision that is "intensive" in the sense that the goal is to watch offenders diligently. Thus, probation and parole officers are given reduced caseloads, and they are expected

Source: *Federal Probation*, Vol. 58, No. 1 (March 1994), 72-78.

to have more frequent contacts with offenders, sometimes unannounced, and over a longer time period. In addition to this scrutiny, ISPs often incorporate other forms of surveillance such as drug testing and home confinement or electronic monitoring. Meanwhile, offender rehabilitation, the cornerstone of traditional community corrections, recedes to secondary importance or is disdained as irrelevant to the program's mission.

This more intrusive control of offenders (and abandonment of treatment), argue ISP advocates, will enhance public safety, help alleviate prison crowding, and save money for governmental jurisdictions facing the expensive proposition of imprisoning a growing number of offenders. First, the increased surveillance and the threat of various sanctions will induce a commensurate fear of punishment for offenders in ISPs. As a consequence, offenders will be less likely to break the law than if they had been placed on traditional probation or parole where monitoring is less frequent and the threat of sanctions is less severe. Second, given the presumed efficacy of intensive supervision in scaring offenders straight, these offenders would, in effect, be diverted from incarceration. Control in the community would maintain public safety and also accomplish a large cost saving by reducing the flow of offenders into overcrowded prisons.

The intractable problem of prison crowding and its corresponding drain on the public treasury has been a catalyst in the proliferation of ISPs over the last decade (Clear & Hardyman, 1990; DeJong & Franzeen, 1993; Petersilia & Turner, 1993). But, more than this has been at work: the prevailing punitive context also must be considered (Currie, 1985; Scheingold, 1984). Unlike traditional community corrections programs that could be discredited as liberal attempts to coddle offenders, ISPs were also touted as a means of policing law-breakers—as another weapon in the arsenal to get tough on crime. Promising control and punishment, in short, struck a responsive chord among policymakers wishing to stem escalating corrections budgets while avoiding the risk of appearing easy on crime.

The growth of ISPs attests to their political attractiveness, but now, after a decade of experimentation, it is time to assess whether they have lived up to their promise. As we review below, the existing evaluation research suggests that ISPs with a strong focus on control are not an effective correctional intervention. However, there is beginning evidence that supervision programs which merge control with rehabilitation achieve more favorable results. When seen in the context of the growing evidence demonstrating the effectiveness of correctional treatment, these latter ISP findings provide a basis for considering a new generation of community corrections programs that not only supervise but also rehabilitate offenders. These programs, which we call intensive *rehabilitation supervision* (IRS), should be informed by the existing knowledge base on offender classification and on the principles of effective correctional treatment. Initial guidelines for integrating this knowledge into future IRS programs are presented.

## The First Generation of Community Supervision Programs

### The Limits of Control

The first generation of ISPs was greeted with enthusiasm, both in the press (e.g., *New York Times*, Dec. 18, 1985) and by criminal justice professionals (e.g., Conrad, 1986). The two prominent ISPs in this regard originated in Georgia and New Jersey and appeared to generate positive results (Erwin, 1986; Pearson, 1988; Pearson & Harper, 1990). This initial optimism, however, proved misleading. Gendreau and Ross (1987) pointed out that the reductions in recidivism reported for offenders in the Georgia ISP compared to those who were incarcerated were modest at best. More importantly, there were no differences in recidivism between the ISP and regular probation groups. In addition, the evaluations of both programs were questioned on a variety of methodological grounds (Byrne, 1990; Tonry, 1990; Tonry & Will, 1988). Finally, the majority of ISP evaluations in other jurisdictions "do *not* support the notion that 'intensive' supervision significantly reduces the risk of offender recidivism" (Byrne & Pattavina, 1992, p. 296, emphasis in original; see also Cullen, Wright, & Applegate, 1993).

Even more pessimistic news has just come from research conducted by Joan Petersilia and colleagues at Rand (Petersilia & Turner, 1993). The scope of the Rand evaluation was impressive as it included 14 sites that used Georgia's control-oriented model of ISP. Offenders were randomly assigned to ISP and regular probation control groups. The original Georgia results were replicated; the recidivism rates for ISP offenders did not differ significantly from those of regular probationers.

In terms of cost savings, the researchers failed to find one site that realized a cost saving. As the authors note, the expenses involved in maintaining an ISP had been underestimated. In fact, ISPs may cost about three times what regular probation does (Gendreau, Paparozzi, Little, & Goddard, 1993), and, in some instances, specific components of ISPs such as drug testing can be prohibitively expensive (e.g., Britt, Gottfredson, & Goldkamp, 1992). In addition, claims that ISPs may be cost-effective (New Jersey and Georgia) are very much open to question (Tonry, 1990).

The failure of ISPs to produce striking results in reducing recidivism would not surprise those familiar with the relevant criminological and psychological research. Underlying ISPs is the theory of deterrence— that is, the notion that offenders can be compelled to behave prosocially by the threat of enhanced punishment. This idea has achieved little empirical support in the criminological literature (Finckenauer, 1982; Paternoster, 1987; Walker, 1989). Furthermore, the results are not at all surprising when the massive psychological literature on punishment and attitude change is considered. This literature has been totally ignored by ISP program designers.

This literature has been summarized in regard to the current crop of punishment-oriented ISPs (Gendreau, 1993; Gendreau & Goddard, 1994; Gendreau & Ross, 1981). Briefly, the major findings from laboratory and clinical studies of punishment show that punishment is effective in suppressing behavior under a limited set of conditions. To be effective, punishment must be: a) immediate, b) at maximum intensity, c) varied (to avoid habituation effects), d) always contingent upon the disapproved behavior, and e) impossible to escape. When these punishment principles are weighed with factors such as the personality characteristics of offenders (e.g., psychopathy, neutralization cognitions that dismiss negative consequences) and socialization experiences that likely make them resistant to punishment, it becomes difficult to imagine why ISPs would have much influence on offenders' behavior. Additionally, there is no solid experimental or clinical evidence that the ISP sanctions currently in use, with the exception of fines, are effective punishers.

To ensure effective punishment, ISPs must *always* adhere to these aforementioned principles, but to do so in the "real world" is far beyond the logistical and ethical scope of any ISP. This conclusion not only applies to ISP programs with a punishment ideology but other community-based programs that stress punishment or the threat of punishment.

## The Promise of Rehabilitation

Despite this bleak picture of ISPs, the current evaluation studies have yielded an important insight: while there is little evidence for the effectiveness of increased surveillance and the threat of punishment, a few intensive supervision programs have reported reductions in recidivism. What kind of ISPs are these?

As it turns out, the ISPs that have demonstrated reductions in recidivism are those that went beyond simple control and also attempted to provide a significant treatment component (Jolin & Stipak, 1992; Paparozzi & Gendreau, 1993; Pearson, 1988). The most compelling data come from the latter two studies which were based New Jersey.

Paparozzi's Bureau of Parole program deliberately targeted only high-risk parolees. Across three indices, the recidivism rates for the ISP group were 21-29 percent lower than for a carefully matched sample of regular parolees. Secondly, critiques of the Pearson (1988) study have overlooked the fact that reductions in recidivism were 30 percent lower for those in ISP versus a comparison group in the case of the highest-risk probationers. It should be noted, however, that the quality of the services in these programs is unknown.

Finally, while the ISPs evaluated by Byrne and Kelly (1989) and Petersilia and Turner (1991) showed no overall reduction in recidivism compared to regular probation control groups, they did find that probationers who received more or better quality services while under supervision had lower recidivism rates.

## IRS: The Second Generation of Community Supervision Programs

Based on the existing empirical evidence, a persuasive case can be made for abandoning intensive supervision programs that seek only to control and punish offenders in favor of programs that give equal primacy to changing offenders. ISPs, moreover, may provide a unique opportunity for effective rehabilitation. Given their extensive contact with offenders, probation and parole officers should have the time needed to enhance the delivery of services and to monitor their clients' progress. We might also add that intensive rehabilitation supervision programs have a good prospect of receiving political support. By retaining "intensive supervision," the programs would not weaken surveillance over offenders, and by systematically incorporating treatment, intensive rehabilitation supervision (IRS) could offer the realistic hope of lower recidivism rates. More generally, research is clear in showing that the public favors correctional interventions that both control and rehabilitate (Cullen & Gendreau, 1989; Cullen, Skovron, Scott, & Burton, 1990).

### Who Gets into IRS:
### Risk/Needs Assessment

A glaring weakness of the first-generation ISPs is that there is no unifying theoretical basis for the selection of offenders for program participation. On the face of it, one would expect that ISPs would be reserved for the higher-risk offender who would supposedly benefit from increased control. However, after yielding to political pressure to get tough on everyone, using subjective as opposed to objective risk assessments, and allowing judges' discretion in sentencing to ISPs, many ISPs are left with a limited range of offenders who fall in the lower-risk categories (Gendreau & Ross, 1987; Tonry, 1990).

While reviewers of the rehabilitation literature may debate the overall potency of treatment, they do not dispute the fact that some treatment programs are effective in reducing recidivism for some offenders. The trick is identifying for *which* offenders treatment is most effective. Andrews, Bonta, and Hoge (1990) described a number of general principles that guide the matching of offender to treatment. The first two principles, the risk and need principles, are particularly relevant to our proposal to marry ISP with treatment in the form of IRS.

The risk principle states that treatment will more likely be effective when treatment services are matched with the risk level of the offender. That is, intensive services should be provided for higher-risk offenders and minimal services for lower-risk offenders. Mismatching level of service with offender risk has seldom shown reductions in recidivism (Andrews & Bonta, 1994; Andrews, Zinger, Hoge, Bonta, Gendreau, & Cullen, 1990). As we have noted, many ISP programs do not target higher risk offenders, although they provide a structural setting for sustaining intensive services. More frequent monitoring and supervision, however, are simply not equivalent to intensive rehabilitation services. After all, hypochondriacs may visit doctors daily, and they do not necessarily get better. What becomes important is what the doctor does with the patient during those visits, and part of the answer comes from the second principle.

The need principle recognizes two types of offender needs: criminogenic and noncriminogenic (e.g., Andrews & Bonta, 1994). Criminogenic needs are actually *dynamic* risk factors. A dynamic risk factor is one that can change over time. Some examples in this regard are an offender's attitudes towards employment, peers, authority, and substance abuse. The importance of criminogenic needs is that they serve as treatment goals: when programs successfully diminish these needs, we can reasonably expect reduction in recidivism. Some examples of noncriminogenic needs are anxiety, depression, and self-esteem; when programs target these types of needs, reductions in recidivism are negligible (Andrews & Bonta, 1994).

From our description of the risk and need principles, we hope that the reader sees the important implications for the design of IRS programs. Basically, IRS programs should target higher-risk clientele and provide rehabilitation services aimed at reducing criminogenic needs. In order to achieve these goals, the first step requires systematic risk-needs assessment.

Most offender assessment/classification instruments are simple risk instruments composed of items measuring an offender's past criminal history (Bonta, 1993). An example is the Salient Factor Score (Hoffman,

1983). All but one of the seven items are historical; that is, they relate to an offender's past, e.g., number of previous convictions, age at first arrest, rather than his or her current behavior and attitudes. Although they may achieve reasonable predictive accuracy and could be helpful in directing higher-risk offenders into IRS programs, they fail to provide the dynamic risk factors needed for effective treatment planning.

In contrast, the more recently developed risk-needs assessment instruments include not only criminal history items but also information of a dynamic quality. The criminogenic needs information can then provide staff assistance in identifying problematic aspects of the offender's situation requiring attention in order to reduce the risk of reoffending.

To our knowledge, there are only three risk-needs classification instruments in widespread use (we do not include personality-based assessments such as the I-Level and Megargee-MMPI because of the general lack of post-program predictive validity; see Andrews & Bonta, 1994). These three instruments are the Level of Supervision Inventory (LSI) (Andrews & Bonta, 1994), the Wisconsin classification system (Baird, 1981), and the Community Risk/Needs Management Scale used by the Correctional Services of Canada (Motiuk, 1993). Only the LSI and the Community Risk/Needs Management Scale were developed specifically with the risk and needs principle considered. At this point in time, only the LSI has shown post-probation dynamic risk validity. That is, changes in offender needs, as measured by the LSI, were associated with changes in recidivism. Analyses of the two other systems show some promise with respect to dynamic risk (Bonta, Andrews, & Motiuk, 1993), but more direct evidence is still lacking.

In short, systematic risk-needs assessment should be used to guide the selection of offenders into IRS programs. Interventions developed for these offenders should be based on specific treatment principles, with risk and need principles forming the general context for treatment.

### Principles of Effective Correctional Treatment

Even though the anti-rehabilitation "nothing works" rhetoric took firm hold in the United States for a variety of sociopolitical reasons (Cullen & Gendreau, 1989), dedicated clinicians and researchers have continued to generate data on the effectiveness of offender rehabilitation programs. For the interested reader, this evidence can be found in a variety of published critical narrative reviews and meta-analyses of the offender-treatment outcome literature (Andrews & Bonta, 1994; Andrews et al., 1990; Cullen & Gendreau, 1989; Garrett, 1985; Gendreau, 1993; Gendreau & Andrews, 1990; Gendreau & Ross, 1979; 1984; 1987;

Gottschalk, Davidson, Mayer, & Gensheimer, 1987; Izzo & Ross, 1990; Lipsey, 1992; Losel, 1993; Palmer, 1992).

What are the results from these studies? First, if one surveys all the treatment studies that had control group comparisons, as Mark Lipsey (1992) did for 443 studies, 64 percent of the studies reported reductions in favor of the treatment group. The average reduction in recidivism summed across the 443 studies was 10 percent. Secondly, according to Lipsey, when the results were broken down by the general type of program (e.g., employment), reductions in recidivism ranged from 10 to 18 percent.

It is not enough, however, simply to sum across studies or to partition them into general programmatic categories. The salient question is, what are the characteristics that distinguish between effective and ineffective programs? What exactly is done under the name of "employment"? Therefore, based on the literature reviews and to a lesser extent on the documented clinical wisdom of our treatment colleagues, we have discovered that programs which adhered to most of the characteristics to be described below, reduced recidivism in the range of 25 to 80 percent with an average of about 40 percent. A summary of these characteristics is provided. As well, we also include a listing of the principles of ineffective programs. Such knowledge is likely just as important as knowing "what works."

### Principles of What Works

A) *Risk principle: Intensive services, behavioral in nature, are provided to higher risk offenders.*

> i) Intensive services occupy 40-70 percent of the offender's time and are of 3 to 9 months duration.

> ii) Behavioral programs range from radical behaviorism (e.g., token economies) to cognitive social learning strategies that employ modeling, cognitive restructuring, and explicit reinforcement of alternatives to antisocial styles of thinking, feeling, and acting.

B) *Need principle: The goal of treatment is to reduce criminogenic needs.*

> i) Therapist and program providers must clearly differentiate criminogenic from noncriminogenic needs and ensure that the program targets criminogenic needs.

> ii) Program success is partly measured by the reduction of criminogenic needs.

C) *Responsivity: The style and mode of treatment is matched to the offender.*

i) The learning style and personality of the offender are matched with the program. For example, impulsive offenders and those who prefer a high degree of structure may benefit from a token economy program.

ii) Offenders are matched with the therapist, e.g., "anxious" offenders may respond better to more relaxed and calmer therapists.

iii) Therapists are matched with the type of program, e.g., therapists who have a concrete conceptual level for problem solving may function best in a radical behavioral program.

D) *Program contingencies/behavioral strategies are enforced in a firm but fair manner.*

i) Reinforcement contingencies are designed with meaningful input from offenders but remain under the control of the staff. Nondirective counseling programs do not seem to work with offenders.

ii) Positive reinforcers outweigh punishers by a 4:1 ratio.

iii) Internal controls are established to maintain prosocial behaviors and discourage antisocial behaviors in the absence of external contingencies.

E) *Therapists relate to offenders in interpersonally sensitive and constructive ways and are trained and supervised appropriately.*

i) Therapists have at least an undergraduate degree or equivalent, with knowledge of the theories of criminal behavior and of the prediction and treatment literature.

ii) Therapists receive 3 to 6 months of formal and on-the-job/internship training in the application of behavioral interventions generally and specific to the program.

iii) Therapists are reassessed periodically on quality of service delivery.

iv) Therapists monitor offender change on criminogenic needs.

F) *The program structure and activities should disrupt the criminal network.*

G) *There is a high level of advocacy and brokerage as long as the community agency offers appropriate services.*

i) Community services should be assessed in as objective a manner as possible, for example, the Correctional Program Assessment Inventory or CPAI (Gendreau & Andrews, 1993), so as to ensure that quality services applicable to the offenders and their problems are provided. All too often this is not the case. In a recent survey of 112 offender substance abuse programs using the CPAI, only 10 percent had programmatic elements that would lead one to believe that an effective service was being provided (Gendreau & Goggin, 1990).

## Principles of What Does Not Work

A) *Programs, including behavioral, that target low-risk offenders.*

B) *Programs that target offender need factors not predictive of criminal behavior (e.g., anxiety, depression, self-esteem).*

C) *Traditional Freudian psychodynamic and Rogerian nondirective therapies.*

These programs, at least in the offender treatment literature, have been characterized as follows:

   i) "talking" cures,

   ii) good relationship with the client is the primary goal,

   iii) unravelling the unconscious,

   iv) gaining insight as the major goal,

   v) resolving neurotic conflicts and self-actualizing,

   vi) externalizing blame to parents, staff, victims, society,

   vii) ventilating anger.

D) *Traditional "medical model" approaches.*

   i) diet change,

   ii) pharmacological, e.g., testosterone suppressants for sex offenders,

   iii) plastic surgery.

E) *Subcultural and labeling approaches.*

For a more complete review of these approaches see Andrews and Bonta (1994). Briefly, they note that interventions based on the following views are ineffective:

   i) Respect offenders' culture.

   ii) Provide legitimate opportunities only.

   iii) Rely on incidental learning. Somehow offenders will "get it" with minimal guidance.

   iv) Divert offenders from the stigmatization of the criminal justice system. This will be sufficient to reduce criminal behavior.

v) Use alternative sanctions with lower levels of punishment; these punishments are supposedly dignified and just, while treatment is coercive and does an injustice to offenders.

F) *Deterrence or "punishing smarter" strategies.*

This category includes the first generation ISPs described in this column, as well as bootcamps, electronic monitoring, scared straight, and shock incarceration. Gendreau and Little (1993) have conducted a preliminary meta-analysis of this literature. Their analysis consisted of 174 comparisons between a "punishment" group and a control group. The punishment in deterrence strategies produced slight increases in recidivism. Also of note is that both Cullen et al.'s (1993) narrative review of this literature and Andrews, Zinger et al.'s (1990) meta-analysis reached similar conclusions.

## Intensive Rehabilitation Supervision: The Future

The empirical evidence regarding ISPs is decisive: without a rehabilitation component, reductions in recidivism are as elusive as a desert mirage. This leaves community corrections somewhat at a crossroad. The choice is between (1) abandoning ISPs and returning to regular probation and parole supervision or (2) incorporating effective rehabilitation programming into the intensive monitoring conducted within ISPs. The first choice would be difficult: too much is invested politically in these programs.

The second choice, a new generation of intensive community programming, is more palatable. IRS holds the hope of reduced recidivism within a context of public support. The switch, however, from ISPs to IRSs will not be easy.

First of all, program developers must familiarize themselves with the extensive rehabilitation and punishment literature. For many, this will be foreign territory. Second, for staff who have become accustomed to a "law enforcement" role, incorporating a therapeutic role may bring confusion and conflict. Tonry (1990) has outlined some of the areas of resistance in this regard. Third, the temptation will be to provide IRS to all clientele instead of targeting the higher-risk offender. Not only would this be in contradiction to the risk principle, but it also would widen the net of state control. Finally, there is the question of costs. Training staff to adopt new roles and learn new skills will certainly require the expenditure of resources.

There are probably other unforeseen obstacles, but they are not, in our view, insurmountable. The principles of effective rehabilitation can be taught, staff supported in the transition to new roles, and objective risk-needs assessments adopted to guide the identification of offenders for IRS. In terms of costs, traditional ISPs along with their adjunct programs (electronic monitoring, urinalysis) are extremely expensive. Diverting this money to rehabilitation programs at least has the promise of producing reduced recidivism. There already seems to be a modest movement towards incorporating treatment into ISPs and targeting higher-risk offenders (see the New Jersey studies), but it is more haphazard rather than planned. We think the time for this movement to accelerate in a systematic and proactive manner is now opportune. To maintain the status quo is clearly unacceptable.

## References

Andrews, D. A. & Bonta, J. (1994). *The psychology of criminal conduct.* Cincinnati, OH: Anderson.

Andrews, D. A., Bonta, J. & Hoge, R. D. (1990). Classification for effective rehabilitation: Rediscovering psychology. *Criminal Justice and Behavior, 17,* 19-52.

Andrews, D. A., Zinger, I., Hoge, R. D., Bonta, J., Gendreau, P. & Cullen, F. T. (1990). Does correctional treatment work? A psychologically informed meta-analysis. *Criminology, 28,* 369-404.

Baird, S. C. (1981). Probation and parole classification: The Wisconsin model. *Corrections Today, 43,* 36-41.

Bonta, J. (1993, November). *Risk-needs assessment and treatment.* Presentation at a conference of the International Association of Residential and Community Alternatives, Philadelphia, PA.

Bonta, J., Andrews, D. A. & Motiuk, L. L. (1993, October). *Dynamic risk assessment and effective treatment.* Paper presented at the annual meeting of the American Society of Criminology, Phoenix, AZ.

Britt, C. II., Gottfredson, M. R. & Goldkamp, J. S. (1992). Drug testing and pretrial misconduct: An experiment on the specific deterrent effects of drug monitoring defendants on pretrial release. *Journal of Research in Crime and Delinquency, 29,* 62-78.

Byrne, J. M. (1990). The future of intensive probation supervision and the new intermediate sanctions. *Crime and Delinquency, 36,* 6-41.

Byrne, J. M. & Kelly, L. (1989). *Restructuring probation as an intermediate sanction: An evaluation of the Massachusetts Intensive Supervision Program.* Final report to the National Institute of Justice, U.S. Department of Justice, Research Program on the Punishment and Control of Offenders, Washington, DC.

Byrne, J. M. & Pattavina, A. (1992). The effectiveness issue: Assessing what works in the adult community corrections system. In J. M. Byrne, A. J. Lurigio & J. Petersilia (Eds.), *Smart sentencing: The emergence of intermediate sanctions* (pp. 281-306). Newbury Park, CA: Sage.

Camp, G. M. & Camp, C. G. (1993). *The corrections yearbook: Probation and parole.* South Salem, NY: Criminal Justice Institute.

Clear, T. & Hardyman, P. L. (1990). The new intensive supervision movement. *Crime and Delinquency, 36,* 42-60.

Conrad, J. P. (1986). News of the future: Research & development in corrections. *Federal Probation, 49*(2), 82-84.

Cullen, F. T. & Gendreau, P. (1989). The effectiveness of correctional rehabilitation: Reconsidering the "Nothing Works" debate. In L. Goodstein & D. MacKenzie (Eds.), *American prisons: Issues in research and policy* (pp. 23-44). New York: Plenum.

Cullen, F. T., Skovron, S. E., Scott, J. E. & Burton, V.S. (1990). Public support for correctional rehabilitation: The tenacity of the rehabilitation ideal. *Criminal Justice and Behavior, 17,* 6-18.

Cullen, F. T., Wright, J. P & Applegate, B. K. (1993, November). *Control in the community.* Presentation at a conference of the International Association of Residential and Community Alternatives, Philadelphia, PA.

Currie, E. (1985). *Confronting crime: An American challenge.* New York: Pantheon.

DeJong, W. & Franzeen, S. (1993). On the role of intermediate sanctions in corrections reform: The views of criminal justice professionals. *Journal of Crime and Justice, 16,* 47-73.

Erwin, B. S. (1986). Turning up the heat on probationers in Georgia. *Federal Probation, 50,* 17-24.

Finckenauer J. O. (1982). *Scared straight! and the panacea problem.* Englewood Cliffs, NJ: Prentice-Hall.

Garrett, C. J. (1985). Effects of residential treatment on adjudicated delinquents: A meta-analysis. *Journal of Research in Crime and Delinquency, 22,* 287-308.

Gendreau, P. (1993, November). *The principles of effective intervention with offenders.* Presentation at a conference of the International Association of Residential and Community Alternatives, Philadelphia, PA.

Gendreau, P. & Andrews, D. A. (1990). Tertiary prevention: What the meta-analysis of the offender treatment literature tells us about "what works." *Canadian Journal of Criminology, 32,* 173-184.

Gendreau, P. & Andrews, D. A. (1993). *The correctional program assessment inventory* (3rd ed.). University of New Brunswick, Saint John, N. B. and Carleton University, Ottawa, Ontario.

Gendreau, P. & Goddard, M. (1994). *The realities of punishment.* Manuscript submitted for publication.

Gendreau, P. & Ross, R. R. (1981). Correctional potency: Treatment and deterrence on trial. In R. Roesch & R. R. Corrado (Eds.), *Evaluation and criminal justice policy* (pp. 29-57). Beverly Hills: Sage.

Gendreau, P. & Ross, R. R. (1984). Correctional treatment: Some recommendations for successful intervention. *Juvenile and Family Court Journal, 34,* 31-40.

Gendreau, P. & Ross, R. R. (1979). Effective correctional treatment: Bibliotherapy for cynics. *Crime and Delinquency, 25,* 463-489.

Gendreau, P. & Little, T. (1993). *A meta-analysis of the effectiveness of sanctions on offender recidivism.* Unpublished manuscript, Department of Psychology, University of New Brunswick, Saint John.

Gendreau, P., Paparozzi, M., Little, T. & Goddard, M. (1993). Punishing smarter: The effectiveness of the new generation of alternative sanctions. *Forum on Correctional Research, 5,* 31-34.

Gendreau, P. & Ross, R. R. (1987). Revivication of rehabilitation: Evidence from the 1980s. *Justice Quarterly*, 4, 349-407.

Gottschalk, R., Davidson, W. S., Mayer, J. & Gensheimer, R. (1987). Behavioral approaches with juvenile offenders: A meta-analysis of long-term treatment efficacy. In E. K. Morris & C. J. Braukman (Eds.), *Behavioral approaches to crime and delinquency: A handbook of application, research, and concepts* (pp. 399-422). New York: Plenum Press.

Hoffman, P. B. (1983). Screening for risk: A revised salient factor score (SFS 81). *Journal of Criminal Justice*, 11, 539-47.

Izzo, R. & Ross, R. R. (1990). Meta-analysis of rehabilitation programs for juvenile delinquents: A brief report. *Criminal Justice and Behavior*, 17, 134-42.

Jolin, A. & Stipak, B. (1992). Drug treatment and electronically monitored home confinement: An evaluation of a community-based sentencing option. *Crime and Delinquency*, 38, 158-70.

Lipsey, M. W. (1992). Juvenile delinquency treatment: A meta-analytic inquiry into the variability of effects. In T. D. Cook, H. Cooper, D. S. Cordray, H. Hartmann, L. V. Hedges, R. J. Light, T. A. Louis & F. Mosteller, (Eds.), *Meta-analysis for explanation* (pp. 83-127). New York: Russell Sage Foundation.

Losel, F. (1993, November). *Evaluating psychosocial interventions in prison and other contexts*. Paper presented at the Twentieth Criminological Conference, Strasbourg, Germany.

Motiuk, L. L. (1993). Where are we in our ability to assess risk? *Forum on Corrections Research*, 5, 14-19.

Palmer, T. (1992). *The re-emergence of correctional intervention*. Newbury Park, CA: Sage.

Paparozzi, M. & Gendreau, P. (1993). *An ISP that works!: Treatment, organizational supportiveness and probation officer roles*. Unpublished manuscript. Bureau of Parole, Trenton, NJ.

Paternoster, R. (1987). The deterrent effect of perceived certainty and severity of punishment: A review of the evidence and issues. *Justice Quarterly*, 4, 173-217.

Pearson, F. S. (1988). Evaluation of New Jersey's Intensive Supervision Program. *Crime and Delinquency*, 34, 437-48.

Pearson, F. S. & Harper, A. G. (1990). Contingent intermediate sentences: New Jersey's Intensive Supervision Program. *Crime and Delinquency*, 36, 75-86.

Petersilia, J. & Turner, S. (1993). Intensive probation and parole. In M. Tonry & N. Morris (Eds.), *Crime and justice: An annual review of the research* (Vol. 17). Chicago: University of Chicago Press.

Petersilia, J. & Turner, S. (1991). An evaluation of intensive probation in California. *Journal of Criminal Law and Criminology*, 82, 610-58.

Scheingold, S. A. (1984). *The politics of law and order: Street crime and public policy*. New York: Longman.

Tonry, M. (1990). Stated and latent functions of ISP. *Crime and Delinquency*, 36, 174-90.

Tonry, M. & Will, R. (1988). *Intermediate sanctions: Preliminary report to the National Institute of Justice*. Washington, DC: National Institute of Justice.

Walker, S. (1989). *Sense and nonsense about crime: A policy guide*. Pacific Grove, CA: Brooks/Cole.

# 15

# Community Service: A Review of the Basic Issues

Robert M. Carter
Jack Cocks
Daniel Glaser

## Introduction

It is clear that the use of community service as a sentencing alternative is a major judicial and correctional trend in the United States. In part driven by tax-limiting initiatives such as Propositions 13 in California and 2.5 in Massachusetts, community service seemingly has high potential in the continued search for more effective and less costly methods of dealing with offenders. The trend toward community service also is driven by economic considerations brought about by the efforts to balance the Federal budget. These efforts forecast that there will be a reduction in Federal funds available to states, counties, and municipalities that will impact the criminal justice systems generally and correctional systems specifically.

Source: *Federal Probation*, Vol. 51, No. 1 (March 1987), 4-10.

In addition to these economic influences, the prospects for community service were significantly bolstered by enactment of the Federal Comprehensive Crime Control Act of 1984, effective November 1, 1987, which states:

> If sentenced to probation, the defendant must also be ordered to pay a fine, make restitution, and/or work in community service.[1]

Changes and directions in the Federal correctional system—probation, parole, and institutions—have often established trends for corrections at state and local levels.

The definition of community service varies in the professional literature, but for purposes of this commentary it is a court order that an offender perform a specified number of hours of uncompensated work or service within a given time period for a nonprofit community organization or tax-supported agency. It clearly is distinguished from monetary *restitution* to the victim or payment of a *fine* to a political jurisdiction: restitution and fine, as in the Federal legislation noted above, also may be part of a court order. In a generic sense, community service has been labeled as "restitution"—a sanction imposed by an official of the criminal justice system requiring an offender to make a payment of money or service to either the direct or substitute crime victim. Community service has had other labels, among them court referral, reparation, volunteer work, symbolic restitution, service restitution, and, for those individuals who perform community service without an adjudication of guilt, pretrial diversion and pretrial intervention.

More pragmatically, however, the specific use of community sanctions is of recent origin, emerging conceptually in England in the late 1960's and operationally in 1972 with Parliament granting the courts authority to order convicted offenders to perform community service. Within just a few years, the program was expanded in England and introduced into the United States and Canada.

Considerable literature on this sentencing and correctional alternative has been generated since that time, and at least two major bibliographies are now available which reflect that growing interest.[2]

There are several issues which should be carefully reviewed prior to the decision to begin community service as a sentencing alternative or enhancement. The purpose of this article is to review the more significant issues and the options available to the judicial and correctional decision-makers as each issue is examined. The issues include, but are not limited to, judicial and correctional philosophy, offender eligibility, criteria for selection, organizational models for community service, community service investigations, sentencing considerations, assignments to community service programs, supervision, and evaluation.

## Judicial and Correctional Philosophy

Community service, as with any other sanction, should support the overall philosophical orientation of the criminal justice system and its judicial and correctional decisionmakers specifically. That philosophical orientation—whether it be rehabilitation, restitution, deterrence, retribution, punishment, or something else, singly or in combination— should be translated into community service program goals, objectives, and orientation. Simply stated, operational decisions should be developed from some shared understandings about community service as a sentencing alternative—an alternative to confinement, to fines, to restitution, and/or to other traditional penalties, with special attention focused upon the offender and the community. Operationally, a community service program developed to increase the penalty to an appropriate level of deterrence or just desert may be significantly different from one established to repay the community for damages that the offenders have done or to help the community meet its needs for unpaid workers.

It is not our purpose to argue here what the purposes for community service should be, but it is important to emphasize the need for decision-makers to specify why community service would be a useful sentencing alternative for them. If they state the goals that they seek with community service, they can design programs to achieve these goals.

## Offender Eligibility

Community service has been utilized mostly by the lower courts for individuals convicted of offenses considered less serious, especially misdemeanors, including traffic violations. An option to be considered is the use of community service for more serious offenders. Within the Federal system, even apart from the Comprehensive Crime Control Act requirements, community service has been ordered for white collar and corporate offenders, and even for corporations. The inclusion of felons, in addition to misdemeanants, appears a rational expansion of community service, providing that the threat to community safety is always considered and minimized. The issue of dangerousness clearly is a critical correctional issue.

Concerns about dangerousness may be reflected in mandated exceptions to the utilization of community service for persons (1) committing certain types of offenses, (2) exhibiting particular traits or characteristics in their background, such as drug addiction, or (3) committing offenses with weapons or violence. Indeed, as the question of offender eligibility is considered, it may be appropriate to consider whether there is any reason why individuals entering into or being processed through the criminal justice system, who otherwise are deemed appropriate for a judicial or correctional release to the community, should be barred from community service. This would include adults and juveniles, felons and misdemeanants, probationers and parolees, individuals and corporations, and those convicted of offenses as well as those diverted from the justice system.

## Selection for Community Service

Selection for community service requires a dual focus: on the offender and on the community. In considering individuals, explicit and objective criteria are necessary to prevent in community service the sentencing disparities which have been so well documented nationwide in other sentencing options. It has been noted that

> (t)he lack of standards or guidelines means that similar offenders can receive very different community service sentences for the same offense from a given judge, from two judges in the same jurisdiction, or from judges in different jurisdictions.[3]

Allegations that community service sentences are applied in an unfair or discriminatory fashion also flow from a lack of criteria. The question of equity assuredly will surface if the community service sanction is applied only to the poor and the minorities or, contrastingly, only to middle- or upper-income offenders.

In determining selection criteria, the assignment of an offender to community service requires attention to community safety, to the offender's attitude and special skills or talents, to the seriousness of the offense, the availability of a suitable community service placement, and the wisdom of selecting other sentencing alternatives. As the community is examined, several other important issues emerge, including the public's attitude toward specific offenses and offenders, as well as the impact of community service on perceptions of the justice system by the citizenry. It is important that the public see community service as both a benefit to the community and a reasonable judicial disposition of the offender.

The process by which the criteria are established may be as important as the criteria themselves. It has been suggested that a "core group of advocates"—consisting perhaps of members of the judiciary, corrections, and the community—join together to establish the standards for selection to community service.[4]

## Organizational Issues:

A community service program of any size requires some administrative structure. The two most common administrative entities are the probation agency or a volunteer bureau. There may also be a combined effort in which the probation agency has some oversight of those functions which are uniquely offender-connected within the volunteer bureau. In this case, the probation office and the private organization have mutually supportive and compatible roles. A third type of administrative entity is the private organization created solely for the purpose of overseeing community service activities. An example of this third type is the Foundation for People, a nonprofit corporation established in Los Angeles under the aegis of the Probation Office of the U.S. District Court for the Central District of California. One of its several activities is to work with Federal courts to arrange as community service for white-collar offenders their assistance in the vocational training, counseling, and job-placement of blue-collar offenders.

There are several important distinctions which enter into the issue of the probation agency, volunteer bureau, or other entity providing the organizational structure for community service.[5] The probation agency and the volunteer bureau are established in the community and have important connections with other organizations that already play a role in community-based corrections which could serve as the foundation for the community service function. Probation, as an established part of the criminal justice system, can provide a legitimacy and stability to a community service program and affect both judicial and community acceptance. Volunteer bureaus long have been involved in identifying and matching community needs with individuals able to offer a variety of services.

Regardless of the agency charged with the community service function, it is assumed in this writing that the order to community service is usually a condition of probation. However, it may be appropriate for community service to be ordered by the court without probation, particularly for less serious offenses, and in those smaller jurisdictions in which the court has continuous firsthand contact with the agency providing the community service function. The organization with the administrative responsibility must be able to provide some form of community service investigation, discussed below, as well as to supervise community service. Therefore, it must have the authority to insure compliance with the court order.

In making an organizational decision, there is a need to focus upon two basic functions—the development of some type of plan for joining offenders with community service and for supervision of these offenders in that service obligation. These functions parallel the traditional investigation and supervision functions of probation, but this similarity is not to be interpreted as a preference for the probation agency option. Let us examine these functions separately.

## The Community Service Investigation

A number of important issues surface in a community service investigation and report, especially in the development of a plan for community service. Some of the issues are:

- What constitutes an appropriate community service investigation?
- What is an appropriate format for a community service report?
- Should there be an investigation and report on all individuals eligible to receive a community service sentence or only on specific individuals? If the latter, is it at the direction of the court, the discretion of the probation agency or volunteer bureau, or upon request by the prosecutor or the defendant or the defense attorney?
- Should a community service investigation and report be separate from, an adjunct to, or part of the formal presentence investigation and report? Indeed, for some minor offenses, would a community service investigation and report be an appropriate substitute for a presentence investigation and report?
- How much (additional) time should be allowed for the investigation, the preparation of a report, and the development of an appropriate plan?
- Does the community service investigation and report require a "specialist" familiar with the community and its needs and able to connect offender and community?
- Should the community service investigation and report be conducted before or after the imposition of a community service requirement?
- Should the agency responsible for the investigation and report also be charged with supervision of the community service?
- From an administrative perspective, how many community service investigations and reports are the equivalent of a presentence investigation and report?

## Some Sentencing Considerations

The addition of community service as a sentencing alternative creates several unique issues for the court. Obviously, traditional considerations relating to the imposition of sentence remain, such as the concern for justice, equity, protection of the community, and rehabilitation. If there is an order of community service in lieu of confinement in a local custodial facility, a question of equivalence arises. At bottom, and as a question — how many hours of community service are the equivalent of a day in custody? Is it a day for a day, two for one, three for one, or some other ratio? If it is a day for a day, then is the equivalent of a 30-day jail sentence 30 8-hour days of community service, or 90 8-hour days? In the interests of fairness and equity, these ratios need to be established.

If on the other hand, the court wishes to impose community service instead of a fine — perhaps because the offender simply will be unable to pay a fine — what is the dollar equivalent of an hour of community service work? Is it the minimum wage, the prevailing wage in the community, or is it equal to the offender's normal hourly rate — perhaps $4 an hour for one offender and $25 an hour for another? Is it more equitable to have a uniform "equivalency" or to have equivalence individualized? If the latter, one of these offenders could work off a $1,000 community service obligation with 250 hours of service; the other could accomplish the same in 100 hours.

Community service can be thought of as providing some of the equity that is credited to the day-fine principle pioneered in Scandinavia and now found in several other nations, including Austria and West Germany.[6] Under this principle, an offender is sentenced to a fine of his or her earnings for a given number of days, so that the amount of money involved varies with the size of the earnings. As administered in Sweden, the fine is collected by that country's equivalent of our Internal Revenue Service, which collects all taxes or other money owed to the government. This agency determines the amount of the fine from its records of the offender's past taxable earnings, deducts an amount for necessities and dependents, but imposes some fine per day of the penalty even on those whose only income is from welfare. They collect almost every fine without jailing by allowing installment payments with interest for those who cannot pay immediately, but attaching salaries and even seizing possessions if there is a persistent failure to pay. Our courts, by imposing a penalty of a specified number of days of community service, are getting the same amount of service from each offender punished in this way, regardless of contrasts in the price that the services of different persons command per day when compensated in the free market.

It seems essential that the court fix both the precise number of hours of community service to be performed and the period of time during which the obligation is to be completed. Regardless of whether the number of hours was determined by the nature of the offense or the background of the offender, some other "arithmetic" needs to be completed. That arithmetic focuses on the balance between the number of hours to be performed and the length of time given for completion of community service. An order for 400 hours of community service approximately equals 1 day or perhaps two evenings of service per week for a year. Is that a reasonable assessment when examining all of the factors — the offense, the offender, the offender's family and employment obligations, the community's needs for the service to be performed, and the feeling that "justice was done"? Or would 400 hours of community service over 2 years be more appropriate considering all of the variables?

One last numeric item — there seemingly should be both a minimum and maximum number of hours which can be ordered. It is assumed that there is some number of hours below which the administrative burden to the agencies involved in the delivery of community services would be inefficient and ineffective, and a number above which the offender could not hope to comply with the order. While we do not intend to be prescriptive here, the courts need to establish a meaningful range; perhaps from a 30-hour minimum, equivalent to 1 day a week for 1 month for a minor offense or offender, to as much as perhaps 400 hours per year for 5 years, a total of 2,000 hours of service, for the most serious offense or offender that still would permit imposition of a community-based correctional alternative.

## Community Service Assignments

Following an investigation and report, and an order by the court for community service, there is a requirement to assign the offender to a specific community activity. As noted, this assignment may be made through a probation agency, volunteer bureau, or other organization designated to administer the community service effort. There are two basic perspectives about the assignment issue. The first argues for a matching of offender and community service on the basis of the skills or talents of the offender and the documented needs within the community. An often cited example is the assignment of a physician ordered to perform community service to a program in which medical skills may be utilized, such as a public health or "free" medical clinic of some sort. This kind of matching of abilities and needs may or may not seem as appropriate as a second type of matching: attempts to connect the community service assignment to the offense committed. For example, the assignment of an offender without medical service skills convicted of driving under the influence to a hospital emergency room — where there is considerable opportunity to see the harm done by drinking drivers — may not provide much relevant service.

An alternative to either of these two types of matching is the more-or-less random assignment of offenders to community activities as offenders become available through the system and community needs are identified. Simply put, if two or three projects are identified as valid community needs requiring the services of 25 individuals, one assigns to these projects the next 25 offenders ordered to community service by the court, regardless of the number of hours ordered or the special abilities of the offender. The offender may be allowed to request participation in one or the other of the community services identified. This method has the advantage of simplicity, and perhaps some basic equity, although it is clear that the hypothetical physician mentioned above is not providing the most meaningful service to the community, particularly if the community service project at that time is clearing trash from the side of the road.

All approaches require basic data about the offense, offender, and the community service requirements, but the matching approach — in contrast to randomness — requires considerably more data about these matters. Personal data about skills and abilities are needed, as is related information about employment schedules, indicating hours of the day and days of the week which are available for service, and special clothing or other needed equipment. Indeed, systems involved in matching also require considerable specificity about the nature of the tasks to be accomplished and the skills required of the offender for their accomplishment. A large matching system most likely would be computer-based, whereas a smaller system might simply use 3- by 5-inch index cards.

A number of other related issues surface about the assignment phenomena: what agencies are eligible to receive community service? Agencies with a religious orientation or involvement might be ineligible because of perceived violations of the doctrine of separation of church and state, while assignments to political organizations, public interest or pressure groups, or controversial collectivities of citizens create other problems. Then, too, there are special problems associated with organized labor and with some citizen perceptions that community service deprives "honest citizens" of employment opportunities. Even apart from the issue of legitimacy of organizations to receive services, there are questions as to whether such community services should be provided to *individuals* as opposed to *organizations* . . . for example, to individual victims of crime.

## Supervision of Community Service

The supervision function, whether performed by a probation agency, volunteer bureau, or other organization, also raises some significant issues. Among them are questions which focus upon *disclosure* about the offender, the offense, and personal background to the community organization receiving the offender's service. Is there a reverse side of that coin which assures the offender at least a minimum right to *privacy*? And during the time that the offender is performing community service, does the community service sponsoring agency—the volunteer bureau, for example—have some degree of *liability* for the offender's behavior? Or if the offender is injured while performing community service, are there *disability* rights vested in that service? And should individuals sponsoring community service activities have *personal insurance* to protect them against a variety of potential legal actions which may grow from the connection to community service? While the *charging of fees* to offenders for probation services has been emerging nationwide, would it be appropriate for similar charges to be extended for community service investigations and supervision? Finally, would it be appropriate for the tax-supported agencies or the nonprofit community organizations receiving community services to pay the court for the services received?

Apart from these issues, there are more traditional questions about community service supervision ranging from the identification of those who provide it, frequency of contact with the offender and the community service supervisor or agency, the nature and schedule of reports, reassignment determinations, and the overall relationship between probation supervision and community service supervision, particularly if two separate agencies are involved.

Under some circumstances, there may be important questions raised about compliance with the community service court order. What constitutes a violation: would it be a failure to complete all of the assigned hours in the prescribed time or, in the shorter time-frame, a failure to appear to perform service on one or more occasions? Would a belligerent or disruptive attitude warrant cessation of a community service order? Probation and parole supervision long have had explicit conditions or standards of behavior: is there a need for a parallel series of community service guidelines for those involved in both the supervision and performance of community service?

## Evaluation of Community Service

At a minimum, two areas of community service need assessment. The first centers upon measures of offender success and failure; the second upon some determination of cost-benefits. The cost-benefit analyses must consider both the criminal justice system *and* the community. In short, effectiveness and efficiency are required targets for analysis.

Definitions of success and failure for offenders involved in the many varieties of community corrections long have been troublesome.

Although we do not address that conflicted arena here, we note that community service does not make those assessments simpler, but rather more complex. An overall evaluation should go beyond that which could be generated by data as to whether or not the offender completed the required number of hours of community service within the court-ordered period of time.

Several examples may illustrate the complexity. The first focuses upon the definition of success and failure by asking about how the two are related in probation *and* community service. As an example: consider an offender who successfully completes a court-ordered community service obligation but is declared in violation of probation for behavior that is not related to the community service. How is that overall offender performance to be assessed?

If costs are the focus of evaluation, two quite different sets of cost data may be examined. The first may be the value of services provided the community—these calculated at some arbitrary hourly or daily rate such as the national minimum wage or an average local wage. The overall dollar value of the services provided is the number of hours of service multiplied by the value of those hours for a given period of time.

A second set of data may be derived from the "savings" obtained by having offenders provide community service instead of being in local custody. This may be calculated as the daily custodial rate multiplied by the number of confinement days not served. It is quite probable that estimates of monies saved by the justice system from non-incarceration of offenders who are performing community service may be markedly different from estimates of the value of the community service developed from hourly or daily wage comparisons, and that the two might be added. This difference would grow if calculated to include welfare assistance given to families of confined offenders. If community service serves as an alternative to the capital costs of constructing a custodial facility, the savings—even when prorated in some fashion—become enormous. And if these community services generate activities and projects which otherwise might not have been accomplished—that is, things which the community could not have done without these court-ordered services—perhaps some other dollar equivalents would be justified.

Finally, improvements in community feelings about "justice" generally and the criminal justice system specifically on one hand or the improvement of the offender's personal feelings of self-worth which may be generated from performing a service to the community on the other, cannot be measured readily, but nevertheless need assessment.

## Some Other Issues

Clearly, the issues identified above are not a complete listing, not only because of space limitations, but also because issues are emerging as the utilization of community service expands and new concerns evolve. At this point, we simply would identify some other questions.

- Because of the rapid growth of the community service sentencing option nationwide, is there now a need for professional community service associations at the national, state, and local levels?
- Is there a need for the development of prescriptions about the use of the community service option and, if prescriptions are appropriate, what organizations and agencies should be involved in standard-setting?
- Should there be statutory authority for the use of community service, or is the use of that option clearly inherent in the sentencing powers of the courts?
- What is the appropriate priority for insuring compliance with court orders that direct two or more actions, for example, a fine, restitution, and performance of community service?
- As related to the very complicated issue of "what" constitutes community service, should offender involvement in education and training programs be credited to the community service obligation?
- Would it be appropriate to order completion of a *project* (an attorney, for example, ordered to prepare a specific number of wills for the elderly poor) instead of a *specified number of hours*?
- And a host of other issues; including the appropriate location for community service offices; whether to focus upon one or two large agencies to receive community service (example: a Veterans Administration hospital and the Red Cross) or divide the available service among many community agencies; how to minimize reporting requirements that might be placed on agencies receiving the service, which are time-consuming and generally considered onerous; the selection, composition, and utilization of local advisory committees; methods for obtaining public understanding and support of community service; and so on.

## Summary

Community service as a sentencing option has an operational history of about 15 years. There is every reason to believe that its utilization in America and elsewhere will expand significantly during the next decade. Because it has evolved and grown so rapidly, there has not yet been adequate time or attention given to identification of the issues that surround its usage or to develop standards for that usage. Indeed, there is some evidence of a failure to understand that the many issues which have been or yet may be identified are completely interrelated, one with the other.

The authors have not been prescriptive but would argue that there is a mandate to examine carefully a number of issues about community service. Some of these have been identified—judicial and correctional philosophies, offender eligibility and selection criteria, organizational arrangements, community service investigations and supervision, sentencing considerations, community service assignments, and evaluation. If community service is to become a truly viable sentencing option, these areas need thoughtful consideration by those academicians, administrators, practitioners, and researchers concerned with criminal justice.

## Notes

[1] 18 U.S.C. 3563 (a) (2) (p.157, 98 Stat. 1993). As quoted in Anthony Partridge, "The Crime Control and Fine Enforcement Acts of 1984: A Synopsis," Federal Justice Center, Washington, DC, January 1985, p. 8.

[2] See, for example, Burt Galaway, Joe Hudson, and Steve Novack, "Restitution and Community Service: An Annotated Bibliography," National Institute for Sentencing Alternatives, Brandeis University, Waltham, Massachusetts, September 1983, 132 pp. and "Community Service: Custom Search," U.S. Department of Justice, National Institute of Justice/NCJRS, Washington, DC, 1986, 266 pp.

[3] M. Kay Harris, "Community Service by Offenders," U.S. Department of Justice, National Institute of Corrections, Washington, DC, January 1979, p. 45.

[4] Ibid., p. 11.

[5] Ibid., pp. 14-15.

[6] See, for example, Hans J. Albrecht, "Recidivism after Fines, Suspended Sentences, and Imprisonment," International Journal of Comparative and Applied Criminal Justice, 8, (Winter 1984), pp. 199-207 and Robert W. Gillespie, "Fines as an Alternative to Incarceration: The German Experience," Federal Probation, 44, (December 1980), pp. 20-26.

# 16

# Electronic Monitors
## Realistically, What Can Be Expected?
## Annesley K. Schmidt

## Introduction

The electronic monitoring equipment presently in use in the United States applies telemetry technology to determine whether an offender is present in the required location at the required times. First used on offenders in 1984, it is presently used daily on at least 12,000 probationers, parolees, work releasees, pretrial releasees, and other offenders under correctional supervision in the community (Renzema).

There are two basic types of electronic monitoring devices. "Continuously signalling devices" constantly monitor the presence of an offender at a particular location. "Programmed contact devices" contact the offender periodically to verify his presence.

A "continuously signalling device" has three major parts: A *transmitter* attached to the offender sends out a continuous signal. Transmitters produced by some manufacturers send an altered signal to alert officials if they are tampered with, and others do not. A *receiver-dialer* located in the offender's home is attached to his telephone and detects signals from the transmitter. It reports to the central computer

Source: *Federal Probation*, Vol. 55, No. 2 (June 1991), 47–53.

when it stops receiving the signal and when it starts receiving it again. A *central computer* accepts reports from the receiver-dialer over telephone lines, compares them with the offender's curfew schedule, and alerts correctional officials to any unauthorized absences. The computer also stores information about routine entries and exits of each offender so that reports can be prepared.

"Programmed contact devices" provide an alternative approach. They contact the offender at intervals to verify that he is at the location where he is required to be. These devices all use a computer programmed to telephone the offender during the monitored hours, either randomly or at specifically selected times. The computer is also programmed to prepare reports on the results of the call. However, each manufacturer uses a different method to assure that the offender is the person responding to the call and is in fact at the monitored location as required. One system uses voice verification technology. Another system requires a "wristlet," a black plastic module, which is strapped to the offender's arm. When the computer calls, the wristlet is inserted into a verifier box connected to the telephone to verify that the telephone is answered by the monitored offender. A third system uses visual verification to assure that the telephone is being answered by the offender being monitored.

"Hybrid" equipment, introduced by several manufacturers, functions as a continuously signalling device. However, when the computer notes that the offender appears to have left at an unauthorized time, it functions similarly to a programmed contact device, contacting the offender by telephone and verifying that the person responding is the offender being monitored either by the use of voice verification technology or the insertion of a "wristlet" into a "verifier box" attached to the telephone. If verification does not occur, notification is made that a violation has occurred.

The role of the telephone, in the electronic monitoring of offenders, requires that certain new telephone technologies are not in use on the offender's telephone. For example, "call forwarding," where the telephone will automatically switch the call to another number, and a portable telephone would make it easier for the offender to respond to calls while away from home. Many programs also prohibit "call waiting" since it might interfere with the equipment's effort to call the central computer or for the verifier box to be attached. The program must review the offender's monthly telephone bill to assure that none of the prohibited services have been acquired.

At present, most of the equipment limits participation in monitoring programs to those who have a telephone at home. However, at least one company produces equipment that allows an officer to drive near the offender's house and tune to the frequency of the offender's transmitter and thus to determine if the offender is home without the officer leaving the car or the offender knowing that monitoring has occurred. Other companies are investigating similar approaches.

Offenders are also monitored without electronic verification. One approach uses the automatic equipment to telephone the offender and records the response. With this approach, verification that the person responding is in fact the monitored offender occurs when the recording is played by someone who recognizes the offender's voice. Another simpler, traditional approach has officers knocking on the door of offenders' homes to assure that they are home.

For the past 6 years, I have been watching the development of these electronic monitoring devices. During that time, which dates almost from the beginning of the correctional application of the technology, I have observed the continuing development, refinement, and improvement of the equipment, along with the beginnings, mergers, demise, and growth of manufacturers. There has also been the parallel development of a related service industry. These companies receive the output of the monitoring and respond to each different agency according to pre-determined specifications.

While the equipment and service industries have been developing, the users have made strides toward defining appropriate uses for the equipment, as well as determining which uses are inappropriate because the technology does not further the program's goals. Programs have also become clearer in their definition of purpose and therefore in deciding which type of equipment is most suitable and whether, in that particular program context, it makes more sense to handle their own monitoring equipment or contract with a service provider.

I have also tried to stay aware of developments in the field. To accomplish this, I have read the literature about monitors, written papers, visited programs, and interviewed monitored offenders, the officers supervising them, and those directing the programs. In addition, I have heard and participated in discussions with proponents and opponents. Much of what I have read and heard appears accurate and realistic, but some seemed to include exaggeration, distortion, misunderstanding, or wishful thinking.

The development of new technology has led to at least the possibility of a different approach to the supervision of offenders in the community. However, it has been only a short 6 years since the first program began, so there are many questions, the answers to which are yet to be learned. In this context, it is not surprising that some misinterpretations, misconceptions, myths, and misunderstandings have also emerged.

The sources of various perceptions and misconceptions are different depending on the nature of the issue. There are the concerns that arise from philosophical objection to the use of any equipment to monitor the behavior of offenders in the community. Some show a misunderstanding about the functioning of the equipment. Others have arisen when the equipment and the program using it have been "oversold" so that no program could possibly accomplish the goals that have been established with the resources given. This overselling often reflects a misunderstanding about money, the potential economic impact that a monitoring program might have (Byrne).

## Philosophical Issues

The development of electronic monitoring has coincided with the increasing discussion of intermediate sanctions. This dialogue examines sanctions that can be applied to criminal behaviors which are less serious than those requiring long-term incarceration, while, at the same time, being more serious than those deserving standard probation. The use of electronic monitors has fitted into this discussion, both when equipment is the sanction and when it is a part of efforts to increase the credibility and viability of probation as a sanction, as can be seen in programs such as intensive supervision.

When electronic monitoring devices are used as a part of correctional supervision in the community, such application may generate controversy. There are some people who feel that monitoring is improper. This point of view is aptly illustrated by the title of a recent paper, "No Soul in the New Machines: Technofallacies in the Electronic Monitoring Movement" (Corbett & Marx). It discusses "fallacies" that can occur in the establishment of programs. Some of the fallacies the authors mention, such as failure to clearly state the program's agenda or purpose, can occur in the establishment of any kind of program, have happened in a few monitoring programs, and should not be permitted to happen in any well-thought-out program of any type. However, it is not a criticism of monitoring programs, in particular, as much as it is a criticism of impulsive program design.

The issues more specific to monitoring programs are related to the purpose of correctional supervision in the community. A recent annual conference and training institute of the American Probation and Parole Association stated the apparent conflict in its title, "Supervision in the 1990s: Surveillance vs. Treatment" (APPA). The descriptive materials about the conference posed a question: "Are the concepts really conflicting or can they be supporting and complementary?" (Ibid, p. 20). The answer to that question must be determined by each agency. In the case of public agencies, the answer is determined by the politicians who chart the agency's course either overtly or through the budget that they provide. That answer, no matter how it is arrived at, will determine whether the use of monitors could make sense in their context.

Electronic monitoring devices are surveillance technology. Therefore, if surveillance is not one purpose of the program, these devices would be inappropriate. By the same token, if surveillance is a purpose of the program, the use of equipment is one way to enhance effort to achieve it, but not the only way. As mentioned earlier, humans knocking on doors would be another way to achieve the surveillance objective.

Another proposition states that monitoring will lead to "net widening." The expression "net widening" is based on an analogy to catching fish in a net. If the net is opened more widely more fish will be caught. Thus, in this context, it refers both to sanctioning those who would not otherwise have been sanctioned and to sanctioning someone more severely than would otherwise have been done. In this case, the concern revolves around hypotheses about what would happen if the program did not exist or what will happen if a program is established. If offenders are being monitored who would otherwise have been incarcerated, the use of the equipment may be seen as a reduction in the severity of the sanction. If, on the other hand, monitors are being used for offenders who might receive probation with little direct supervision, the level of the sanction appears to have been increased, and the question becomes, "Is the community receiving a needed increase in protection?"—a very different issue.

When "net widening" is discussed, the issue has two distinct ends with abundant space in between. At one end is the concern that the use of monitors may increase the level of sanctioning and therefore cause "net widening." At the other end is the argument that presently offenders are being sanctioned at a lesser level than is appropriate because of prison crowding. Therefore, if there is an increase in the level of sanctioning, it is an increase to an appropriate level. Differences among programs make a general resolution of this issue impossible, and specific resolutions must occur in the context of the handling of individual cases by individual programs.

Another issue has been expressed as: Monitors spy on people and reveal their secrets (Marx, 1985 & 1986). We have all seen the spy movie where the olive in the martini is really a transmitter revealing the plans of "the bad guys" to "the good guys" so that the good guys can come and save the day. It seems plausible that such technology is available, but the present electronic monitoring equipment used on offenders does not have that capacity. Whether future equipment will have that capacity is unknown, and, if it does, whether it would be used is dependent on the ethics of those operating the program. Furthermore, some people would contend that an officer, entering an offender's home during a surveillance check, is likely to learn more about the activities in the house and the interaction of the members of the household.

There is equipment on the horizon with the capacity to track the offender. When this becomes available, programs will be able to plot a route for the offender to use when traveling to and from work and learn of deviations from that, as well as know about unauthorized departures from work. This new knowledge may be reassuring to those concerned about detailed monitoring of activities. At the same time, those who question the appropriateness of surveillance will have a further basis for their questions.

When considering these philosophical issues, it needs to be kept in mind that there is a distinction between the equipment and the program that uses it. It is the program that makes and enforces the rules and responds to what it learns from the equipment. The equipment provides information which can be responded to immediately, later, or not at all, with a phone call or a visit, as specified by the program's procedures.

## Misunderstandings About the Equipment

Assuming that any potential philosophical misgivings are answered, it is important that the program designers are realistic about what the equipment can and cannot accomplish. For example, as mentioned earlier, equipment that tracks offenders is expected to come onto the market, but it is not presently available. However, the present equipment is often incorrectly assumed to have the capacity to track the offender as he moves around the community.

Since the introduction of the equipment, some have posited: This is new and it's technology, so it must be "good." As the pioneers who first used the equipment learned, the equipment and the computer programs that convert the signal from the equipment into something meaningful, needed to be tried, tested, refined, and modified in the real world. Vast strides have been made in the technology, and its reliability has increased greatly. At the same time, it seems unlikely that it will ever be 100 percent perfect.

A closely related erroneous assumption is: Monitors are technology so they must be an improvement. Any program that acquires monitors will obtain more information about those being supervised than was previously available. Whether or not this new information is an improvement depends on the use to which it is put. If more paper is added to files, and little else is done, then a question can be raised about the value of the information from the equipment. In addition, when the offender learns by experience that violations are of little or no consequence, the credibility of the program is undermined. On the other hand, if violations are responded to, the offender learns that the program means what it says, and greater control is achieved. Thus, the program establishes its credibility with offenders and the public.

Even when the equipment is functioning correctly, it cannot *prevent* violations, as some have hoped. The offender is free to leave any time he decides to do so, and nothing about the equipment will stop him. In addition, the offender can leave as if he were going to work and then go anywhere. Unless the officer happens to check with the place of employment, he'll find out that the offender did not go to work when he sees reduced hours on the pay stub or when the offender is fired. Finally, there is no information about what the offender is doing when he is home which could be anything from something innocuous like watching TV to something as heinous as drug dealing or inflicting physical abuse on another member of the household. The equipment simply provides information showing that the offender is present within range of the receiver-dialer.

Any program has to determine how it will respond to the increase in information, realizing that the additional information may well mean that the program is now aware of failures that would have previously been unknown. This newly acquired information must be responded to by the staff if the program is to maintain its credibility with the offenders and with the public. If the staff is overworked and unable to respond to the information that it now receives, acquiring more information from monitors will only increase the staff frustration and decrease the program's credibility.

Some manufacturers of continuously signalling equipment provide a special feature in the band that holds the transmitter on the offender. When present, the nature of the signal changes when the band is tampered with. At first blush, this tamper-resistant band appears to prevent violations. However, tamper signals may occur when the equipment is twisted or otherwise handled roughly but not actually tampered with. On the other hand, the tamper signal can only be perceived if the offender is within range of the receiver-dialer. Outside that range, it will signal, but there is no way it can be "heard."

Monitoring requires that an offender have a home with a telephone and that he remain there. Some offenders do not have homes, and others have homes without telephones. Secondly, if others in the household are not supportive of the offender's participation in the monitoring program, they can sabotage the offender. For example, if the household contains teenage phone users who are not willing to limit their calls or relinquish the phone to the equipment, the offender cannot successfully participate. Moreover, there are situations when a house is not a home— at least not one for home confinement. This would be especially true if abuse is present.

# Money: What Monitors Can Save

Program funders often hope or assume that they can buy equipment and save money directly or indirectly by decreasing staff or, at the very least, not increasing it. First, capital or money is required if the equipment is purchased. But, equipment can be and often is obtained by lease or lease-purchase arrangements which do not require a large initial outlay. Second, the caseloads of monitoring programs are usually about 25 while regular probation programs frequently have caseloads of over 100 offenders. In addition, monitoring programs require substantial labor if reported violations are responded to on a 24-hour, 7-day per week basis. This may have implications for staff, staffing costs, and labor-management agreements if the staff is required to be available during times which have not been traditionally considered to be working hours. Additionally, the outputs of equipment will provide staff with previously unavailable information to which staff now must respond.

The actual cost obviously depends on the type of equipment, the number of units, and whether the equipment is purchased or leased. In addition to staffing, extra costs may be incurred because of telephone charges. The In-House Arrest Work Release Program of the Sheriff's Stockade in Palm Beach County, Florida, charges participants in the voluntary program $9 per day (Garcia, 1986). Within the first 14 months of program operation, the program's investment in equipment had been returned by offender fees. However, if the initial amount invested is more or less, if fees are charged at a lower or higher rate, or not at all, or if the equipment is in use a greater or lesser proportion of the time, then the pay-back period will change. Also, the costs have changed as the competition between the manufacturers has increased. During the same time, staff salaries have increased, and many programs have been established in sites that are not routinely staffed 24 hours a day, 7 days a week. And, most importantly, there are many who do not feel that it is appropriate to charge offenders for their supervision. This philosophical consideration has been the subject of numerous booklets and articles and is mentioned here. Detailed consideration of this point is outside the scope of this article but an important financial and philosophical issue for program designers to consider.

The staff of some agencies has become concerned that monitors will replace people. However, this loses sight of the fact that monitors are just equipment. People are required for a number of purposes by a program that uses monitors. First, people must screen participants and attach the equipment. Once participants are in the program, staff is required to interpret the output from the equipment. Then, based on that interpretation, staff has to respond to the offender. Additionally, there are things only people can do, such as counseling, job placement, and employment verification. Given the smaller caseloads needed to respond to the additional information provided by the monitors, it seems unlikely that programs will be able to replace staff with the equipment, and many have found that more staff is required.

Many jurisdictions have justified the acquisition of electronic monitors with assurances that it will alleviate prison and jail crowding. This view may be optimistic, for a variety of reasons. First, in addition to issues related to what a community can, will, and should be expected to tolerate, it should be reiterated that monitors are technological devices potentially useful in a variety of program contexts. The population selected as the focus of monitoring programs may or may not be one that might otherwise be sent to jail or prison if monitors were not available. Second, consideration needs to be given to the likely impact on the total problem. In a thousand-man jail, the release of 20 monitored inmates would reduce the population by only 2 percent. One hundred monitored inmates would have to be released before the population would be affected by 10 percent. In a smaller jail, more impact would be achieved by a system the size of the typical initial purchase of 20 units, if all units were being used at the same time. In the prison systems of many states with much larger populations, more monitored inmates would have to be released before a significant reduction in population could occur. Furthermore, the cost of a monitoring program cannot be directly compared to per diem costs of incarceration. The largest component of per diem costs is staff salaries. Therefore, until the number of released inmates is large enough to affect staffing of the facility, the only savings achieved are in marginal categories such as food.

Closely related to the assertion that monitors will solve crowding is the assertion that monitors save money because monitoring is less expensive than jail. The arguments seem to rest on faulty mathematics and inappropriate comparisons when comparing the per diem of jail with the per diem costs of monitoring. Jails are labor intensive, with about 80 percent of the costs being staffing. Therefore, unless staffing can be affected or construction becomes unnecessary, the only cost savings are marginal items such as food and medical care. It is also important to note that this comparison is based on the assumption that all monitored offenders would otherwise be in jail. The experience of many programs makes this assumption at least questionable.

All of the assertions made about monitors in the corrections literature and the popular press lead to the assumption that the use of monitors is widespread. However, Marc Renzema's latest 1-day count shows about 12,000 to 14,000 offenders being monitored (Renzema). At the same time, the Bureau of Justice Statistics tells us that there are 2.6 million offenders under supervision in the community (BJS). As can be readily seen, monitors are used on only a very small proportion of offenders.

## Some Strategies to Avoid Misunderstandings

During the short period that monitors have been available, experience has taught some of the issues that must be resolved before or during the establishment of a monitoring program. There are myriad decisions which must be made, few of which have known "right" answers. However, if the questions are answered clearly, many myths can be laid to rest and misunderstandings avoided.

The program needs to provide the context in which the equipment is to be used. If that is lacking, there will be the inappropriate situation of "equipment in search of a program." The program needs to be defined in terms of how an offender enters the program, who will make the decision, and on what will the decision be based—risk, need, offender status, etc.; then, how long people will remain in the program.

The program's statement of purposes and objectives should supply a clear rationale for the use of monitors, which means that at least one of the program goals should be offender surveillance and control. If this is not a goal, there seems little reason to use monitoring equipment and little justification for it.

Then, the program needs to determine what type of equipment will be used, keeping in mind both the cost and surveillance implications of the choice. It should be noted that different features are available on different equipment, even equipment of the same type. These choices should be evaluated in terms of how the features relate to goals of the program. The equipment decision should consider the cost and desirability of certain features to determine whether the program wishes to monitor consistently or intermittently; whether tamper-resistance is required or visual inspection for damage will be sufficient; and what the nature and size of the equipment itself is.

If equipment seems appropriate in the context of the program, the next question is financial. What will be purchased? The usual choice is one of two possibilities—equipment or service. Either the agency obtains the equipment and uses its staff to provide the service or the agency contracts for service with a company that will provide both monitoring equipment and monitoring. The equipment may be acquired through a lease, purchase, or lease with an option to purchase.

The equipment is going to provide information which was previously unknown. This will range from simple facts, such as what time the offender left for work or that the offender was late leaving and therefore was probably late for work. The program will also learn that the offender is not at his residence when he is supposed to be. The program needs to anticipate these issues and determine in advance how it will respond. For the simpler issues, responses may be as simple as telephoning the employer to determine that the offender is, in fact, at work. The response to reported violations may vary. It may be by phone or in person, at the time when it first becomes known or during the next workday.

The decisions about response to violation have implications for costs and staff. They must also be made considering what the responsible authorities—usually a court or parole board—are going to require as proof of violations. When planning the response to violations, the program should consider the possibility that false alarms may occur and that equipment may be damaged accidentally or purposely.

Once these decisions, and many others, have been made, it is important that the program plan allow time to test and get acquainted with the equipment and to train staff.

As the program plan is being developed, there are a variety of other issues which need to be considered. All the elements of the criminal justice system need to be involved in the planning so that their issues and agendas can be considered. Cooperation of the courts and probation and parole will likely be required. Additionally, many times, planning also may involve the sheriff, other law enforcement agencies, and others. As with any multi-agency effort, the lines of responsibility must be clear and the cooperation between them developed. For example, if the program is going to monitor the output of the equipment around the clock, then the base is optimally located where 24-hour staffing is already present. This facility might be a jail operated by the sheriff. If the program, on the other hand, is being operated by the probation office, the division of responsibilities and expectations should be clearly specified, preferably in writing. At the same time, at least some elements of the broader community should be involved, such as the press and political action groups concerned about criminal justice issues, such as MADD (Mothers Against Drunk Driving).

The establishment of a monitoring program in some areas has provided an opportunity for the agency to be proactive, reaching out to the public and the press. This contrasts with the reactive posture often assumed by corrections and may lead to the development of relationships with the press which may be useful in other contexts.

In summary, when starting a program, it is important to be *realistic* about why the program is being established and what it is expected to accomplish. In addition, the program needs to be placed in a context that is well thought out, has consistent policies and procedures, and documents events that occur and specific expectations. Above all, monitoring equipment should never be "equipment in search of a program."

## References

American Probation and Parole Association. (1988, Spring). *Perspectives.*

Bureau of Justice Statistics. (1988, March). *Report to the nation on crime and justice.* Washington, DC: U.S. Government Printing Office.

Byrne, J. M., Kelly, L., & Guarino-Ghezzi, S. (1988, Spring). Understanding the limits of technology: An examination of the use of electronic monitoring in the criminal justice system. *Perspectives,* pp. 30–37.

Corbett, R. P., Jr., & Marx, G. T. (1990, November). No soul in the new machines: Technofallacies in the electronic monitoring movement. Paper presented at the Annual Meeting of the American Society of Criminology, Baltimore, MD.

Garcia, E.D. In-house arrest work release program. February 16, 1986, xeroxed, six pages, and personal communication.

Marx, G. T. (1986, Winter). I'll be watching you. *Dissent,* pp. 26–34.

_____. (1986, May-June). The new surveillance. *Technology Review, 45,* 43–48.

Rensema, M., personal communication, March 29, 1991.

Rensema, M., & Skelton, D. T. (1990, November/December). *The use of electronic monitoring in the United States: 1989 update (NIJ Reports),* pp. 9–14.

# Part IV

# The Effectiveness Issue

Since the first edition, the system of corrections has continued to grow at an unprecedented rate. It appears that while the rate of crime in certain crime categories has slowed, the only factor influencing incarceration appears to be the availability of bedspace. In only a few states have voters expressed disapproval when asked to fund prison construction. California and Michigan are two such examples in recent years. The increase in the offender population under community correctional supervision continues at a rate which is more than twice the number of inmates confined in prisons and jails. Probation continues to be the disposition of choice in virtually every jurisdiction.

"The Effectiveness Issue" section continues to emphasize the importance of program evaluation in community corrections. The field has benefited from many of the works contained within this section as the profession seeks to identify practices and programs that "work." The literature on community corrections is replete with various definitions of effectiveness and success. Factors such as prior criminal record, rearrest during the supervision term, age, length of sentence, educational attainment, race, marital status, and others have been shown to play a role in predicting success or failure under supervision. Success can also be multifaceted. Offenders who violate the rules or conditions in one jurisdiction may continue under supervision and eventually be successfully discharged from supervision, while within a neighboring jurisdiction an offender may violate similar rules, be revoked, and sentenced (or returned) to prison, naturally resulting in the label of case failure.

In the first selection, Patrick Donnelly and Brian Forschner identify factors which contribute to success in a co-correctional halfway house, one of a limited number of studies of residential community correctional programs. As expected, strong socialization ties to the community and few prior contacts with the criminal justice system contribute significantly to client success.

In "Measuring the Performance of Community Corrections," Joan Petersilia discusses concerns which have plagued the field of community correction for years. First is the need for the profession to articulate its mission or at least come to an agreement as to the most appropriate indicators of successful performance. The identification of methods of accomplishing its mission and goals is a vital link between the development of a clear mission and the measurement of the extent to which the activities are performed and goals attained.

Although it is the most frequently used criminal disposition, probation is often criticized for its inability to rehabilitate the offender and to deter offenders from additional crime. Since the 1960s, dozens of studies have identified probation failure rates, figures which range from 14 to 60 percent. In addition, various sources have reported the factors associated with success and failure of offenders while on probation supervision. The most frequent outcome measures reported were rearrest, reconviction, revocation or absconding. In "Factors Influencing Probation Outcome: A Review of the Literature," Kathryn Morgan reviews the professional literature focusing on outcome measures in probation. She finds that the "legal factors" cited previously are frequently used to measure "success." Morgan suggests that there exists a need for additional research on probation as a correctional alternative.

Utilizing recidivism or rearrest as the primary measure of success or failure, the authors of "The Effectiveness of Institutional and Community-Based Programs for Juvenile Offenders," Larry Webb and John Scanlon, conclude that community programs can be as successful as their institutional counterparts in reducing recidivism among juvenile offenders. This selection is significant to the study of community corrections in that it addresses the concerns of the critics who believe that community correctional programs do little to deter the offender or to reduce criminal activity. During a period when the costs associated with incapacitation continue to be staggering, this work can direct our attention to less expensive forms of corrections without compromising community safety.

When intensive probation supervision programs came upon the scene in the early 1980s, they were presented as an alternative to prison which would reduce crowding, a cost saving device, and as a form of offender supervision which would tell that these were lofty, often unattainable goals. Still, the promotion if ISP programs as surveillance-oriented forms of offender supervision, more stringent than "regular" probation supervision, continue to expand in most jurisdictions. In their National Institute of Justice sponsored research, Joan Petersilia and Susan Turner focus attention on the ISP programs in 14 evaluation sites throughout the United States. Most significant was that ISP programs were effective as a form of surveillance, although there was no clear relationship between the level of offender contact and recidivism. Rearrest of ISP offenders were reported higher than the control group in most sites, a result which may be explained by the ability of the system to detect crime through increased surveillance. If cost comparisons are made, ISP programs are significantly more expensive than regular probation programs, although they are cheaper than prison. High violation rates and incarceration rates increased the estimated supervision costs to $7,200, compared to $4,700 on routine supervision. This selection contains several policy implications which could significantly affect the results of future ISP outcome evaluations. For consideration, the authors recommend that ISPs consider increasing treatment within the context of this surveillance-oriented program option as well as de-emphasizing the importance of technical violations.

# 17

# Predictors of Success in a Co-Correctional Halfway House: A Discriminant Analysis

Patrick G. Donnelly
Brian E. Forschner

## Abstract

*Considerable research and debate have focused on the effectiveness of community correctional programs. Much of the research does not address the issue of the effectiveness of programs for persons with different types of problems or criminal histories. This article utilizes discriminant analysis to determine the characteristics of persons most likely to succeed in one halfway house. The results indicate that strong socializing and integrating ties in the community and few previous contacts with the criminal justice system are major predictors of success in a halfway house program. The seven discriminators for females are used to accurately predict 87 percent of the female misdemeanants while the nine discriminators for male felons correctly predict 63 percent of the cases.*

Source: *Journal of Crime and Justice*, Vol. 10, No. 2 (1987), 1-22. Copyright © 1987 by Anderson Publishing Co. Reprinted with permission.

# Introduction

While halfway houses existed in the United States as early as 1864, most of the interest and growth in the halfway house movement occurred in the 1960s and '70s (Reid, 1981). The federal government did not use halfway houses until 1961 and, by 1965, there was no more than a few dozen correctional-oriented houses. Recently the International Halfway House Association listed almost 2,300 facilities containing over 100,000 beds (Gatz and Murray, 1981).

This growth may be attributed to both practical and ideological factors. The parole system was expanding and frequently it required that offenders have employment before their release. Since most prisoners found themselves in rural areas far removed from their home communities, finding a job was often difficult. Halfway houses enabled prisoners to return to their communities to search for jobs while the correctional system maintained control over them. In addition, during the 1960s and '70s, many people began to recognize the failure of many rehabilitative efforts in prison. Bailey (1966) and Lipton, Martinson and Wilks (1975) provided much of the evidence of this failure in their reviews of studies evaluating various treatment programs. Finally, the perceived cost-effectiveness of halfway houses over prisons contributed to their growth (Gatz and Murray, 1981).

While these practical considerations gave impetus to the increased use of halfway houses, other factors also played a role. Humanitarian interests sought to eliminate the devastating psychological and economic effects of prisons and the prisonization process. Prisons were suffering from overcrowding, gross idleness of prisoners, and unsafe and unhealthy physical plants. The President's Commission in 1967 stated that "Life in many institutions is at best barren and futile, at worst unspeakably brutal and degrading" (1967:159). There was also a growing realization that criminal behavior originates in the community, that it is a response to a whole set of factors present in the community including school systems, economic conditions, urban decay and racism. This led some reformers to argue that the responsibility for dealing with criminal behavior must begin in the community. The development of the reintegrative model, which found expression in the President's Task Force on Corrections (1967), called for greater emphasis on rebuilding strong ties between the offender and family and community institutions.

More recently, there has been an increasing number of attacks on community-based corrections and louder calls for a renewed emphasis on institutionalization (Allen and Seiter, 1976; Reid, 1981; Scott, 1978). These changes are also due to practical and ideological factors. They result, at least in part, from the findings of numerous research projects that show that the reintegration or community rehabilitation programs are not effective in reducing future criminality (van den Haag, 1975). Segments of the public create political pressure and call for reinstitutionalization when the local media report that parolees in the community repeat the same heinous violent crimes for which they were originally incarcerated. The ideological element underlying many of the attacks on community-based corrections is the turn toward a more conservative political climate in the country during the late 1970s and early 1980s. This climate leads to efforts to punish rather than rehabilitate individuals for their criminal acts. This movement finds support in the just deserts model of criminal justice which generally emphasizes retribution rather than treatment, recommends flat sentencing and the elimination of parole (Fogel, 1975).

What is underemphasized or ignored by many critics of community-based programs is that these programs may work for many people. Newspapers do not report when parolees and probationers do *not* commit crimes again. Critics may claim that 50 percent of the clients in one program or another later commit another crime. They do not emphasize that 50 percent did not. Frequently, the researchers or evaluators of a program are at fault. Researchers evaluating programs frequently do not examine the effectiveness of the programs for subgroups of the population. They do not analyze whether the programs are more effective for people with certain types of problems or histories (Glaser, 1975; Palmer, 1974). Correctional programs with an overall success rate of 50 percent may be successful 80 percent of the time for one subgroup and 20 percent of the time for another group. Before old programs are thrown out or new programs are created, researchers need to focus on this issue.

This paper will review some of the literature that does attempt to assess the effectiveness of halfway houses, describe the program utilized in one halfway house, and use discriminant analysis to determine the characteristics of persons most likely to succeed in the halfway house environment.

## Review of the Literature

The traditional measure of the success or failure of a correctional program is recidivism. This is consistent with the goal of the whole criminal justice system to reduce crime. However, this may not be a realistic goal of any aspect of the criminal justice system. The causes of crime are too complex to be handled by one arm of the government. Measuring the effectiveness of correctional programs by recidivism rates may be inappropriate since they have only limited control over the conditions and causes of criminal behavior. Correctional programs cannot eliminate unemployment, poverty or discrimination. The individual participating in the correctional program can acquire academic diplomas or degrees, extensive vocational training, psychological counseling, and interpersonal skills, yet still return to crime upon his release. The job market for his skills and educational level and the reaction of family and friends are two areas over which the correctional program has no control. If the well-trained ex-convict cannot find a job, despite an array of skills acquired in the correctional program, he may be pressured into returning to crime. If an ex-inmate's family and friends shun her upon her release from a halfway house, she may begin associating with those who will accept her — other criminals. This may induce her to return to crime. These are only two examples of conditions that lead some people to commit crime for which correctional programs today cannot be held accountable.

Considering these limitations, it might be expected that the rehabilitative and reintegrative capabilities of the halfway house would be tempered by the external conditions. Studies evaluating the post-release recidivism rates of halfway house clients suggest that this does occur. A report by Seiter et al. (1977) that was later updated by Latessa and Allen (1982) examines 44 studies addressing the post-release recidivism rates of halfway house clients. The degree of methodological rigor varies considerably in these studies. Neither of the two studies using true experimental designs found any significant difference between the recidivism rates of halfway house clients and a control group.

There were 23 studies that used a quasi-experimental design. Twelve of these reported lower recidivism rates (or better behavioral assessments) for ex-parolee halfway house residents than for the comparison group although only three of these 12 revealed statistically significant differences. Six of the quasi-experimental studies found no significant differences between the experimental and comparison groups. Five studies showed that ex-halfway house clients actually had slightly higher recidivism rates although none of these were statistically significant. There were 19 nonexperimental studies reporting recidivism or failure rates but because of the varying operational definitions and the lack of a control group, the authors could not indicate whether or not the halfway houses were effective in lowering recidivism.

A recent study that is not included in the Latessa and Allen evaluation was conducted on a California halfway house for female offenders (Dowell et al., 1985). It compared the recidivism rates of a group of female halfway house clients with rates of a comparable group of females released directly into the community. The former halfway house clients were significantly less likely to commit offenses in the follow-up period. When they did commit crimes, they were less serious offenses than those committed by the comparison group.

Seiter et al. (1977) conclude that there is some evidence to support the idea that halfway houses reduce the recidivism rates of former clients in comparison to ex-offenders who are released directly into the community. They readily admit that the few significant findings do not lend much reliability to this claim. Latessa and Allen (1982) suggest that the more conservative conclusion is that halfway houses are at least as effective as parole in deterring recidivism. Given that halfway house clients are probably a higher risk group than parolees and that recidivism rates are similar for the two groups, halfway houses may be doing a better job than the evaluations can measure.

There are a number of other goals that correctional programs seek to attain. Seiter (1978) surveyed halfway house directors and staff, and probation and parole officers to determine what they perceived to be the goals of the halfway houses. Some 30 different goals were identified by the respondents. They ranged from very broad goals, such as reintegration of the offender and providing for the safety of society, to very specific ones including the provision of particular programs dealing with the educational, vocational, psychological and spiritual needs of clients. One of the more obvious but often unstated goals of halfway houses is that clients utilize these existing services and programs. Clients who do not volunteer to participate or who refuse to participate in the programs obviously are not fulfilling the tasks assigned to them by the correctional authorities. The success or failure of a halfway house is often defined in terms of the number or percent of the residents who complete the halfway house program. Seiter et al. (1977) report success rates ranged from 26 percent to 93 percent of the clients who entered the program.

Some of these studies and others published since then examine the characteristics of persons who are most likely to succeed in the programs. A study by Moran et al. (1977) of one halfway house found that the most important predictors of success were the length of time on a single job prior to admission and the highest grade completed in school. Persons with longer periods of time on one job and those with more years of schooling were more likely to be successful in the halfway house. For males, age and IQ were also important. Older males and those with higher IQs were more likely to succeed. Females who were older when they were first arrested and admitted, who were incarcerated for longer periods of time and who did not have a psychiatric history were more likely to succeed in the halfway house program. A study by Moczydlowski (1980) found that clients with fewer prior arrests, no history of alcohol problems and higher levels of educational achievement were more likely to succeed in the halfway house program. Beha's (1977) study of Brooke House in Boston found that clients without a history of drug use, who had been on a single job for longer periods of time and who came from outside Boston were more likely to succeed in the program. Clients with more limited previous experience with the prison system were also more likely to be successful.

A 1984 study by Donnelly and Forschner indicated that gender, education, length of time on a single job, referral source, previous outpatient therapy, age at first arrest, the number of adult convictions and incarcerations, the number of months incarcerated and the number of days in the halfway house were all related to success or failure. Females and persons with more years of education and longer periods on a single job were more likely to be successful. Persons referred from municipal and federal sources were more likely to be successful than those referred from state or county sources. Clients with fewer convictions and incarcerations and fewer months of incarceration were also more likely to succeed. The client's success or failure was also related to his or her age at first arrest. Those whose first arrest came later in their lives were significantly more likely to succeed in the halfway house than were those who were arrested earlier in their lives.

These findings may not hold up in all halfway houses either because houses may have very different programs and services or they may deal with different types of clients. Even those with similar programs may have slightly different emphases. These differences may make a difference in terms of who is successful and who is not.

While in-program success rates may not impress those who argue that the real goal is reduced recidivism, it should be noted that there is an inverse relationship between program completion and recidivism. Persons who successfully complete the halfway house program are significantly less likely to be recidivists than those who failed in the program (Beha, 1977; Meta Metrics, 1983) or those parolees released directly into the community (Meta Metrics, 1983).

This research will utilize program completion as its measure of successful clients. Like some of the previous research, we examine the characteristics of successful and unsuccessful clients. Unlike previous research, we are examining a halfway house with a very heterogeneous population. It is made up of referrals from federal, state, county and city agencies. Its clients include felons and misdemeanants, parolees, probationers and pre-releasees. Another major difference is that this study will examine female and male residents in a co-correctional halfway house. Like most of the research on criminals and criminal justice, most of the previous research on halfway houses focuses only on men. Studies of female clients generally examine all-female halfway houses. Finally, this research will use a sophisticated, multivariate statistical analysis to examine the relationship between a set of independent variables and the outcome measure. While bivariate analyses are helpful in suggesting what factors might be helpful in predicting success or failure in the halfway house program, they suffer from a number of weaknesses. Frequently, a fairly large number of variables are related to the outcome making it difficult to determine which factors are the most important. More importantly, bivariate analysis fails to control for the interaction between the variables.

## Description of Cope House

Cope House is a nonprofit, community-based correctional agency whose primary function is the rehabilitation and reintegration of adult offenders. Founded in 1975 under the aegis of Talbert House, Inc., of Cincinnati, Ohio, it became independently incorporated, with its own Board of Trustees, in 1976. It is a diversified halfway house which accepts adult male and female referrals from the Federal Bureau of Prisons, the Department of Corrections of the State of Ohio, the Montgomery County Probation Department, and female referrals only from the city of Dayton Municipal Court. Cope House became co-correctional in January of 1981. Its clientele is a mixture of Federal pre-releasees, State parolees, County probationers, and City misdemeanants doing workhouse time.

Cope currently has a 22-bed capacity. Cope administrators select residents on the basis of information sent from institutions, probation and parole departments, as well as other available social data. Where it is possible, residents are interviewed. Not all types of offenders are admitted. Generally, chronic violent offenders, rapists, severe drug and alcohol users, those clinically diagnosed as arsonists, psychotics or severely retarded are not accepted. However, Cope does accept offenders with a broad range of social and psychological problems, as can be seen in Table 1.

Upon arrival, clients are restricted to the house for a 48-hour period of orientation. During this time they are introduced to the staff, residents, rules, and regulations of the facility. A distinction should be made between internal and external rules and regulations. While Cope House rules and regulations are generally the same for all clients, external ones differ according to referral source. Federal clients tend to have the greatest structure and restrictions placed upon them, with State parolees having the least.

Cope's programming revolves around a behavioral contract called a Mutual Agreement Plan (MAP), a plan modeled after that used by the Massachusetts Halfway House Association. This contract is client need-oriented and focuses on employment, education and training, finances, housing, and social service needs. Needs are mutually identified between the client and counselor during the orientation period. Specific completion dates and times are emphasized. This MAP is monitored and updated when necessary.

Clients leaving the house during the day for education, training, job seeking or employment are monitored by phone contacts with representatives at their destinations. These contacts are made randomly and without jeopardizing the client's position. All residents are required to see their counselor weekly, and attend the weekly house meeting. Unemployed clients are expected to meet daily for a "job seeking" meeting where results of the day are analyzed. Job seeking classes are held weekly at Cope House for the unemployed. These may be formal or informal depending on the size.

Residents are also assigned weekly house chores, and are expected to keep their beds made and rooms tidy. They are also required to perform two hours of community service work weekly. Residents are also informed that they may be subjected to periodic urine monitoring for drugs and alcohol. Observance of rules and regulations leads to greater liberty in the form of extended curfews, overnight and weekend passes. Major and minor infractions of rules and regulations can lead to sanctions. These sanctions range from minor ones such as house restriction and loss of curfew and passes, to removal from the program and return to prison.

Staffing at Cope House generally includes four to five full-time professional staff and five to seven part-time staff. The staff seeks to avoid duplication of existing community services when trying to provide for the clients' needs. This not only reduces costs but also allows residents to reintegrate into the community and begin socializing with the non-offender population. For example, instead of offering an Alcoholics Anonymous (A.A.) program in-house, clients are encouraged to attend the weekly A.A. programs in the community. A primary emphasis of all programs is to enable residents to begin developing life skills and support groups in the community. In order to complete the program, they must be able to address the issues of employment, finances, and housing. More generally, however, the program seeks to allow residents to answer the question, "Where do you belong?" Consequently, the program emphasizes social and psychological integration in the community. It is a strong programming belief that these "roots" will inhibit recidivism as much as, or more than, employment.

## Methods and Data

Upon entering Cope, all clients are interviewed by a staff member who administers a standard intake questionnaire to them. This questionnaire was developed by the International Halfway House Association and meets the requirements of the Commission on Accreditation for Corrections. Another standard form is completed upon the client's termination from Cope. The data collected on these forms, therefore, rely on client self-disclosure. If warranted, some of the information is verified by a check of the client's file. These questionnaires provide the data for this study.

Information on the intake forms deals with the demographic characteristics, social background and legal history of the client. The client's age, race and gender are recorded. The social background characteristics include marital status, living arrangements prior to incarceration, employment history, and previous psychological or drug treatments. Among the legal characteristics are the referral source, age at first arrest, number of adult arrests and convictions and the number of times and length of incarceration as an adult.

The data were collected on all 417 clients entering Cope between January 1, 1980, and December 31, 1982. Table 1 presents a profile of the 276 men and 129 women on whom complete or near complete information was available. In general, females tended to have less education, fewer community ties (family and employment) and less previous involvement with the criminal justice system (arrests, convictions and length of incarceration) than did the males.

Large proportions of both groups had less than 12 years of schooling, unstable if any employment records, and were legally and residentially separated from spouses and other family members. This profile is not surprising since these characteristics of Cope clients are generally consistent with those of prison inmates and persons in other stages of the criminal justice system.

The vast majority (80 percent) of the women admitted to Cope House during the three year period were referred by municipal sources for misdemeanor offenses. The majority of the men, on the other hand, were from federal, state or county sources for felony offenses (91 percent). Because of these significant differences we therefore decided to do a separate analysis for men and women and limit our analysis to the 103 female misdemeanants and to the 252 male felons. Eighty-two percent of the females and 58 percent of the males in these groups successfully completed the program.

The dependent variable is the client's success or failure in the Cope program. This is determined by the reason the client leaves the program. There are three ways in which clients failed in the program: they absconded from the house; they committed a different, new criminal offense and were removed; or they were removed due to misbehavior in the house. This usually occurred when clients consistently broke house rules and regulations. When this happened, they were sent back to their referral source. Success in the program is simply the converse

Table 1

**Characteristics of Male and Female Halfway House Clients (In Percents)**

| Variable | Male | Female |
|---|---|---|
| Age | | |
| 18-24 | 36.9 | 40.8 |
| 25-35 | 45.2 | 43.8 |
| 36+ | 17.9 | 15.4 |
| Highest Grade Completed | | |
| 0-11 | 44.4 | 56.9 |
| 12 | 41.9 | 30.0 |
| 13+ | 13.7 | 13.1 |
| Marital Status | | |
| Married | 13.0 | 7.0 |
| Never Married | 46.7 | 45.7 |
| Divorced/Separated/Other | 40.2 | 47.3 |
| Last Community Residence | | |
| With Relatives/Friends | 75.3 | 64.1 |
| Alone/Other | 24.7 | 35.9 |
| Number of Jobs Held in Last Two Years | | |
| 0 | 22.8 | 41.1 |
| 1-2 | 52.2 | 46.5 |
| 3+ | 12.0 | 12.4 |
| Number of Months on Longest Job | | |
| Less than 8 | 56.9 | 70.5 |
| 8+ | 43.1 | 29.5 |
| Percent of Weeks Full-Time Active | | |
| 50 and less | 66.2 | 80.6 |
| 51-99 | 12.0 | 5.4 |
| 100 | 21.8 | 14.0 |
| Prior Admission to Drug Treatment Program | | |
| No | 76.1 | 79.2 |
| Yes | 23.9 | 20.8 |
| Prior Alcohol Treatment | | |
| No | 80.7 | 90 |
| Yes | 19.3 | 10 |
| Outpatient Therapy for Psychological Problems | | |
| No | 80.4 | 76.2 |
| Yes | 19.6 | 23.8 |
| Hospitalized for Psychological Problem | | |
| No | 86.0 | 85.4 |
| Yes | 14.0 | 14.6 |

| Variable | Male | Female |
|---|---|---|
| Age at First Arrest | | |
| 8-17 | 56.9 | 26.4 |
| 18-25 | 34.1 | 46.3 |
| 26 + | 9.0 | 27.3 |
| Number of Adult Arrests | | |
| 1 | 16.3 | 28.2 |
| 2-5 | 51.8 | 47.7 |
| 6 + | 31.9 | 24.1 |
| Number of Adult Convictions | | |
| 1 | 31.0 | 43.8 |
| 2-5 | 59.1 | 46.9 |
| 6 + | 9.9 | 9.3 |
| Number of Adult Incarcerations | | |
| 0 | 4.7 | 34.6 |
| 1-2 | 59.5 | 41.6 |
| 3-15 | 35.8 | 23.8 |
| Number of Months Incarcerated as Adult | | |
| 0 | 7.0 | 45.4 |
| 1-2 | 4.1 | 23.1 |
| 3-12 | 30.5 | 14.5 |
| 13 + | 58.4 | 17.0 |

of failure. Most often, it means that the clients completed the halfway house program. However, it is not limited to this. It also includes those who had their legal status discontinued and those removed by the referral source. This latter circumstance usually occurred when Cope was only meant to be a temporary assignment. These persons are considered successful because, at the time of the departure, they were making satisfactory progress in the Cope program and had not committed any law or rule infractions.

The independent variables used in this analysis are presented in Table 1. These were chosen based on their significance as determined by previous research. Because separate analyses are done for males and females, gender is not used as an independent variable. For the discriminant analysis, the marital status variable was made into two dummy variables. One represents a married-nonmarried distinction while the other is a divorced or separated versus a nondivorced or nonseparated category.

The relative importance of these characteristics in determining the success or failure of clients in the halfway house is examined using discriminant analysis. This technique is most helpful when the dependent variable is a dichotomy. In this case, clients either fail or succeed in the Cope program. Discriminant analysis provides the independent variable set that is most useful for distinguishing between the groups of clients that fail in the program and those that succeed. A stepwise discriminant is used with variables selected for inclusion in the set based on minimizing Wilks lambda.[1]

# Results

Because Cope House is somewhat unique in that it is co-correctional, separate analyses are run for males and females. The number of cases in the discriminant analyses was reduced to 93 females and 228 males due to missing data on one or more of the independent variables. The data presented in Table 2 suggest the set of independent variables that is useful in discriminating between successful and unsuccessful halfway house clients. For female misdemeanants, the Wilks lambda, an inverse measure of discriminating power, is utilized for distinguishing between the successful and unsuccessful female clients. Thirty-six percent of the variance in the derived function is explained by the composition of the two groups of women.

Table 2 also presents the relative impact of the variables on outcome. The magnitude of the standardized discriminant coefficients ranges from – .574 for prior admissions to a drug treatment program to .217 for outpatient therapy for psychological problems.

Women with a history of admissions to drug treatment programs are less likely to successfully complete the program. This may indicate that their drug or drug-related problems are continuing and that the halfway house program is not meeting the needs of these clients. The second highest discriminant function is that for the number of adult arrests. Women with many previous arrests may be more firmly committed to a criminal career and may not accept the structured program that the halfway house offers. While the remaining standardized coefficients are somewhat smaller, they indicate that successful clients are likely to be older, have completed more years of school, have been living alone and have no experience with outpatient therapy for psychological treatment. These findings indicate that more mature or socially stable women with no history of psychological or drug problems are more likely to succeed in Cope House.

The discriminant procedure also serves as a classification technique. Based on a person's scores on the discriminating variables, cases are assigned to either of the two groups. These are then compared with the actual outcome of that case in the program. The set of discriminating

Table 2

**Discriminant Analysis for Male and Female Halfway House Clients**

| MALES | | |
|---|---|---|
| Variable | Wilks Lambda* | Standardized Discriminant Coefficient |
| Highest grade | .932 | .530 |
| Prior alcohol treatment | .912 | .502 |
| No. of adult incarcerations | .890 | -.323 |
| Outpatient psych. therapy | .872 | .392 |
| No. of jobs (last two years) | .860 | .248 |
| Age at first arrest | .849 | .267 |
| Married | .840 | .269 |
| No. admissions to drug treatment | .836 | -.197 |
| Pct. weeks full-time active | .832 | .178 |

| Eigenvalue | Wilks Lambda | Canonical Correlation |
|---|---|---|
| .202 | .832 | .410 |

Percent correctly classified: 63.49

| FEMALES | | |
|---|---|---|
| Variable | Wilks Lambda* | Standardized Discriminant Coefficient |
| No. of adult arrests | .794 | -.550 |
| No. admis'ns to drug treatment | .742 | -.574 |
| Age | .708 | .251 |
| Months on longest job | .684 | .343 |
| Highest grade | .668 | .260 |
| Last community residence | .655 | .229 |
| Outpatient psych. therapy | .645 | .216 |

| Eigenvalue | Wilks Lambda | Canonical Correlation |
|---|---|---|
| .551 | .645 | .596 |

Percent correctly classified: 87.38

* All values significant at $< .001$ level.

variables for the female misdemeanant clients led to the correct classification of 87 percent of the cases.

For the male felony clients of Cope House, 9 of the 17 independent variables met the criteria to be discriminators. The Wilks lambda for the men, .832, indicates that this set of variables is not as powerful as the set for the female misdemeanants. Only 17 percent of the variance in the derived function is explained by the variables. The standardized discriminant coefficients range from a high of .530 for the education variable to a low of arrest. Men with more years of schooling were more likely to succeed in the program than those with less schooling. Men who had no history of outpatient therapy for psychological problems and those with some prior treatment for alcohol problems were also more likely to succeed. While the remaining relationships are somewhat weaker, there is some tendency for men who had been incarcerated fewer times, whose first arrest came at later ages, who are married, who held more jobs that kept them more active and with no admissions for drug treatment to be more successful than other groups. Using this set of discriminating variables, 63 percent of the cases in this sample would be correctly classified.

## Discussion

It would appear that for both males and females who fail in the program critical socializing and integrating factors have been retarded. Such traditional integrating factors as tenure relative to education, residency, and employment for females, and marriage, education and employment for men are important discriminators between successful and unsuccessful clients.

Both males and females were more likely to succeed in the program if they had no history of drug treatment or out-patient counseling. An individual's need for drug treatment and counseling might very well be symptomatic of the lack of social integration and educational and occupational skills characterized by the other discriminators in the study. The only exception to this appears to be males who have sought help for problems stemming from alcohol abuse. Due to the ready availability of such groups as Alcoholics Anonymous and the relative legitimacy of drinking versus drugs, this may not be a conflicting or confounding factor.

Age and contacts with the criminal justice system also appear to be strong discriminators. In males, this was witnessed by strong predictors, such as number of adult incarcerations, and, to a lesser extent, age at first arrest. Among females, the number of adult arrests was a very strong predictor while age was also important.

It should be emphasized that the female group was a very homogeneous grouping composed primarily of city misdemeanants, while, on the other hand, the males were a mixture of felons from diverse jurisdictions—federal, state, and county. This relative homogeneity possibly accounts for the strength of the predictive capabilities of the female discriminators. Using the seven discriminators for the female group, the analysis is accurate in correctly classifying 87 percent of the women, while the nine discriminators for the men allow the correct classification of 63 percent of that group.

Finally, the characteristics distinguishing between success and failure in the two groups were quite similar, with predictions of success centering around older ages, fewer contacts with the criminal justice system, absence of drugs, alcohol, and emotional problems, and strong socializing and integrating ties in the community—witnessed by higher educational levels, length of employment, and stability of residence.

## Implications and Conclusions

While no major changes or reforms in community based corrections should be made on the basis of a single study of one halfway house, the implications of this research need to be carefully considered. We show that most female misdemeanants are successful in this halfway house program while 58 percent of the male felons are successful. By using discriminant analyses, this research draws a profile of those characteristics which are most important in distinguishing between successful and unsuccessful clients. These findings can be utilized in either of two ways by halfway house administrators. First, halfway houses can choose to accept only those clients who are most likely to succeed. For example, halfway house administrators, where possible, may only accept older, well-educated women with stable employment careers who had limited previous involvement with the police. By not accepting those who are likely to fail in the existing program, the houses will have more room for those likely to obey house rules and regulations and successfully complete the program.

A second way to utilize these findings is to implement new programs or redesign existing ones to assist those who are likely to fail. For example, since female clients who had participated in previous drug treatment or outpatient psychological treatment programs were less likely to be successful, administrators may seek to implement or strengthen programs designed to deal with these problems. This might mean that the halfway house would increase referrals to local community mental health agencies and to support groups for former drug abusers. Since the education variable was a discriminator for the male clients, more emphasis might be placed on providing additional schooling for those in the program. This might involve enrollment in local two-year or four-year college programs in addition to the more common high school or GED programs.

Programs that teach job seeking skills might be developed. This can emphasize both the technical and social skills necessary to find and keep employment. For example, the program could include sessions on writing resumes and how to locate job openings. It should also provide the basic communication and interactional skills necessary to do well in interview situations and in the job itself.

Attempts should be made at all program levels to integrate clients into the community mainstream. One way that this can be done is by contracting for various drug, alcohol, and other social services outside the halfway house. This often has a twofold effect. It reduces costs and facilitates meeting new individuals and provides fresh feedback and interaction. Emphases should also be placed on community responsibility through restitution, community service work and voluntarism. Every area of programming should focus on treating the client, not as an isolated individual, but as a member of the community where he or she must find a niche.

While these implications are important, there is a broader issue that must be addressed not only by halfway house administrators but also by those in the political system who make policies affecting the criminal justice system. It is unlikely that any set of discriminating variables will ever predict human behavior with 100 percent accuracy. Even in this study, which correctly classified a very high percent of the outcomes for female misdemeanants, there are 13 percent of the cases which would have been incorrectly predicted. The discriminating variables found for this group predicted 26 failures and 77 successes. Ten of the 26 which were predicted to be failures were actually successful in the program. Only three clients predicted to be successful were unsuccessful. For the men, 75 of the 136 cases that were predicted to be failures were actually successful. Thirty-one of the 116 cases that were predicted to be successful were failures. In both male and female groups, the discriminating variables tended to overestimate the likelihood of failure. Any model or prediction table seeking to forecast human behavior is going to have this "error" factor since humans are complex actors in a world that may influence or constrain but not determine their actions.

Administrators and policymakers need to consider whether the predictive capability of this or any model or set of variables is sufficiently accurate to allow its use. While this research provides a set of variables that has a high-to-moderate predictive capability, and while it tends to predict on the conservative side, i.e., more predicted failures that succeed and fewer predicted successes that fail, it is a model that needs to be tested on other programs before it is adopted.

In summary, this research demonstrates that a politically and sexually diversified program can be successful for certain groups of offenders. This is a critical point for halfway house administrators and trustees exiting an era when funding was abundant and when they will be called upon more frequently to justify their program's existence. In addition, this research suggests the need for a broader, more culturally defined concept of reintegration. Some criminologists call contemporary criminals "unmeltables," who have not been absorbed into the American "melting pot." Consequently, reintegration cannot be defined simply in terms of housing and employment factors. It must go beyond these physical and economic conditions to consider the more purely social factors such as relationships with family and friends and coping mechanisms that can help individuals avoid drug, alcohol and psychological problems.

## References

Allen, Harry E., and Seiter, Richard P. (1976). "The Effectiveness of Halfway Houses: A Reappraisal of a Reappraisal." *Chitty's Law Journal*, 24, 196-200.

Bailey, Walter C. (1966). "Correctional Outcome: An Evaluation of 100 Reports." *Journal of Criminal Law, Criminology and Police Science*, 57, 153-60.

Beha, James A. (1977). "Testing the Functions and Effects of the Parole Halfway House: One Case Study." *Journal of Criminal Law and Criminology*, 67, 335-50.

Carter, Timothy (1979). "Juvenile Court Dispositions: A Comparison of Status and Non-status Offenders." *Criminology*, 17, 3, 38-44.

Donnelly, Patrick, and Forschner, Brian (1984). "Client Success or Failure in a Halfway House." *Federal Probation*, September, 38-44.

Dowell, David; Klein, Cecelia; and Krichmar, Cheryl (1985). "Evaluation of a Halfway House for Women." *Journal of Criminal Justice*, 13, 217-26.

Fogel, David (1975). *We Are the Living Proof: The Justice Model for Corrections*. Cincinnati, OH: W. H. Anderson.

Gatz, Nick, and Murray, Chris (1981). "An Administrative Overview of Halfway Houses." *Corrections Today*, 43, 52-54.

Glaser, Daniel (1975). "Achieving Better Questions: A Halfway Century's Progress in Correctional Research." *Federal Probation*, September, 3-9.

Klecka, William (1975). "Discriminant Analysis." In N. Nie et al. (Eds.), *Statistical Package for the Social Sciences* (pp. 434-67). New York: McGraw-Hill.

Latessa, Edward, and Allen, Harry (1982). "Halfway Houses and Parole: A National Assessment." *Journal of Criminal Justice*, 10, 2, 153-63.

Lipton, Douglas; Martinson, Robert; and Wilks, Judith (1975). *The Effectiveness of Correctional Treatment: A Survey of Treatment Evaluation Surveys*. New York: Holt, Rinehart and Winston.

Meta Metrics, Inc. (1983). *Evaluation of Connecticut Community Programs.* Washington, DC: Meta Metrics, Inc.

Moczydlowski, K. (1980). "Predictors of Success in a Correctional Halfway House for Youthful and Adult Offenders." *Corrective and Social Psychiatry and Journal of Behavior Technology, Methods and Therapy,* 26, 5, 9-72.

Moran, E.; Kass, W.; and Munz, D. (1977). "In-program Evaluation of a Community Correctional Agency for High Risk Offenders." *Corrective and Social Psychiatry and Journal of Behavior Technology, Methods and Therapy,* 23, 48-52.

Palmer, Ted (1974). "The Youth Authority's Community Treatment Project." *Federal Probation,* 38, 1, 3-14.

President's Commission on Law Enforcement and the Administration of Justice (1967). *Challenge of Crime in a Free Society.* Washington, DC: U.S. Government Printing Office.

Reid, Susan Titus (1981). *The Correctional System: An Introduction.* New York: Holt, Rinehart and Winston.

Scott, Ronald J. (1978). "Contract Programming in Probation: Philosophical and Experimental Bases for Building a Model." *The Justice System Journal,* 4, 49-70.

Seiter, R. (1978). *Evaluation Research as a Feedback Mechanism for Criminal Justice Policy Making: A Critical Analysis.* San Francisco: R and E Research Associates, Inc.

Seiter, R.; Carlson, Ed.; Bowman, H.; Grandfield, J.; and Beran, N. (1977). *Halfway Houses: National Evaluation Program: Phase I, Summary Report.* Washington, DC: U.S. Department of Justice.

van den Haag, Ernest (1975). *Punishing Criminals: Concerning a Very Old and Painful Question.* New York: Basic Books.

## Note

[1] Discriminant analysis is a technique which statistically distinguishes between two or more groups. The appropriate multivariate analysis is largely determined by the measurement level of the dependent variable. If the dependent variable is continuous or if we can assume equal intervals, regression is appropriate. In this study, the dependent variable is a dichotomy. Clients either succeed or fail. The mathematical objective of discriminant analysis is to weight and linearly combine the discriminating variables to make the groups as statistically distinct as possible. The objective of this research is to determine the independent variable set that is most helpful for distinguishing between those that succeed and those that fail. This analysis utilizes a stepwise selection method which selects variables for entry into the analysis on the basis of their discriminating power. First, it selects the variable with the highest value on the selection criterion. The second variable selected is the one which, when it is paired with the first, produces the highest value on the selection criterion. The selection criterion utilized here is the overall multivariate F ratio for the test of differences among the group centroids. The variable which maximizes the F ratio also minimizes Wilks lambda which is a measure of group discrimination. Wilks lambda, then, is an inverse measure of discriminating power (Carter, 1979; Klecka, 1975).

# 18

# Measuring the Performance of Community Corrections
## Joan Petersilia

## Introduction

The 1980s saw tremendous growth in community corrections' populations—from about 1.4 million persons at the start of the decade to 3.2 million by 1990—a more than 130 percent increase. This increase was larger than that experienced by either prisons or jails over the same time period (Hindelang et al., 1981; Jankowski, 1992). Today, 3 out of every 4 persons under correctional supervision in the United States are on some form of community-based custody—mostly probation or parole—although community corrections also includes halfway houses, residential centers, work furlough, and all other programs for managing the offender in the community.[1]

Despite its wide usage, community corrections is often the subject of intense criticism. Probation and parole suffer from a "soft on crime" image and, as a result, maintain little public support. Their poor (and

Source: *Performance Measures for the Criminal Justice System* Bureau of Justice Statistics-Princeton University Study Group on Criminal Justice Performance Measures, 1993, 61-84.

some believe, misunderstood) public image leaves them unable to compete effectively for scarce public funds. Nationally, community corrections receives less than 10 percent of State and local government expenditures for correctional services, which includes jails and prisons (Flanagan and Maguire, 1992). And their budgets are declining at a faster rate when compared to other criminal justice components. Over the last decade in Los Angeles, for example, the county Superior Court budget grew more than 200 percent, the sheriffs' and district attorneys' budgets grew about 50 percent, while that of probation grew by a mere 10 percent—even though probation populations more than doubled over this time period.

It is also true that those offenders being sentenced to probation and parole are more serious than in the past—in terms of their crimes, prior criminal records, and substance abuse histories (Petersilia and Turner, 1990). In New York, for example, 77 percent of probationers are felons (not misdemeanants), and fully a third of active cases are people who have been found guilty of violent crimes—yet these persons are supervised on caseloads of several hundred persons (*Los Angeles Times*, February 7, 1993:A20). The Los Angeles situation is even more critical. The L.A. County Probation Department, the largest in the world, supervises 90,000 adult offenders—80 percent of all those convicted in the county. But three-quarters of those offenders are monitored only by computer, by probation officers with caseloads of about 1,000 each. As a result, Chief Probation Officer Barry Nidorf estimates that his deputies have, on average, only 1 hour and 47 minutes per year to devote to each probationer (*Los Angeles Times*, February 8, 1993:A12).

Why does community corrections fare so poorly? It is not that its services are undervalued. Quite the contrary: every national study and commission beginning with the President's Commission on Law Enforcement and Administration of Justice (1967) up to the more recent President's *National Drug Control Strategy* (1990) has recommended expanding community corrections. In fact, the National Advisory Commission on Criminal Justice Standards and Goals (1973:311) referred to community corrections as the justice system's "brightest hope." Public opinion polls also show wide support for community-based sentencing for nonviolent offenders (Doble, 1987; Jacoby and Dunn, 1987).

But while there is general support for the *concept* of community sanctions, current programs are seen as inadequate. Most of the commissions that endorse community corrections go on to state that current programs are unable to provide effective offender supervision or rehabilitation. Furthermore, their minimal supervision is not seen as adequate punishment for most serious crimes. As DiIulio notes in *No Escape: The Future of American Corrections* (1991:68),

Most Americans think that criminal sanctions that make little or no use of incarceration fail to protect the public adequately, to deter would-be criminals, and to prevent convicted offenders from finding new victims. Furthermore, they simply do not feel that alternatives to incarceration are an adequate moral response to the pain and suffering imposed upon innocent victims by often calculating and remorseless victimizers.

In their defense, "community corrections" remains an ambiguous concept. It is a legal status, an alternative to incarceration, a service-delivery mechanism, and an organizational entity. As an organizational entity, it has objectives and performs a wide range of activities—some totally unrelated to offender supervision and/or treatment. One survey found that probation departments were responsible for more than 50 different activities, including court-related civil functions (for example, step-parent adoption investigations, minority age marriage investigations) (Fitzharris, 1979). The time-worn controversy over whether community corrections (particularly probation) is punishment, treatment, or an amalgam of both further confuses discussions of its mission. As David Fogel (1984) observed: "probation lacks a forceful imagery that other occupations in criminal justice can claim: police catch criminals, prosecutors try to get them locked up, judges put them in prisons, wardens keep them there, but what do probation officers do?"

So while it is true that study panels continually endorse the expansion of community corrections, none has specified exactly what functions it should perform, or when and how it should be used. Having been founded more than 150 years ago, community corrections still has an unclear primary mission, with confusion about what activities contribute to that mission and how best to assess their performance. Many observers have urged community corrections to quantify what they do, with whom, and to what benefit (Cochran et al., 1991; Petersilia et al., 1985; Clear and O'Leary, 1983; McAnany et al., 1984; Blair et al.,1987).

Without a clear public mandate or an effective constituency, community corrections has been vulnerable to political pressures. It has fallen prey to the weakness described by the adage: "If you don't stand for something, you'll fall for anything." In the 1970s, when rehabilitation was in favor, it promised to rehabilitate. In the 1980s, when the public mood turned tough-on-crime, it promised toughness. But with budget cuts, observers have noted that community corrections ends up promising much but being able to deliver very little (Clear and Byrne, 1992).

As DiIulio (1992) points out, to some extent these problems are endemic to all public agencies. However, they seem particularly problematic in community corrections agencies for two reasons. First, there is a serious lack of consensus—and in fact, widespread disagreement—among community corrections staff as to goals and mission. The leadership, as well as line staff, differ—both within and among departments—as to the importance of the surveillance/control model versus the treatment service model. Of course, supervision usually combines elements of both, but studies have shown that supervision activities do differ significantly, depending on which model the staff endorses (Ellsworth, 1992). The controversy over whether community corrections is punishment, treatment, or both has now been enlivened. A number of large community corrections agencies (for example, Los Angeles) have now openly embraced a surveillance model—quite different from the meshing of the two major goals in previous years.

Thus, there is a major disagreement *within the leadership* of community corrections about what the primary mission of their agencies is.

The second major difficulty—closely related to the first—is that community corrections has, by and large, never been able to show that it "works." Historically, recidivism rates—an offender's return to crime after some intervention—have been the gauge by which community corrections has been evaluated. And after hundreds of research studies (most poorly done), the weight of evidence shows that community corrections programs have not been able to reduce recidivism (Lipton et al., 1975; Gottfredson and Gottfredson, 1980; Petersilia and Turner, 1993). A recent report by the Bureau of Justice Statistics revealed that 43 percent of felons on State probation were rearrested for another felony within 3 years (Langan and Cunniff, 1992).

After a long history of being unable to affect recidivism significantly, probation and parole leaders have begun to question the outcome measure itself—not whether recidivism should be included at all, but whether it should be the sole or primary measure of their performance. They note that crime is the result of a long line of social ills— dysfunctional families, economic and educational deprivation, and so on—and these social problems are clearly beyond the direct influence of probation/parole agencies. As the BJS/Princeton Study Group concludes (1992):

> to evaluate the system's performance chiefly in terms of recidivism
> measures is to exaggerate the system's ability to affect the prevalence
> and severity of crime in society, to miss other important measures
> of the system's day-to-day performance, and to obscure the role that
> citizens can and should play in promoting secure communities
> (DiIulio, 1992).

Corrections officials also argue persuasively that recidivism rates measure just one function, while ignoring other critical probation/parole tasks, such as preparing presentence investigations, collecting fines and fees, monitoring community service, and so on. Adequate performance indicators should reflect the multitude of an agency's goals and activities.

The American Probation and Parole Association (1992) has recently called for including other intermediate outcomes in program evaluations. These would measure the offenders' activities while on probation or parole supervision (for example, rates of employment, drug use, participation in work and education). The association argues that programs do affect offender behavior, and that the effects would be shown if these mediating outcomes were measured.

Corrections practitioners also question whether their performance should be judged by how the offender behaves once he is *off* formal probation/parole supervision. After all, other components of the justice system are not judged by their ability to affect the future criminal behavior of offenders, and corrections should not be either. Charles Logan (1992) agrees and writes:

> The police, prosecutor, and courts are judged by more proximate outcomes (such as arrest and conviction rates). It is only when the system switches to corrections, that changing the offenders' crime behavior becomes the primary measure of success.

An additional difficulty has recently emerged regarding the recidivism measure. Specifically, even if one accepts that recidivism is a useful measure of success, it is not clear which *direction* indicates success. If one believes that the major mission of community corrections is to protect the public—emphasizing the *surveillance* function—then perhaps *increasing* recidivism rates (for example, returns to prison) is a positive— not negative—performance indicator. If offenders are convicted of a crime and incarcerated, then public safety is being served. But if *rehabilitation* is the primary goal, as it has historically been, then *decreasing* recidivism indicates success. For example, a recent evaluation of intensive probation/parole supervision programs found that closer supervision increased technical violations and returns to jail and prison. The *Los Angeles Times* called the probation program a "dismal failure" since it failed to decrease recidivism. Barry Nidorf, Chief Probation Officer in Los Angeles County, used the higher recidivism figures to argue that the ISP program had succeeded. He wrote:

> Reducing recidivism was not listed as the highest priority . . . holding offenders accountable was of primary importance . . . given the stated project goal of protecting the community, a significantly lower recidivism rate was not expected.

> For years, probation has been measured only by recidivism rate . . . . In today's environment, with over 70 percent of the probation caseload consisting of felony offenders, is it still realistic to use only

> this one criterion? Why is revocation and sentencing of a probation violator not considered a "success"? I believe it should be . . . (Nidorf, 1991a).

Without consensus about whether the major criminal justice outcome—recidivism—should be increasing or decreasing as a result of interventions, the research field is likely to become even more muddled.

It does appear that community corrections, more than other public agencies, has had difficulty articulating its mission and reaching agreement as to appropriate performance indicators. But as budgets shrink, public stakeholders will be increasingly asking what they are getting—in objective, measurable terms—for their dollar. Within this context, probation and parole will become increasingly vulnerable to budget cuts if they cannot clearly articulate what they do, with whom, and to what effect.

This paper is designed to address that need. Specifically, it attempts to—

1) articulate a mission statement for community corrections
2) identify the goals contained within the mission statement
3) specify methods or activities that address each goal
4) identify measurable performance indicators for each goal.

This paper is clearly just a first step and is meant to stimulate discussion and further work. Other goals could be added to the mission statement (for example, educate the public, prevent crime), and additional (or different) methods and performance indicators could be substituted for those indicated. Community corrections agencies should customize their mission statement, methods, and performance indicators so that they reflect local resources and priorities.

## Step 1: Specify a Mission Statement for Community Corrections

A necessary first step toward developing performance indicators is to articulate the organization's goals and mission. As Peters and Waterman, authors of *In Search of Excellence*, put it: "Figure out what your value system is. Decide what your company stands for . . ." (1982:227). The same principle applies to social, nonprofit organizations. Before community corrections agencies can evaluate their performance, they must first define what they are attempting to accomplish.

As noted above, probation and parole have historically had difficulty defining their mission (McAnany et al., 1984; Petersilia et al., 1985). Different goals are often given by administrators and staff within the same department. And sometimes the same person gives different messages to different audiences, depending on his or her perception of their support for rehabilitation versus enforcement activities. In some instances, agencies adopt a mission or goal statement that they think will sell their services to the external community, but that staff do not sincerely support. And the goals of the staff might not be shared by their principal sponsors or customers (the judiciary, county funders, and the public, in the case of community corrections). The result is that the mission statements of many agencies become public relations gimmicks as opposed to working statements that assist internal agency operations.

DiIulio (1991) advises criminal justice agencies to develop mission statements that—

1) include only activities that the agency can reasonably and realistically be expected to fulfill
2) are fairly narrow and consistent in scope
3) contain activities that are unique to the justice agency, rather than conflated with functions of other social institutions such as schools and welfare agencies.

His major message is that the mission statement should not ask the agency to "do the impossible" and it should contain activities over which it has direct control, rather than seek the achievement of more distant ends.

Nidorf (1991b) adds an additional requirement: mission statements must be responsive to expectations held by the community and by other justice agencies. He argues persuasively that community corrections operates *within* the justice system, not independent from it, and that its goals and activities—and eventual survival—depend heavily on how well it meets the expectations of the public and peer agencies (police, courts).

Several attempts have been made to develop mission statements for community corrections, most recently by the American Correctional Association (1986) and the California Corrections Policy Project (1992). These statements, as well as those of earlier years (see Fitzharris, 1979; McAnany, 1984; Clear and O'Leary, 1983), all embrace the notions of public protection and offender rehabilitation. For instance, the California Corrections Policy Project's statement is:

> The mission of community corrections is to protect the community;
> support the rights of victims; enforce court-ordered sanctions; and
> assist offenders to change (CCPP, 1992).

The statement of the American Correctional Association (ACA) is broader, simply stating that the community corrections mission as sanction is to "enhance social order and public safety" (1986:58).

The American Probation and Parole Association (APPA) (1992) says that the goals of community corrections are to: "protect the community;

deter criminal and drug activity; punish and rehabilitate offenders.''

In fact, all of the mission statements identified were quite similar in their mention of public protection and offender rehabilitation. Some also included assisting the court in sentencing decisions, public education, and aiding victims (Fitzharris, 1979).

For purposes of this paper, the author adopts the following mission statement, which comes from reviewing the literature as well as talking with the leadership of the APPA, National Association of Probation Executives (NAPE), and the California Probation/Parole and Correctional Association (CPPCA).

> **The mission of community corrections is to assist the court and/or parole board in assessing candidates' suitability for community placement; and once offenders are placed in the community, to enforce the court-ordered sanctions, protect the community, assist offenders to change, and support the rights of their victims.**

## Step 2: Identify Methods Designed to Accomplish Each Identified Goal

The major objective in developing a clear mission or goal statement is that it defines what the agency is about, what it hopes to achieve. This makes the next step possible: specifying the agency activities that are designed to achieve (or move toward achieving) the various goals. Table 1 takes the mission statement adopted for this paper, breaks it down into individual goals, and then identifies specific community corrections methods or activities that are designed to accomplish each goal. For example, the first goal pertains to advising the court about an offender's suitability for community placement. Community corrections staff do this in two principal ways: conducting presentence investigations, and conducting investigations of parole or probation violations. Methods are linked to each of the five major goals contained in the study group's original mission statement.

## Step 3: Specify Performance Indicators for Each Method or Activity

Once the agency has identified its goals and the methods it uses to address each goal, it can specify objective (measurable) performance criteria that determine the extent to which the activities are being performed and the goals are being achieved.

Identifying indicators of probation and parole success is not as easy as it sounds. As Clear and O'Leary (1983:67) note, many probation and parole staff are like social-service workers and tend to frame the substance of their work in terms of broad attitudinal or otherwise

The mission of community corrections is to assist the court and/or parole board in assessing candidates' suitability for community placement; and once offenders are placed in the community, to enforce the court-ordered sanctions, protect the community, assist offenders to change, and support the rights of their victims.

# Community corrections: Goals, methods, and performance indicators

| Goals | Methods/Activities | Performance Indicators |
|---|---|---|
| **1. Assess offender's suitability for placement:** Community corrections advises the court and/or parole board on suitability of community placement | Conduct presentence investigations (PSI)<br>Conduct investigations of violation reports | Accuracy and completeness of PSI<br>Timeliness of revocation and termination hearings<br>Validity of classification/prediction instrument<br>Percent of offenders receiving recommended sentence or violation act<br>Percent of offenders recommended for community who violate |
| **2. Enforce court-ordered sanctions:** The court permits the offender to remain in the community if he/she adheres to certain conditions, which always includes no new crime and may include financial obligations and prohibitions on alcohol/drug use, peer associations, unemployment, etc. | Monitor police arrest and investigation reports<br>Monitor victim restitution and court fees<br>Monitor community service<br><br>Conduct personal contacts and other monitoring (such as electronic)<br>Verify employment, school performance, peer associations<br>Test for drug and alcohol use | Number of arrest and technical violations during supervision<br>Percent of ordered payments collected<br>Number of hours/days performed community service<br>Number of favorable discharges<br><br>Number of days employed, in vocational education or school<br>Drug-free and/or alcohol-free days during supervision |

| Goals | Methods/Activities | Performance Indicators |
|---|---|---|
| **3. Protect the community:** Offenders are to be closely observed so that violations are noted, and if serious enough, result in the offender's being removed from the community. | Risk/needs instruments to assign classification status<br>Conduct personal contacts with offender<br>Conduct telephone contacts and collateral contacts<br>Limit offender freedom/mobility (e.g., curfews)<br>Conduct drug and alcohol testing<br>Coordinate with police on investigations/warrants<br>Monitor arrest records<br>Restrict offender travel outside designated community | Number and type of supervision contacts<br><br>Number and type of technical violations during supervision<br><br>Number and type of arrests during supervision<br>Number of absconders during supervision |
| **4. Assist offenders to change:** Offenders should be given the opportunity to participate in activities designed to reduce their long-term return to crime. | Refer to educational/vocational activities<br><br>Refer to drug/alcohol treatment<br><br>Refer or conduct personal counseling | Number of times attending treatment/work programming<br>Employment during supervision<br>Number of arrests and/or technical violations during supervision<br>Number drug-free and/or alcohol-free days during supervision<br>Attitude change |
| **5. Restore crime victims:** Crime victims have a right to be involved in the justice system, provided necessary financial support and social services, and protected from harm and intimidation. | Monitor restitution payments<br>Inform victim of potential contact/danger<br>Inform victims of services for them | Payment of restitution<br>Extent of victim satisfaction with services and department |

nonspecific changes. Officers frequently identify the outcomes in terms of changes in the client—but in often vague or ambiguous terms such as "ability to deal with authority," or "improved self-image." These broad changes are difficult to define operationally because they are subject to individual judgment—one officer's definition of progress might be quite different from another's—and because there are few objective measures for determining whether the goal has been met. For purposes of performance measurement, we need objective, measurable outcome statements that are tied to specific targeted activities that are believed to be related to the mission.

Column 3 of table 1 ("Performance Indicators") specifies performance indicators for each of the major goals in the mission statement. For example, one of the major goals of community corrections is to protect the public. This is done by monitoring the offender's behavior (through officer contacts), drug and alcohol testing, and so forth. To objectively measure whether these activities protect the public, one would record the number and types of arrests that occur during supervision and the number of offenders who abscond during supervision. Likewise, one goal is to "assist the offender to change." "Success" in achieving this goal might be measured by the number of drug-free or alcohol-free days, number of times attending treatment, and objective tests of attitude change.

It is important to mention two things at this point:

1) the performance indicators listed in table 1 are quite different from those currently used and include much more than recidivism, and

2) the measurements (including recidivism) reflect only activities that occur *while the offender is formally on community corrections status, not beyond.*

It may be quite interesting to track offenders for some time period after their supervision has ended and record their recidivism, but those rates should not be used, as they have historically, as the primary measure of probation and parole effectiveness. Criminal behavior is motivated by social and other factors over which the justice system has little, if any, direct control. Hawkins and Alpert (1989) suggest that to ask the justice system to assume responsibility for post-program behavior is akin to asking high schools to assume responsibility for post-graduation employment. Success in high school is defined as completing the course of study (not dropping out) and attaining some level of knowledge and skills assessed by grades and standardized tests. Schools do not follow up their graduates to see if they slip back into ignorance or fail to hold a job after leaving school. But corrections programs are judged not on their immediate impact but on their long-term effects: does the person refrain from crime after formal supervision has ended?

**It is the belief of the BJS/Princeton Study Group that the performance
of community corrections agencies ought not to be evaluated mainly
or exclusively in terms of their effects on recidivism rates, and that the
success of community corrections should not be based on some
postprogram assessment of behavior.**

## Why Bother with Performance Indicators?

Community corrections agencies do not currently collect information
on most of the performance indicators listed in table 1. To do so, agencies
would first need to define their mission, identify activities related to
that mission, and collect relevant performance indicators. Given their
current budget woes, why would they want to take on this additional
task?

There are a number of reasons. Completing such an exercise would
assist them in prioritizing activities and allocating resources. When the
agency implemented a new program or policy, data would be readily
available to monitor (or even project) the program's impact. Collecting
data on the performance indicators in table 1 should also increase staff
morale, since these indicators measure activities they do control and
will likely show some success. Also, going through the exercise of
defining mission, activities, and performance indicators helps the
organization—top management and field staff—reach consensus on key
issues. It also helps identify those priority areas that have few related
program activities. The most important reason, however, for completing
this exercise and collecting the necessary data is a practical one: without
such information, community corrections remains vulnerable to
continued budget cuts. It has been shown that those who can quantify
what they do, with whom, and to what effect have a strong competitive
advantage in budget negotiations.

Donald Cochran, Commissioner of Probation in Massachusetts
(1991:38), articulates the practical advantages of engaging in such an
exercise:

> Probation managers need to use information to accurately determine
> what work needs to be done, the outcomes the agency will produce
> if resources are added, or likely program outcomes and organizational
> practices if resources continue to be reduced . . . *information and
> knowledge driven probation programs can and will be funded*
> (Cochran, 1991:36, emphasis in original).

Ronald Corbett (1991) expands by noting:

in a time when agencies are increasingly called to define their existence, the absence of a clearly articulated philosophy will leave agencies vulnerable, unable to offer a compelling vision of their contribution to the common good in a manner that justifies continued existence . . . an agency that cannot offer a clear and convincing statement of its reason for being will not survive the rough and tumble of competition for shrinking tax dollars.

When public agencies fail to define their mission internally, political influences are more apt to define it for them. And when they fail to articulate how they should be evaluated, outcome measurements such as recidivism rates will likely be imposed upon them.

Over time, community corrections policy has become heavily influenced, not by those practitioners who are most knowledgeable about it, but instead by public opinion, fear, and political hype. One of the biggest challenges now facing community corrections is to regain control of its profession. One direct and effective way to do this is by defining a mission and showing—in measurable terms—that the agency is achieving it. With more solid information, community corrections should again be able to inspire the confidence of policymakers and the public, and ultimately secure the dollars necessary to perform adequately the activities that help accomplish their mission.

## Note

[1] Probation is often confused with parole. Probation is a sentence the offender serves in the community while under supervision; parole is the conditional release of an inmate from incarceration under supervision after a portion of the prison sentence has been served.

## References

American Correctional Association (1986). *Public Policy for Corrections*. College Park, MD: American Correctional Association.

American Probation and Parole Association (1992). Working Draft on Intensive Supervision Probation-Parole Training Manual.

Blair, Louis H., Harry P. Hatry, Karan Bunn et al. (1971). *Monitoring the Impacts of Prison and Parole Services: An Initial Examination*. Washington, DC: The Urban Institute.

California Corrections Policy Project (1991). *California Corrections Policies for the Future: Mission and Policy Statement*. Sacramento: California Corrections Policy Project.

Clear, Todd R., and James M. Byrne (1992). "The Future of Intermediate Sanctions: Questions to Consider," in James M. Byrne, Arthur J. Lurigio, and Joan Petersilia (eds.), *Smart Sentencing: The Emergence of Intermediate Sanctions*. Newbury Park, CA: Sage Publications.

Clear, Todd R., and Vincent O'Leary (1981). *Controlling the Offender in the Community.* Lexington, MA: Lexington Books.

Cochran, Donald (1991). "Classification/Information Systems" in Donald Cochran et al., *Managing Probation with Scarce Resources: Obstacles and Opportunities.* Washington, DC: National Institute of Corrections.

Cochran, Donald et al. (1991). *Managing Probation with Scarce Resources: Obstacles and Opportunities.* Washington, DC: National Institute of Corrections.

Corbett, Ronald P., Jr. (1991). "How Did We Get in this Mess?" in Donald Cochran et al., *Managing Probation with Scarce Resources: Obstacles and Opportunities.* Washington, DC: National Institute of Corrections.

DiIulio, John J., Jr. (1991). *No Escape: The Future of American Corrections.* New York: Basic Books.

_____ (1992). *Rethinking the Criminal Justice System: Toward a New Paradigm.* Washington, DC: U.S. Department of Justice, Bureau of Justice Statistics.

Doble, John (1987). *Crime and Punishment: The Public's View.* New York: Public Agenda Foundation.

Ellsworth, Thomas (1992). "The Goal Orientation of Adult Probation Professionals: A Study of Probation Systems," in Thomas Ellsworth (ed.), *Contemporary Community Corrections.* Prospect Heights, IL: Waveland Press.

Fitzharris, Timothy L. (1979). *Probation in an Era of Diminishing Resources.* The Foundation for Continuing Education in Corrections. Sacramento: The California Probation, Parole, and Correctional Association.

Flanagan, Timothy J., and Kathleen Maguire (eds.) (1992). *Sourcebook of Criminal Justice Statistics, 1991.* U.S. Department of Justice, Bureau of Justice Statistics. Washington, DC: U.S. Government Printing Office.

Fogel, David (1984). "The Emergence of Probation as a Profession in the Service of Public Safety: The Next Ten Years," in Patrick D. McAnany, Doug Thomson, and David Fogel (eds.), *Probation and Justice: Reconsideration of Mission.* Cambridge, MA: Oelgeschlager, Gunn and Hain.

Gottfredson, Michael R., and Don M. Gottfredson (1980). *Decisionmaking in Criminal Justice.* Cambridge, MA: Ballinger.

Hawkins, Richard, and Geoffrey P. Alpert (1989). *American Prison Systems: Punishment and Justice.* Englewood Cliffs, NJ: Prentice Hall.

Hindelang, Michael J., Michael R. Gottfredson, and Timothy J. Flanagan (eds.) (1981). *Sourcebook of Criminal Justice Statistics, 1980.* Washington, DC: U.S. Department of Justice, Bureau of Justice Statistics.

Jacoby, Joseph E., and Christopher S. Dunn (1987). "National Survey on Punishment for Criminal Offenses." Unpublished paper. Bowling Green State University, Bowling Green, OH.

Jankowski, Louis W. (1992). *Correctional Populations in the United States, 1990.* Washington, DC: U.S. Department of Justice, Bureau of Justice Statistics.

Langan, Patrick A., and Mark A. Cunniff (1992). *Recidivism of Felons on Probation, 1986-89,* Special Report. Washington, DC: U.S. Department of Justice, Bureau of Justice Statistics.

Lipton, D., R. Martinson, and J. Wilks (1975). *The Effectiveness of Correctional Treatment and What Works: A Survey of Treatment Evaluation Studies.* New York: Praeger Publishers.

Logan, Charles H. (1992). "Criminal Justice Performance Measures for Prisons," *Performance Measures for the Criminal Justice System*. Washington, DC: U.S. Department of Justice, Bureau of Justice Statistics.

McAnany, Patrick, Doug Thomson, and David Fogel (1984). *Probation and Justice: Reconsideration of Mission*. Cambridge, MA: Oelgeschlager, Gunn and Hain.

National Advisory Commission on Criminal Justice Standards and Goals (1973). *Report on Corrections*. Washington, DC: U.S. Government Printing Office.

Nidorf, Barry (1991a). "'Nothing Works' Revisited," *Perspectives*, Vol. 15, No. 3, pp. 12-13.

_____ (1991b). "External Relations," in Donald Cochran et al., *Managing Probation with Scarce Resources: Obstacles and Opportunities*. Washington, DC: National Institute of Corrections.

Peters, Thomas, and Robert Waterman, Jr. (1982). *In Search of Excellence*. New York: Harper & Row.

Petersilia, Joan, and Susan Turner (1990). *Intensive Supervision Probation for High-Risk Offenders: Findings from Three California Experiments*. R-3936-NIJ/BJA. Santa Monica, CA: RAND.

_____ (1993). "Intensive Probation and Parole Supervision: Research Findings and Policy Implications," in Michael Tonry (ed.), *Crime and Justice*, Vol. 17. Chicago: University of Chicago Press.

Petersilia, Joan, Susan Turner, James Kahan, Joyce Peterson (1985). *Granting Felons Probation: Public Rise and Alternatives*. R-3186-NIJ. Santa Monica, CA: RAND.

President of the United States (1990). *National Drug Control Strategy*. Washington, DC: U.S. Government Printing Office.

President's Commission on Law Enforcement and Administration of Justice (1967). *The Challenge of Crime in a Free Society*. Washington, DC: U.S. Government Printing Office.

# 19

# Factors Influencing Probation Outcome
## A Review of the Literature
### Kathryn D. Morgan

## Introduction

For much of correctional history, the criminal justice community has relied upon various programs designed to serve as alternatives to incarceration. Probation has been and continues to be one of these correctional alternatives. Recent statistics published by the Department of Justice (Bureau of Justice Statistics, 1992) indicate that in December 1990, there were approximately 3 million offenders under Federal and state probation supervision, with 83 percent of the total being under active supervision. Petersilia (1985) estimates that between 60 percent and 80 percent of all convicted criminals are sentenced to probation. Despite the proliferation of intermediate punishments such as intensive probation, home confinement, and electronic surveillance, probation has survived as a sentencing alternative.

Although used extensively, probation has been the center of much controversy and criticism for its failure to rehabilitate and deter offenders placed under the supervision of probation departments. Much of this criticism can be attributed to the decline of the rehabilitative ideal and the rise of the Justice Model in the 1970s and the "get tough on crime"

Source: *Federal Probation*, Vol. 57, No. 2 (June 1993), 23-29.

philosophy of the 1980s. The controversy and criticism that have surrounded probation since the 1930s focus on several issues which include: having caseloads too large for supervising officers to be effective; inadequate funding which often results in understaffed and underpaid probation departments; and failure of probation to rehabilitate offenders or deter their future criminal actions.

Because such a large number of correctional clients are under probation supervision, it is important that we understand the effectiveness and outcome issues related to probation and assess factors which influence probation outcome and probation effectiveness. Past research has provided some important insight into what factors influence probation outcome and which offenders are more likely to succeed or fail under probation supervision.

## Review of the Literature

Although used extensively, probation has been criticized for its failure to rehabilitate and deter offenders. Many studies have shown that the failure rate for probationers under supervision is high. Tippman (1976), who studied 790 male felons, found the failure rate to be 40 percent. Rogers (1981), with a sample of 1,014 probationers, concluded that 60 percent of those placed under probation supervision fail. Many studies have cited such factors as age, gender, employment, educational attainment, and marital stability as related to probation success or failure. Roundtree, Edwards, and Parker (1984) and Tippman (1976) found prior criminal record to be the most significant predictor of probation outcome. Other studies have identified probation supervision variables including the length of sentence and types of conditions assessed as being predictors of probation outcome. The studies which focus on probation outcome can be classified into three categories: (1) studies that report probation failure rates only (Irish, 1977; Rogers, 1981; General Accounting Office, 1976); (2) studies that report failure rates but also indicate significant factors correlated with that failure (Caldwell, 1951; England, 1955; Frease, 1964; Davis, 1964; Landis, Mercer, & Wolff, 1969; Tippman, 1976; Kusuda, 1976; Missouri Division of Probation and Parole, 1976; Roundtree et al., 1984); and (3) studies that discuss factors influencing probation outcome only (Ditman, 1967; Lohman, 1966; Wisconsin Corrections Division, 1972; Bartell & Thomas, 1977; Renner, 1978; New Jersey Administrative Office of the Courts, 1980; Holland, Holt, & Beckett, 1982; Scott & Carey, 1983; Cuniff, 1986; McCarthy & Langworthy, 1987; Petersilia, 1987; Kane County Diagnostic Center, no date; California Bureau of Statistics, 1977).

## Studies Reporting Probation Failure Rates

The first group of studies report failure rates for probation samples (see table 1).

Table 1

**Summary of Studies Reporting Failure Rates Only**

| Year | Researcher | Failure Rate |
|------|------------|--------------|
| 1976 | General Accounting Office | 55% |
| 1977 | Irish | 30% |
| 1981 | Rogers | 60% |
| 1985 | Vito | 22% |

The General Accounting Office (1976) studied probation outcome in four counties in the United States: Maricopa County, Arizona; Multnomah County, Oregon; Philadelphia County, Pennsylvania; and King's County, Washington. In these counties, approximately 77 percent of all offenders were placed under probation supervision. The sample consisted of 1,100 closed probation cases which were tracked for 22 months after discharge from probation and 50 current cases. Recidivism was defined as having probation revoked while still on probation or during the follow-up period. The results showed that only 4 or 5 out of every 10 complete their probation without arrest, conviction, or revocation.

Irish (1977) attempted to assess probation effectiveness by examining probation outcome. His conclusions indicated that three-fourths of those under study made a successful adjustment while on probation, and two-thirds conformed to law-abiding behavior after probation. Thus, he concluded that probation was successful in accomplishing its outcome.

Rogers (1981) analyzed data on 1,104 male and female probationers to identify factors related to recidivism. She used three measures of recidivism: reconvictions during probation; reconvictions between date that the probation order was issued and 24 months following termination; and sentences assessed between the date the probation order was issued and 24 months following termination. She found that one of every five probationers was convicted while under probation supervision. Within the 24-month period following termination, the number had increased to one in three probationers being convicted, with 60 percent of those convicted being given sentences of incarceration.

Among probationers receiving intensive probation supervision, reconviction rates were much higher (60 percent) than for probationers given minimum or no supervision.

Vito (1985) concluded that felony probation is effective in controlling recidivism when his examination of 317 felony probationers in Kent, Ohio, indicated a failure rate of 22 percent.

## Studies Reporting Failure Rates and Related Factors

The second category of studies reports probation failure rates but also describes factors significantly correlated with probation failure and success (see table 2).

Caldwell (1951) studied Federal probationers whose cases had been terminated during the period of July 1, 1937, through December 31, 1942. In the analysis of 337 probationers who violated conditions while under supervision, youthfulness and low socioeconomic status were characteristics of violators. Educational attainment was similar for both recidivists and nonrecidivists. In the second part of the study, 403 postprobationers were selected to examine postprobation outcome. Results indicated that there were 66 probation failures or probationers who were convicted of crimes following probation release. Fifty-eight of the 66 failures were due to arrests for minor offenses. Factors related to postprobation success included high occupational skill, full employment, adequate income, and marriage with children.

England (1955) studied 500 Federal offenders whose probation was terminated between January 1, 1939, and December 31, 1944. He followed these offenders for a period of 6 to 12 years. He defined failure as convictions for misdemeanor and felony offenses. With a 17 percent failure rate, factors associated with failure included previous criminal record, youthfulness, personal instability, and lower socioeconomic background. Most postprobation convictions were for minor offenses such as gambling, theft, and disorderly conduct. England (1955) used findings from his study of 490 adult felony and misdemeanor probationers who had completed terms between 1939-44 to suggest that selection for probation and daily probation operations might provide more insight into understanding probation outcome. These probationers were not subjected to any intensive, individualized social casework procedures. They were simply exposed to routine surveillance. The data showed that by 1951, only 17.7 percent of the offenders had recidivated. He argued that other variables besides "social work" are important in the probation experience, including the fact of being under surveillance; being publicly branded an offender; and the threat of a jail term.

Table 2

**Summary of Studies Reporting Failure Rates and Related Factors**

| Year | Researcher | Failure Rate | Related Factors |
|------|-----------|--------------|-----------------|
| 1951 | Caldwell | 19% (termination) | Failure correlated with youth and low socioeconomic status. |
|  |  | 16% (postprobation) | Postprobation success related to full employment, adequate income, marriage with children. |
| 1955 | England | 17% | Failure related to instability, prior criminal record, low socioeconomic status, and youth. |
| 1964 | Frease | 20% | Success related to being female, no felony commitments, educational attainment, marriage, positive family support. |
| 1964 | Davis | 30% | Age and sex highly related to outcome. |
| 1969 | Landis et al. | 52% | Failure related to frequent job changes, prior criminal record, marital instability, and low educational attainment. |
| 1975 | Cockerill | 39% | Failure related to employment, marital status, time of most recent previous conviction. |
| 1976 | Tippman | 40% | Failure correlated with adult criminal record. |
| 1976 | Kusuda | 18% | Success correlated with full employment, realistic goals, stable marriage, nonuse of alcohol and drugs, being 55 +, and income of $400 or more per month. |
| 1976 | Missouri Dept. of Corrections | 20% | Failure related to age, educational attainment, marital status, employment, adequate income, prior incarceration, alcohol and drug use, and conviction offense. |
| 1984 | Roundtree et al. | 14% | Failure related to prior arrests, length of supervision, age at first arrest, school grade completed. |
| 1987 | Petersilia | 51% | Failure related to conviction offense, prior juvenile and adult convictions, income at arrest, living arrangements. |

Frease (1964) studied 605 probationers under supervision from July 1, 1961, through June 30, 1962, to identify factors related to probation outcome. He defined failures as those who had been served a bench warrant or whose probationary status had been revoked. The data indicated the following factors to be associated with probation success: being female; no prior felony commitments; 5 years or more residence in Washington; a fourth grade education or more; nondrinking; married; and positive family support.

Defining failure as two or more violations and revocation, Davis (1964) used a cohort approach to study probation effectiveness. The sample consisted of a cohort made up of all defendants granted probation in 56 California counties in the years 1956 (3,199); 1957 (3,970); and 1958 (4,469). The highest revocation rate was for probationers convicted of minor offenses, including forgery and check offenses. The lowest revocation rate was for homicide and sex offenses. Age and sex were more significantly correlated with probation outcome; females and older people are more successful on probation.

Landis et al. (1969) analyzed variables related to success or failure on probation for 791 adult offenders in California. Three categories of variables for the 415 probation successes and 376 failures were identified: social background, antisocial behavior, and conditions of probation. Social background variables included educational achievement, occupational achievement, work history, marital status, and use of intoxicants. Antisocial behavior variables included type of military discharge, prior juvenile record, prior adult record, type of offense, and type of property offense. Conditions of probation were length of probation, jail as a probation condition, and restitution as a condition of probation. Of the three categories of variables, antisocial behavior variables were more highly correlated to probation failure. Probationers with a past history of disciplinary problems, a juvenile record, or an adult record are more likely to fail on probation. Probation failures commit more property crime. As it relates to social background, failures are more likely to have lower educational achievement and lower socioeconomic status, marital instability, and a tendency to move from job to job.

Of the 2,726 offenders convicted of criminal offenses in Alberta Canada, in the years 1967-71, Cockerill (1975) took a subsample of those offenders who had been placed on probation. The data showed that the group had a failure rate of 39 percent with employment, marital status, and time of most recent conviction being significantly related to failure. He also found that racial origin was a significant variable.

Tippman (1976) studied 790 male felons 1 year after they were placed on probation. Within a year after placement on probation, 17 percent had committed new felonies, and 23 percent had committed misdemeanors or violated probation conditions. He found the best predictor of recidivism to be adult criminal record with race, age, and juvenile record having only a slight impact on recidivism. He concluded that recidivism rates can be predicted and explained by prior criminal record. He also found that large numbers of poor probation risks are being placed under probation supervision.

Kusuda (1976) examined factors related to recidivist behavior for 7,147 male and female probationers who had been terminated from the Wisconsin Division of Corrections. The study defined failure as revocation of probation for a new offense, rules violation, or absconding. The results indicated a 19 percent failure rate with failures being due to absconding and minor offenses. Success was linked to such factors as stable marriage; full-time employment; per month income of more than $400; nonuse of drugs and alcohol; and probation terminated at age 55 or older.

The Missouri Division of Probation and Parole (1976) examined probation and postprobation outcomes using data for 5,083 probationers placed under supervision from July 1, 1968, to June 30, 1970. Data indicated that approximately 20 percent of the probationers under supervision failed, with failure being related to age, educational attainment, marital status, employment, adequate income, prior incarceration, and alcohol and drug abuse. The results also indicated that the type of conviction offense is related to failure. Those convicted of armed robbery, forcible rape, motor vehicle theft, and forgery are likely to fail. A simple random sample of 216 cases was selected from the population of probationers who had successfully completed probation. During the follow-up period which lasted from 6 months to 7 years, 30 percent of the 216 cases failed. Of the failures, only one probationer was arrested for a crime similar to the original conviction offense.

Roundtree et al. (1984) isolated offender characteristics related to recidivism. A random sample of 100 probationers was selected from a total population of 2,419 adult probation cases that had been closed between January 1, 1975, and December 31, 1978. Of the cases making up the sample, 14 percent were revoked and 86 percent completed probation successfully. Significant relationships were found between recidivism and school grade completed, prior criminal record, age at first arrest, number of prior arrests, offender classification, and length of probation sentence. Factors not significantly related to recidivism included race, sex, age left school, marital status, employment status at the time of the offense, age at the time of present offense, and time of the offense.

Petersilia (1987) conducted research to determine how felons perform under probation supervision. Taking a sub-sample of 1,672 from a sample of 16,000 felons convicted in the California Superior Court, she reported a 51 percent failure rate for probationers. Data showed that those originally charged with property crimes were more likely to recidivate; they tended to be arrested more than those convicted of violent or drug offenses. Factors correlated to probation failure included prior juvenile and adult convictions, income at arrest, and household composition. The greater the number of prior convictions, the higher the probability of probation failure; regardless of the source or amount, the presence of income at the time of arrest reduces possibility of failure; and living with spouse and/or child reduces the probability of failure.

In a study of 266 felony probationers in Tennessee, Morgan (1991) found probation failure significantly related to employment, hourly wage, marital status, prior felony commitments, and conviction offense. Probationers who are unemployed, making less than minimum wage, unmarried, with two or more prior felony commitments and a conviction for a property offense are more likely to experience probation failure. In this study, failure was measured by revocation, absconding, or being sentenced for a new offense.

### Studies Reporting Factors Related to Probation Outcome

The third category of studies report findings of research that focus primarily on factors that are highly correlated to probation success or failure (see table 3). Whereas the second category of studies focuses on failure rates and factors highly correlated to those failure rates, this third category attempts to identify factors related to probation outcome.

Ditman (1967) examined the relationship between alcohol rehabilitation treatment and probation success rates. He defined success as not having any rearrests. The study tracked 2,713 offenders for a 6-month treatment period. For the 6-month treatment period, 472 offenders had successful probation outcomes. Of the 146 probationers who had violated probation conditions during this 6-month period, 62 percent were successful and had no further violations after serving a 30-day sentence and receiving additional alcohol treatment.

Lohman (1966) found little difference in the type of supervision and success or failure. He compared intensive, ideal, and minimal supervision and their relationships to probation outcome. Using a sample size of 307, he studied males and females between the ages of 20 and 60 who had been under ideal, intensive, or minimal supervision status. The study found that violation rates for intensive supervision were much higher than for ideal and minimal supervision.

Data from the Wisconsin Corrections Division (1972) provide insight into probation outcomes for adult and juvenile probationers. They defined outcome as success or failure under supervision. Data regarding

Table 3

**Summary of Studies Identifying Factors Related to Probation Outcome**

| Year | Researcher | Related Factors |
|------|-----------|-----------------|
| 1967 | Ditman | Failure correlated with alcohol abuse. |
| 1966 | Lohman | Failure correlated with level of supervision. |
| 1972 | Wisconsin Corrections Division | Failure correlated with age, drug and alcohol abuse, employment, and length of probation sentence. |
| 1976 | McGinnis & Klockseim | Most important factor related to success is employment and length of supervision. |
| 1977 | Bartell & Thomas | Best predictors of probation failure are age, prior arrests, and burglary as a conviction offense. |
| 1977 | California Bureau of Statistics | Probation outcome related to age, race, prior criminality, and being convicted of a property offense. |
| 1978 | Renner | Failure related to employment, alcohol, drugs, and longer periods of supervision. |
| 1980 | New Jersey Administrative Office of the Courts | Failure related to unemployment and prior criminal record. |
| 1982 | Holland et al. | Failure highly related to being a property offender. |
| 1983 | Scott & Carey | Failure related to serious physical injury in the conviction offense, unemployment, and prior incarcerations. Age, race, and prior convictions have no significant effect. |
| 1986 | Cuniff | Failure related to being convicted of property offense (burglary), age, employment, and sex. |
| 1987 | McCarthy & Langworthy | Failure highly related to age—males 50 and over are more successful. |
| no date | Kane County Diagnostic Center | Probation outcome most significantly related to highest grade completed, income, number of dependents, prior incarcerations, marital status. |

successful outcomes indicate that females are more successful under supervision than males. Drug and alcohol use, being unemployed, and long periods of supervision were highly correlated with failure.

Bartell and Thomas (1977) studied recidivist practices for 100 probationers and incarcerated felons. They found that the best predictor of failure for both groups was age, which was inversely related to recidivism. Those who were the lowest risks for recidivism were offenders age 28 and above. Offenders arrested for burglary are more likely to be rearrested, with the new charge most often being another burglary.

Renner (1978) profiled 1,905 probationers in Ontario and concluded that the factors most often related to failure were employment, alcohol and drugs, and longer and more intense periods of probation supervision.

A 1980 study by the New Jersey Administrative Office of the Courts analyzed recidivism rates for 651 probationers who had been terminated in 1975. The study found that one-third of all probationers recidivated either prior to termination or after discharge. Employment status and a prior criminal record were strongly related to recidivism rates.

Holland et al. (1982) studied probation outcome for 198 male offenders over a period of 32 months. The researchers concluded that nonviolent failure is more common; the nonviolent criminal is more likely to recidivate. Persistent nonviolent criminality reflects a propensity for criminality. Because violence is a transitory psychological state, it is not a good predictor of future criminality.

Using 498 felons placed on probation and in a residential treatment facility, Scott and Carey (1983) found failure to be highly correlated with unemployment, prior incarcerations, and whether or not there was serious physical injury in the previous offense. Age, race, and prior convictions had no significant effect on outcome for probationers or inmates.

Cuniff (1986), taking a subsample of 226 from a larger sample, found that probation failures are more likely to be males, in the mid-twenties, living at home with family and convicted of property crimes. When probationers are rearrested, It is most often for burglary.

McCarthy and Langworthy (1987) compared probationers aged 50 and older (N = 95) with younger probationers (N = 82). They argued that being older, married, and employed with no drug use contributed to a higher success rate for older offenders. They also stated that older offenders are usually violent offenders rather than property offenders, a fact which possibly contributes to higher success rates for older offenders.

Kane County Diagnostic Center in Illinois found variables most related to probation outcome included highest grade completed, income, number of dependents, prior incarceration, and marital status. McGinnis and Klockseim (1976) concluded that employment is the most important factor in probation success.

When comparing probationers given straight probation time with offenders given probation and jail time and offenders given straight jail time, a California (1977) study found that probationers with straight probation time did better than the other two groups. With straight probation, females were more successful than males; sex offenders were more successful than property offenders; and younger offenders ($<30$) were the most likely to fail within the first year. The study indicated age, race, prior criminality and being convicted of a property offense were significantly correlated to probation outcome.

## Summary of the Literature Review

Much of the prior research on probation outcome measures outcome as success or failure while under supervision or during the postprobation period. Failure in a majority of these cases was measured by reconviction, revocation, or absconding. Success was measured by the completion of the probation term without reconviction, revocation, or absconding. Much of the reviewed research indicated that probation is effective as a correctional alternative. Failure rates ranged from 14 percent (Roundtree et al., 1984) to 60 percent (Rogers, 1981). Factors most often associated with failure included employment status, prior criminal record, low income, age, sex, and marital status. Young males who are unemployed or underemployed with a low income and prior criminal record are more likely to fail. Instability, as measured by employment status, marital status, and length of stay at residence, was also related to probation failure or success. Probationers who were married with children, adequately employed, and had lived in an area for more than 2 years, were often successful under supervision. When discussing probation failures, most of the studies indicated that reconviction offenses tended to be minor misdemeanors rather than felonies.

According to Latessa, Eskridge, Allen, and Vito (1985), it is important to exercise care when reporting the results of probation research. He points out that methodological problems occur when trying to assess probation effectiveness from past research. Definitions of failure, follow-up periods, and types of offenders used in the sample often differ from study to study. These problems prevent adequate assessment of probation and determination of effectiveness.

In the literature review for the present study, there were questions and issues in the different studies which are crucial to probation research designed to assess the effectiveness of probation as a correctional alternative. In the studies reviewed, there was little uniformity in the definition of failure. Many of the studies used failure to indicate termination from probation due to reconviction, revocation, or absconding. Other studies used failure to refer to arrests for both misdemeanors and felonies, reconvictions, and revocation. In these studies, absconding or disappearance without notification was not considered to be failure.

None of the studies indicated the use of a control group for comparison. Although the experimental design with random assignment represents the best way for determining effectiveness, it is seldom possible in corrections research. However, the use of a comparison group based on matching would be beneficial to probation research.

Studies of postprobation outcome used different follow-up periods. Some used 6 to 12 years; 4 to 11 years; 22 months; 5-1/2 to 11 years; 3 to 4 years; and 6 months to 7 years.

Study populations were different. Some studies used only felons, while others used both felons and misdemeanants. Federal probationers comprised the population in two studies, while the remaining studies used probationers supervised by state probation agencies.

The purpose of this article was to examine past research regarding probation outcome. A major underlying theme of this past research has been whether probation as a nonincarcerative alternative is fulfilling its objectives. There is a tremendous need for more empirical investigation of probation as a correctional alternative. More research is needed into issues including whether probation "widens the net" of social control, what probation can and cannot do, and for whom probation works best.

### References

Bartell, T. & Thomas, W. (1977) Recidivist impacts of differential sentencing practices for felony offenders. *Criminology, 15*, 387-96.

Bureau of Justice Statistics. (1992). Probation in 1990. *Correctional populations in the United States, 1990.* Washington, DC: Department of Justice.

Caldwell, M. (1951). Preview of a new type of probation study made in Alabama. *Federal Probation, 15*(2), 3-11.

California Bureau of Statistics. (1977). Superior court probation and/or jail sample.

Cockerill, R. (1975). Probation effectiveness in Alberta. *Canadian Journal of Criminology and Corrections, 17*(4).

Comptroller General of the United States. (1976). *State and county probation: Systems in crisis.* Washington, DC: U.S. Government Printing Office.

Cuniff, M. (1986). *A sentencing postscript: Felony probationers under supervision in the community.* Washington, DC: National Criminal Justice Planning Association.

Davis, G. (1964). A study of adult probation violation rates by means of the cohort approach. *Journal of Criminal Law, Criminology and Police Science, 55*, 70-85.

Ditman, K. S. (1967). A controlled experiment on the use of court probation for drunk arrests. *American Journal of Psychiatry, 124*(2), 160-63.

England, R. (1955). A study of postprobation recidivism among five hundred federal offenders. *Federal Probation, 19,* 10-16.

Frease, D. (1964). Factors related to probation outcome. Olympia, WA: Department of Institutions, Board of Prison Terms and Parole.

General Accounting Office. (1976). *State and county probation systems in crisis.* Washington, DC: U.S. Government Printing Office.

Holland, T., Holt, N. & Beckett, G. (1982). Prediction of violent versus nonviolent recidivism from prior violent and nonviolent criminality. *Journal of Abnormal Psychology, 91,* 178-82.

Irish, J. (1977). Probation and its effect on recidivism: An evaluative study of probation in Nassau County, New York. Mineola, NY: Nassau County Probation Department.

Kane County Diagnostic Center. (no date). *Probation prediction models and recidivism.* Geneva, IL.

Kusuda, P. (1976). *1974 probation and parole terminations.* Madison: Wisconsin Corrections Division.

Latessa, E., Eskridge, C., Allen, H. & Vito, G. (1985). *Probation and parole in America.* New York: The Free Press.

Landis, J., Mercer, J. & Wolff, C. (1969). Success and failure of adult probationers in California. *Journal of Research in Crime and Delinquency, 6,* 34-40.

Lohman, J. (1966). *Ideal supervision caseload: A preliminary evaluation.* (The San Francisco Project Research Report #9). Berkeley: University of California School of Criminology.

McCarthy, B. & Langworthy, R. (1987). *Older offenders: Perspectives in criminology and criminal justice.* New York: Praeger.

McGinnis, R. & Klockseim, K. (1976). *Probation and employment: A report to the Bergen County New Jersey Probation Department.*

Missouri Division of Probation and Parole. (1976). *Probation in Missouri, July 1, 1968-June 30, 1970: Characteristics, performance and criminal reinvolvement.* Jefferson County, MO: Division of Probation and Parole.

Morgan, K. (1991). *An analysis of factors influencing probation outcome.* Unpublished dissertation, Florida State University.

New Jersey Administrative Office of the Courts. (1980). *Adult probation in New Jersey: A study of recidivism and a determination of the predictive utilities of a risk assessment model.* Trenton, NJ.

Norland, S. & Munn, P. (1984). Being troublesome: Women on probation. *Criminal Justice and Behavior, 11,* 115-35.

Petersilia, J. (1985). *Granting felons probation: Public risks and alternatives.* Santa Monica, CA: The Rand Corporation.

Petersilia, J. (1987). Probation and felony offenders. *Federal Probation, 51*(2), 56-61.

Renner, J. (1978). *The adult probationer in Ontario.* Ontario, Canada: Ministry of Correctional Services.

Rogers, S. (1981). *Factors related to recidivism among adult probationers in Ontario.* Ontario, Canada: Ontario Correctional Services Ministry.

Roundtree, G., Edwards, D. & Parker, J. (1984). A study of personal characteristics related to recidivism. *Journal of Offender Counseling Services and Rehabilitation, 8,* 53-61.

Scott, M. & Carey, H. (1983). Community alternatives in Colorado. *Criminal Justice and Behavior, 10*(1), 93-108.

Tippman, D. (1976). *Probation as a treatment alternative for criminal offenders: An analysis of variables related to performance on probation in a sample of men placed on probation.* Ph.D dissertation, Wayne State University.

Vito, G. (1985). Probation as punishment: New directions and suggestions. In L. Travis III (Ed.), *Probation, parole and community corrections.* Prospect Heights, IL: Waveland Press.

# 20

# The Effectiveness of Institutional and Community-Based Programs for Juvenile Offenders

## Larry Webb
## John R. Scanlon

### Introduction

The effectiveness of institutional and community-based programs for juvenile offenders has been widely debated in recent years. Many in the juvenile justice field argue that community-based programs are a more cost-effective and less oppressive treatment alternative for troubled youth.[1] Institutional programs have been called dehumanizing and isolating.[2] Consequently, the number of community-based programs has increased dramatically in recent years.[3] Koshel noted that:

> . . . Some observers apparently felt that society's best interests are served by noninstitutional arrangements for all delinquents. They

Source: *Juvenile and Family Court Journal*, Vol. 32, No. 3 (August 1981), 11-16. Copyright 1981 by the National Council of Juvenile and Family Court Judges. Reprinted with permission.

claim that the harmful effects of an institutional experience eventually surface in the form of higher recidivism rates and that these higher recidivism rates obviously affect everyone. It is on this basis that some authorities argue against sending any delinquent children to custodial institutions, believing that no alternative is less effective than institutions in reducing recidivism.[4]

The widely publicized closing of institutions by the Massachusetts Department of Youth Services (DYS) in the early 1970s is the best example of radical reform of an existing system. Others have suggested that community services need to be improved and firmly established before institutions are closed.[5] The California Youth Authority's ambitious Community Treatment Project (CTP) sought to test the effectiveness of community-based treatment. Palmer, in discussing the CTP, pointed out that:

> Within and outside of corrections, many concerned individuals are currently engaged in an ideological battle over whether to ''keep almost all offenders, on the streets,'' or else ''lock up nearly all offenders except for first-timers.'' . . . the facts which have emerged from California's 12-year experiment thus suggest that both of the above positions may be too extreme, and that a more differentiated or flexible approach may be appropriate.[6]

A review of research on the comparative effectiveness of institutional and community-based programs reveals no clear pattern. Palmer reported ''that boys who participated in the CTP program performed substantially better than those in the traditional (institutional) program at least during the 2-to-4 year, typical duration of their Youth Authority jurisdiction.''[7] However, Lerman analyzed the same data and concluded that ''CTP did not have an impact on youth behavior that differed significantly from the impact of the control program.''[8] Coates, Miller and Ohlin studied the Massachusetts experience and offered the following conclusion:

> . . .when looking at indicators of recidivism over time, representing the training-school system of the late sixties and the community-based system of the middle seventies, we saw that the absolute rate had increased slightly (8%). Numerous explanations are possible for this increase, reflecting changes in the makeup of the DYS population over time, broader societal trends in youth crime, changing attitudes toward females, and changes in police and court resources. Nonetheless, it is clear that the reforms in DYS did not bring about a decrease in the recidivism rate, and it is equally clear that the reforms did not generate an explosive youth crime wave. Short-term outcomes such as improved self-image, improved perception of others, and enhanced expectations and aspirations increase in settings that can be described as more normalized within the programs and the community. Again, the data support the notion

that the department, in replacing the training-school system with a community-based system, made a move in the right direction. While the overall results are not perhaps as outstanding as the proponents of reform had hoped, the results do suggest strongly that the vast majority of committed delinquents can be handled in relatively noninstitutional settings. Even youths requiring secure facilities can be handled in smaller, more humane settings than the traditional large training school.[9]

In another study, Koshel discussed projects in Essexfields and Colledgefields, N.J., and Provo, Utah: "While all three of these projects could be classified as successful, they were not significantly more successful than traditional treatment alternatives (probation and custodial institutions) in reducing recidivism."[10]

The purpose of this study is to assess the adjustment of juvenile offenders served in institutional and community-based programs. Selection of outcome criteria was not a simple task. The effects of "people changing" organizations are sometimes subtle and almost always difficult to measure. Recidivism, although sometimes overrated, is probably the single best measure for correctional programs. Measurement of recidivism is recognized as a useful tool and is utilized frequently by researchers.[11] The effects of treatment programs on interpersonal, familial, vocational and educational problems are areas for study.[12] Psychological test score changes are also analyzed.[13] Other researchers have used treatment staff ratings or self reports on client adjustments.[14]

Outcome measures utilized in this study are recidivism and treatment staff ratings of adjustment in counseling, educational and vocational settings. Recidivism rates of samples of youths placed in institutional and community-based programs will be measured and differences will be tested for significance. Similarly, the study will include an analysis of differences in staff ratings.

## Methodology

### Research Design

The best method for comparison of the effectiveness of the two types of programs would be to randomly assign offenders and conduct a study with an experimental design. However, ethical and legal considerations obviated serious consideration of such an approach. This study employs a quasi-experimental design in which samples of youths served by each type of program are matched according to key characteristics. Campbell and Stanley and other researchers recognized the constraints of "real-world" research and promoted the utilization of matched-group designs.[15] Matching is considered to be a useful and acceptable method as long as care is taken in the selection of variables for matching and in identifying populations to which the results can be generalized.[16]

### Samples, Procedures and Definitions

From a population of 400 male youths committed by juvenile courts to the Georgia Department of Human Resources, Division of Youth Services, in the last half of 1976, 127 were selected for study (64 institutional placements and 63 community placements). Youths who had been committed previously were excluded and the variables age, race, type of offense leading to commitment and number of prior offenses were controlled in the selection process. Table 1 shows that the two groups were well-matched, since none of the chi-square values were significant.

Treatment staff were surveyed to obtain program adjustment data. Recommitment data were obtained from records in the central office of the Division of Youth Services. Prison entry data were obtained from records provided by the Georgia Department of Corrections.

The outcome variables are operationally defined as follows:

(1) "Reported favorable adjustment to counseling"—Response from youth's supervising worker indicating that, during the placement, the youth's response to counseling was "somewhat improved" or "improved."

(2) "Reported favorable educational program adjustment"—Response from youth's supervising worker that, during the placement, the youth's progress in an academic program had been "average" or "above average."

Table 1

## Characteristics of the Samples

|  | Institutional Placements | Community Placements | Chi-Square Value (Significance) |
|---|---|---|---|
| Sample Size | 64 | 63 | — |
| No. and % White | 35 (55%) | 32 (51%) | 0.193 (p > .66) |
| No. and % under age 15 | 16 (25%) | 16 (25%) | 0.372 (p > .99) |
| No. and % committed for felonies | 47 (77%) | 52 (85%) | 3.343 (p > .18) |
| No. and % with: No prior adjudications 1-3 prior adjudications More than 3 adjudications | 14 (22%) 39 (61%) 11 (17%) | 15 (24%) 38 (60%) 10 (16%) | 0.289 (p > .99) |

(3) "Reported favorable vocational program adjustment" —Response from youth's supervising worker that, during the placement, the youth's progress in a vocational program had been "average" or "above average."

(4) "Recidivism"—Within three years, recommitment by a juvenile court to the Georgia Division of Youth Services and/or admission to a Georgia State Prison.

## Results

Tables 2 and 3 illustrate the differences in outcome between the two samples. The findings are as follows:

(1) There was not a significant difference in the overall recidivism rate of the two samples. The slightly higher percentage of recommitments in the community sample, though not significant in isolated analysis, contributed to this result.

(2) A significantly higher percentage of youths in the institutional sample entered state prisons (20 percent compared to 5 percent for the community sample).

(3) There was not a significant difference in the percentages of juvenile court recommitment of the two samples. The percentage was 32 percent for the community sample and 23 percent for the institutional sample, but the difference can be attributed only to chance.

(4) There was not a significant difference in the ratings of treatment staff in the area of response to counseling.

(5) The institutional sample was reported to have significantly more favorable adjustments in education settings.

(6) There was no significant difference in the reported vocational program adjustment of the two samples. However, the institutional sample received favorable ratings that approached statistical significance.

(7) The offenses committed by recidivists during the three-year follow-up period were predominantly property-related. Of the 64 institutional placements, only three, or 5 percent, went on to commit violent acts. Of the 63 community placements, only two, or 3 percent, went on to commit violent acts.

## Discussion

The findings indicate that there were some short-term advantages to institutional placement of juvenile offenders, but that impact on

Table 2

## Recidivism Rates and Treatment Staff Ratings
## of Institutional and Community-Based Samples

|  | Institutional Placements | Community Placements | Chi-Square (Significance) |
|---|---|---|---|
| **Recidivism Rates**<br>No. and % of sample entering state prison within 3 years | 13 (20%) | 3 (5%) | 6.972 (p < .01) |
| No. and % of sample recommitted by juvenile courts within 3 years | 15 (23%) | 20 (32%) | 1.099 (p < .30) |
| Overall recidivism | 28 (44%) | 23 (37%) | 0.6918 (p < .35) |
| **Treatment Staff Ratings**<br>No. and % of sample reported as responding favorably to counseling | 41 (72%) | 36 (63%) | 0.424 (p < .45) |
| No. and % of sample with favorable adjustment in educational setting | 48 (77%) | 22 (39%) | 16.186 (p < .0001) |
| No. and % of sample with reported favorable adjustment in vocational setting | 25 (40%) | 15 (25%) | 3.2459 (p > .05) |

recidivism did not follow. While youths placed in community-based programs were reported by counseling staff to have greater difficulty adjusting in educational programs, they had lower prison recidivism rates and comparable overall recidivism rates. The fact that institutions offer more structure is borne out by the results of this study. However, it appears that this short-term structure does not have lasting benefit for some youth.

The results indicated that prison is more likely to be the "next step" for recidivists who have been in juvenile institutions than for those who have not been institutionalized. Both judicial and treatment staff attitudes are probably relevant in this regard. The apparent lack of relationship between staff ratings of in-program adjustment and subsequent recidivism is consistent with the findings of other studies.[17]

As stated earlier, the "matched group" approach of this study is a less rigorous research design than an experimental approach. The possibility exists that the institutional and community groups differed in ways

Table 3

**Offenses Committed By Recidivists**

| Offense | Institutional Placements who were Recidivists | Community Placements who were Recidivists | Totals |
|---------|:---:|:---:|:---:|
| Burglaries | 11 | 7 | 18 |
| Theft | 3 | 6 | 9 |
| Motor Vehicle Theft | 4 | 2 | 6 |
| Forgery | 2 | 0 | 2 |
| Rape | 1 | 0 | 1 |
| Robbery/Armed Robbery | 1 | 1 | 2 |
| Criminal Damage | 0 | 2 | 2 |
| Aggravated Assault | 1 | 1 | 2 |
| Drug Offense | 0 | 1 | 1 |
| Terroristic Threats | 1 | 0 | 1 |
| Unruly | 1 | 0 | 1 |
| Disorderly Conduct | 1 | 0 | 1 |
| Simple Battery | 1 | 0 | 1 |
| Violation of Aftercare | 1 | 0 | 1 |
| Violation of Curfew | 0 | 1 | 1 |
| Fornication | 0 | 1 | 1 |
| Criminal Attempt | 0 | 1 | 1 |
| Totals | 28 | 23 | 51 |

not identified in the matching process. Matching for extraneous, but possibly relevant, variables such as quality of aftercare service, family and peer influence and job opportunities would require a prohibitively large study population. Consequently, this study should not be interpreted as a definitive statement on the comparative effectiveness of the two types of programs. It was beyond the scope of this study to conduct a comprehensive "evaluation" of all aspects of the programs. However, there are clear indications here, as in the findings of other studies, that community-based programs can be utilized as successfully as institutional programs.

### Notes

[1] James McSparron. "Community Correction and Diversion." *Crime and Delinquency* 26, no. 2 (1980):228.
Richard E. Isralowitz. "Deinstitutionalization and the Serious Juvenile Offender." *Juvenile and Family Court Journal* 30, no. 3 (1979):21.

[2] Maurice J. Boisvert, Helen J. Kenney, and William C. Kvaraceus. "Massachusetts Deinstitutionalization: Data on One Community-Based Answer." *Juvenile Justice* 27, no. 2 (1976):35.

Mercedese M. Miller, ed. *Evaluating Community Treatment Programs: Tools, Techniques, and a Case Study* (Lexington, MA: D.C. Heath and Co., 1975), p. xiii.

[3] Ibid.

[4] J. Koshel. *Deinstitutionalization: Delinquent Children* (Washington, DC: The Urban Institute, 1973), p. 50.

[5] Holland M. Gary. "A Small County's Answer to Community-Based Programs." *Juvenile Justice* 26, no. 2(1975):26.

John P. Conrad. "There Has to Be a Better Way." *Crime and Delinquency* 26, no. 1 (1980):85.

[6] Ted Palmer. "The Youth Authority's Community Treatment Project," *Federal Probation* 38, no. 1 (1974):11.

[7] Ibid., p. 6.

[8] Paul Lerman. *Community Treatment and Social Control: A Critical Analysis of Juvenile Correctional Policy* (Chicago: The University of Chicago Press, 1975), p. 67.

[9] Robert B. Coates, Alden D. Miller, and Lloyd E. Ohlin. *Diversity in a Youth Correctional System: Handling Delinquents in Massachusetts* (Cambridge: Ballinger Publishing Co., 1978), pp. 172-77.

[10] Koshel. *Deinstitutionalization*, p. 22.

[11] Daniel Glaser. *Routinizing Evaluation: Getting Feedback of Effectiveness of Crime and Delinquency Programs*, Crime and Delinquency Series (Rockville, MD: National Institute of Mental Health, 1973), p. 17.

Paul Gendreau and Bob Ross. "Effective Correctional Treatment: Bibliotherapy for Cynics." *Crime and Delinquency* 25, no. 4 (1979):486.

McSparron. "Community Correction." p. 231.

William E. Wright and Michael C. Dixon, "Community Prevention and Treatment of Juvenile Delinquency." *Journal of Research in Crime and Delinquency* 14, no. 1 (1977):59.

Boisvert, Kenney, and Kvaraceus. "Massachusetts Deinstitutionalization," p. 39.

[12] Gendreau and Ross. "Effective Correctional Treatment," p. 486.

Glaser. *Routinizing Evaluation*, p. 5.

[13] Lerman. *Community Treatment*, p. 22.

Ted B. Palmer. "California's Community Treatment Program for Delinquent Adolescents," in *Readings in Juvenile Delinquency*, ed. Ruth S. Cavan (Philadelphia: J.B. Lippincott Co., 1975), p. 503.

[14] Lerman. *Community Treatment*, p. 22.

Wright and Dixon. "Community Prevention," p. 50.

[15] Donald T. Campbell and Julian C. Stanley. *Experimental and Quasi-Experimental Designs for Research* (Chicago: Rand McNally and Co., 1963), p. 34.

Bruce W. Tuckman. *Conducting Educational Research* (New York: Harcourt, Brace, Jovanovich, Inc., 1972), p. 83.

Dwight C. Jarvis. *Institutional Treatment of the Offender* (New York: McGraw-Hill, Inc., 1978), p. 286.

[16] Howard E. Freeman and Clarence C. Sherwood. *Social Research and Social Policy*, Prentice-Hall Series in Social Policy (Englewood Cliffs, NJ: Prentice-Hall, Inc., 1970), p. 117.

Glaser. *Routinizing Evaluation*, p. 65.

Delbert C. Miller. *Handbook of Research Design and Social Measurement* (New York: David McKay Co., Inc., 1964), p. 38.

[17] Gene Kassebaum, David Ward, and Daniel Wilner. *Prison Treatment and Parole Survival: An Empirical Assessment* (New York: John Wiley and Sons, Inc., 1971), p. 316.

Glaser. *Routinizing Evaluation*, p. 19.

# 21

# Evaluating Intensive Supervision Probation/Parole

## Results of a Nationwide Experiment

### Joan Petersilia
### Susan Turner

Sentencing practices in this country suggest that offenses can be divided into two categories. When the crime is relatively serious, offenders are put behind bars; when it is less so, they are put on probation, often with only perfunctory supervision. This two-fold division disregards the range of severity in crime, and as a result, sentencing can err in one direction or another: either it is too harsh, incarcerating people whose crimes are not serious enough to warrant a sanction this severe, or too lenient, putting on probation people whose crimes call for more severe punishment. This need for more flexible alternatives—punishments that in harshness fall between prison and probation—led many States to experiment with intermediate sanctions, such as intensive supervision probation/parole (ISP).[1]

Intensive supervision probation/parole is a form of release into the community that emphasizes close monitoring of convicted offenders and imposes rigorous conditions on that release. Most ISP's call for:

Source: *National Institute of Justice, Research in Brief*, U.S. Department of Justice, May 1993, 1–11.

- Some combination of multiple weekly contacts with a supervising officer.
- Random and unannounced drug testing.
- Stringent enforcement of probation/parole conditions.
- A requirement to participate in relevant treatment, hold a job, and perhaps perform community service.

Interest in ISP's has been generated in part by the increased proportion of serious offenders among the probation population, a group whose needs and problems may not be effectively addressed by routine probation. Another reason for interest in ISP's is the greater flexibility in sentencing options that they permit. They are better able than the traditional alternatives—prison or probation—to fit the punishment to the crime.

## The Problem

The population on probation is a particular focus of ISP's. This population has been growing, increasing 5 to 7 percent each year from 1985 to 1990. At the end of 1990, two-thirds of all people who were under correctional supervision were on probation.[2] More importantly, the type of offender on probation has also changed. More of the current probation population consists of people convicted of felonies than misdemeanors.[3]

As a sentencing option, routine probation was neither intended nor structured to handle this type of offender. One reason is that felons are not good risks for routine probation. A recent report by the Bureau of Justice Statistics revealed that 43 percent of felons on State probation were rearrested for another felony within 3 years.[4] This threat to public safety underscores the need for sentencing alternatives. Moreover, the need is even greater in view of budget cuts at probation agencies.

At the other extreme, reliance on imprisonment has limitations. Prison populations have tripled since 1975. States have responded to the increased need with enormous investments in prison construction. Yet the level of violent crime is now substantially higher than it was a decade ago, indicating that the prospect of imprisonment has not had the deterrent effect that investment in prisons hoped to buy.[5] It has also meant that 36 States are currently operating all or part of their correctional systems under court orders or consent decrees to reduce crowding.[6]

## The Rationale for ISP's

Since neither prison nor routine probation can fully respond to the current situation, ISP's have increasingly been viewed as an alternative. Indeed, these programs have been hailed by many as the most promising criminal justice innovation in decades. Between 1980 and 1990 every State adopted some form of ISP for adult offenders.[7] The Federal system has not been as aggressive as the States in ISP experiments, although there are a few programs in selected districts.

---

### Types of ISP's

ISP's are usually classified as prison diversion, enhanced probation, and enhanced parole. Each has a different goal.

**Diversion** is commonly referred to as a "front door" program because its goal is to limit the number of offenders entering prison. Prison diversion programs generally identify lower risk, incoming inmates to participate in an ISP in the community as a substitute for a prison term.

**Enhancement** programs generally select already sentenced probationers and parolees and subject them to closer supervision in the community than regular probation or parole. People placed in ISP enhanced probation or enhanced parole programs show evidence of failure under routine supervision or have committed offenses generally deemed to be too serious for supervision on routine caseloads.

---

A growing number of jurisdictions have come to believe that by providing increased supervision of serious offenders in the community, ISP's can both relieve prison crowding and lessen the risks to public safety that such offenders pose—and all at a cost savings. In addition to these practical considerations, many believe ISP's should be adopted as a matter of principle, to meet the need for greater latitude in sentencing and to achieve the sentencing objective of just deserts.

The practical argument is the one advanced most often. ISP's are believed to be cost-effective, either in the short run or the long run. Prison-diversion programs (see "Types of ISP's") are thought to be able to reduce corrections costs because they presumably cost less than prison. Probation-enhancement programs are believed to prevent crime because the close surveillance they provide should deter recidivism. With lower recidivism, the need for imprisonment is also reduced, since fewer offenders will be reprocessed by the system.

Assumptions about the effect of ISP's on crime control involve comparisons of various types of sanctions. Prison is assumed to provide the strongest, and routine supervision the weakest, crime control. ISP's are a middle ground, with more control than routine supervision but less control than prison. Theoretically, offenders in ISP programs are deterred from committing crimes because they are under surveillance, and they are constrained from committing crimes because the conditions of the program limit their opportunities.

## Initial Reactions to ISP's

Some of the enthusiasm for ISP's was generated by early reports from programs like that of the Georgia Department of Corrections, which seemed to bear out many of the assumptions and to produce a number of benefits.[8] Many ISP programs claimed to have saved at least $10,000 a year for each offender who otherwise would have been sentenced to prison.[9] Participants in the Georgia program, which served as the model for programs adopted elsewhere, had low recidivism, maintained employment, made restitution, and paid a monthly supervision fee.

In other places where ISP's were adopted, evaluations produced mixed results, with some sites reporting cost savings (Illinois and New Jersey, for example), while others did not (such as Massachusetts and Wisconsin); and some reporting reduced recidivism (Iowa, for example), while others did not (such as Ohio and Wisconsin).

The ambiguous results of these programs indicate that assumptions about the ability of ISP's to produce practical results—relieve prison crowding, lower costs, and control crime—may not have been well-founded. Reservations have been raised by independent agencies (such as the U.S. General Accounting Office), as well as by a number of scholars, including proponents of the ISP concept.[10] It appears not that the ISP's themselves have failed, but that the objectives set for them may have been overly ambitious, raising expectations they have been unable to meet.

The evidence seems better able to support the argument based on principle. That is, because ISP's are more punitive than routine probation and parole and because they provide for greater surveillance, they may be able to achieve the goal of permitting needed flexibility in sentencing.

## The Demonstration Project

To test the relative effectiveness of ISP's and traditional sanctions, NIJ evaluated a demonstration project sponsored by the Bureau of Justice

Assistance (BJA). The demonstration, which involved 14 programs in 9 States, ran from 1986 to 1991 and involved about 2,000 offenders. NIJ commissioned the RAND Corporation to evaluate the programs in a project supported by the Institute as well as BJA.

The participating jurisdictions (see exhibit 1) were asked to design an ISP program and were given wide latitude in doing so. Only two sites (Marion County, Oregon, and Milwaukee, Wisconsin) selected prison diversion programs, in which lower risk offenders who would have entered prison were diverted into the community. All others chose either probation enhancement or parole enhancement programs for the more serious offenders who were then under community supervision.

The offenders whom the jurisdictions chose to target had to meet only two criteria: they had to be adults and they could not be currently convicted of a violent crime. Once these criteria were met, the jurisdictions were free to focus on whatever type of offender population they wished: probationers and/or parolees, people currently in jail, or people who were prison bound.

They were also free to tailor their programs to meet local needs. For example, several sites designed their programs specifically for drug offenders. However, for a variety of reasons, the agencies were unable to place many offenders in drug, alcohol, or other such treatment programs. Thus, the ISP's evaluated were not primarily service and treatment programs, but rather were oriented more toward surveillance and supervision. (See "Study Methods.")

---

*Exhibit 1.* **The 14 Demonstration/ Evaluation Sites**

---

Contra Costa County, California

Los Angeles County, California

Seattle, Washington

Ventura County, California

Atlanta, Georgia

Macon, Georgia

Waycross, Georgia

Santa Fe, New Mexico

Des Moines, Iowa

Winchester, Virginia

Dallas, Texas

Houston, Texas

Marion County, Oregon

Milwaukee, Wisconsin

---

## Effectiveness of ISP's

The demonstration was intended to answer the question of how participation in an ISP affected offenders' subsequent criminal behavior (that is, its effect on recidivism). The evaluation was intended to bring to light information about cost-effectiveness and extent of offender participation in counseling, work, and training programs. The effect of ISP's on prison crowding was not a study aim, but it has been a major policy interest in all ISP programs. The participating sites had their own objectives and interests. Most wanted to learn whether ISP's are an effective intermediate sanction, in which probation and parole conditions are monitored and enforced more credibly.

Overall, the results revealed what *cannot* be expected of ISP's as much as what *can* be. Most notably, they suggest that the assumptions about

---

## Study Methods[11]

### Program Design

All jurisdictions selected by the Bureau of Justice Assistance for participation in the demonstration and evaluation were asked to design and implement an ISP program that was to be funded for 18 to 24 months. The jurisdictions also were required to receive training and technical assistance, both provided by outside consultants.[12] In addition, they took part in the independent evaluation, which required their gathering data about the program.

The population studied consisted of approximately 2,000 adult offenders who were not currently convicted of a violent crime (homicide, rape, robbery, and assault). The vast majority of the offenders were men in their late 20s and early 30s, and most had long criminal records. In other respects, sites varied. Some, for example, chose offenders with more serious prison records than others. The nature of their offenses varied, as did their racial composition. The proportion of offenders in Dallas had served a prison term, while for Contra Costa the figure was only 5 percent.

Because each site was allowed to design its own ISP, no two programs were identical. They adopted whatever components of the general ISP model they wished (such as random urine testing, curfews, electronic monitoring, and treatment referrals).

Close supervision of offenders was one of the few required program components. It consisted of weekly contacts with the officers, unscheduled drug testing, and stricter enforcement of probation/parole conditions.

### Random Assignment

The study was conducted as a randomized experiment. Indeed, the study may well be the largest randomized experiment in corrections ever undertaken in the United States. At each site, along with the experimental group, a control group of offenders was set up to serve as a comparison. The offenders in the control group were not part of the program but instead were given a different sanction (either prison or routine probation or parole, for example).[13] After the jurisdictions selected the pool of offenders they deemed eligible for ISP programs, the researchers assigned them randomly to one or the other of the two groups.

Having a control group with which to compare findings ensured that the results were the product of the manipulated variables of the ISP program rather than of differences among the offenders in the two groups. Previous ISP evaluations lacked matching comparison groups.

### Data Collection

For each offender, in both the experimental and the control groups, data collection forms were completed by the participating agency in the respective jurisdictions. A *background assessment* recorded demographic information, prior criminal record, drug dependence status, and similar information. The other forms—*6- and 12-month reviews*—recorded probation and parole services received, participation in treatment and work programs, and recidivism during the 1-year followup. Also recorded on this form were the number of drug tests ordered and taken, the types of drugs for which the offender tested positive, and the sanction imposed.

### Measuring Program Effects

Separate calculations were devised for estimating costs and for measuring program implementation, the effect of the ISP's on recidivism, and the effect on social adjustment (percentage of offenders who attended counseling, participated in training, were employed, and the like).

---

the ability of ISP's to meet certain practical goals—reduce prison crowding, save money, and decrease recidivism—may not have been well-founded and that jurisdictions interested in adopting ISP's should define their goals carefully. Other study findings indicate that ISP's were most successful as an intermediate punishment, in providing closer supervision of offenders and in offering a range of sentencing options between prison and routine probation and parole.

*The programs were effective as surveillance.* The ISP programs were designed to be much more stringent than routine supervision, and in every site they delivered more contacts and monitoring than did the routine supervision provided in the control groups. Most of the ISP's were significantly higher than the control programs in number of face-to-face contacts with supervisors, telephone and collateral contacts, law enforcement checks, employment monitoring, and drug and alcohol testing. (See exhibit 2 for findings on contacts and drug tests.)

The data reveal no straightforward relationship between contact levels and recidivism; that is, it is not clear whether the surveillance aspect

**Exhibit 2.** **Number of Monthly Face-to-Face Contacts and Drug Tests During 1-Year Followup**

| | Face-to Face Contacts | | Drug Tests | |
| | ISP | Controls | ISP | Controls |
| --- | --- | --- | --- | --- |
| Contra Costa County, California | 2.7 | 0.5* | 1.7 | 0.2* |
| Los Angeles County, California | 4.1 | 0.6* | 0.5 | 0.2* |
| Seattle, Washington | 3.4 | 0.8* | 0.4 | 0.1* |
| Ventura County, California | 7.4 | 3.0* | 2.7 | 1.3* |
| Atlanta, Georgia | 12.5 | 14.9 | 4.8 | 4.9 |
| Macon, Georgia | 16.1 | 17.7 | 5.8 | 3.7* |
| Waycross, Georgia | 22.8 | 22.4 | 14.2 | 1.6* |
| Santa Fe, New Mexico | 10.6 | 2.8* | 2.9 | 1.1* |
| Des Moines, Iowa | 5.8 | 3.8* | 2.8 | 1.0* |
| Winchester, Virginia | 8.1 | 1.9* | 1.5 | 0.4* |
| Dallas, Texas | 3.3 | 1.5* | 0.1 | 0.0* |
| Houston, Texas | 4.0 | 1.9* | 0.7 | 0.0* |
| Marion County, Oregon** | 12.2 | n/a | 2.2 | n/a |
| Milwaukee, Wisconsin | 8.8 | n/a | 0.7 | n/a |
| AVERAGE | 5.8 [a] | 1.6 [b] | 1.4 [a] | 0.2 [b] |

* Indicates that ISP and control are significantly different, $p < .05$.

** Based on 6-month followup only.

[a] Weighted average of ISP in all sites.
[b] Weighted average of routine probation in Contra Costa, Los Angeles, Seattle; routine probation/parole in Santa Fe, Des Moines, Winchester; routine parole in Dallas and Houston.

of the ISP had a positive effect on offenders' subsequent behavior. For example, although the average number of face-to-face contacts in Seattle was 3.4 per month and the average in Macon was much higher at 16.1, the percentage of ISP offenders arrested at both sites was about the same—46 percent in Seattle and 42 percent in Macon.

This finding must, however, be qualified by the nature of the data. The ISP programs were "packages" of contacts and services, and for this reason it is difficult to distinguish the specific effect of individual components of a package (such as contact level, drug testing, and electronic monitoring) on recidivism.

*The programs were effective as intermediate sanctions.* In a sense, this issue is the same as the preceding one if more frequent contacts and drug testing are viewed as punishment. Most of the ISP's had significantly higher levels of the features that curtail freedom.[14] Both coercion and enforced diminution of freedom were higher for most ISP's than for the control group when measured by the criminal justice system response to offenders' technical violations.[15] In fact, the response to this type of violation gives ISP's their greatest punitive value. The rate of technical violations was high, making the resultant coercion and diminution of freedom experienced by the offenders an added punitive sanction as well as creating a public safety benefit.

The General Accounting Office, in its report on intermediate punishments, noted that if judged by a standard of zero risk, all ISP programs fail to protect public safety.[16] However, what most of these programs try to achieve is a more stringent punishment for at least some of the serious offenders who now receive only nominal supervision. Judged by that criterion, virtually all of the sites succeeded. It is also possible that the closer surveillance imposed on ISP participants may increase the probability that they are caught for a larger percentage of the crimes they commit.

To test this effect, researchers conducted interviews with ISP participants in the Contra Costa site to discuss their perceptions of the harshness of the program. The interview findings confirmed that these offenders viewed the likelihood of their being caught for probation violations to be higher than for offenders who were on routine probation. They felt this to be particularly true when the violations involved drugs. In addition, the ISP offenders believed they would be treated more harshly for most types of violations than would their counterparts who were on routine supervision.

Evidence also suggests that some offenders may view ISP's as even more punitive and restrictive of freedom than prison. Among offenders at the Oregon site, 25 percent who were eligible for prison diversion chose not to participate. The reason may be that Oregon's crowded prisons made it unlikely that anyone sentenced to a year would serve the full term, while offenders assigned to ISP's could be certain of a full year of surveillance in the program. As prisons become more crowded and length of sentence served decreases, ISP's may come to seem increasingly punitive to offenders.

## The Effect on Recidivism

The major recidivism outcome measures were officially recorded arrests and technical violations. On these measures, the ISP programs were not as successful as on others.

ISP participants were not subsequently arrested less often, did not have a longer time to failure, and were not arrested for less serious offenses than control group members. The findings reveal that in 11 of the 14 sites, arrest rates during the 1-year followup were in fact higher for ISP participants than for the control group (although not significantly so). At the end of the 1-year period, about 37 percent of the ISP participants and 33 percent of control offenders had been arrested. (See exhibit 3.)

These findings should be interpreted with caution, because officially recorded recidivism may not be as accurate an indicator of an individual's criminality as it is a measure of the impact of the ISP program on the criminal justice system. That is, officially recorded recidivism measures enforcement—the system's ability to detect crime and act on it (through arrests).

As noted earlier, with an ISP program, surveillance may be so stringent as to increase the probability that crimes (and technical violations) will be detected and an arrest made. In this way ISP's may increase officially recorded recidivism. Thus, it may be that an ISP offender is committing the same number or fewer crimes than someone on routine supervision, who has a lower probability of being arrested for them. The ISP offender, whose behavior is more closely monitored, may be caught in the enforcement net, while the offender on routine probation or parole may escape it.

*Effect of technical violations.*   If technical violations are interpreted as another measure of recidivism, the findings are also less positive for the ISP's than the controls. An average of 65 percent of the ISP clients had a technical violation compared with 38 percent for the controls. (See exhibit 3). However, technical violations can be interpreted as effects of the program itself rather than as evidence of criminal activity or recidivism. For one thing, the view of technical violations as a proxy for crime commission is only an assumption. Non-compliant behavior such as disregarding curfews, using alcohol and drugs, and missing treatment sessions may not necessarily signal that the ISP participant is going to commit "new" or "real" crimes.

To test the hypothesis that revoking offenders for technical violations prevents arrests for new crimes, the researchers examined the ISP programs in California and Texas. They computed correlations between number of arrests and number of technical violations and found few statistically significant relationships. In other words, offenders who committed technical violations were no more likely to be arrested for new crimes than those who did not commit them. Moreover, when convictions for arrests during the 1-year followup were examined for all sites, the researchers found no difference in the rates of the ISP offenders and the control group.

ISP's were consistently associated with higher rates of technical violations because of the closer supervision given to those in the programs. If stringent conditions are imposed and people's behavior is monitored, they have more opportunities for violations and for being found out than if there are few conditions and few contacts. For example, the requirement of frequent drug testing alone is virtually guaranteed to generate a large number of technical violations. Few of the sites had many low-risk[17] offenders. The higher the risk, the more likely that offenders are involved with drugs. At most of the sites, drug-related technical violations accounted for a large proportion of all technical violations. Offenders under routine supervision were not subjected to such close scrutiny and would not therefore have had as many opportunities to commit technical violations of the conditions of their probation or parole.

*Effect of type of ISP program.*   Because only 2 of the 14 sites implemented prison diversion programs and their programs experienced difficulties, the research remains inconclusive regarding the ability of this type of ISP to relieve prison crowding. (See "The Experience of the Prison Diversion Programs.")

The findings for parole and probation enhancement ISP's suggest that commitments to prison and jail may actually increase under the program. The reason is the large number of technical violations, which lead to a higher percentage of ISP offenders than controls being recommitted to jail and prison. At a minimum, ISP programs attempt to increase the credibility of community-based sanctions by making certain that the conditions ordered by the court, including those considered "technical" in nature, are monitored, enforced, and if violated, punished by imprisonment. Depending on how severely ISP staff and their respective courts choose to treat ISP infractions, commitments to prison and jails may rise precipitously.

*Exhibit 3.* **Offender Recidivism During 1-Year Followup**

| | Percentage of Offenders With Any Arrest | | Percentage of Offender With Technical Violations | | Percentage of Offenders Returned to Prison | |
|---|---|---|---|---|---|---|
| | ISP | Controls | ISP | Controls | ISP | Controls |
| Contra Costa County, California | 29 | 27 | 64 | 41* | 2 | 4 |
| Los Angeles County, California | 32 | 30 | 61 | 57 | 26 | 22 |
| Seattle, Washington | 46 | 36 | 73 | 48* | 6 | 5 |
| Ventura County, California | 32 | 53* | 70 | 73 | 23 | 28 |
| Atlanta, Georgia | 12 | 04 | 65 | 46 | 23 | 4 |
| Macon, Georgia | 42 | 38 | 100 | 96 | 8 | 21 |
| Waycross, Georgia | 12 | 15 | 38 | 31 | 4 | 0 |
| Santa Fe, New Mexico | 48 | 28 | 69 | 62 | 14 | 17 |
| Des Moines, Iowa | 24 | 29 | 59 | 55 | 39 | 23 |
| Winchester, Virginia | 25 | 12 | 64 | 36* | 14 | 8 |
| Dallas, Texas | 39 | 30 | 20 | 13 | 28 | 17 |
| Houston, Texas | 44 | 40 | 81 | 33* | 35 | 20* |
| Marion County, Oregon | 33 | 50 | 92 | 58 | 50 | 25 |
| Milwaukee, Wisconsin | 58 | 03* | 92 | 17* | 35 | 3* |
| AVERAGE | 37 [a] | 33 [b] | 65 [a] | 38 [b] | 24 | 15 |

* Indicates that ISP and control are significantly different, p <.05.

[a] Weighted average of ISP in all sites.
[b] Weighted average of routine probation in Contra Costa, Los Angeles, Seattle; routine probation/parole in Santa Fe, Des Moines, Winchester; routine parole in Dallas and Houston.

## The Experience of the Prison Diversion Programs

Prison diversion programs in this study did not provide data on the effect of ISP's on prison crowding. Of the two participating sites that implemented prison diversion programs in the demonstration, one had too few eligible offenders to yield usable results. In the other, the use of randomization was overridden by the jurisdiction, thereby foiling its purpose. The selection process at these two sites therefore makes it impossible to state with certainty the effect of ISP's in reducing prison crowding.

The experience of the two sites (Marion County, Oregon, and Milwaukee, Wisconsin) does reveal a number of insights into the issues jurisdictions face when making decisions about selecting convicted offenders for diversion into the community.

### Marion County, Oregon

Marion County set eligibility requirements so stringent that few offenders could qualify for the prison diversion ISP. The study's mandated criterion of excluding offenders currently convicted of violent crimes was extended to exclude offenders with any prior record of violence. Examination of the Marion County data revealed that, in addition, a large percent of potential participants who had current burglary convictions were rejected. Although this offense is considered nonviolent, evidently Marion County did not wish to place burglars into ISP programs.

The three criteria—exclusion of violent offenders, people with any history of violence, and convicted burglars—shrank the pool of eligibles considerably. Furthermore, the local Marion County judge imposed the requirement of informed consent from the offender, producing a sample too small to yield statistically reliable results.

### Milwaukee, Wisconsin

In Milwaukee, judges and probation/parole officers overrode the researchers' random assignment of offenders into the experimental and control groups. Milwaukee initially had two pools of eligibles: "front-end" cases consisting of high-risk offenders newly convicted of nonviolent felonies, and "back-end" cases consisting of probation or parole violators who were facing revocation. Regardless of the random designation made by the researchers, most front-end cases were sentenced to prison rather than diversion to an ISP. Of the back-end cases, more than half were sent to routine probation or parole.

That only two sites chose prison diversion suggests the level of concern on the part of the criminal justice system about the risks involved in sending convicted offenders into the community. Further evidence of this concern is the response of these two sites in placing additional restrictions on program implementation.[18]

Data from the Houston site illustrate this point. The Houston ISP was a parole-enhancement program that targeted people under supervision who had a high probability of returning to prison. ISP participants were not arrested for new crimes more often than the controls (who were on routine parole), but were returned to prison more frequently for more technical violations. Fully 81 percent of the ISP offenders had technical violations, compared with 33 percent of offenders in the control group. As a result, five times as many ISP offenders were returned to prison for technical violations as those on routine supervision (21 percent versus 4 percent), and at the end of the 1-year followup, about 30 percent of ISP participants were in prison, compared with only 18 percent of the control group.[19]

Thus, in Houston, putting people on ISP added more offenders to the prison population than did routine parole. This is interpreted as an effect of the ISP program itself—which tends to generate more technical violations—rather than the result of differences between the ISP experimental and control groups. Any other differences were eliminated through random assignment of offenders to both groups.

## Cost Benefits

Are ISP's a cost-saving alternative? Like other questions about ISP's, this too has an ambiguous answer—one that depends on what is being compared to what. Compared with routine probation, ISP's are more costly because they are highly labor intensive. Because supervision is intensive, ISP's require lower caseloads—typically 25 offenders per supervisor or team of supervisors. An increase of only 100 offenders in an ISP would call for hiring and training 4 to 8 new employees.

If the cost of ISP's is compared to that of imprisonment, the opposite is true. Virtually no one would question the claim that it is more expensive to keep an offender in prison than on probation. The costs per day for imprisonment are much higher per offender than the costs per day for an ISP. Obviously, ISP's cost less than building new prisons.

Length of time under each sanction also has to be taken into consideration when comparing costs of prison and ISP's. The average cost per year per imprisoned offender is $12,000 and per ISP offender only $4,000. However, if the ISP offender would have otherwise served time in prison (had he or she not been placed in an ISP) for a period of only 3 months, the cost would be $3,000—less than the $4,000 it costs for 1 year of an ISP program. In addition, some of the ISP participants spent part of the followup year incarcerated rather than in the ISP program, thus eliminating part of the cost savings of diversion from prison.

Again, it should be kept in mind in interpreting these findings that the ISP programs resulted in more incarcerations and consequently higher costs than routine probation/parole because of the higher number of technical violations. Across the 12 probation/parole enhancement programs, high violation and incarceration rates for ISP offenders drove up the estimated costs, which averaged $7,200 per offender for the year, compared with about $4,700 for the control group on routine supervision.

## Results for Treatment

Treatment and service components in the ISP's included drug and alcohol counseling, employment, community service, and payment of restitution. On many of these measures, ISP offenders participated more than did control group members (see exhibit 4); and participation in such programs was found to be correlated with a reduction in recidivism in at least some sites.

When figures from all sites are examined, they reveal that participation in counseling was not high in either the experimental or control groups, but it was higher for ISP offenders. Forty-five percent of ISP offenders received some counseling during the followup period, compared with 22 percent of the controls.

Overall figures indicate that more than half of the ISP participants were employed compared with 43 percent of the offenders who were on routine supervision. In 4 of the 14 sites (Contra Costa, Los Angeles, Seattle, and Winchester), ISP offenders were significantly more likely than controls to be employed.

Participation in community service varied considerably by site. The highest rate (more than two-thirds of offenders) was reported in the three Georgia sites, where community service has historically played a major role in the ISP design. In seven of the ISP programs, 10 percent or fewer offenders participated in community service, and at no site did ISP offenders participate significantly more often than routine supervision offenders.

Although restitution was paid by only a small minority of offenders, the rate was higher among ISP offenders than those on routine supervision (12 percent and 3 percent, respectively, paid some restitution).

Analysis of the programs in California and Texas revealed a relationship between treatment participation and recidivism. A summary score was created for each offender, with one point assigned for participation in any of four treatment or service programs. Analysis revealed that higher levels of program participation were associated with a 10- to

*Exhibit 4.* **Representative Program Participation**

| | Percentage of Offenders in Any Counseling During 1-Year Followup | | Percentage of Offenders With Any Paid Employment During 1-Year Followup | |
|---|---|---|---|---|
| | ISP | Controls | ISP | Controls |
| **Contra Costa County, California** | 39 | 14* | 41 | 26* |
| **Los Angeles County, California** | 16* | 02 | 45 | 18* |
| **Seattle, Washington** | 42 | 14* | 31 | 08* |
| **Ventura County, California** | 78 | 76 | 80 | 79 |
| **Atlanta, Georgia** | 48 | 48 | 54 | 65 |
| **Macon, Georgia** | 65 | 50 | 85 | 71 |
| **Waycross, Georgia** | 100 | 88 | 92 | 96 |
| **Santa Fe, New Mexico** | 100 | 59* | 86 | 79 |
| **Des Moines, Iowa** | 59 | 41* | 76 | 70 |
| **Winchester, Virginia** | 32 | 12 | 89 | 56* |
| **Dallas, Texas** | 04 | 02 | 37 | 33 |
| **Houston, Texas** | 55 | 32* | 61 | 61 |
| **Marion County, Oregon** | 50 | n/a | 33 | n/a |
| **Milwaukee, Wisconsin** | 54 | n/a | 54 | n/a |
| **AVERAGE** | 45 [a] | 22 [b] | 56 [a] | 43 [b] |

* Indicates that ISP and control are significantly different, p <.05.

[a] Weighted average of all sites.
[b] Weighted average of routine probation in Contra Costa, Los Angeles, Seattle; routine probation/parole in Santa Fe, Des Moines, Winchester; routine parole in Dallas and Houston.

20-percent reduction in recidivism. However, because offenders were not randomly assigned to participate in these activities within the experimental and control groups, it is not possible to determine whether the lower recidivism was the effect of the treatment or of selection bias. In other words, the positive outcomes may be a function not of the treatment but of the type of offender who entered the treatment program. Nevertheless, the results are consistent with literature showing positive outcomes of treatment.

The ISP programs in the demonstration project were by design oriented more toward surveillance than treatment, with funds used largely for staff salaries rather than for treatment service. Sites had to rely on existing treatment programs, which in some communities were quite minimal. This raises the issue of whether participation in treatment would have been higher had more resources been allocated to it.

## Policy Implications

Jurisdictions that wish to adopt ISP's might want to revise the model represented in the demonstration to create a better "fit" with their particular needs.

*Making controls more stringent.* ISP contact levels were greater than with routine supervision, but it might be argued that the programs were not "intensive" enough. It appears that more stringent conditions could be required of ISP's. In the demonstration, ISP contact of any type amounted, on average, to a total of less than 2 hours per month per offender (assuming that 20 minutes, on average, was spent per face-to-face contact). The same is true of drug testing—the average for all sites was just over two tests per month. If the amount of time spent in contacts were greater (that is, if conditions were tougher), the result might be less recidivism. Jurisdictions would have to decide how much more restrictive the conditions should be and would have to weigh possible benefits against the probable higher cost.

*Increasing treatment.* Jurisdictions might want to strengthen the treatment component of ISP's in hopes of a positive behavioral effect that would lower recidivism. As stated earlier, at the California and Texas sites the recidivism of offenders who received any counseling (for drugs or alcohol), held jobs, paid restitution, and did community service was 10 to 20 percent lower than those who did not.

Overall outcomes might have been even more positive had a greater proportion of the offenders participated in treatment.[20] Participation in drug treatment, in particular, might have had a high payoff. In all the sites, about half the offenders were judged drug dependent by their probation or parole officers. Yet ISP staff often reported difficulties obtaining drug treatment for these people, and at some sites a large percentage of all offenders in need of drug treatment went untreated.[21] It comes as no surprise, therefore, that about one-third of all new arrests were drug-related. A high priority for future research would be evaluation of ISP programs in which treatment plays a major role.[22]

*Deemphasizing technical violations.* Jurisdictions might want to reexamine the assumption of technical violations as a proxy for criminal behavior. Offenders who commit this type of violation constitute a considerable proportion of the prison population. On any given day, about 20 percent of new admissions nationwide consist of parole or probation violators, and the resultant crowding means early release for other offenders.

The experience of the State of Washington in rethinking parole and probation revocations is instructive. There, the State legislature, responding to the heavy flow of technical violations attendant on stringent parole and probation conditions, set new rules. The rules require conditions be set according to the specific offense and the particular offender's past criminal behavior; they effectively bar the imposition of conditions affecting all offenders. In addition, the new rules state that prison cannot be used as a sanction for technical violations; the maximum sentence is 60 days in jail.[24]

No empirical studies have been performed yet, but Washington officials believe that as a result of the new rules, revocations for technical violations have decreased while arrest rates for new crimes have remained roughly the same.[25] If Washington is successful, it may mean that jurisdictions will have more prison space for really serious offenders and therefore increase public safety by decreasing the number of people sent to prison for technical violations of parole and probation.

*Handling costs.* When considering the issue of affordability, jurisdictions need to keep in mind its relation to program goals. The more constraints a program imposes and/or the more it is service- and treatment-oriented, the higher will be the cost. In Ventura and Houston, for example, stringent conditions and rigorous response to technical violations drove up costs. On the other hand, future evaluations might reveal that the return on investment in programs with these types of emphasis may be lower recidivism.

*Judging outcomes.* In assessing the success of ISP's (and deciding whether to invest further in them), jurisdictions need to use the same criterion for deciding whether a program is affordable; that is, does it achieve the goals set? One of the study's strongest implications is that jurisdictions need to establish very clearly their intentions for the ISP's they develop and structure the programs accordingly. If jurisdictions are interested primarily in imposing intermediate sanctions, even if the result is not lower recidivism, that goal should be made clear. Otherwise, the public may interpret the recidivism rates as an indication of program failure.

If jurisdictions are primarily interested in reducing recidivism, prison crowding, and system costs, ISP programs as currently structured may not meet all their expectations. These more "practical" objectives were set on the basis of overly ambitious assumptions and on the early results of a few programs that received a great deal of attention and perhaps unwarranted enthusiasm. The findings of this evaluation provide further evidence that surveillance-oriented ISP's will have difficulty in fully achieving these objectives.

If jurisdictions target objectives based more on intermediate sanctions principles, ISP's hold promise. By setting this type of objective, they may be able to impose more stringent controls on offenders than are possible without probation and parole, and they may achieve greater flexibility in sentencing decisions by punishments that more closely fit the crimes committed. Developing an array of sentencing options is an important and necessary first step to creating a more comprehensive and graduated sentencing structure. This goal alone can provide the justification for continued development of ISP and other intermediate sanctions.

*Is prison diversion viable?*   The evaluation findings indicate that prison diversion and, by extension, reduction of prison crowding, is particularly difficult to implement. This difficulty is reflected in the decision by only 2 of the 14 sites to adopt this type of program. The criteria these two jurisdictions used to assign offenders to the programs also suggest a measure of reluctance. (See "The Experience of the Prison Diversion Programs.") The experience with prison diversion in this study indicates that the criminal justice system and the general public do not at present seem receptive to this type of ISP. A targeted public and judicial education campaign would be required to overcome that reluctance.

## Future Research

The major issue for further research is determining whether ISP, a concept that may be sound in theory, might be structured and implemented differently to produce better results. The experience of the California sites suggests, for example, that certain program components could be manipulated. At these sites, a higher level of offender participation in treatment and service programs was associated with lower recidivism. In Ventura, which had the highest levels of surveillance, arrest rates were lower than among the controls. A revised ISP model could answer these and other questions:

- Would ISP's reduce recidivism if resources were sufficient to obtain treatment drug offenders need?
- Would more intensive surveillance lower recidivism?
- Would more selective conditions of parole and probation lower revocation rates?
- What combination of surveillance and treatment would produce the best results?

The study findings indicate a number of additional areas for research:

*The potential of ISP as prison diversion.* The limited number of study sites selecting this option and their restrictions on the programs indicate major concerns about ISP for prison diversion. Researchers may want to examine the nature of the potential pool of eligibles, document the most commonly utilized criteria for ISP eligibility, and depending on the criteria, simulate the prison population that would qualify.

*Testing of different offender populations.* The ISP model in this study was tested primarily on drug-involved offenders who had committed serious crimes. Studies have shown that the more experienced the offenders, the lower they rate the risk of being caught and confined.[26] For this reason, models using a population of less serious offenders might result in greater deterrence.

*The effects of different ISP components.* The random assignment in this study permitted testing the effect of the entire ISP "package," but made it impossible to test the effect of a particular program component. By extension, it was not possible to determine how changing a component might change the effects. Future research could be designed specifically to test the incremental impact of various ISP conditions (such as drug testing and drug and alcohol treatment) on offender behavior.

*Effectiveness over time.* Recent research indicates that a 1-year followup, the time period on which the evaluation of outcomes was based, may not be long enough.[27] Future research might focus on whether longer followup might ultimately result in behavioral differences between ISP offenders and controls.

*Technical violations and criminal behavior.* The study revealed that technical violations resulted in many recommitments to prison and jail. As noted earlier, the view that such recommitments prevent crime may be only an assumption. The policy significance of technical violations suggests that research is needed in a number of areas:

- Empirical evidence of the relationship of technical violations to criminal behavior.
- The types of technical conditions currently imposed at sentencing.
- How technical conditions are used by community corrections to manage offenders, encourage rehabilitation, and protect the community.
- Trends in the growth of the technical violator population and the effect on jails and prisons.
- Innovative programs, policies, and statutes that have emerged to deal with technical violators.

*Appropriate outcome measures.* Recidivism is a key outcome used in evaluating all types of interventions, and because success in rehabilitation has been far from complete, it is almost the only measure used in corrections.

In reaffirming its commitment to ISP and to its focus on rehabilitation, the American Probation and Parole Association issued a position paper that identifies behavioral change, not recidivism, as the appropriate outcome measure. Such change includes negotiation skills, managing emotions, and enhanced values and attitude shifts.

Given the centrality of recidivism to research and practice, it is essential to examine its appropriateness as a measure for certain interventions. For some programs, recidivism may be one of many measures, but perhaps not the primary one.

These are not the only issues for a future criminal justice research agenda, but they are currently the most pressing for research on the future of intensive supervision probation and parole.

## Notes

1 The results of NIJ-sponsored research into four major types of intermediate sanctions are summarized in Gowdy, Voncile B., *Intermediate Sanctions*. Research in Brief. Washington, DC: U.S. Department of Justice, National Institute of Justice, 1993.

2 Bureau of Justice Statistics, *Probation and Parole 1990*. Bulletin. Washington, DC: U.S. Department of Justice, Bureau of Justice Statistics, November 1991.

3 The figure for felonies is 48 percent, and for misdemeanors, it is 31 percent, according to Bureau of Justice Statistics, *Correctional Populations in the United States, 1990*. Washington, DC: U.S. Department of Justice, Bureau of Justice Statistics, July 1992.

4 Langan, Patrick A., and Mark A. Cuniff. *Recidivism of Felons on Probation, 1986–89*. Special Report. Washington, DC: U.S. Department of Justice, Bureau of Justice Statistics, February 1992.

5 A discussion of recent findings about the rise in the rate of violent crime despite the increase in the number of people incarcerated is presented in the National

Research Council's *Understanding and Preventing Violence*, ed. Albert J. Reiss, Jr., and Jeffrey A. Roth, Washington, DC: National Academy Press, 1993: 292–294.

[6] Macguire, Kathleen, and Timothy J. Flanagan, eds. *Sourcebook of Criminal Justice Statistics—1991*. Washington, DC: U.S. Department of Justice, Bureau of Justice Statistics, 1992.

[7] General Accounting Office. *Intermediate Sanctions: Their Impacts on Prison Crowding, Costs, and Recidivism Are Still Unclear*. Gaithersburg, Maryland: General Accounting Office, 1990.

[8] For descriptions of the Georgia program, see Erwin, Billie S. "Turning Up the Heat on Probationers in Georgia." *Federal Probation*, vol. 50 (1986):2. See also: Petersilia, Joan. *Expanding Options for Criminal Sentencing*. Santa Monica: RAND Corporation, 1987. Byrne, James M., Arthur J. Lurigio, and Christopher Baird. "The Effectiveness of the New Intensive Supervision Programs." *Research in Corrections*, vol. 2 (1989). The results of a National Institute of Justice evaluation of the program are presented in Erwin, Billie S., and Lawrence A. Bennett. *New Dimensions in Probation: Georgia's Experience With Intensive Probation Supervision (IPS)*. Research in Brief. Washington, DC: U.S. Department of Justice, National Institute of Justice, January 1987.

[9] Byrne, Lurigio, and Baird, "The Effectiveness of the New Intensive Supervision Programs."

[10] General Accounting Office, *Intermediate Sanctions*. See also Morris, Norval, and Michael Tonry. *Between Prison and Probation: Intermediate Punishments in a Rational Sentencing System*. New York: Oxford University Press, 1990.

[11] For more information on the experiences of the site in implementing the experiments, see Petersilia, Joan. "Implementing Randomized Experiments: Lessons for BJA's Intensive Supervision Project." *Evaluation Review*, vol. 13, 5.

[12] The training component was directed by Rutgers University, the technical assistance by the National Council on Crime and Delinquency.

[13] In the Georgia and Ventura sites, the control programs were another form of intensive supervision. References to all ISP's mean all 14 experimental programs. References to ISP enhancement programs mean all experimental ISP's except Milwaukee and Marion, which adopted prison diversion programs. References to routine supervision probation and parole mean the control programs in eight sites: Contra Costa, Los Angeles, Seattle, Santa Fe, Des Moines, Winchester, Dallas, and Houston.

[14] This meets the definition of effective sentencing proposed by Morris and Tonry. It involves "the curtailment of freedom either behind walls or in the community, large measures of coercion, and enforced diminutions of freedom." (*Between Prison and Probation*)

[15] A violation that does not consist of committing a crime or is not prosecuted as such is usually called a technical violation. It is behavior forbidden by the court order granting probation or parole but not forbidden by legal statute. Examples are failure to observe curfew, abstain from alcohol, or attend treatment sessions.

[16] General Accounting Office, *Intermediate Sanctions*.

[17] The risk score was constructed from the following variables: drug treatment needs, age at first or current conviction, previous probation terms, previous probation and parole revocations, previous felony convictions, and type of current offense.

[18] NIJ has provided support to RAND to evaluate a prison diversion program in Minnesota that promises to furnish more reliable evidence on the impact of this type of sanction.

[19] Turner, Susan, and Joan Petersilia. "Focusing on High-Risk Parolees: An Experiment to Reduce Commitments to the Texas Department of Corrections." *Journal of Research in Criminology and Delinquency*, vol. 29, 1 (1992):34–61.

[20] Some recent literature gives credibility to this notion. See Anglin, M. Douglas, and Yih-Ing Hser. "Treatment of Drug Abuse." In *Crime and Justice: An Annual Review of Research, Volume 13: Drugs and Crime.* ed. Michael Tonry and James Q. Wilson. Chicago: University of Chicago Press, 1990; and Paul Gendreau and D. A. Andrews. "Tertiary Prevention: What the Meta-Analyses of the Offender Treatment Literature Tell Us About 'What Works.'" *Canadian Journal of Criminology*, vol. 32 (1990):173–184.

[21] For a more complete presentation of this finding, see Petersilia, Joan, Susan Turner, and Elizabeth Piper Deschenes. "Intensive Supervision Programs for Drug Offenders." In J. Byrne, A. Lurigio, and J. Petersilia. *Smart Sentencing: The Emergence of Intermediate Sanctions.* Newbury Park, CA: Sage Publications, 1992.

[22] NIJ is providing RAND with support for a randomized field experiment, currently being conducted in Maricopa County, Arizona, that will test the impact on probationers of different levels of treatment.

[23] Petersilia, Joan, and Susan Turner. "Reducing Prison Admissions: The Potential of Intermediate Sanctions," *The Journal of State Government*, vol. 62 (1989):2.

[24] Washington State Sentencing Guidelines Commission. *Preliminary Evaluation of Washington State's Sentencing Reform Act.* Olympia: Washington State Sentencing Guidelines Commission, 1983.

[25] Greene, Richard. "Who's Punishing Whom?" *Forbes*, vol. 121, 6 (1988):132–133.

[26] Paternoster, R. "The Deterrent Effect of the Perceived Certainty and Severity of Punishment: A Review of the Evidence and Issues." *Justice Quarterly*, 4 (1987).

[27] Anglin, M. D. and W. H. McGlothlin. "Outcomes of Narcotic Addict Treatment in California." In *Drug Abuse Treatment Evaluation: Strategies, Progress, and Prospect,* ed. F. M. Tims and J. P. Ludford. National Institute on Drug Abuse Research Monograph No. 51. Rockville, MD: U.S. Department of Health and Human Services, National Institute on Drug Abuse, 1984.

# Part V

# Legal and Ethical Issues in Community Corrections

As with most professions, community corrections has a legal as well as an ethical foundation. Professionals in the field are constantly exposed to legal liabilities in such areas as probation presentence investigations, supervision practices, and revocation. The parole of prisoners has also been a source of litigation, challenging such issues as parole guidelines, the right (or privilege) to parole, and revocation practices, to name a few. Moreover, the development of a series of alternative sanctions has created a new set of legal considerations for community corrections practitioners. For example, electronic monitoring and house arrest have been criticized as too intrusive and an invasion of privacy.

Since the decision granting probation in every jurisdiction is a judicial one, we must ask ourselves the question, "What legal authority do probation officers have in the supervision of the offender granted probation once assigned by the court?" Concisely, do probation officers enjoy judge-like immunities by virtue of their position and relationship with the court? Mark Jones and Rolando del Carmen address this issue in "When Do Probation and Parole Officers Enjoy the Same Immunity as Judges?" It is unlikely that probation and parole officers will be entitled to absolute immunity solely by virtue of their position, though they can qualify for quasi-judicial immunity "if they are performing functions which are intimately associated with the judicial process." Previous case law has described this "process" as applicable in the writing of pre-sentence reports, pretrial release, revocations, and certain aspects of offender supervision.

"Legal Issues in the Use of Electronic Surveillance in Probation," by del Carmen and Joseph Vaughn, focuses on the legal issues surrounding the use of electronic surveillance. The Fourth Amendment to the Constitution and accompanying case law serve to establish the parameters for the use of electronic surveillance in community corrections, including the belief that the convicted offender has diminished rights while under supervision. In addition, the authors note, authorities which grant probation have received broad discretion in the setting of conditions and terms of supervision. While the rules or conditions vary from state to state, with several common conditions, del Carmen and Vaughn outline the circumstances which must be met for the rules or conditions to be valid. Legal challenges to the use of electronic surveillance are viewed within the context of previous case law decisions and an interpretation of the Constitution, especially the Fourth, Fifth and Eighth Amendments.

In the third selection, "The Ethics of Community-Based Sanctions," noted scholar Andrew von Hirsch argues that the expanded use of noncustodial sanctions makes it imperative that we study the ethical considerations surrounding their use. There is great potential for misuse and abuse if the system is left unchecked. The Constitution, von Hirsch points out, "does not give consideration to the treatment of convicted offenders." Only the Eighth Amendment restricts "disproportionate punishment," but it is the states' responsibility, according to von Hirsch, to safeguard the just deserts requirements set forth by law.

The articles in this section are important to the study of community corrections in that policy development and practice are governed by the rule of law. In the absence of a clear mandate specifying action, ethical considerations should fill the void in defining the limits of our activities involving both the rehabilitation of the offender and the protection of society.

# 22

# When Do Probation and Parole Officers Enjoy the Same Immunity as Judges?

Mark Jones
Rolando V. del Carmen

## Introduction

The 1980s and early 1990s have witnessed a dramatic increase in community-based offender populations. The number of adults on probation in the United States increased from a total of approximately 2 million in 1985 to 2,670,234 in 1990. Between 1989 and 1990 alone, the number of adults on probation increased by 6.1 percent. Parole populations also increased during the 1980s, despite several jurisdictions having abolished parole. At the end of 1990, 1 in every 43 adults in the United States was under some form of correctional supervision; 1 in every 24 males was under supervision.[1]

As these populations have increased and changed, so have line officer and administrator concerns about liability. A review of case law indicates

Source: *Federal Probation*, Vol. 56, No. 4 (December 1992), 36-41.

that more courts are granting probation and parole officers quasi-judicial immunity, but court decisions have provided no clear guidelines for determining under what circumstances quasi-judicial immunity applies.

This article examines the types of defenses a probation or parole officer enjoys in civil liability suits. It focuses on the concepts of absolute, quasi-judicial, and qualified immunity. Prior court decisions indicate that probation and parole officers generally enjoy only qualified immunity, meaning they are immune only when the action was taken in good faith. This article suggests that rules regarding the types of defenses available to field officers may be changing in favor of more immunity for the line officer, but the limits are vague and undefined.

Several means of redress are available to offenders wishing to sue probation or parole officers, one of the most common being a claim for damages under state tort law. A tort is defined as a "private or civil wrong or injury other than breach of contract, for which the court will provide a remedy in the form of an action for damages."[2] Tort law, however, varies from state to state in specifics.

The main source of civil liability under Federal law is 42 U.S.C. Section 1983, often referred to as Section 1983 or Federal tort cases.[3] Two basic elements are required for a Section 1983 case to succeed, namely: The defendant must be acting under "color of law,"[4] and the violation must be of a constitutional or a federally protected right.

## Types of Immunity

The two most frequently invoked defenses in liability suits are official immunity and good faith. Official immunity generally means that certain public officers are immune from liability on the theory that they are acting for the state, which enjoys sovereign immunity. Good faith, on the other hand, means that there is no liability unless the officer violated a clearly established constitutional or statutory right of which a reasonable person would have known.[5]

Courts have traditionally recognized three types of official immunity: absolute, qualified, and quasi-judicial. Under absolute immunity, civil suits are dismissed without going into the merits of the claim, the assumption being that there is no reason to delve into the merit or demerit of the allegation since, regardless of fault, no liability ensues. Absolute immunity has been applied primarily to judges, legislators, and prosecutors.[6] In *Stump v. Sparkman*,[7] the Court held that judges are not liable for errors or acts done maliciously or in exercise of authority, but only for acts in the "clear absence of all jurisdiction." Legislative immunity has two meanings. The first is that except in cases of treason, felony, and a breach of the peace, legislators are "privileged from arrest during their attendance" at sessions and, second, that "for any speech or debate in either House, they shall not be questioned in any other place."[8] In *Imbler v. Pachtman*,[9] the Supreme Court ruled that prosecutors enjoy absolute immunity for decisions to prosecute or for activities "intimately associated with the judicial phase of the criminal process."[10]

Another type of official immunity is qualified immunity, meaning that the officer is immune only if he or she acted in good faith. With few exceptions and until recently, probation and parole officers enjoyed only qualified immunity because they are members of the executive department.[11] That, however, may be changing in the direction of more absolute immunity for probation and parole officers in some instances, as some cases discussed in this article suggest.

Qualified immunity has two formulations, depending upon jurisdiction. First, under state tort law, qualified immunity usually applies if an official performs a discretionary act, meaning an act that requires personal deliberation and judgment, as opposed to a ministerial act, meaning an act that amounts only to the performing of a duty. Second, qualified immunity is related to the good faith defense in Federal cases. In Federal cases (Section 1983), an officer is exempt from liability if he or she does not violate a clearly established constitutional right of which a reasonable person should have known.

A recent case that involved this defense is *Hunter v. Bryant*,[12] in which two Secret Service agents were sued for arresting a man for threatening President Reagan. The Supreme Court held that the agents were entitled to qualified immunity because their decision was reasonable, even if mistaken. The Court held that the qualified immunity standard provides ample room for judgment errors and protects all but those who are plainly incompetent or those who knowingly violate the law.

Absolute immunity generally applies only to officials in the judicial and legislative branches of government, while qualified immunity applies to officials in the executive branch. Some officials, however, have both judicial and executive functions; such officials include court personnel, parole board members (when making a decision to release or not to release an inmate on parole), and some probation officers. Under this immunity, judicial-type functions that involve discretionary decision making or court functions are immune from liability, while other functions (such as the ministerial duties of a job) are not. The emphasis therefore is on the function performed rather than on the officer performing the function.[13]

While absolute immunity generally applies to judicial and legislative officials, and qualified immunity usually applies to members of the executive branch, quasi-judicial immunity, the third type of immunity, typically applies to persons performing both judicial and executive functions. Court personnel, parole officers, and probation officers performing judicial-type functions fall under this category.

The quasi-judicial immunity defense used to apply only to cases when probation officers prepared and wrote a presentence report. A number of presentence investigation (PSI) cases, both old and recent, illustrate the use of this type of immunity for probation officers. Some of the more notable cases are presented in table 1.

In each of these cases the court ruled that conducting a presentence investigation is an integral part of the judicial process and is carried out because of judicial order, hence quasi-judicial immunity applies.

## Cases Rejecting the Quasi-Judicial Immunity Doctrine

Some recent cases, not involving a presentence report, have resulted in liability being imposed on line officers (see table 2). In these cases, the officers unsuccessfully tried to shield themselves from liability by claiming they were performing a judicial function. In *Crawford v. State*,[14] a prison inmate, Kenneth Maynard, while in a work furlough program, was instructed to attend an Alcoholics Anonymous (AA) session. Maynard absconded while being allowed to leave the furlough center to attend the session. Two months later, Maynard was arrested and charged with aggravated murder. He was convicted and sentenced to life in prison. The murder victim's widow filed a wrongful death suit against the state; the lower court granted summary judgment for the defendants, and the plaintiff appealed.

The Ohio Supreme Court held the state liable, saying that the employees were not acting upon a judicial directive and that the decision to send an inmate to a "non-educational" program such as AA is not a basic policy decision. Chances were that if attendance at AA had been court-ordered, or if AA had been directly recognized by state parole authorities as a viable educational or rehabilitative program, the state would not have been held liable. Since center authorities were acting on their own accord in sending Maynard to the program, rather than on judicial directive, liability was imposed.

Uncertainty remains as to the kinds of activities included in the phrase "intimately associated with the judicial process." The *Crawford* case, above, clarifies the ambiguity to some extent, but *Brunsvold v. State*,[15] decided in 1991, paints a less clear picture of what the phrase means. Brunsvold had been placed on probation for a bad check charge. He was subsequently arrested on a new bad check charge. While revocation was pending, the Montana Department of Institutions, acting on court orders, began crediting good time allowances on sentences where defendants were on probation while serving a suspended or deferred adjudication sentence. The probation officer calculated the discharge date, but Brunsvold was incarcerated beyond the date anyway. He filed suit against the prison warden and the probation officer.

Summary judgment was granted at the local level for all defendants, but the Montana Supreme Court reversed in part. The court ruled that the warden was acting as an agent of the judiciary but that the probation officer was acting as an agent of the executive branch and thus was not entitled to the same immunity as the warden. The court concluded that the officer was performing an administrative, rather than a judicial, task. Regarding the judicial immunity, or "intimately associated with the judicial phase" concept, the court stated that expanding the doctrine in accordance with this case would create a bright clear line and simplify application of the quasi-judicial doctrine. But the court also stated that the quasi-judicial doctrine is not intended to cover any government employee having any contact with a judicial act or proceeding.[16]

In *Mee v. Ortega*,[17] the court held that initiation of revocation proceedings is not blanket protection from liability. In *Mee*, a parole officer held a parolee in jail for 1 month awaiting a revocation hearing. The Parole Board decided against having a hearing and ordered Mee to be released. Mee filed suit against the parole officer; the officer maintained that he was performing a function analogous to that of a prosecutor and therefore enjoyed absolute immunity. Mee also alleged that the officer perjured himself at a habeas corpus hearing.

The court ruled that the officer was entitled to absolute immunity regarding the perjury allegation. But the court also held that the officer was only entitled to qualified immunity in reference to Mee's incarceration. The court said that, in this instance, the officer's function was more closely related to that of a police officer than of a prosecutor.

## Cases Broadening the Quasi-Judicial Immunity Doctrine

A number of recent cases, such as those listed in table 3, appear to broaden the concept of judicial immunity, extending it to other phases of probation and parole work. An example is *Triparti v. United States Immigration and Naturalization Service*.[18] Triparti faced deportation based on Federal criminal charges. He sued the Immigration and Naturalization Service, the U.S. attorney who prosecuted him, an immigration officer who participated in the deportation proceedings, and two Federal probation officers. The probation officers were sued for allegedly making false statements in a presentence report and a pretrial bond report.

Table 1

**PSI Cases Where Public Officers Successfully Invoked the Quasi-Judicial Immunity Defense**

| Case | Party Involved | Function Performed | Liability Imposed? | Reason for Decision |
|---|---|---|---|---|
| *Friedman v. Younger*, 282 F.Supp. 710 (CD Cal. 1969) | Prosecutor & probation officer | PSI | No | Officers were performing a quasi-judicial function which is an integral part of the judicial process |
| *Burkes v. Callion*, 433 F.2d 318 (9th Cir. 1970) | Probation officer & medical examiner | PSI | No | Probation officer performing quasi-judicial functions is entitled to same immunity as judges |
| *Spaulding v. Nielsen*, 599 F.2d 728 (5th Cir. 1979) | Federal probation officer | PSI | No | An integral part of the sentencing process |
| *Hughes v. Chesser*, 731 F.2d 1489 (11th Cir. 1984) | State probation officer | PSI | No | Immunity granted Federal probation officers is applicable to the state probation officers |
| *Crosby-Bey v. Jansson*, 586 F.Supp. 96 (DDC 1984) | Probation officer | PSI | No | A probation officer is entitled to share a judge's absolute immunity from the charge that false and erroneous information in presentence report persuaded the judge to impose an unduly harsh sentence |
| *Demoran v. Witt*, 781 F.2d 155 (9th Cir. 1986) | State probation officer | PSI | No | Absolute immunity applies even amid allegations of bad faith and malice |
| *Dorman v. Higgins*, 821 F.2d 133 (2nd Cir. 1987) | Federal Probation officer | PSI | No | Immunity is needed to avoid intimidation while exercising a high degree of discretion |

Table 2

**Cases Rejecting the Quasi-Judicial Immunity Doctrine**

| Case | Party Involved | Liability Imposed | Function Performed | Reason for Decision |
|---|---|---|---|---|
| *Crawford v. State*, 566 N.E.2d 1233 (Ohio Sup. Feb 1991) | State of Ohio | Yes | Sending an inmate to non-court-ordered treatment | Not a basic policy decision |
| *Zavalas v. Department of Corrections*, 809 P.2d 1329 (Or.App. April 1991) | State probation officer | Yes | Supervision | Probation officer who failed to report known drug violations to court is not entitled to absolute immunity (claiming to act as an agent of the court) when probationer killed people while operating a vehicle under the influence, as this was not a judicial function |
| *Brunsvold v. State*, 820 P.2d 732 (Mont.Sup. Oct. 1991) | State probation officer | Yes | Calculation of prison discharge date | Is not so intimately associated with judicial act as to be an agent of the judiciary |
| *Mee v. Ortega*, 967 F.2d 423 (10th Cir. 1992) | State probation officer | A) Yes B) No | A) holding parolee in jail for one month pending a hearing (which was never held) B) Testimony at a Habeas Corpus hearing | A) Closer to a police function than a prosecutorial one B) Witnesses in judicial proceeding enjoy absolute immunity |

The district court dismissed the suit against all defendants. In the case of the probation officers, the district court stated that the probation officers were covered by qualified immunity because they were performing a narrowly defined judicial function. The Tenth Circuit Court of Appeals agreed that the probation officers were entitled to immunity, but based on different grounds. The court stated that the officers were entitled to absolute immunity if they were performing "quasi-judicial" functions. Stating that probation officers who conduct presentence and pretrial release reports perform "critical roles," the court held that when the challenged activities of a Federal probation officer are "intimately associated with the judicial phase of the criminal process,"[19] that officer is absolutely immune from liability.

In *Farrish v. Mississippi State Parole Board*,[20] a convicted drug offender was imprisoned, paroled, and rearrested for parole violations because of subsequent drug charges. Throughout the revocation proceedings, Farrish insisted on the appearance of an individual who he alleged could provide favorable testimony. Parole officials concluded they had no subpoena power, hence his request was denied. The witness never appeared, and Farrish's parole was revoked. He filed a Section 1983 lawsuit, alleging that his constitutional rights to due process were violated. The district court agreed; it also ruled, however, that the governor, members of the Mississippi Parole Board, and the members of the Board of Corrections were immune since they did not personally engage in conduct violative of Farrish's due process rights. The court held the corrections commissioner liable for failure to establish rules or policies for conducting preliminary parole proceedings. The district court also held the two parole officers involved liable. The commissioner and the two officers appealed.

Even though Farrish's due process rights were violated, the Fifth Circuit Court of Appeals held that the parole officer enjoyed absolute immunity from liability. It concluded that the parole revocation process was even more adjudicatory in nature than the initial process of paroling an inmate from prison. Inasmuch as the individual officers were conducting activities associated with this adjudicatory process, i.e., the role of a prosecutor, they enjoyed absolute immunity.

Absolute immunity for parole officers also prevailed in *Brown v. Nester*.[21] In this case, Brown's parole was revoked based on an armed robbery charge, a weapons possession charge, failure to report, and failure to abide by curfew. Brown sued his parole officer, alleging that he was subjected to onerous reporting conditions and that nonproven allegations were submitted to the parole board for consideration. Brown also alleged that he should not have been revoked based on the armed robbery charge because he had not been indicted, but was merely a suspect. Citing *Farrish*, the court ruled that the parole officer was entitled

Table 3

## Cases Broadening the Quasi-Judicial Immunity Doctrine

| Case | Party Involved | Function Performed | Liability Imposed? | Reason for Decision |
|------|----------------|--------------------|--------------------|---------------------|
| *Triparti v. U.S. INS*, 784 F.2d 345 (10th Cir. 1986) | Federal probation officer | Pretrial release | No | Intimately associated with the judicial phase of the criminal process |
| *Chitty v. Walton*, 680 F.Supp. 683 (D.Vt. 1987) | Prison caseworker & parole officer | Preparole report | No | Closely associated with parole board's quasi-judicial function |
| *Farrish v. Mississippi State Parol Board*, 836 F.2d 969 (5th Cir. 1988) | State parol officer & preliminary hearing officer | Preparation for revocation hearing | No | Revocation process is adjudicatory in nature |
| *Cooney v. Park County*, 792 P.2d 1287 (Wyo. 1990) | State probation officer | Testifying in revocation hearing | No | Revocation is intimately associated with judicial phase of criminal proceeding |
| *Kipp v. Saetre*, 454 N.W.2d 639 (Minn.App. 1990) | State probation officer | Revocation process | No | Acted on judge's directive |
| *Brown v. Nester*, 753 F.Supp. 630 (S.D.Miss. 1990) | State probation officer | Supervision, submission of parole violations to parole board | No | Function analogous to that of prosecutor |

to absolute immunity because he was performing a role analogous to that of a prosecutor.

In *Kipp v. Saetre*,[22] the Court of Appeals of Minnesota addressed the question of whether a probation officer is entitled to absolute or qualified immunity from a civil suit under 42 U.S.C. Section 1983. Kipp, a West German national, entered a guilty plea to a charge of selling cocaine. As a condition of his sentence, Kipp was ordered to return to West Germany and remain on unsupervised probation for 5 years. The supervision probation officer subsequently heard rumors that Kipp had returned to the United States. He reported these rumors to the sentencing judge, who ordered that an arrest warrant be issued. Kipp, however, had been arrested and charged with several new offenses. The original sentencing judge signed a revocation order without granting Kipp a revocation hearing. An appellate court ruled that Kipp's due process rights were violated because he did not receive a formal hearing. The court also ruled that Kipp's return to the United States did not constitute a probation violation.

Kipp subsequently filed a Section 1983 suit against the sentencing judge, the prosecutor, and the probation officer. The Minnesota Court of Appeals held that the judge and prosecutor were entitled to absolute immunity. It also held that the probation officer was entitled to absolute immunity because he was acting upon the directive of a judge, adding that the decision not to hold a hearing was the judge's, not the probation officer's. The court ruled that "absolute immunity attaches to those activities of a county prosecutor and a county probation officer which are associated with the judicial phase of the criminal process.[23] The court stated that to deny absolute immunity under such circumstances "would set a precedent inimical to the functioning of our system."[24]

Even when a probation/parole officer may have committed a criminal act in the course of a revocation proceeding, civil liability is not necessarily imposed because of quasi-judicial immunity. In *Cooney v. Park County*,[25] the Supreme Court of Wyoming held that a probation officer enjoyed absolute immunity even though he knowingly gave false testimony during a revocation hearing. Since the officer in this case was conducting activities intimately associated with the judicial process, he enjoyed absolute immunity from liability, though not from criminal prosecution.

## Conclusion

Two related themes are identifiable in cases where quasi-judicial immunity applies. First, the court focuses on the *function* performed by the officer rather than on who the officer may be. It is unlikely that probation or parole officers will ever be entitled to absolute immunity by virtue of their position alone. Second, in order for quasi-judicial immunity to apply, the function performed must be intimately associated with the judicial phase of the criminal process. What this means is far from certain and appears to change and evolve over time. Earlier cases limited its meaning to the preparation and writing of PSI reports; the cases in table 3, however, include such functions as pretrial release, preparole reports, preparation for a revocation hearing, revocations, and submissions of parole violations. These deviate from previously decided cases that extended quasi-judicial immunity primarily to instances when probation officers performed PSI functions. The limits appear to be expanding, but the rationale remains the same.

Case law indicates that probation and parole officers have better chances of successfully invoking the quasi-judicial immunity defense if they are performing functions that are intimately associated with the judicial process. An officer should examine whether the function being performed is more analogous to that of a judicial official, such as a prosecutor or judge, as opposed to that of a law enforcement officer. As is evident in *Crawford*, officers will be subject to the less protective qualified immunity doctrine when acting in a nonjudicial or supervisory capacity. That may not make sense to officers who say that they are judicial or parole board employees and that just about everything they do is upon orders of the judge or parole board. The quasi-judicial immunity defense, however, has not gone that far. Despite current trends toward expansion, the chances of the courts extending absolute immunity to all acts performed by probation or parole officers appears unlikely. The limits may be expanding, but the rationale for granting quasi-judicial immunity—only when the function performed is intimately associated with the judicial process—remains the same.

## Notes

[1] Bureau of Justice Statistics (1991). *Probation and Parole 1990*. Washington, DC: U.S. Department of Justice.

[2] *Black's Law Dictionary*, 5th Edition, 1979, at 1335.

[3] Section 1983 states: Every person who, under color of any statute, ordinance, regulation, custom, or usage, of any State or Territory, subjects, or causes to be subjected, any citizen of the United States or other persons within the jurisdiction thereof to the deprivation of any rights, privileges, or immunities secured by the Constitution and laws, shall be liable to the party injured in an action at law, suit in equity, or other proper proceeding for redress.

[4] A person acting under color of law does so when he/she is clothed with authority of state law.

[5] *Harlow v. Fitzgerald* (457 U.S. 800, 1982).

[6] See *Stump v. Sparkman*, 435 U.S. 349 and *Pierson v. Ray*, 386 U.S. 547 (1967).

[7] 435 U.S. 349 (1978).

[8] *Black's Law Dictionary*, 5th Edition (West Publishing Company) 1979, at 810.

[9] 424 U.S. 409 (1976).

[10] However, this standard may be changing as well. The Supreme Court, in *Burns v. Reed*, 59 U.S.L.W. 4536, ruled that prosecutors may be held liable for the legal advice they provide law enforcement officers.

[11] *Thompson v. Burke*, 556 F.2d 231 (3rd Cir. 1977).

[12] 112 S.Ct. 534 (1991).

[13] R. V. del Carmen, *Potential Liabilities of Probation and Parole Officers*, Anderson Publishing Company, 1985, at 35.

[14] 566 N.E.2d 1233 (Ohio Sup. Feb 1991).

[15] 820 P.2d 732 (Mont.Sup. Oct. 1991).

[16] Id.

[17] 967 F.2d 423 (10th Cir. 1992).

[18] 784 F.2d 345 (10th Cir. 1986).

[19] *Triparti v. U.S. INS*, 784 F.2d 345, 348 (10th Cir. 1986).

[20] 836 F.2d 969 (5th Cir. 1988).

[21] 753 F.Supp. 630 (S.D. Miss. 1990).

[22] 454 N.W.2d 639 (Minn.App. 1990).

[23] Id., at 640.

[24] Id., at 645.

[25] 792 P.2d 1287 (Wyo.Sup. April 1990).

# 23

# Legal Issues in the Use of Electronic Surveillance in Probation

Rolando V. del Carmen
Joseph B. Vaughn

## I. Introduction

Jail and prison overcrowding has generated a reexamination of the concept of imprisonment and the use of alternative forms of sentencing for those who would normally be incarcerated if space were available. From 1972 to 1982, the population in Federal and state prisons throughout the United States more than doubled. In 1981 and 1982 there was a 12 percent growth rate each year in the number of offenders sentenced to state and Federal prisons. In 1984 more than 430,000 men and women were incarcerated in those institutions.[1] That does not include the thousands more held in local and county jails.

Solutions to the overcrowding have been mandated by the courts in some 39 states, the District of Columbia, Puerto Rico, and the Virgin

Source: *Federal Probation*, Vol. 50, No. 2 (June 1986) 60-69.

Islands.[2] The traditional response to overcrowding has been to build more prisons. There is a growing realization, however, that this response may not be economically or politically feasible. Initial construction costs are prohibitive and the public has shown signs of reluctance to expend public funds for institutionalization. A new prison cell is estimated to cost from $25,000 to $75,000.[3] The State of Illinois has appropriated $150 million to capital expenditures for prisons, representing 50 percent of all capital spending during that time period.[4] Moreover, experts disagree on whether or not the construction of new prisons is the answer. Some maintain that new prisons are needed to alleviate overcrowded conditions; others believe that prison construction would merely widen the net and lead to more incarceration.[5]

Recent articles indicate a growing belief that alternatives to incarceration should be utilized both as a means to alleviate prison overcrowding and as a more humane and effective form of offender treatment.[6] Proposed alternatives include restitution, community service, prerelease programs, early parole, intensive probation supervision, and house arrest. Others have even suggested a return to corporal punishment.[7]

Probation in diverse forms has been used in all states as a viable alternative to incarceration; but its cost-effectiveness has also been questioned. While probation is admittedly less costly, it is far from inexpensive. For example, California spends approximately $1,600 per year for each person on probation. In that state 1 out of every 83 people between the age of 9 and 65 is now on probation.[8]

One proposed incarceration alternative is intensive supervision through the use of electronic devices to monitor offenders. The solution is now technologically feasible and is being used in a few jurisdictions. This article examines the current use of the device and some possible constitutional and legal challenges to its use. There have been no court cases decided to date which deal specifically with the issue, hence the article will focus on the use of electronic surveillance based on cases where similar issues have been raised. It concludes with an assessment of the constitutionality of such use in probation cases.

## II. The Monitoring System

While the full extent of its use is unknown, widespread use of the monitoring system has not yet occurred. Among the first users of the system were West Palm Beach County, Florida; Lake County, Illinois; Albuquerque, New Mexico; Kenton County, Kentucky; and Washtenaw County, Michigan.[9]

The monitoring systems currently used are usually composed of three parts — a control computer located at the controlling agency, a receiver unit located in the offenders home, and a transmitter device worn by the offender. The style of the transmitter varies from those that are worn on the ankle to those that are worn on the wrist or around the neck. The ankle transmitting device, which is about the size of a cigarette package and weighs 5 ounces, is strapped just above the ankle with a rubberized watch-type strap which is said to be tamperproof. Although the offender conceivably could remove the device by cutting the strap or stretching it and taking it off over his foot, an electronic circuit within the device detects such tampering and sends an alarm to the receiving unit.[10]

In one program the ankle device is viewed as a part of the punishment process. There is no provision for its removal. While technology exists to make the unit much smaller, advocates of the program do not want the offender to forget that he is wearing it. The weight of the device serves to remind the person of its presence, enhancing its use as a punishment. In one program, out of the 60 people on whom the ankle device has been placed, only 1 has had an adverse physical reaction to it.[11]

The receiver, located in the offender's home, communicates with the control computer through a telephone connection. Like the ankle device, the receiver is designed to be tamperproof. There is an internal battery to supply power in the event the unit is unplugged or the electricity goes off in the home. The receiver communicates with the control computer at randomly selected times. If the message is not sent at the selected time, the control computer automatically calls the receiver to check and alerts the operator if there is a problem. Additionally, the receiver keeps a log of the times the offender comes and goes from the house. To facilitate work-release programs, the computer can be set to allow the person to leave and return home at certain times without triggering an alarm.

The control computer, like the receiver, has an alternate power supply to allow its continued operation in the event the electric service is interrupted. It provides a print-out of the times an individual enters or leaves the area of confinement, thus preserving a record of any violations of the restrictions placed upon him.[12]

The system is reported to be accurate 85 percent of the time in monitoring violations.[13] Inaccurate reports can be generated, according to one user, by power failures or severe thunderstorms that interfere with the telephone line transmissions. One operation problem has been discovered in the system itself. If a person places his body in a fetal position, as sometimes occurs during sleep, and his body mass is between the ankle device and the receiver, the signal is blocked and a false alarm is sent to the computer indicating that the user has left home. When the user rolls over and his body mass is no longer blocking the signal the receiver will indicate he has returned. According to the system supplier, it is necessary to rely on a human's analytical ability to distinguish between false readings and actual violations.[14]

The system is designed for selective use and is not for everyone. "It is for a select group of non-violent offenders who really want to make it work; it is for the person who has good motivation."[15] In West Palm Beach County, Florida, it was initially utilized only for persons convicted of driving while intoxicated. Currently, approximately 50 percent of the offenders in that program are such persons, while the remainder have been convicted of a broad spectrum of nonviolent misdemeanors. It is used "for people who appear to be those who could make it on the street if their activities were curtailed somewhat. The system is a curfew device, it doesn't control his (the offender's) activities."[16]

Aside from intensive supervision, the system has also been utilized to monitor pretrial detainees who, because of prior record, would normally not be eligible for release on a personal recognizance bond. The system is used in lieu of pretrial detention in jail. In these instances, the alternative is provided only to those nonviolent offenders who have a permanent place to live and are employed. If there is a shortage of equipment and no units are available the person must remain in jail until his trial if he is unable to post a bond.[17]

The system can be operated either publicly by the probation department or privately on a contract basis with a corporation. Under the second option, the private corporation in effect assumes the duties of a probation department in providing the supervision of the offenders. Additionally, programs can be devised to accept only misdemeanants or only felony offenders or any combination of offense types. The cost of the program can be financed totally by the government or it can be partially paid for by the offender through fees.

## III. Constitutional Issues

### Electronic Surveillance

Supervision of probationers requires a varying degree of surveillance by probation officers. The use of house arrest and monitoring devices to supervise clients must comply with the fourth amendment which prohibits unreasonable searches and seizures. That amendment provides the foundation for cases decided by the United States Supreme Court which involve the use of electronic surveillance. Since 1928, the United States Supreme Court has decided a series of cases which indicate the parameters within which electronic surveillance and devices may be used.

The seminal case in electronic surveillance is *Olmstead v. United*

*States*,[18] decided in 1928. In *Olmstead*, the Court held that a wiretap executed without an accompanying trespass in an individual's home was not a fourth amendment violation. The central issue of trespass, on which *Olmstead* was based, formed the basis for two subsequent decisions dealing with the use of electronic "bugging" devices. *Goldman v. United States*,[19] involved police officers who electronically monitored a conversation through a wall of an adjoining office. In *On Lee v. United States*,[20] a former-friend-turned-informant, who was wired with a transmitting device, entered the defendant's laundry with defendant's consent. In both cases the Court held that the electronic surveillance was constitutional because there was no trespass to property.

The modern landmark case on electronic surveillance and its fourth amendment restrictions was decided by the Court in 1967. In *Katz v. United States*,[21] government agents, without the defendant's knowledge or consent, attached a monitoring device to the outside of a public telephone booth and recorded only the defendant's conversation. The Court ordered the tape recorded evidence excluded because no warrant had been issued authorizing the surveillance. Overruling *Olmstead* and *Goldman*, the Court held that the absence of a trespass into the public telephone booth did not justify violating the defendant's "reasonable expectation of privacy," saying that "the Fourth Amendment protects people, not places."[22] *Katz* is significant because it eliminated trespass as a requirement for unconstitutionality. More importantly, it made the right to privacy in effect portable in that such right now attaches to a person rather than to a protected place. The *Katz* case has been the foundation upon which recent right to privacy cases have been decided.

The *Katz* decision did not overturn *On Lee*, although some lower courts held otherwise. In deciding a case similarly circumstanced, *United States v. White*,[23] the Court reaffirmed the decision in *On Lee*. In *White*, an informer had consented to wear a microphone and have his conversations with the defendant recorded. The Court held that no fourth amendment violation had occurred because a defendant does not have a "justifiable and constitutionally protected expectation that a person with whom he is conversing will not then or later reveal the conversation to the police." The Court believed that if there was no reasonable expectation of privacy, the use of electronic equipment to record the conversation could not be construed as creating a violation of the defendant's constitutional rights.

In *Berger v. New York*,[25] the Court dealt specifically with the constitutional requirements for a wiretap. It held that the language of a New York statute authorizing wiretapping was too broad and therefore violative of rights under the 4th and 14th amendments. The Court went on to say that a valid warrant authorizing any form of electronic surveillance, including wiretapping, must satisfy the following requirements: (1) The warrant must describe with particularity the conversations which are to be overheard; (2) A showing of probable cause to believe that a specific crime has been or is being committed must be made; (3) The wiretapping must be for a limited period of time; (4) The suspects whose conversations are to be overheard must be named; (5) A return of the warrant must be made to the court, showing what conversations were intercepted; and (6) The wiretap must terminate when the desired information has been obtained. In very specific terms, *Berger* spelled out the constitutional requirements for electronic surveillance. States have since complied with these requirements by statute or court decisions.

## Federal Legislation

In 1968 Congress passed Title III of the Omnibus Crime Control and Safe Streets Act to regulate the electronic and mechanical interception of wire and oral communications. That law requires law enforcement officials to obtain a court order to intercept wire and oral communications. The act governs only the interception of *contents* of oral or wire communications and therefore leaves open a wide variety of other electronic surveillance devices which may be utilized without obtaining a court order.[26] Title III regulates only the interception of the contents of oral and wire communications, hence the use of monitoring devices which track locations of people, absent any state enacted statute, is governed only by the Constitution.

In 1977, the Supreme Court, in *United States v. New York Telephone Co.*,[27] directly addressed the issue of whether or not Title III applied to governmental use of pen registers. In that case the Court found that such devices are not regulated by the act because they do not intercept actual telephone conversations, but merely record telephone numbers dialed from a telephone. Two years later, in *Smith v. Maryland*,[28] the constitutional issue of whether or not the use of pen registers constituted a search within the meaning of the fourth amendment was resolved. The Court held that the attachment of a pen register at the telephone company office to record the numbers dialed on a phone did not constitute a search because there was no legitimate expectation of privacy.

*United States v. Knotts*,[29] decided in 1983, represents the first time the Supreme Court considered the use of "beeper"[30] devices to trace the location of an object or person. In that case a "beeper" was placed in a container of chemicals which was later purchased by the defendant for use in the manufacture of drugs. Police followed the defendant by utilizing the beeper and located a cabin where he was staying. The Court held that there is no reasonable expectation of privacy as to a person's movement on public highways and therefore no search occurred. The Court did not rule on whether the installation of the "beeper" was constitutional because *Knotts* did not raise the issue. Prior to *Knotts*, the lower court's decisions on the utilization of electronic surveillance devices to track a vehicle on a public highway generally held that no warrant need be obtained.[31]

A year later, in *United States v. Karo*,[32] the Court addressed an issue left unanswered in *Knotts* — whether the use of a "beeper" would constitute a search under the fourth amendment if it revealed information that could not have been obtained through visual surveillance. In *Karo*, government agents learned from an informer that the defendants had ordered a quantity of ether for use in manufacturing cocaine. The agents supplied to the manufacturer a canister containing a beeper which was later sold to the defendants. Installation of the beeper did not constitute a violation of the fourth amendment. The can belonged to the government agents at the time the beeper was installed and therefore the defendants could not have had any legitimate expectation of privacy in it. Even if the beeper had been placed in one of the canisters owned by the manufacturer, the consent of the manufacturer to its placement would have been sufficient to comply with the requirements of the fourth amendment. The Court also held that the transfer of the canister to the defendants, under these circumstances, did not constitute a search or a seizure.

While concluding that no fourth amendment right was infringed by the installation of the beeper or the transfer of the canister containing the beeper to the defendants, the Court found that their privacy interests were violated by the monitoring of the beeper. Over a period of several months the electronic device was utilized to monitor the movement of the canister until agents obtained a search warrant for the home of one of the defendants. The device was used not only to track movements of the canister in public places, but to confirm that it was located in a specific residence, information that could not have been obtained by observation from outside the curtilage of that residence.

*Karo* differs from *Knotts* in that in *Knotts*, the beeper was utilized to monitor the movements of the automobile and the arrival of the canister in the area of the cabin, something that could have been done by the naked eye. The beeper was not utilized to monitor the canister while it was inside the cabin. In *Karo* the beeper was used to monitor the canister inside the residence belonging to the defendant, something which could not be done by the naked eye alone. It is this distinction, monitoring in a private versus a public place, which constitutes a violation of the right to privacy.

The aforementioned cases indicate that the use of electronic devices by law enforcement officials does not constitute a search within the meaning of the fourth amendment when there is no interception of oral or wire communication and when the device does not reveal information that could not have been obtained through visual surveillance. It could therefore be argued that the use of an electronic device which merely indicates whether a person is complying with his curfew restriction, would not constitute a search. The ankle device currently utilized as a condition of probation is not capable of monitoring conversations, nor can it determine what the individual is doing inside the confines of his home. Its sole purpose is to ensure that the probationer is complying with the conditions of probation. It is true that the ankle device generates information which could not otherwise be obtained by visual surveillance, but that alone should not taint the device because its installation is with the client's consent. Additionally, under a system of house arrest and under most probation conditions, the officer would have a right anyway to verify whether the person is complying with such restrictions through visual surveillance and unannounced home visits. The use of the ankle device, therefore, merely enhances the ability of the officer to conduct surveillance even in a place where a client has a "reasonable expectation of privacy"; something which a probation officer is generally authorized to do.

Fourth amendment protection for persons incarcerated is less than that afforded the public at large. In *Hudson v. Palmer*,[33] the Court said that the fourth amendment right against unreasonable searches and seizures affords an inmate absolutely no protection for searches and seizures in his cell. Courts have traditionally been reluctant to interfere with searches in prisons and jails, particularly where the security and orderly operation of the institution is at stake. The use of electronic devices to record and monitor the private conversations of prisoners is one of many areas where the needs of the institution have been held to justify what would otherwise have been an impermissible practice if noninstitutionalized individuals were involved. In *Lanza v. New York*,[34] the Supreme Court noted that a jail shares none of the attributes of privacy of a home, an automobile, an office, or a hotel room. And in *Bell v. Wolfish*,[35] a case involving the rights of pretrial detainees, the Court said that any expectation of privacy of a prisoner necessarily would be of a diminished scope.

## Constitutionality of Probation Conditions—in General

As a general rule, the authority granting probation has broad discretion in setting terms and conditions. Restrictions on constitutional liberties which have been upheld by the courts include warrantless searches by probation officers, freedom of association, freedom to travel, requiring the regular reporting to a probation officer, regulating the freedom to travel, change jobs, or choose a residence.[36] The courts have held that a probationer may be subject to these restrictions as a condition of receiving the privilege of probation even though they could not be imposed upon the citizenry in general. "The court may surround probationers with restrictions and requirements which a defendant must follow to retain his probationary status."[37]

Most state statutes suggest probation conditions which are optional with the sentencing judge. In the aggregate, decided cases show that there are four general elements for the validity of a probation condition. These are:

1. The condition must be protective of society and/or rehabilitative of the probationer;
2. The condition must be clear;
3. The condition must be reasonable; and
4. The condition must be constitutional.

Protection of society and/or rehabilitation of the probationer are all-encompassing and convenient justifications for the imposition of a condition. Because justifications are easy to establish, challenges to probation conditions seldom succeed. Just about any probation condition can be broadly justified as either protective of society or rehabilitative of the individual. These two rationales may, however, be antithetical in that what may be protective of society may not necessarily be rehabilitative of the individual. In these cases courts balance the interests involved on a case-by-case basis. Protection of society and rehabilitation of the client are such strong justifications that they may validate conditions which are otherwise violative of fundamental rights. This was implied in *Porth v. Templar*,[38] where the Tenth Circuit Court of Appeals said that probation conditions must bear a relationship to the treatment of the offender and protection of the public. The court then added that "The case stands for the proposition that absent a showing of a reasonable relationship between a release condition and the purpose of release the abridgement of a fundamental right will not be tolerated.[39]

The second requirement for the validity of a probation condition is that the condition must be clear, meaning that the probationer must know what acts are violative of the condition. In *Panko v. McCauley*,[40] the condition forbidding the probationer from "frequenting" establishments selling alcoholic beverages was not upheld because there was no evidence that the probationer understood what that term meant. This case implies that there may be a duty to explain conditions of probation which are unclear.

Reasonableness mandates that the condition be fair and can be carried out properly. For example, a probationer was ordered to abstain from alcohol for 5 years. Evidence that he was an alcoholic led the court to deny probation revocation when the condition was violated, the court claiming unreasonableness because of the probationer's condition.[41] Similarly, a former serviceman convicted of accepting kickbacks was placed on probation on condition that he forfeit all personal assets and work without compensation for 3 years or 6,200 hours. The condition was struck down as unduly harsh in its cumulative effect.[42]

Conditions which are unconstitutional are invalid unless validly waived. A waiver obtained where the alternative is incarceration is not always a voluntary waiver, particularly if it involves the violation of a fundamental right. The courts are particularly protective of first amendment rights, such as the freedoms of religion, speech, press, and association. In one case, the court held that a condition which requires a convicted person to attend church services is improper.[43] The same is true with conditions limiting freedom of speech, unless there is a showing of a reasonable relationship between the release condition and the abridgement of a fundamental right.[44]

The use of electronic surveillance needs to be analyzed in the context of the above requirements. Arguably, the wearing of an electronic device is protective of society and rehabilitative of the individual. Setting a curfew for a convicted offender might protect society and instill a sense of discipline which can be rehabilitative for the probationer. Clarity of conditions poses no problem in electronic surveillance cases because the client obviously knows what is happening and how the condition might be breached. Where the practice may run into probable difficulties is in the reasonableness and constitutionality requirements. Reasonableness is closely linked to the Equal Protection provision of the 14th amendment, basically meaning that the requirement be fair and just. There is nothing inherently unfair or unjust with electronic surveillance when viewed in isolation, but when applied to an aggregate where financial capability becomes a determinant to obtaining probation, equal protection considerations might arise, particularly where no provisions are made for accommodating indigent defendants.

Of even greater concern than reasonableness are questions concerning the constitutionality of the condition, viewed in the light of specific constitutional provisions. Electronic surveillance therefore needs to be analyzed in the context of constitutional guarantees, specifically the following rights: privacy, self-incrimination, cruel and unusual punishment, equal protection, and warrantless searches.

### Right to Privacy

It is axiomatic that the rights of probationers are limited; the courts have consistently held that they have a limited expectation of privacy.

In one case, a probationer who was required to report his employment and financial condition to his counselor argued that his right of privacy was being violated. In rejecting his argument, the court said that some restrictions on privacy were permissible in order to accomplish the legitimate goal of monitoring the behavior of probationers.[45] In other cases, the right to privacy has been invoked to challenge conditions restricting contact with family members or barring pregnancy or marriage.[46]

Conditions of probation which infringe on the privacy rights of the probationer are examined by the courts under a doctrine of *reasonableness* to determine if they are designed to meet the rehabilitation needs of the offender or if they serve the interests of the state or public in maintaining order. The electronic device currently used is designed to enforce curfew and travel restrictions, both of which the courts have upheld as valid conditions of probation. In reality, all the device does is allow the probation officer to become more proficient at enforcing curfew and travel limitations. Theoretically, the officer could watch each probationer to ensure that he is complying with those restrictions. The courts have refused to hold that scientific enhancement raises any constitutional issues which visual surveillance would not also raise. In *Knotts* the Court refused to equate police efficiency with unconstitutionality and rejected the petitioner's argument that scientific devices (in this case a "beeper" used to show location) are unconstitutional. In the *Karo* case the Court reaffirmed that doctrine. It did not find that the use of the device was unconstitutional, only that the manner in which it was used was unlawful. It follows, therefore, that if the conditions of probation are reasonable, the use of technology to enhance the probation officer's efficiency in enforcing them would not be unconstitutional. All the technology accomplishes is increased surveillance proficiency.

## The Right Against Self-Incrimination

The fifth amendment provides that no person may be compelled in a criminal proceeding to be a witness against himself. In probation, this right has been invoked in cases where an offender is required to answer a counselor's questions,[47] submit to a search by a probation counselor or policeman,[48] or provide a juror or prosecutor with information.[49]

Conviction does not remove or lessen a person's constitutional right not to testify against himself. Two courts of appeals recently were faced with probation conditions regarding tax returns. In one case, a probationer was ordered to file tax returns despite his claim of a fifth amendment privilege.[50] In the other, a probationer was ordered to file amended tax returns.[51] The first of those conditions was held to be improper, while the second was upheld. In the latter case, while the filing of amended returns was called for—and presumably complete returns were what the court had in mind—there was no attempt to interfere with the probationer's possible exercise of a constitutional right; he could comply with the condition, literally, and on the amended return claim his fifth amendment privilege. This would not violate the condition, hence probation could not be revoked for exercising an explicit right. In the former case, however, the mere assertion of the right not to incriminate himself placed the probationer in danger of revocation.

Another fifth amendment issue arises when the probationer is required by a condition, such as regular polygraph tests, to disclose information which could be used in a new criminal proceeding. In these cases, the result of a fifth amendment challenge to the condition has turned on: (1) whether the government could reasonably have expected incriminating evidence to be forthcoming, (2) whether use immunity was promised, and (3) whether fifth amendment rights were voluntarily, knowingly, and intelligently waived.[52]

In *Minnesota v. Murphy*,[53] the Supreme Court clarified the muddied waters on this issue, saying that a state "may validly insist on answers to even incriminating questions and hence sensibly administer its probation system, as long as it recognizes that the required answers may not be used in a criminal proceeding and thus eliminates the threat of incrimination."[54] The Court added that "a defendant does not lose this Fifth Amendment protection by reason of his conviction of a crime; notwithstanding that a defendant is imprisoned or on probation at the time he makes incriminating statements, if those statements are compelled they are inadmissible in a subsequent trial for a crime other than that for which he has been convicted."[55]

Whether or not the fifth amendment protects a probationer against self-incrimination generally depends on the type of proceeding wherein the evidence is to be used. If the evidence is to be used in a revocation proceeding, the fifth amendment argument usually fails. On the other hand, if the claim is raised in a subsequent criminal trial, the claim is usually upheld.[56]

In the case of electronic devices, violation of the right against self-incrimination is remote for a number of reasons. The evidence obtained will be used only for purposes of revocation since only a probation condition is violated and no criminal act is involved. The device certainly serves the system's needs, particularly the need to monitor the activities of a probationer and to help control burgeoning prison populations. An even stronger reason is that such devices do not per se violate the right against self-incrimination because what that right protects is merely the right against testimonial, not physical self-incrimination.[57] If any incrimination at all is involved in the use of an electronic device, such incrimination is physical, not testimonial. Some cases appear to indicate, however, that when the probation conditions require incriminating information, the fifth amendment entitles the client to some form of immunity against the use of the evidence obtained.[58]

### Cruel and Unusual Punishment

The eighth amendment of the Constitution proscribes cruel and unusual punishment. Although the provision is often invoked in prison cases, it is seldom used in probation perhaps because the terms of probation are seldom severe or oppressive. Nonetheless, some cases have held that conditions which are excessively harsh or impossible to comply with may fall under this category.[59] In one case, the condition that the defendant leave the country was deemed cruel and unusual, hence unconstitutional;[60] similarly, a condition that an alcoholic refrain from drinking was found to be unconstitutional.[61]

The use of an anklet device does not appear to violate the cruel and unusual punishment standard used by the courts in corrections cases.[62] Its effects are not oppressive, nor does it subject the user to humiliation or degradation. Compared to incarceration, it is certainly less restrictive and much more humane.

### Payment of Costs and Equal Protection

Requiring probationers, as a condition of probation, to reimburse the state for its costs has been upheld by the state courts. In *Arizona v. Smith*,[63] the state appeals court allowed the imposition of a probation condition that the defendant spend 30 days in the county jail and pay for the cost of that incarceration. The condition was allowed, even though there was no specific statutory authorization to do so. The decision was justified under the broad discretion of the court to determine conditions of probation. In that case, there was no claim of indigency on the part of the defendant.

Under a slightly different set of facts, the Arizona Court of Appeals in 1982 considered the issue of requiring payment of costs as a condition of probation. The court found that:

> To require a probationer to help defray the state's costs of supervising his probation should be beneficial in the rehabilitation of the defendant, and such reimbursement into the probation fund will strengthen the criminal justice system's ability to finance its probation services. We find there is nothing unconstitutional in the Arizona Legislature enacting legislation that requires a financially capable probationer to help defray the state's cost of maintaining him while on probation.[64]

The courts, in these cases, have held that a probationer who is not indigent may be required to repay costs. The decisions are based on the rationale that such a requirement is directly related to the rehabilitative goal of probation and that it serves a legitimate state interest.

A slightly different situation is presented in probation revocation cases when the probationer is unable to pay court costs or restitution. In *Bearden v. Georgia*,[65] decided in 1983, the Court held that a judge cannot properly revoke a defendant's probation for failure to pay a fine and make restitution — in the absence of evidence and finding that the probationer was somehow responsible for the failure or that alternative forms of punishment were inadequate to meet the state's interest in punishment and deterrence. In essence, the decision holds that a probationer can be revoked for refusing, but not for inability caused by indigency, to pay restitution and court costs.

In at least one system currently in operation, the probationer is required to pay the costs of utilizing the ankle device to monitor his presence in the home during the required hours.[66] It is in this area that a challenge under the Equal Protection clause of the 14th amendment is foreseen. Prior court decisions which have upheld the requirement that offenders reimburse the state for financial costs dealt with offenders who could afford to pay. The issue is different when indigent defendants who would have been eligible for probation must face incarceration because they cannot afford to pay. This presents a real problem because a monitoring device at present costs approximately $5 per day.[67] The Court has said that "there can be no equal justice where the kind of trial a man gets depends on the amount of money he has."[68]

### Warrantless Searches

"With few exceptions it has been held that the United States Constitution is not violated by the requirements that a probationer submit to warrantless searches as a condition of probation."[69] The courts, however, disagree to whether the requirement is valid as to searches by probation officers only, or whether the probationer may be required to submit to warrantless searches by police officers as well.

The Ninth Circuit Court of Appeals ruled in *United States v. Consuelo-Gonzalez*,[70] based upon the Federal Probation Act, that Federal probationers are subject to warrantless searches by probation officers only. The court, however, expressly pointed out that states may implement a different rule which would be constitutional, saying:

> It is obvious, however, that opinions differ as to what controls are improper, and we express no opinion here regarding the extent to which the states constitutionally may impose conditions more intrusive on the probationer's privacy than those we have here indicated are proper under the Federal Probation Act.[71]

Relying on the above case, the Arizona Supreme Court, in 1977, upheld the imposition of a probation condition allowing a warrantless search by both police and probation officers.[72] That endorsement, however, was qualified by the belief that in the majority of the cases, the probationer should not be required to submit to a warrantless search by police officers in addition to submitting to such searches by probation officers. The court feared that warrantless searches by police might interfere with the rehabilitative effort.

Six years earlier, the California Supreme Court upheld the imposition of the same conditions, finding that the requiring of a narcotics offender to submit to searches by police officers as well as probation officers was reasonably related to the person's prior criminal conduct and was aimed at deterring or discovering subsequent criminal offenses. They reasoned that the offender would be less inclined, under those conditions, to be in possession of narcotics.[73]

Some states, however, are more restrictive. Utah has held that a parole officer may only conduct searches that are rationally and substantially related to the performance of his duties. Warrantless conditions of probation are not a waiver of the probationer's constitutional rights.[74]

While it is not currently foreseen that the use of an ankle device to monitor the presence of the probationer in his home during the required times constitutes a search under the meaning of the fourth amendment, the requirement that a probationer submit to reasonable warrantless searches of his home would authorize probation authorities to utilize the device if the court should sometime in the future determine that its use constitutes a search.

# IV. Other Legal Concerns

### The Use of Curfew Restrictions

In establishing a curfew which requires a person to be in a certain place at a certain time, the courts will generally uphold the condition if it is shown that the restriction will facilitate supervision and discourage harmful association. Such conditions have been viewed by the courts in terms of whether or not they are reasonably related to the rehabilitation of the offender and whether they accomplish the essential needs of the state and public order.

In *State v. Sprague*[75] the Oregon Court of Appeals upheld the imposition of a 10 p.m. curfew of a 20-year-old female after she was convicted of interfering with a friend's arrest during which she struck a police officer. The trial judge determined that her continued association during the late evening hours with her friends would be detrimental to her rehabilitation. Other decisions have upheld a curfew from 10 p.m. to 6 a.m.,[76] while another upheld prohibiting a probationer from driving a car between midnight and 5:30 a.m. on the belief that it would minimize the opportunity to contact persons involved in criminal activities.[77]

The condition, however, must be reasonably related to rehabilitation. The imposition of a curfew for 5 years has been held invalid because there was no showing that it was reasonably related to the rehabilitation of the offender.[78] If the use of a curfew and electronic surveillance is reasonably related to rehabilitation, given the offense committed, questions of legality or constitutionality should not be of any major concern.

### Waiver of Rights and the Right to Refuse Probation

Court decisions on the validity of waivers of rights in probation and parole cases are mixed. Traditionally, courts have relied on express waivers or have invoked the "act of grace" or "constructive custody" doctrines to strip offenders of most of their constitutional rights.[79] In the last decade, however, courts have re-examined this approach. As a result, new doctrines have emerged such that the whole issue should be considered unsettled. This doctrinal uncertainty is reflected in the cases discussed below, each adhering to differing doctrines. On the one hand, the Court has ruled that a person may pre-waive his rights voluntarily. In *Zap v. United States*[80] the Court said:

> The law of searches and seizures as revealed in the decisions of this Court is the product of interplay of the Fourth and Fifth Amendments. But those rights may be waived. And when petitioner, in order to obtain the government's business, specifically agreed to permit inspection of his accounts and records, he voluntarily waived such claim to privacy which he otherwise might have had . . .[81]

In this case the petitioner had contracted with the government and as a condition of that contract agreed to allow inspection of his records. During an audit of the records evidence was uncovered which led to his conviction for fraud.

Applying the rationale of *Zap*, the Supreme Court of California ruled that when a probationer, in order to obtain probation, specifically agrees to a warrantless search condition, he has "voluntarily waived whatever claim of privacy he might have otherwise had."[82] Note, however, that *Zap* was not a probation or parole case.

Claims that attaching such conditions to probation amount to coercion and not a voluntary waiver of a person's rights have not been favorably received by some courts. In one case, the Nebraska Supreme Court reasoned that:

> If acceptance of this term of probation to avoid going to prison amounts to coercion, the same argument would apply equally to any condition attached to the granting of probation, and the coercion rule would consequently invalidate all conditions of probation.[83]

The claim of a New Mexico appellant that the choice between going to prison and signing a probation agreement is no choice, and therefore could not constitute a valid waiver, met a similar fate in that state's court of appeals. The court refused to even consider the argument, deciding the case on a broader issue, finding that probationers are not automatically granted full constitutional protection. The court held that a probationer's rights are more limited than the rights of a person not on probation.[84] What the court in essence held was that there could have been no coercion, resulting in an invalid waiver, because the appellant was not entitled to the constitutional protection claimed.

Because probation is viewed as a privilege, the state may impose restrictions which aid in the rehabilitative process or prove a reasonable alternative to incarceration as punishment for a crime committed. If the probationer finds the terms and conditions of that probation to be unacceptable, he may reject the probation and ask to be incarcerated instead. The decision to accept or reject probation has been viewed by the courts as constituting a voluntary choice and not coercion. Court decisions take the position that as long as the conditions of probation are reasonable, the probationer is given a free choice to either accept the probation or to reject it and go to jail. Probation reflects the benevolence of the state and no one is forced to accept it; however, if anybody does he may be required to submit to reasonable intrusions by the state.

The above cases indicate that waiver of rights is valid. On the other hand, however, later cases provide some authority for the proposition that a parole or probation condition waiving fourth amendment protection is illegal or ineffective. In one case where a consent to search had been signed by a state parolee, the consent was thrown out by a Federal court in a collateral challenge.[85] The court reasoned that since the prisoner could only secure his release on parole by accepting the condition, his consent was not voluntarily given. The prospect of 8 years of additional confinement was coercive, according to the court.

Even in the Ninth Circuit, which recognizes a waiver condition as valid, the terms of the condition must be narrowly drawn. The Ninth Circuit disapproved as overly broad a condition that appeared to extend the benefits of a Federal probation condition to all law enforcement officers.[86] This holding was based on the coerciveness of the circumstances that gave rise to a consent waiver.

The mere act of agreeing to the terms of probation does not mean that a legal challenge is foreclosed. An example is *Sobell v. Reed*[87] where a Federal parolee asserted that his first amendment rights had been violated by a condition prohibiting him from going outside the limits of the Southern District of New York without permission from the parole officer. On a number of occasions, Sobell sought and obtained permission to travel to and speak at various places; however, on other occasions, such requests were denied. The court held that the board violated Sobell's exercise of his rights of speech, expression, or assembly, except when it could show that withholding permission was necessary to safeguard against specifically described and highly likely dangers of misconduct by the parolee. In *Porth v. Templar*,[88] a case involving a first amendment right, the Tenth Circuit Court of Appeals stated that probation conditions must bear a relationship to the treatment of the offender and the protection of the public for it to be valid. Reliance on a waiver will therefore not legitimize an otherwise invalid condition. The court added that absent a showing of a reasonable relationship between a release condition and the purpose of release, the abridgement of a fundamental right will not be tolerated. The aforementioned cases imply that release conditions abridging fundamental rights can be sustained only if they serve a legitimate and demonstrated rehabilitative objective. The claim by the state that waiver by the probationer or parolee cures any constitutional infirmity will no longer be upheld consistently.

In the case of electronic surveillance, refusal to waive what primarily amounts to a right to privacy may mean incarceration instead of probation. Using the standard of reasonableness, however, it can be said that diminution of privacy in exchange for freedom is reasonable when the alternative is no freedom at all and a greatly diminished right to privacy in case of incarceration. Moreover, the right to privacy does not enjoy the same degree of protection and preference as do first amendment rights.

## V. Conclusion

Jails and prisons are overcrowded, and their use as a rehabilitative tool is suspect. There is a growing belief that alternatives to incarceration should be utilized both as a means to alleviate overcrowding and as a more humane and effective form of offender treatment. Technology has provided and shows promise as an alternative to incarceration for those who may be given a second chance to become useful members of society. It provides intensive supervision in the form of movement restriction which regular probation otherwise cannot supply.

Providers of the system foresee a continued growth in its utilization, particularly in any area where there is a court mandated ''cap'' on the number of prisoners which may be held in a facility.[89] Electronic surveillance technology is relatively new, hence expansion into other areas is still clouded. Whatever the future portends, a review of decided cases in probation and parole indicates that while the use of electronic devices raises constitutional issues, its constitutionality will most likely be upheld by the courts, primarily based on the concept of diminished rights. It is important, however, that the use of electronic devices be governed by specific guidelines that comport with state statutes in those states which have applicable laws. Moreover, the issue of device availability to indigents must be addressed so as to remove any possibility of a successful constitutional challenge based on equal protection. It is this article's conclusion that the constitutionality of the use of electronic devices in probation is strongly defensible. Whether or not such use is cost-effective, politically acceptable, or administratively feasible is an entirely different matter.

## Notes

[1] J. Thompson, "Prison Crowding: A Symposium," 78 U. Ill. L.R. 203 (1984).

[2] "Lock 'Em Up? There's No More Room!," 69 A.B.A. J. 1352 (1983).

[3] G. Kennedy, Control Data Corporation, Minneapolis, Minnesota. Interview conducted April 11, 1985.

[4] *Supra* Note 1 at 204.

[5] For a full discussion of the issue, see Conrad and Rector, *Should We Build More Prisons? A Debate*, 1977 National Council on Delinquency (1977).

[6] Corbett and Fersch, "Home As Prison: The Use of House Arrest," *Federal Probation*, March 1985, pp. 13-17.

[7] See G. Newman, *Just and Painful: A Case For the Corporal Punishment of Criminals*, MacMillan (1983).

[8] "California Probation Problems May be Five Years Ahead of Nation," 16 *Corrections Digest*, February 13, 1985, at 7.

[9] *Supra* Note 2 at 1352; *Houston Chronicle*, February 17, 1985, at A22, col. 1; Berry, "Electronic Jails: A New Criminal Justice Concern," 2 *Justice Quarterly*, March 1985 at 3; *Houston Chronicle*, March 13, 1985, at A10, col. 1. The program at Washtenaw County was scheduled to begin April 1, 1985 for a 6-month trial basis.

[10] *Supra* Note 3.

[11] F. Rasmussen, Pride, Incorporated, West Palm Beach Florida. Interview conducted April 11, 1985.

[12] *Supra* Note 3.

[13] *Supra* Note 11.

[14] *Supra* Note 11.

[15] *Supra* Note 3.

[16] *Supra* Note 11

[17] *Supra* Note 11

[18] 227 U.S. 438 (1928).

[19] 316 U.S. 129 (1942).

[20] 343 U.S. 747 (1952).

[21] 389 U.S. 347 (1967).

[22] *Id.* at 351.

23 401 U.S. 745 (1971).

24 *Id.* at 749. *See also Hoffa v. United States*, 385 U.S. 293 (1966). Court held the Constitution does not protect a person's misplaced belief that a person he reveals illegal activities to will not later reveal them to police.

25 388 U.S. 41 (1967).

26 18 U.S.C. 2510-2520 (Codified 1976).

27 434 U.S. 159 (1977).

28 442 U.S. 735 (1979).

29 460 U.S. 276 (1983).

30 A "beeper" is a transmitting device which emits a signal to a receiver which allows a person to determine the location of the beeper.

31 *See United States v. Brock*, 667 F.2d 1311 (9th Cir. 1982), *cert. denied*, 103 S.Ct. 1271 (1983); *United States v. Sheikh*, 654 F.22d 1057 (5th Cir), *cert. denied*, 455 U.S. 991 (1982); and *United States v. Michael*, 654 F.2d 252, (5th Cir.), *cert. denied*, 454 U.S. 950 (1981).

32 104 S. Ct. 3296 (1984).

33 35 Cr.L. 3230 (1984).

34 370 U.S. 139 (1962).

35 411 U.S. 520 (1979).

36 See R. del Carmen, *Potential Liabilities of Probation and Parole Officers*, 34-37 (1982).

37 *State v. Smith*, 542 P.2d 1115, (Ariz. S.Ct. 1975).

38 453 F.2d 330 (10th Cir. 1971).

39 Note, "Fourth Amendment Limitations on Probation and Parole Supervision," 1976 Duke, L. J. 71, 75 (1976).

40 473 F. Supp. 325 (D.C. Wisc. 1979).

41 *Supra* Note 36, at 37.

42 *Supra* Note 36, at 36.

43 *Id.*

44 *Sobell v. Reed*, 327 F. Supp. 1294 (S.D.N.Y. 1971).

45 *United States v. Manfredonia*, 341 F. Supp. 790 (S.D.N.Y.), affirmed, 459 F.2d 1392 (2nd Cir.), *cert. denied*, 409 U.S. 851 (1972).

46 *State v. Livingston*, 53 Ohio App. 2d 195 (1976).

47 *State v. Johnson*, 202 NW 2d 132 (1972).

48 Note, "The Search and Seizure Condition of Probation: Supervisory or Constitutional?," 22 South Dakota L. Rev. 199 (1977), as cited in N. Cohen and J. Gobert, *The Law of Probation and Parole* (1983).

49 See in general N. Cohen and J. Gobert, *The Law of Probation and Parole* (1983).

50 *United States v. Conforte*, 624 F.2d 869 (9th Cir.) *cert. denied*, 449 U.S. 1012 (1980).

51 *United States v. McDonough*, 603 F.2d 19 (7th Cir. 1979).

52 See R. V. del Carmen, *Potential Liabilities of Probation and Parole Officers*, revised edition, 103 (1985).

53 104 S.Ct. 1136 (1984).

54 *Id.* at 1147.

55 *Id.* at 1142.

56 *Supra* Note 49, at 236.

57 *Schmerber v. California*, 384 U.S. 757 (1966).

58 *Supra* Note 49, at 234.

59 *Supra* Note 49, at 215.

60 *Dear Wing Jung v. United States*, 312 F.2d 73 (9th Cir. 1962).

61 *Sweeny v. United States*, 353 F.2d 10 (7th Cir. 1965).

62 See Legal Responsibility and Authority of Corrections Officers, American Correctional Association, 51-53 (1982).

[63] 576 P.2d 533 (Ariz. App. 1978).

[64] *State v. Means*, 654 P.2d 29 (Ariz. App. 1982) at 32.

[65] 33 CrL 3103 (1983).

[66] *Supra* Note 11.

[67] *Supra* Note 11.

[68] *Griffen v. Illinois*, 351 U.S. 12 (1956) at 19.

[69] 79 ALR 3d at 1803.

[70] 521 F.2d 259 (9th Cir. 1975).

[71] *Id.* at 266.

[72] *State v. Montgomery*, 566 P.2d 1329 (Ariz. S.Ct. 1977).

[73] *People v. Mason*, 488 P.2d 630 (Calif. S.Ct. 1971).

[74] *Utah v. Valasquez*, 672 P.2d 1254 (Utah S.Ct. 1983).

[75] 629 P.2d 1326 (Or. Ct. App. 1981).

[76] *Johnson v. State*, 291 S.E. 2d 94 (Ga. Ct. App. 1982).

[77] *State v. Cooper*, 282 S.E. 2d 436 (Ga. S.Ct. 1981).

[78] *State v. Labure*, 427 So. 2d 855 (1982).

[79] *See U.S. v. Pattman*, 535 F.2d 1062 (8th Cir. 1976).

[80] 328 U.S. 624.

[81] *Id.* at 628.

[82] *People v. Mason*, 488 P.2d 630 (Cal. S.Ct. 1971) at 634.

[83] *State v. Morgan*, 295 N.W. 2d 285 (Nev. S.Ct. 1980) at 289.

[84] *State v. Gallagher*, 675 P.2d 429 (N.M. App. 1984).

[85] *U.S. ex. rel. Coleman v. Smith*, 395 F. Supp. 1155 (W.D.N.Y. 1975).

[86] *U.S. v. Consuelo-Gonzalez*, 521 F.2d 259 (9th Cir. 1975).

[87] 327 F. Supp. 1294 (S.D.N.Y. 1971).

[88] 453 F.2d 330 (10th Cir. 1971).

[89] *Supra* Note 11.

# 24

# The Ethics of Community-Based Sanctions

## Andrew von Hirsch

*The reviving interest in noncustodial penalties makes it urgent to explore the ethical limits on their use. This article explores three kinds of limits: proportionality (desert) constraints, restrictions against humiliating or degrading punishments, and concerns about intrusion into the rights of third parties. In connection with the second of these limits, the concept of "acceptable penal content" is developed.*

Imprisonment is a severe punishment, suited only for grave offenses. Crimes of lesser and intermediate gravity should receive nonincarcerative sanctions. Such sanctions long were underdeveloped in the United States, and it is gratifying that they are now attracting interest. Noncustodial penalties, however, raise their own ethical questions. Is the sanction proportionate to the gravity of the crime? Is it unduly intrusive, upon either defendants' human dignity or the privacy of third persons?

In the enthusiasm for community-based sanctions, such issues are easily overlooked. Harsh as imprisonment is, its deprivations are

Source: Andrew von Hirsch, *Crime and Delinquency*, Vol. 36, No. 1 (January 1990), 162-73.

manifest—and so, therefore, is the need for limits on its use. Noncustodial penalties seem humane by comparison, and their apparent humanity can lead us to ignore the moral issues. As Allen (1964) warned us two decades ago, it is precisely when we seem to ourselves to be "doing good" for offenders that we most need to safeguard their rights.

This essay will address two kinds of ethical issues involved in noncustodial sanctions. One concerns just deserts: that is, the proportionality of the sanction to the gravity of the crime of conviction. The other issue—or, as we will see, cluster of issues—concerns the "intrusiveness" of the sanction, that is, the constraints that are needed to prevent punishments in the community from degrading the offender or threatening the rights of third parties.

## Proportionality and Desert

The issue of proportionality in community-based sanctions has suffered a double neglect. Desert theorists, when writing on proportionality and its requirements, tended to focus on the use and limits of imprisonment, paying little attention to community sanctions. Reformers involved in developing these sanctions, meanwhile, gave little thought to proportionality.

The disregard of proportionality has reinforced a tendency to assess community-based sanctions principally in terms of their effectiveness. If a program (e.g., an intensive supervision scheme) seems to "work" in the sense of its participants having a low rate of return to crime, then it is said to be a good program. Seldom considered are questions of the sanction's severity and of the seriousness of the crimes of those recruited into the program.

Imprisonment is obviously a severe punishment, and its manifestly punitive character brings questions of proportionality into sharp relief. Noncustodial measures, however, are also punishments—whether their proponents characterize them as such or not. A sanction levied in the community, like any other punishment, visits deprivation on the offender under circumstances that convey disapproval or censure of his or her conduct. Like any other blaming sanction, its degree of severity should reflect the degree of blameworthiness of the criminal conduct.[1] In other words, the punishment should comport with the seriousness of the crime.

The punitive character of noncustodial sanctions, however, is often less visible to those who espouse them. Because these sanctions are often advertised as more humane alternatives to the harsh sanction of imprisonment, the deprivations they themselves involve are often overlooked. Because the offender no longer has to suffer the pains of confinement, why cavil at the pains the new program makes him or her suffer in the community?

Such attitudes are particularly worrisome when it comes to the newer noncustodial sanctions, which include such measures as intensive supervision, community service, home detention, and day-fines.[2] These sanctions often involve substantial deprivations: intensive supervision and home detention curtail an offender's freedom of movement, a community-service program exacts enforced labor, a day-fine may inflict substantial economic losses. Part of the attraction of these programs has been that their more punitive character gives them greater public credibility than routine probation and, hence, makes them plausible substitutes for imprisonment. In short, these are sanctions of intermediate severity. But then it *must* be asked: Are the offenses involved serious enough to make the sanction a proportionate response? Often, the answer to this question is no. Clear (this issue) points out that intensive supervision programs tend to be applied to offenders convicted of the *least* serious felonies because program organizers feel that such persons would be more likely to "cooperate."

When devising community penalties, reformers should ask themselves about the proportionality of the sanction. They might begin by posing a few simple questions. First, how serious are the crimes that the proposed sanction would punish? Seriousness is a complex topic (see von Hirsch, 1985, ch. 6), but rough-and-ready assessments should be possible. For example, several sentencing commissions (most notably, those of Minnesota, Washington, and Pennsylvania) have explicitly ranked the gravity of crimes on a rating scale (von Hirsch, Knapp, and Tonry, 1987); those rankings could be drawn upon, supplemented by common-sense arguments about the appropriateness of particular rankings.

Second, how severe is the proposed sanction? Severity is likewise a complex topic (see von Hirsch, Wasik, and Greene, 1989), but, again, a common-sense assessment is possible. If one assumes routine probation to be lenient and imprisonment to be severe, one can make a comparative judgment of the onerousness of the proposed sanction. This would involve inquiring about the extent of restriction of freedom of movement, of monetary deprivation, etc., and it should yield a rough assessment of whether the sanction is mild, intermediate, or more severe. In assessing severity, the preventive as well as punitive aspects of the sanction should be considered. An intensive supervision program that, for example, involves curfews or periods of home detention invades personal liberty to a significant extent, and is therefore quite severe. This holds true whether the purpose of the detention is to punish or to restrain or cure.

Asking such questions will put reformers in the position to begin to make judgments about commensurability. Potential mismatches will begin to become apparent, for example, the imposition of sanctions of intermediate or higher severity on lesser crimes.

There are more sophisticated models available for gauging commensurability that are applicable to noncustodial penalties. One actual project—the Vera Institute's day-fine project in Staten Island, New York—has developed explicit standards: Crimes are rated on a seriousness scale, and monetary penalties are arrayed accordingly (Greene, 1988). Theoretical models are also beginning to develop. I refer interested readers to a general account of how desert principles apply to community punishments, (von Hirsch et al., 1989), as space does not permit me to summarize these views here.

## Common Fallacies of "Intrusiveness"

When we consider the potential intrusiveness of sanctions, we enter less-explored territory. Whereas an extensive literature on desert exists,[3] less thought has been devoted to what makes a punishment unacceptably humiliating or violative of others' privacy. We might begin by clearing away the underbrush, that is, putting aside some commonly heard fallacies.

One fallacy is the *anything-but-prison theory.* Intervention in the community is tolerable irrespective of its intrusiveness, this theory asserts, as long as the resulting sanction is less onerous than imprisonment. This is tantamount to a carte blanche: Because imprisonment (at least for protracted periods) is harsher than almost any other community punishment, one could virtually never object.

The anything-but-prison theory is a version of the wider misconception that an individual cannot complain about how he or she is being punished if there is something still worse that might have been done instead. The idea bedeviled prison policy for years: Prisoners should not complain of conditions because they might have fared worse—been held longer or in nastier conditions, or even been executed. The short answer is that a sanction needs to be justified in its own right, not merely by comparison with another—possibly more onerous—punishment.

The theory also rests on the mistaken factual supposition that all those who receive the proposed community sanction would otherwise have been imprisoned. That is almost never the case. Many, if not the bulk, of those receiving the new community sanctions are likely to be persons who otherwise would have received a conventional noncustodial sanction such as probation instead (see Clear, this issue).

A second fallacy is that *intrusiveness is a matter of technology.* The installation of an electronic monitor on an offender's telephone elicits comparisons to "Big Brother," but no similar issues of privacy are assumed to arise from home visits by enforcement agents. The mistake should be obvious: Orwell's totalitarian state may have relied on two-way television screens, but the Czarist secret police achieved plenty of intrusion without newfangled gadgetry. The same point holds for noncustodial sanctions. Intrusion depends not on technology but on the extent to which the practice affects the dignity and privacy of those intruded upon. Frequent, unannounced home visits may be more disturbing than an electronic telephone monitor that verifies the offender's presence in the home but cannot see into it.

A third fallacy is *legalism*. Intrusiveness, in this view, is a matter of whether the practice infringes on specific constitutional requirements. The U.S. Constitution does not give much consideration to the treatment of convicted offenders, and such provisions as are germane have been restrictively interpreted. Those provisions do not exhaust the ethical requirements the state should abide by in the treatment of offenders. This has been understood where proportionality is concerned. The Eighth Amendment (as now construed) outlaws only the most grossly disproportionate punishments,[4] but the state should go (and some jurisdictions have gone) further in safeguarding desert requirements.[5] The same should hold true for the present issues of "intrusiveness." When a program is developed, its sponsors should ask themselves not only whether it passes constitutional muster but whether there are any substantial ethical grounds for considering it humiliating or intrusive.

## Dignity and "Acceptable Penal Content"

The idea of "intrusiveness" is actually a cluster of concepts, and we need to identify its component elements. One important element is the idea of *dignity*—that offenders should not be treated in a humiliating or degrading fashion. We need to inquire why convicted criminals should be punished with dignity and how this idea can be put into operation in fashioning punishments.

***The Rationale for "Dignity" in Punishment.*** To inquire into the rationale for the idea, we might begin with a passage from the philosopher Jeffrie Murphy:

> A punishment will be unjust (and thus banned on principle) if it is of such a nature as to be degrading or dehumanizing (inconsistent with human dignity). The values of justice, rights and desert make sense, after all, only on the assumption that we are dealing with creatures who are autonomous, responsible, and deserving of the special kind of treatment due that status. . . . A theory of just

punishment, then, must keep this special status of *persons* and the
respect it deserves at the center of attention [Murphy, 1979, p. 233].

What this passage reflects is the idea that convicted offenders are still
members of the moral community and that they remain persons and
should be treated as such. Someone's status as a person would ordinarily
militate against *any* sort of insulting or demeaning treatment. With
offenders, however, there is a complication — the nature of punishment
itself. Punishment not only serves as a deprivation but also conveys
blame or censure (von Hirsch, 1985, ch. 3). Blame, because it embodies
disapproval of the offender for his or her conduct, is necessarily
unflattering. What is left, then, of the idea that punishment should not
humiliate its recipient?

The answer lies in the communicative character of blaming. Blame,
Duff (1986) has pointed out, conveys disapproval addressed to a rational
agent. The function of the disapproval is not only to express our
judgment of the wrongfulness of the act but to communicate that
judgment to offenders in the hope that they will reflect upon it and
reevaluate their actions. We may wish offenders to feel ashamed of what
they have done, but the shame we are trying to elicit is their *own* shame
at the conduct, not merely a sense of being abased by what we are doing
to them. The more one treats wrongdoers in a demeaning fashion, the
more this entire moral process is short-circuited. When prisoners are
made to walk the lockstep — to shuffle forward, with head down and
eyes averted — they are humiliated irrespective of any judgment they
might make about the propriety of their conduct. The shame comes not
from any acceptance of the social judgment of censure but simply from
the fact that they are being treated as inferior beings.

Punishments, therefore, should be of the kind that can be endured
with self-possession by persons of reasonable fortitude. These
individuals should be able to undergo the penalty (unpleasant as it
inevitably is) with dignity, protesting their innocence if they feel they
are innocent or acknowledging their guilt if they feel guilty — but
acknowledging it as a person, not a slave, would do. A person can endure
the deprivation of various goods and liberties with dignity, but it is hard
to be dignified while having to carry out rituals of self-abasement,
whether the lockstep, the stocks, or newer rituals.

*Acceptable Penal Content*.    How do we apply this idea of dignity? One
way would be to try to identify and list the various kinds of intrusions
we wish to rule out as undignified. But as intrusion on dignity is a matter
of degree, this would be no easy task. It would be particularly difficult
for noncustodial sanctions because these may be so numerous and
variable in character.

A better approach, I think, is through the idea of "acceptable penal content." The penal content of a sanction consists of those deprivations imposed in order to achieve its punitive and preventive ends. Acceptable penal content, then, is the idea that a sanction should be devised so that its intended penal deprivations are those that can be administered in a manner that is clearly consistent with the offender's dignity. If the penal deprivation includes a given imposition, X, then one must ask whether that can be undergone by offenders in a reasonably self-possessed fashion. Unless one is confident that it can, it should not be a part of the sanction.

Where prisons are concerned, we already have the kernel of this idea, expressed in the maxim that imprisonment should be imposed *as* punishment but not *for* punishment. The idea is that the deprivation of freedom of movement should be the main intended penal deprivation — that while it is severe (and hence suitable only for serious crimes), such deprivation *per se* can be endured without self-abasement. According to this maxim, the intended penal content should not include various possible sanctions within the prison because we have no guarantee that these can be undergone with dignity. It thus would be inappropriate, for example, to prescribe solitary confinement as the punishment for designated crimes. And notice that one need not determine whether each possible sanction-within-the-prison is unduly humiliating. The idea that prison exists only as and not for punishment serves precisely as a prophylactic rule, to endorse only that deprivation — of liberty — that we think can be decently imposed and not to authorize all kinds of further impositions whose moral acceptability is in doubt. Granted, the reality of American prisons is different, with numerous unconscionable deprivations occurring. But we consider them unconscionable precisely because they lie outside the sanction's acceptable penal content.

Once we have specified the acceptable penal content of the sanction, we may also have to permit certain ancillary deprivations as necessary to carry the sanction out. Imprisonment, for example, involves maintaining congregate institutions and preventing escapes or attacks on other inmates and staff. Segregation of some violent or easily-victimized offenders for limited periods may be necessary for such purposes, even if not appropriate as part of the intended penal content in the first place. But these ancillary deprivations must truly be essential to maintaining the sanction.

Can these ideas be carried over to noncustodial penalties? I think they can. The first step would be to try to identify the acceptable penal content for such penalties. Certain kinds of impositions, I think, can be undergone with a modicum of self-possession, and thus would qualify. These would include deprivations of property (if not impoverishing);

compulsory labor, if served under humane conditions (community service, but not chain-gang work); and limitation of freedom of movement. Clearly excluded, for example, would be punitive regimes purposely designed to make the offender appear humbled or ridiculous. An example is compulsory self-accusation, e.g., making convicted drunken drivers carry bumper stickers indicating their drinking habits. There is no way a person can, with dignity, go about in public with a sign admitting himself or herself to be a moral pariah. We may wish the offender to feel ashamed of what he or she has done—but not act as though he or she is ashamed, whatever he or she actually feels. This list of acceptable and unacceptable intrusions is far from complete, and I shall not try to complete it. I am merely suggesting a mode of analysis.

That analysis should be applied not only to the expressly punitive but also to the supposed rehabilitative features of a program. Deprivations administered for treatment are still penal deprivations and can be no less degrading than deprivations imposed for expressly punitive or deterrent ends. I would, for example, consider suspect a drug program in the community that involves compulsory attitudinizing. One may wish to persuade the offender of the evils of drug use and, for that purpose, deny him or her access to drugs or other stimulants. But if we try to *compel* the offender, as part of the program, to endorse attitudes about drug use that he or she does not necessarily subscribe to, we are bypassing his or her status as a rational agent.

After we have specified the acceptable penal content, there comes the question of ancillary enforcement measures. These are measures that are not part of the primary sanction—the intended penal deprivation—but are necessary to ensure that that sanction is carried out. An example is home visits. Such visits are not a part of acceptable penal content: It is not plausible to assert that, without any other need for it, the punishment for a given type of crime should be that state agents will periodically snoop into one's home. The visits could be justified only as a mechanism to help enforce another sanction that *does* meet our suggested standard of acceptable penal content.

What might such a sanction be? Consider the sanction of community service, which I have suggested does meet the primary standard. To assure attendance at work sites and check on excuses for absences, occasional home visits may be necessary and indeed are part of the enforcement routine of the Vera Institute's community service project (McDonald, 1986). Because home visits are justified only as an ancillary enforcement mechanism, their scope must be limited accordingly, that is, be no more intrusive than necessary to enforce the primary sanction. If home visits are ancillary to community service, they should occur only when the participant has failed to appear for work, and their use should be restricted to ascertaining the offender's whereabouts and checking on any claimed excuse. The less connected the visits are with such enforcement and the more intrusive they become, the more they are suspect. General, periodic searches of the offender's home could not be sustained on this theory.

Telephone monitoring can be analyzed in similar fashion. A phone monitor, used to enforce a sentence of home detention, would be an acceptable ancillary measure if designed so that the defendant can simply register his or her presence. Repeated and searching verbal phone inquiries would be another matter.

***Unresolved Issues.*** The analysis still has a number of loose ends. Thus:

(1) Are there any principled limits on the ancillary enforcement sanctions, other than their being essential to enforce the primary penalty? Enforcement sanctions that are grossly humiliating should be ruled out, even if needed as an enforcement tool for a particular kind of primary sanction. If X is an acceptable sanction but needs Y — a morally repulsive one — to enforce it, then the appropriate solution would be to give up X in favor of some other sanction that can be enforced less intrusively. I leave to future discussion how we might specify more clearly such a limit on enforcement measures.

(2) Can one ever argue *for* intrusions on dignity in order to create noncustodial sanctions with a punitive "bite" comparable to that of imprisonment? Consider a range of fairly serious crimes for which imprisonment would normally be the sanction. May one substitute home detention, with specially intrusive conditions designed to make the sanction "equivalent" to the prison? My instinct would be to resist such a suggestion if those conditions are sufficiently demeaning to infringe on the principles just described. For here, imprisonment is not an undeserved response, given the seriousness of the conduct. The alternative *is* objectionable because of its degrading character.

(3) What of choices of evils? Suppose a jurisdiction *inappropriately* uses imprisonment for crimes of intermediate or lesser severity and is prepared to substitute a noncustodial sentence only if it is made highly intrusive. Here, proportionality concerns collide with concerns about dignity — and may require one to decide which value should be accorded higher importance. Such an apparent choice, however, is most likely to arise in poorly regulated sentencing systems in which proportionality constraints and controls over discretion are weak. That, however, is precisely the kind of system in which such purported "alternatives" to incarceration so easily become, instead, substitutes for traditional and less noxious noncustodial penalties.

## The Rights of Third Parties

The prison segregates the offender. The segregation, whatever its other ills, means the rights of third parties are not directly affected. If X goes to prison, this does not restrain Y's rights of movement, privacy, etc. Granted, Y still suffers if he or she is attached to X or economically dependent. But Y, nevertheless, is not restrained.

Noncustodial penalties reintroduce the punished offender into settings in which others live their own existence. As a result, the offender's punishment spills over into the lives of others. Home visits, or an electronic telephone monitor ringing at all hours of the day, affects not only the defendant but any other persons residing at the apartment— and it is *their* as well as his or her dwelling place.[6]

The third-party question is distinct from the issue of the offender's dignity, as discussed earlier. That is true even when the latter issue is affected by the presence of third parties. Consider home visits. Such visits may be potentially shaming to the defendant in part because of the presence of unconvicted third-party witnesses, that is, the other residents of the home. But the visits also affect those other residents, diminishing *their* own sense of privacy.

However, such other persons, are often affected because they have some consensual[7] relation to the defendant, for example, they share the defendant's home. Here lies the difficulty: Granted that the quality of their lives may suffer, but have they not in some sense assumed that risk? When A chooses to live with B, will not A inevitably suffer indirectly from whatever adverse consequences legitimately befall B as a consequence of his or her behavior? It is *this* issue—the extent to which third parties lose their right to complain—that requires more reflection. I have not been able to think of a general answer to this relinquishment-of-rights question. The following modest steps, however, might help to reduce the impact of noncustodial punishments on third parties:

(1) Often, it is not the primary sanction itself but its ancillary enforcement mechanism that intrudes into the lives of third parties (to cite a previous example, home visits used to enforce community service). In such cases, the enforcement mechanism should be limited to enforcing the primary sanction and should not be used to investigate the general extent to which other persons abide by the law. When the defendant's home is visited to check on his or her excuse for being absent at the work site, for example, that should *not* be used as an occasion to gather evidence of law violations by others in the apartment.

(2) The impact on third persons should be one of the criteria used in choosing among noncustodial penalties. Often, the sanctioners may have several sanctions of approximately equal severity to choose from, any

of which would comport with crimes of a given degree of seriousness. Where that choice is available, the sanctioner should, other things being equal, choose the sanction that affects third parties least. Suppose, for example, that the choice lies between home detention (enforced by a telephone monitor) and a fairly stiff schedule of community service (enforced by home visits to check the offender's presence, but only when he or she fails to appear at the work site). Suppose, for the sake of argument, that the penalties have been calibrated to be of approximately equal severity (see von Hirsch et al., 1989). If we conclude that the occasional home visits used to enforce community service are less disturbing to other residents than a (frequently ringing) telephone monitor used with home detention, that would be reason for preferring community service.

## Conclusions

This essay provides more questions than answers. Concerning the first issue, that of proportionality, I have some sense of confidence because there has been an extensive literature on desert. Concerning the second issue, that relating to dignity and humiliation, I have tried to offer the rudiments of a theory, but it stands in need of development. Concerning the third, intrusion into the rights of third parties, I have done little more than raise some issues.

Because innovative noncustodial penalties are only beginning to be explored in this country, little thought has been devoted to limits on their use. Such thinking is now urgently necessary. With adequate ethical limits, community-based sanctions may become a means of creating a less inhumane and unjust penal system. Without adequate limits, however, they could become just another menace and extend the network of state intrusion into citizens' lives. We should not, to paraphrase David Rothman,[8] decarcerate the prisons to make a prison of our society.

### Notes

[1] For a discussion of how the idea of censure or blame underlies the principle of proportionality, see von Hirsch (1985, chs. 3, 5).

[2] For a survey of such penalties, see Tonry & Will (1989).

[3] See e.g., von Hirsch (1976,1985), Singer (1979), and Duff (1986).

[4] See e.g., Rummel v. Estelle, 445 U.S. 263(1980), Solem v. Helm, 463 U.S. 277(1983).

[5] In particular, the states that have adopted sentencing guidelines that emphasize desert principles. See von Hirsch, Knapp, and Tonry (1987, chs. 2,5). Some foreign jurisdictions — most notably Sweden — have also adopted statutes on choice of sentence, stressing ideas of proportionality and desert. See von Hirsch (1987) and, for the English-language text of the statute as enacted, von Hirsch and Jareborg (1989).

⁶ For a brief previous discussion of this question of third parties, see von Hirsch and Hanrahan (1979, pp. 109-12).

⁷ Any children present will not have actually consented, however.

⁸ The original quotation appears in von Hirsch (1976, pp. xxxv-xxxvi).

## References

Allen, Francis A. 1964. *The Borderland of Criminal Justice*. Chicago: University of Chicago Press.

Duff, R. A. 1986. *Trials and Punishments*. Cambridge, England: Cambridge University Press.

Green, Judith A. 1988. "Structuring Criminal Fines: Making an 'Intermediate Penalty' More Useful and Equitable." *Justice System Journal* 13:37.

McDonald, Douglas C. 1986. *Punishment Without Walls: Community Service Sentences in New York City*. New Brunswick, NJ: Rutgers University Press.

Murphy, Jeffrie G. 1979. *Retribution, Justice, and Therapy*. Dordrecht, Netherlands: D. Riedel.

Singer, Richard G. 1979. *Just Deserts: Sentencing Based on Equality and Desert*. Cambridge, MA: Ballinger.

Tonry, Michael and R. Will. 1989. *Intermediate Sanctions*. Washington, DC: Government Printing Office.

von Hirsch, Andrew. 1976. *Doing Justice: The Choice of Punishments*. New York: Hill & Wang. Reprinted 1986, Boston: Northeastern University Press.

_____. 1985. *Past or Future Crimes: Deservedness and Dangerousness in the Sentencing of Criminals*. New Brunswick, NJ: Rutgers University Press.

_____. 1987. "Principles for Choosing Sanctions: Sweden's Proposed Sentencing Statute." *New England Journal on Criminal and Civil Confinement* 13:171.

von Hirsch, Andrew and K. J. Hanrahan. 1979. *The Question of Parole: Retention, Reform, or Abolition?* Cambridge, MA: Ballinger.

von Hirsch, Andrew and N. Jareborg. 1989. "Sweden's Sentencing Statute Enacted." *Criminal Law Review*: 275.

von Hirsch, Andrew, K. A. Knapp, and M. Tonry. 1987. *The Sentencing Commission and Its Guidelines*. Boston: Northeastern University Press.

von Hirsch, Andrew, M. Wasik, and J. A. Greene. 1989. "Punishments in the Community and the Principles of Desert." *Rutgers Law Journal* 20:595.

# Part VI

# The Future of
# Community Corrections

Just as I have attempted to detail the past trends in community corrections, it is also important to consider the future. Many of the changes in sentencing practice that have affected corrections will continue to produce their result: Prisons will continue to be overcrowded, probation and parole will be overutilized, and so on. The future of community corrections is affected by numerous variables, many of which are beyond the scope of this text. The one factor that is within our grasp, however, is the *community*.

James M. Byrne provides a thoughtful, detailed discussion of the importance of the community context in "Reintegrating the Concept of *Community* into Community-Based Corrections." The concept of community-oriented policing is used by the author to point out the need for community corrections to more effectively communicate and interact with the community. This concept has been utilized by law enforcement to both improve the community's attitude toward the police, as well as the officers' view of the general community. As law enforcement utilizes a problem-oriented style of interaction in solving problems in the community, it is argued that community correctional administrators are continuing to use traditional policing practices of surveillance, control, and apprehension. This traditional approach, according to Byrne, under-emphasizes the need to "examine (and change) the underlying community context of offender behavior." Community attitudes toward crime affect the decisions made about offenders. The community supervision model presented here focuses on the use of community corrections to achieve crime control, rather than correctional control. It is through the use of models such as the one proposed by Byrne that community corrections will, in the future, achieve its goal of being truly community-oriented.

421

# 25

# Reintegrating the Concept of *Community* into Community-Based Corrections

## James M. Byrne

Police administrators across the country are developing a range of
community-oriented policing strategies at a time when community
corrections administrators are moving in the opposite direction by
applying traditional, offender-based policing concepts to probation
and parole practice. I highlight the limitations of this new wave of
intermediate sanction programs and then discuss the importance of
community context (i.e., community attitudes, tolerance, support,
and structure) to the development of effective adult supervision
strategies. I conclude by describing the four key characteristics of
a community-oriented approach to probation and parole supervision:
(1) service brokerage, (2) advocacy for offenders and victims, (3)
triage, and (4) location in the community.

Source: James M. Byrne, *Crime & Delinquency*, Vol. 35, No. 3 (July 1989), 471-99. Copyright
© 1989 Sage Publications, Inc. Reprinted by permission of Sage Publications, Inc.

## Introduction: Community-Oriented Policing and Current Community-Corrections Practice—Different Directions

In recent years a new term has been added to the police nomenclature: *community-oriented policing*.[1] This label has been placed on a wide range of police initiatives designed to solve underlying community problems rather than to respond to specific incidents or calls for service. Wilson and Kelling (1989, p. 49) offer the following simple description of the community-oriented approach to policing:

> Community-oriented policing means changing the daily work of the police to include investigating problems as well as incidents. It means defining as a problem whatever a significant body of public opinion regards as a threat to community order. It means working with the good guys, and not just against the bad guys.

The basic problem-solving techniques employed in these initiatives are certain to be familiar to community corrections administrators across the country: service brokerage and advocacy. A number of examples of the successful implementation of community-oriented policing in U.S. cities are provided in a recent article by Wilson and Kelling (1989):

> In Newport News, Virginia, the police department decided to take a new approach to a housing project that was plagued by drug users and, not surprisingly, also had the highest burglary rate in the city. They went into the project and talked to the residents about their concerns. The police found that both crime *and* deteriorated, inadequate housing were priority areas. They subsequently began the task of coordinating improvements in the housing project with other city agencies [p. 46].

> In Los Angeles, when residents in one neighborhood "complained to the police about graffiti on walls and gang symbols on stop signs, officers assigned to the Community Mobilization Project did more than just try to catch the gang youths who were wielding the spray cans; they also organized citizens' groups and Boy Scouts to paint over the graffiti as fast as they were put up" [p. 48].

> And in New York City, when local merchants in one neighborhood "complained to the police about homeless persons who created a mess on the streets and whose presence frightened away customers, the officer who responded did not roust the vagrants but instead suggested that the merchants hire them to clean the streets in front of their store every morning. The merchants agreed, and now the streets are clean all day and the customers find the store more attractive" [p. 48].

These three examples are certainly illustrative of a new set of priorities in many police departments across the country, in tacit recognition of the need to focus our crime control policies on efforts to "change places, not people" (Sherman, Gartin, and Buerger, 1989, p. 47). By directly involving police officers in such a community change effort, community-oriented policing reforms are expanding the role of police to include functions traditionally associated with other agencies, both inside (e.g., probation, parole) and outside (e.g., social welfare, mental health) the criminal justice system.

One apparent byproduct of this process of role redefinition is the change in police officers' view of the general community:

> Traditionally, police officers after about three years get to thinking that everybody's a loser. That's the only people you're dealing with. In community policing you're dealing with the good citizens, helping them solve problems [Officer Robin Kirk, Houston Police Department, as quoted by Wilson and Kelling, 1989, p. 52].

Similarly, the results of a number of community-oriented police experiments suggest that the *community's* attitude toward the police also improves when these programs are implemented. To many observers, this change may be the most significant aspect of the reform effort, because it suggests a strategy for improving not only police-community relations, but also the relations between the courts and the community, and corrections and the community.

Ironically, it appears that as police administrators move to embrace a *problem*-oriented style of interaction with offenders and communities, *community corrections* administrators are introducing traditional (offender-based) policing concepts — utilizing surveillance, control, and incident-based apprehension strategies — which deemphasize the need to examine (and change) the underlying community context of offender behavior. The design and development of such *intermediate* sanctions as intensive supervision, house arrest, electronic monitoring, and split sentencing has been guided by a need to demonstrate to the public that punishment and control, rather than offender treatment, are now the primary task of community corrections. For example, in the name of punishment and "control," we now (1) conduct random drug and alcohol tests, (2) set strict curfews and then monitor compliance utilizing home visits and/or electronic surveillance techniques, (3) require probation fees and/or community service, (4) establish *mandatory* treatment conditions (e.g., mandatory referrals in the areas of employment, education, substance abuse, individual/family problems), and (5) use a short prison sentence to "shock" offenders into compliance. Moreover, the probation and parole officers who monitor offenders' compliance with the multiple conditions of supervision are expected to return offenders to prison or jail if they refuse to abide by these conditions. As Todd Clear recently observed: "The new probation officer is just as likely to bust a felon as encourage him to attend Alcoholics Anonymous'' (Clear, 1987, as quoted by Petersilia, 1988, p.4).

In one sense, this strategy is a response to the community, in that the public's perception is that offenders deserve more punishment (and require more control) than they currently receive in this country.[2] However, it is also apparent that the reason community members call for more punishment is that *they simply want to make their neighborhoods safer places to live*, and they are apparently convinced that punishment, rather than rehabilitation, is the most effective mechanism for accomplishing this goal. Clear and Cole (1986, p. 532) emphasize the futility of this approach:

> A move to meet public demands for punitiveness detracts in the long run from public confidence in corrections. Punishments increase, prisons are filled to overflowing, and still there is crime in the streets. This is a cycle that is nearly impossible to break: the experience of crime leads to a public outcry for punishment as a means to prevent crime, but because the increased punishment has little direct effect on the amount of crime, the cry for more punishment continues unabated.

It is precisely because of this misplaced focus on offender punishment and control — rather than community safety — that the current wave of intermediate sanctions has been explicitly designed to monitor closely and swiftly *react* to early evidence of offender noncompliance. In actuality, punishment and control are simply means to an end: neighborhood safety. However, it is difficult to envision how a strategy designed to punish and control a relatively small number of offenders could have a significant effect on neighborhood safety. In this respect, it seems clear that if the new wave of intermediate sanction programs is to become something more than a short-term solution to prison and jail crowding, program administrators will have to find a way to redefine these programs in terms of *community* protection rather than *offender* punishment and control.

In this article, I describe the interaction between offenders and communities in some detail. I then discuss the potential impact of *community-oriented* probation and parole interventions on the quality of life in our communities. These interventions are a natural extension of the current wave of intermediate sanctions programs that are *already in place* across the country. Drawing on the results of a recently completed evaluation of intensive probation supervision in Massachusetts, I suggest four key elements of a proactive, community-oriented supervision strategy: (1) the coordination and development of community resources to assist offenders with problems in the areas of substance abuse, employment/education, and marital/family relations;

(2) the generation of support for the deescalation of both community-based and institution-based sanctions; (3) a focus on the problems and needs of communities as well as offenders; and (4) the direct placement of probation officer teams in neighborhoods, with responsibility for resource development (as well as offender control) within a specific geographic area. These recommendations for reform are based on a belief that it is time now for the "panacea pendulum" to swing back in the direction of *community-based* solutions to the crime problem.[3] Community-oriented policing represents one important step in this direction, but the development of community-oriented probation and parole supervision strategies is also needed.

## Offenders, Communities, and the Issue of Control

Each year, approximately three-fourths of all offenders under correctional "control" are supervised in community settings. In 1987, for example, 64.8% of the adult correctional population (which totaled 3,460,960) was placed on probation, while an additional 10.5% was placed on parole. It is interesting to consider that while the *prison* crowding problem has received much recent attention (e.g., Blumstein, 1983; Petersilia, 1987; Irwin and Austin, 1987), very few commentators have highlighted the fact that our probation and parole populations have been increasing at a *faster* rate than our prison and jail populations (e.g., Tonry and Will, 1988). During the five year period between 1983 and 1987, the overall adult correctional population increased by 39.8%, from 2,475,100 to 3,460,960. However, the parole (47% increase) and probation (41.6% increase) populations grew faster than the prison (32.6% increase) and jail (32.7% increase) populations during this period.

It should be apparent that probation and parole crowding pose a more *immediate* threat to the community than either prison or jail crowding, since it is probationers and parolees who are currently "at risk" in the community. In fact, a number of these offenders do fail while under community supervision, due to rearrest, reconviction, or technical violations. A recent review of new state prison admissions (Byrne and Kelly, 1989) revealed that between 30% and 50% of new prison admissions in a given year were community supervision failures. Clearly, any discussion of possible *solutions* to the correctional crowding problem must recognize that many offenders move back and forth between community and correctional control during their criminal careers.[4] I highlight this point in Figure 1.

The obvious question becomes: How can we break this cycle of failure? One obvious answer is that we should continue to expand intermediate

Figure 1

**The Interaction Between Community and Correctional Control**

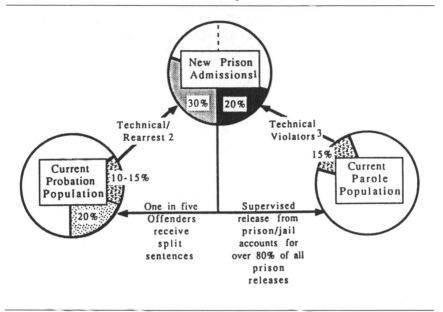

SOURCE: Byrne and Kelly (1989).

NOTE: Data on the movement of offenders from community to correctional control are from a variety of sources, but see the 1986 *Sourcebook of Criminal Justice Statistics* (Table 6.24). Blumstein (1983) has provided perhaps the most comprehensive assessment of demographic effects on prison crowding. For a review of recent shifts in sentencing policy, see Clear (1984) and Tonry and Will (1988). For an overview of the crowding problem, see Gottfredson and Taylor (1983) and Petersilia (1987).

1. We do not depict the interaction between prison and jail populations in this figure. However, prison crowding has a "trickle down" effect on jail crowding (see Bureau of Justice Statistics, 1988a, 1988b 1988c), since statebound offenders (as well as parole violators) are held in county/local jails when the prison system is over capacity.

2. Estimated from the Bureau of Justice Statistics Bulletin (1984, Table 6). For example, in 1985, there were 1,870,132 adults on probation. A *conservative* estimate of the failure rate for these offenders is included above.

3. The figure is for new supervised releases during a *one year* follow-up period. See *Examining Recidivism*, reprinted in Bureau of Justice Statistics (1988a, p. 111). Once again, our estimate of the percentage of all parolees returned to prison in a given year (e.g., 15% of the 277,438 offenders on parole in 1985) are rather conservative.

sanctions as front-end sentencing alternatives, while reducing our reliance on incapacitation. As Lauen (1988, p. 117) suggests, we need to "(1) view prison as a finite resource, (2) reduce the number of people sent to prison, and (3) reduce the length of stay of select inmates." However, such true diversion is difficult to achieve for two reasons. First,

front-end alternatives often "widen the net" of social control, with little
overall effect on the prison population (Baird, 1988). Second, since the
primary focus of these new intermediate sanctions is offender
punishment and control, a significant number of these offenders are
being returned to prison or jail as technical failures after only short
periods of community supervision (Pearson, 1987; Byrne and Kelly,
1989). This suggests that for intermediate sanctions to be effective, they
must be understood and accepted by "in/out" decision makers (Clear
and Baird, 1987) as alternatives to prison and/or jail. In addition,
program administrators need to develop supervision strategies that are
proactive and community oriented rather than reactive and offender
oriented. I will expand on both of these points later in this article.

To assess the appropriateness of a community-oriented supervision
strategy, it is necessary to consider the broad community context of
offender behavior and to identify the interaction among offenders, peers,
and family members in these settings. An examination of the professional
criminology literature reveals that researchers have "rediscovered" (and
revised) the concept of community as originally presented by Shaw and
McKay in the 1920s (Bursik, 1988; Stark, 1987; Reiss, 1986; Byrne and
Sampson, 1986). A review of this literature provides a strong conceptual
framework for community-oriented probation and parole supervision
strategies.[5]

## The Impact of Offenders on Communities

Offenders affect their immediate communities in a number of direct
and indirect ways. For example, the use of probation for a serious (i.e.,
felony) or repeat offender may erode public confidence in the criminal
justice system. This is especially true if neighborhood residents see no
*visible* evidence of the correctional system's control over these offenders.
As Wilson and Kelling (1989, p. 48) observe: "Every police officer knows
that most crimes don't get solved if victims and witnesses do not
cooperate." When the result of such "cooperation" is the immediate
return of the convicted offender to the community with no apparent
"control" by the correctional system, it is easy to understand the current
support for a more punitive sentencing policy.

Of course, it is not simply the fact that these offenders receive
probation that is at issue; rather, it is their attitudes and behavior while
in the community that concerns residents. The life-styles of high-risk
offenders often challenge existing community *control* standards, due to
their public (e.g., motor vehicle violations, license/liquor law violations,
littering) and private (e.g., nonsupport, family relationships) behavior.
These same offenders may also challenge *public order* in a number of

ways (e.g., disorderly person, loitering, failure to disperse, prostitution, drug use) that require community residents to request additional police resources for the area. And finally, these offenders may threaten *community protection* and *public safety* by committing (and getting arrested for) a wide range of felonies and misdemeanors, often in their own community.[6] Since there are obviously many other offenders in each community who are never arrested and/or convicted, the public's desire to punish those who *are* caught is understandable, especially when these more serious violations are viewed by community residents as an outgrowth (or escalation) of other (earlier) forms of disorder that have not been controlled.

We can begin to understand the adverse effects of offenders on communities by examining the findings from a variety of empirical studies of communities and crime. Blumstein et al. (1986), for example, have estimated the impact of *known* offenders on the crime rates of the communities in which these offenders reside.[7] Other researchers have examined such related issues as the impact of crime rates on neighborhood deterioration (Bursik, 1986a, 1986b) and fear of crime (Greenberg, 1986; Skogan, 1986; Skogan, this issue). In addition, a number of researchers have attempted to estimate the social, economic, and political impact of current sentencing and correctional policies on communities. The *social* costs of community supervision are felt when offenders challenge informal neighborhood social controls. For example, offenders represent negative role models for young residents and thus their presence in the community may change the way parents supervise their children as well as the form and extent of neighborhood organization (McGahey, 1986). The *economic* cost of the community supervision of offenders is found in the financial loss associated with the crimes these offenders subsequently commit and in the cost of control itself (Michalowski and Pearson, 1987). And finally, the *political* cost of the community supervision of offenders can best be understood by considering the "stakes" involved in releasing certain types of offenders into the community, and, consequently, the use of crime as a political issue (Finckenauer, 1978, 1982). In this regard, the impact of the Willie Horton case on the recent Presidential campaign provides a classic illustration of the consequences of a single release decision on the community's attitude toward a correctional policy (i.e., furloughs for offenders serving life sentences). My point is simple: Offenders affect communities in a number of ways that not only influence the form and content of sentencing and correctional policies, but also influence the way the community views itself.

# The Impact of Communities on Offenders

While it is true that offenders change communities, it is also true that communities change offenders in a variety of ways that can be either directly or indirectly related to offender recidivism. There are four elements of community context that can be identified: (1) community attitudes, (2) community tolerance, (3) community support/resource availability, and (4) community structure. Byrne and Kelly (1989, p. 4) recently highlighted the influence of these community context variables on adult supervision practices:

(1) *Community Attitudes* toward punishment and various offender control strategies help shape both sentencing and correctional policy.

(2) *Community Tolerance* for various forms of misbehavior (e.g., drug and alcohol abuse, vandalism, gang control of certain areas) will affect both who ends up in court and how [convicted offenders] are supervised in community settings.

(3) *Community Support* (i.e., resource availability) for individuals at risk, due to substance abuse, unemployment, a plethora of individual and family problems, and general living conditions, will directly affect probation officers' assessments, referrals, and follow-up procedures.

(4) *Community Structure* defines the general context in which traditional, offender-based community control strategies must operate, in that "certain kinds of community structure either weaken forms of social control that induce conformity to law-abiding norms or generate controls that inhibit conformity" (Reiss, 1986, p. 15). For example, legal and illegal community opportunity systems . . . may be directly related to the success of various community control strategies (e.g., the use of special conditions mandating employment, drug testing, or curfews).

It is only by examining the influence of each of these elements of community context on *current* policies and practices that we can begin to develop a specific strategy for reintegrating the concept of community into community-based corrections. In the following section, we discuss each of these elements of the community context of correctional control policies.

## Community Attitudes

*Community attitudes* toward punishment and various offender control strategies help shape a number of decisions about offenders: Who should be incarcerated and for how long? Under what conditions should offenders be released (if ever)? How intensively should offenders be supervised in community settings? Under what circumstances should offenders be returned to prison? An examination of the Willie Horton case underscores the potential impact of community attitudes on current correctional control policies and practices. The facts of this case are generally known by most Americans:

> On April 4, 1987, William Horton was arrested in Maryland and charged with the rape of a woman and assault and battery with a knife of her fiance after breaking into the couple's home. At the time of his arrest, Horton was an escapee from the Northeast Correctional Center in Massachusetts, where he was serving a life sentence (with no parole) for first degree murder and armed robbery, stemming from his 1975 conviction for the fatal knifing of a 17-year-old gas station attendant in Lawrence, Massachusetts (on October 26, 1974). Horton had escaped from the Northeast Correctional Center by simply not returning from an unsupervised furlough (his eleventh) in June of 1986. A number of questions about the appropriateness of allowing furloughs for first degree murderers arose in the spring of 1987 and followed Governor Dukakis throughout the presidential campaign. Bowing to intense community opposition to the state's furlough program, the governor placed an official ban on furloughs for first degree lifers in December of 1987, and in April of 1988 he signed legislation to ban furloughs for first degree lifers.[8]

The legislation to ban furloughs for first degree lifers was developed in response to an initiative petition by a community group called CAUS—Citizens Against Unsafe Society—in the fall of 1987, which garnered 52,407 petitions in support of a furlough ban (Bidinotto, 1988). The legislation was also affected by the intense media coverage of the event. A local newspaper—the *Lawrence Eagle Tribune*—ran over 200 stories on the furlough issue, as well as such related topics as the public's right to offender record information. The reporters who covered the story (Susan Forrest and Barbara Walsh) received the Pulitzer Prize for Journalism in 1988, an accomplishment that both large and small newspapers across the country certainly noticed. Consequently, correctional policymakers and administrators are likely to be monitored more closely in the future by both the media and "public interest" organizations. In anticipation of closer scrutiny, I suspect that decision makers will reassess their current policies and practices and—in areas with potential "Willie Horton effects"—they will restructure their decision-making apparatus to ensure greater accountability and control.

It is in this respect that the consequences of the Willie Horton case transcend the individual impact of Horton's actions on his victims and the general impact of the Horton issue on the presidential campaign. They also move beyond a discussion of who should be furloughed and under what conditions. The Horton case raised the decision-making stakes for each of the key decision makers in the correctional system: for politicians who develop sentencing policy, for prison administrators who must control the institutional behavior of offenders and make difficult release decisions in crowded institutions, and for community corrections administrators who must decide on the type and intensity of community supervision that is needed for offenders. The Horton case also did something else: It raised the stakes for communities considering the request for the siting of a new institution, halfway house, or group home in their area. Not surprisingly, the success of the furlough reform effort has heightened general community opposition to alternatives to incarceration. Apparently, this is true not only in Massachusetts, but across the country. When faced with such opposition, the easy, short-term solution is to utilize *more control* in both institutional and community settings. However, the simple truth is that while getting "tough" with offenders is certainly good *politics*, it is not necessarily good policy.

The recent community support for the use of imprisonment is a good example. A study by Petersilia, Turner, and Peterson (1986) revealed that a selective incapacitation strategy for "high-rate" offenders may indeed have a short-term suppression effect that is counterbalanced by two factors: (1) noticeably higher recidivism rates by these offenders once they are released from prison or jail, and (2) the fact that current prediction models used to identify high-rate offenders often have false positive rates of over 50%. Even if the false positive rate *could* be lowered, it appears that what the community might gain from locking these offenders up is lost further down the road. These findings are supported by the results of the recent evaluation of intensive probation supervision in Massachusetts: During a one-year follow-up period, offenders with a recent history of incarceration were much more likely to fail (i.e., rearraignment for a felony or a misdemeanor) than offenders who were not incarcerated (Byrne and Kelly, 1989).[9] I highlight this point in Figure 2. Contrary to the public's perception, the results of this study suggest that the increased use of prisons and jails results in communities that are less, not more, safe.

It should be recognized, however, that public opinion about crime and the criminal justice system is not adequately reflected by the two catchphrases "get tough" and "lock 'em up." A recent nationwide opinion survey revealed the following:

• In total, 76% of the respondents agreed that "judges should use probation for certain offenders as an alternative to prison."

• In total, 82% of the respondents agreed that "for some offenders, parole supervision is useful in deterring crime and in helping the individual to adjust to the community."

Figure 2

**Cumulative Proportion of Massachusetts IPS Offenders Who Survive (Rearraignment for a Felony or Misdemeanor) by Jail Time (Yes/No)**

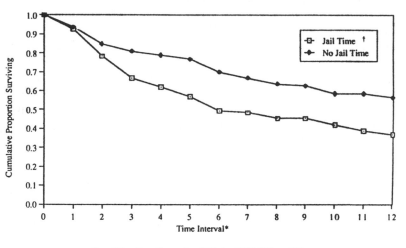

Overall Lee-Desu Comparison Statistic: 7.846 df(1), p=.005

---

SOURCE: Byrne and Kelly (1989).

* Months 1-12. Offenders who were incarcerated due to a technical revocation have been censored at their date of termination.
+ Jail time includes split sentences and/or incarceration in the one year prior to disposition. Proportion surviving until the end of the follow-up period is .57 for offenders with no recent jail time and .37 for offenders with jail time.

---

- In total, 64% of the respondents agreed that parole "performs a valuable safety net function that controls for sentencing disparities at earlier stages" [Research and Forecasts, Inc., 1985, as summarized in Jamieson and Flanagan, 1987, p. 88].

Perhaps even more interesting is the public's response to the question: "What should we do about prison overcrowding?" While 75% did agree that we should build more prisons, 67% of the respondents indicated that we should divert more offenders into alternative programs and 71% recommended that we "reserve prisons primarily for those whose crimes are the most severe" (Jamieson and Flanagan, 1987). How should we interpret these findings? Does the public really want to increase the capacity of *both* prisons and alternatives to prison? Do they believe that we would need more of *both* types of correctional programs if we did, in fact, restrict the use of prisons to only the most "severe" offenders?

One possible answer is that the public is ambivalent about current correctional strategies, but unsure of how to proceed. Up to this point, the new wave of intermediate sanctions (in particular, electronic monitoring) has been "marketed" to the public as an intermediate *punishment*, and the high level of surveillance required by these programs has been emphasized. While it is certainly possible that "surveillance-oriented community corrections is here to stay" (Petersilia, 1988, p. 4), it is also possible that residents will become disillusioned with these new programs once they recognize that increased punishment of a relatively small number of offenders does not accomplish what they are most interested in: safer communities.

### Community Tolerance

Communities may have an effect on offenders in other ways as well. *Community tolerance* for various forms of misbehavior (e.g., drug and alcohol abuse, vandalism, gang control of certain areas) will affect local police practices and sentencing decisions, and, ultimately, how offenders are supervised in community settings. Moreover, *police* tolerance of different types of behavior in different types of neighborhoods will affect traditional adult supervision strategies in ways that are important to understand. For example, Douglas Smith's (1986) recent analysis of the neighborhood context of police behavior in three large U.S. cities revealed the following: (1) "Police patrol both people and places" (p. 337) and (2) "suspects confronted by police have a higher average probability of being arrested in lower-status neighborhoods than in higher-status areas" (p. 337). As I mentioned earlier, one consequence of a more punitive probation and parole system is a higher return to prison rate for offender misbehavior. To the extent that an offender's likelihood of return is affected by *where* they live as well as *what* they have done, we have found yet another mechanism for race and/or class-based disparity.[10] Program developers must recognize this possibility as they develop community-oriented supervision strategies.

### Community Support

A third aspect of the community context of adult supervision strategies is the level of *community support* for individuals at risk, due to substance abuse, unemployment, a plethora of individual and family problems, and general living conditions. Although such support can be manifested in a number of ways, it is resource availability that offers the initial challenge to probation officers seeking help for offenders. Specifically, probation officers conduct an *initial* assessment of offender problems utilizing community resources (e.g., a variety of agencies conduct psychological assessments, educational assessments, alcohol/drug use assessments, and family assessments). Decisions on appropriate referrals and follow-up procedures are based on the availability, cost, and quality of these treatment resources. Of course, the issue of resource availability is less critical to the success of adult supervision strategies if we accept the notion that treatment programs do not reduce recidivism.[11] However, a review of the research on this issue does not support this position (see, e.g., Gendreau and Ross, 1987; Byrne and Kelly, 1989) and, therefore, it seems reasonable to suggest that resource availability is an important factor to consider.

The link between resource availability and offender change was highlighted in the Massachusetts IPS evaluation, where initial offender improvement in the areas of substance abuse, employment, and marital/family relationships resulted in *significant* reductions in offender recidivism (i.e., rearraignments) during a one-year follow-up period (Byrne and Kelly, 1989). The authors point out that the offenders who were seen the most often by probation officers were the *most* likely to improve in experimental courts, but the *least* likely to improve in control courts. They explain this difference as follows:

> It is evident that the implementation of this element of intensive supervision [quantity] results in a *proactive* style of probation supervision, whereby offenders are seen before (and not after) a problem arises. In contrast, probation officers in control courts appear to utilize a *reactive* style of supervision in that it is only *after* offenders begin to fail that they are seen more often by their probation officers. Thus, it is not only the *volume* of contacts but also the *timing* of contacts that is related to offender improvement in substance abuse, employment, and marital/family relationships [Byrne and Kelly, 1989, p. 273].

In the Massachusetts model of intensive supervision, the rationale for closer supervision was not surveillance, but service brokerage. The assumption was that "it takes time" to address the employment, substance abuse, and family treatment needs of offenders by linking offenders with problems to the appropriate treatment resource. Despite these generally positive findings about the impact of intensive supervision on offender change, it was also apparent that resource availability varied greatly from community to community in Massachusetts. A recent assessment of these rehabilitative services by Spangenberg Associates (1987, p. 110) revealed the following:

Only a patchwork system of social services within and outside the probation system has been developed in the Commonwealth. As a result, services that may be available in one community are totally lacking in others. The availability of services in any given community is likely to be the result of a great many factors including the demographics of the area, the urban or rural character of the community, proximity to social work schools and related programs, the personal persuasiveness of the first justice or C.P.O., and, at times, pure chance.

The consequence of this service delivery shortfall for *offenders* is straightforward: Offenders with problems do not get the treatment they need. As a result, these offenders are more likely to continue their "careers" as criminals (and, in many cases, their movement from community to institution and back again). A recent analysis of the reason for eventual return to prison among several thousand prisoners in North Carolina underscores this point:

The type of individual most likely to return to prison (and most likely to have a *small* time until recidivism) is a young, black male with a large number of previous incarcerations, who is a drug addict and/or alcoholic, and whose previous incarceration was lengthy and for a crime against property [Schmidt and Witte, 1988, p. 87].

These results underscore the futility of developing supervision strategies that allocate limited correctional resources to offender monitoring, apprehension, and punishment rather than to offender control through treatment (Clear and O'Leary, 1983).

### Community Structure

A fourth element of community context is *community structure*. Reiss recently reviewed the available evidence on the interaction between offenders and communities and concluded that

The empirical foundation of policies and programs calling for community interventions to reduce crime is that the structure and organization of communities affect the crime rate *independent* of the individual characteristics of residents and offenders or the culture and organization of the society. Offender characteristics contribute to predictions of recidivism, and so does the density of offenders in a community and its social organization. *Each of these factors has an effect on recidivism independent of the others.* Thus a crime reduction program for delinquent recidivists may require intervention into the lives of delinquents, their families and communities [Reiss, 1986, p. 24, emphasis added].

Reiss's assessment of community structure suggests that *offender-based* community control strategies are incomplete, since they take a "closed system" view of correctional interventions: *change the offender and not the community*. Offender improvement in such areas as substance abuse, employment, education, and marital/family relationships is an admirable goal in itself, given the link between offender change and recidivism reduction (Byrne and Kelly, 1989). However, such improvement may be made more (or less) difficult by a variety of community factors, which are important to understand.

A number of recent empirical studies support this position. For example, Gottfredson and Taylor (1986) recently reported that the risk of recidivism posed by parolees released into 90 Baltimore neighborhoods was at least partially explained by a set of previously overlooked socioenvironmental variables, including such factors as level of incivility, deterioration of the neighborhood, and other situational factors. According to the authors, it is the "interaction effects of environmental and offender characteristics" that hold the key to understanding patterns of recidivism. Other researchers have also examined the impact of community characteristics on offender behavior. Stark (1987, pp. 894-895) reviewed this *ecological* research and concluded that "there are five aspects of urban neighborhoods that characterize high deviance areas of cities. . . . These essential factors are (1) density; (2) poverty; (3) mixed use; (4) transience; and (5) dilapidation." According to Stark (1987, p. 895), these factors result in the following responses by area residents: "(1) moral cynicism among residents; (2) increased opportunities for crime and deviance; (3) increased motivation to deviate; and (4) diminished social control." If this scenario is accurate, it points to the need for probation and parole officers to act as *advocates for change* in the communities where offenders reside. Elliot Currie recently described the complexity of this community-level change effect:

> If we are serious about attacking the roots of this American Affliction [crime], we must build a society that is less unequal, less depriving, less disruptive of family and community ties, less corrosive of cooperative values. In short, we must begin to take on the enormous task of creating the conditions of community life in which individuals can live together in compassionate and cooperative ways [Currie, 1985, pp. 225-226, as quoted by Gibbons, 1988, p. 22].

Figure 3 depicts the range of person-environment interactions that social ecologists suggest are related to offender behavior. In this model, individual behavior is viewed as the product of a variety of influences, including individual, family, peer, and neighborhood characteristics. What can *not* be depicted in this model is the mechanism for successful interventions in each of these areas by probation and parole agencies, given current community attitudes, tolerance, and support. I describe

Figure 3
**Person-Environment Interactions and the Prediction of Recidivism**

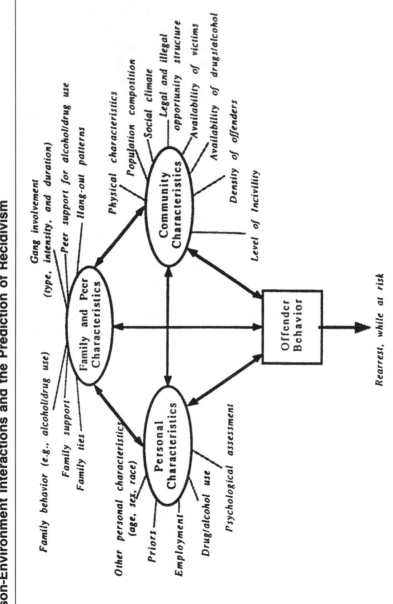

SOURCE: Byrne and Kelly (1989).

the necessary conditions for one possible *community-oriented* intervention strategy in the following section.

## A Strategy for Reintroducing the Concept of Community into Community-Based Corrections

The paradoxical effect of the current correctional crisis is evident in that it offers both an impediment to change (i.e., we define the problem as one of prison crowding rather than community control) and an opportunity for reform (i.e., decision makers must consider new alternatives during this period). Unfortunately, a review of the new wave of intermediate sanctions—such as intensive supervision, split sentencing, house arrest, and electronic monitoring—does not suggest that we are about to return to a community-oriented approach to offenders in the near future. Instead, we appear to be embracing the very tactics that police executives across the country are rejecting: a focus on specific *incidents* rather than on underlying *community problems*.

The basic philosophy of community-oriented policing has much to offer community corrections administrators. This is not surprising, since the community intervention techniques—brokerage and advocacy—are borrowed from the not so distant past of probation and parole.[12] However, it is clear that any attempt to introduce a community orientation to the *current* wave of intermediate sanctions must recognize that community attitudes have become more punitive and that community protection, rather than individual offender rehabilitation, must be the primary concern of program administrators. Dean-Myrda and Cullen (1985, p. 26) underscore this point:

> The punitive panacea at present has no competition, and all evidence suggests that its influence in the correctional arena is growing. Unless those with more reformist impulses begin to offer policy agendas that at once reveal the inadequacies of "getting tough" and furnish answers to the crime problem, the salience of the conservatives' vision of justice thus promises to remain undiminished in the time immediately ahead.

Ironically, the opportunity to infuse a *community* orientation into existing intermediate sanctions is provided by the current correctional crowding crisis itself. The primary force behind the development of such intermediate sanctions as electronic monitoring, house arrest, and intensive supervision is prison crowding and its associated cost. Commenting on the development of intensive supervision, Petersilia (1988, p. 11) recently observed that "the entire movement towards ISP is economically driven. It is commonly acknowledged that if prison crowding disappeared tomorrow, thereby eliminating the need to create less expensive sanctions, so would the incentive to develop ISP.''

Of course, program administrators not only promise diversion and cost effectiveness, they also promise increased community protection through intensive surveillance and control tactics. However, a recent review of the evaluation research on the effectiveness of these intermediate sanctions by Tonry and Will (1988) does not support the early claims of diversionary impact and cost-effectiveness.[13] One reason for these generally negative findings is that when *policing* strategies are used to achieve community protection, the "cost" of a low rearrest/rearraignment rate is a high return to prison rate. As Clear (1987), Petersilia (1987, 1988), and others have suggested, by promising too much to too many, the new wave of intermediate sanctions is setting itself up for failure.

A recent evaluation of New Jersey's intensive probation supervision program underscores this point. Pearson (1987) reported that over 40% of the offenders placed on intensive supervision were returned to prison within one year, and approximately 75% of these offenders were returned for technical violations rather than evidence of recidivism. Since the vast majority of these technical violations were drug test failures (Pearson, 1987), it appears that the program's emphasis was on the *incident* (in this case, detection of drug use) rather than the *underlying problem* (i.e., the offender's continued use of drugs). According to Pearson (1987), one consequence of close surveillance and a strict, incident-based revocation policy is a low rearrest rate while offenders are in the program. However, we do pay a price for such control, and the price is related to (1) the crowding of prisons, (2) the associated costs of reincarceration, and (3) the impact of imprisonment on the subsequent criminal careers of these offenders. In addition, when the development of these new sanctions draws resources away from an already overcrowded *probation* system, we should also anticipate higher return to prison rates among these offenders. Unless these programs are redesigned, the long-term effect of the current wave of intermediate sanction programs on communities will be negative in two important respects: (1) increased cost, and (2) a higher concentration of "ex-offenders" who not only have substance abuse, employment, and family problems, but now also have a recent history of incarceration.

Dean-Myrda and Cullen (1985, p. 9) offer a cogent assessment of our current dilemma: "[The] Panacea phenomenon—characterized by a cycle of unrealistic expectations, failure and dissatisfaction leading to the search for yet another foolproof elixir for the crime problem—has pervaded the entire history of American correctional policy." One reform strategy advocated by Dean-Myrda and Cullen (1985) is to reintroduce an "old" panacea, community-based corrections, but this time with an emphasis on the community control of offenders. Existing intermediate sanction programs attempt to provide short-term community control by utilizing such *offender*-based strategies as drug/alcohol testing, curfew checks, surveillance (via high contact levels), and strict revocation procedures to induce compliance with treatment. However, the primary purpose of these activities is detection and apprehension, rather than treatment and control. As Clear and O'Leary (1983) and Palmer (1984) have suggested, the most effective method of crime control is treatment. For most offenders, this involves help in one or more of the following three general areas: substance abuse, employment and education, and marital/family relationships. The results of previous research on community supervision indicate that offenders who do not show improvement in these areas are much more likely to recidivate than offenders who do show improvement (Byrne and Kelly, 1989). If our objective is community control, then it makes more than a little sense to require probation officers to act first as *service brokers*, linking up offenders with problems to the necessary community resources. Since this social service network often involves a complex array of public and private agencies, specific training on both resource availability and networking strategies will be needed.

When it is apparent that treatment resources are not available in a particular area (e.g., drug treatment, alcohol treatment, employment training), it will also be necessary to have probation and parole officers act as resource *advocates*. The "scope and methods" of this advocacy role will be enhanced by assigning probation officers to specific geographic *areas*, rather than to specific offender caseloads, and by developing intervention strategies that focus on changing both people *and* places (Felson, 1987). The parallels between this approach and the "cop of the block" and "team policing" strategies recommended by community-oriented policing advocates are obvious.[14] Lauen (1988, p. 93) recently emphasized the need for this type of advocacy function:

> Corrections needs to change its image in the minds of community members where communities-managed programs are located by expanding its role. Corrections should be viewed as part of the "helping professions" along with mental health, employment counseling, substance abuse treatment, etc. Unless this kind of change occurs, corrections will continue to be seen exclusively as a social control system, an arm of local law enforcement, with all of the attendant roles, problems, and expectations that this implies.

The scope of the probation and parole officer's advocacy role and brokerage function should not be limited to offenders; the problems and needs of victims should also fall within the purview of a community-oriented supervision strategy. As I commented earlier, the physical location of probation and parole officers in communities should be an important part of such a strategy, given such factors as (1) ongoing offender/victim relationships, and (2) the need to coordinate victim restitution and community service efforts. One of the unfortunate by-products of current community supervision practices is that probation and parole officers are often out of touch with the life-styles of community members generally and offenders in particular. Perhaps more important, both administrators and line staff may often become fearful of entire neighborhoods and this fear undermines the development of an effective intervention strategy. It is only by taking probation and parole officers out of the office and locating them in the community that we can begin to overcome this problem. How can we expect support for community-based corrections from residents who must *live* in the areas where probation and parole officers do not wish to enter? Probation and parole officers need to enter these communities and, as Lauen (1988, p. 118) suggests, "create forums for the public to participate in correctional plans and programs."

Finally, it should be obvious that for our current probation and parole system to embrace fully the community-oriented strategy I have just described, one of three things must occur: (1) we reallocate a much greater proportion of existing correctional resources to community-based corrections; (2) we develop policies that result in significantly fewer offenders under direct correctional supervision/control; or (3) we increase our overall correctional spending. Of these three alternatives, I suspect that efforts to reduce the *size* of the overall correctional population would have the most positive effect on the quality of life in our communities. Bennett (1987) has called this approach "Triage" because it is based on a decision about who we need to control actively either in institutional or community settings — and who we can (or must) let go. A number of commentators have recommended that we reduce our reliance on imprisonment and develop a structured hierarchy of alternative sanctions (e.g., Reiss, 1986; Petersilia, 1987; Clear and O'Leary, 1983). However, we must also move to the *other* end of the sentencing scale and develop an equally creative system of alternatives to active probation supervision. Wasik and von Hirsch's (1988) recent recommendations for the expanded use of day fines is one possible approach, and the use of community service orders is certainly a second possible strategy (Morris, 1987). The implementation of these *nonsupervision* sanctions may require the application of another policing strategy — split policing — to probation and parole. If we are serious about community supervision, we may need to do two things: (1) dedicate a significant portion of current probation and parole personnel to that task alone; and (2) make collections (and other court-support services) the responsibility of the remaining personnel. For those offenders who *are* placed on *active supervision* (regardless of program type) and those offenders for whom *nonsupervision* sanctions are deemed appropriate, we need to consider Morris's (1987, p. 5) admonition:

> We must begin to help judges to be serious about the proposition that the law must keep its promises. It makes no sense to threaten that which we are not going to do — to impose fines that we are not going to collect — to order supervision that we are not going to provide. In child care, if one wished to confirm a child in misconduct, one would make a series of unenforced threats. What we do, to put it rather vulgarly, is we repeatedly threaten offenders with a variety of sanctions, and then, finally we send them away for a long, long time saying, "look at all the chances we gave you!" It is an irrational way to act.

## Conclusion

The community-oriented supervision strategy described in this article will obviously be very difficult to implement, but our current correctional crowding crisis does provide strong motivation for policymakers to consider alternative strategies. The recent development of intermediate sanctions to act as front-end alternatives to prison and jail is one indication that the change process has begun. Similarly, intensive community supervision has been utilized to justify early release of offenders from both prison and jail. The problem with these alternatives is that they are currently designed to focus exclusively on the behavior of *offenders* and ignore the problems of the *communities* in which these offenders reside (Reiss, 1986; Sherman, Gartin, and Buerger, 1989).

The community supervision model I propose would allow the correctional system to make *community crime control*, rather than *correctional crowding*, the driving force behind innovation and change in the system.[15] The parallels between community-oriented policing and the community-oriented probation and parole supervision strategies I recommend are important to consider. Police administrators across the country have begun the long, difficult, incremental change process that the development of community-oriented policing entails; it is time now for corrections administrators to do the same. Again.

### Notes

[1] Other labels for the community policing model include "community policing" and "community-based policing." An excellent discussion and critique of this general approach is provided by Murphy (1988). See also Moore, Trojanowicz, and Kelling (1988), or Kelling (1988).

[2] A nice discussion of public attitudes toward punishment and control is provided by Cullen and Gilbert (1982). They point out that despite the current wave of support for

punishment and control, the public *still* thinks we should initially attempt to rehabilitate adult offenders. See also Dean-Myrda and Cullen (1985) and Jamieson and Flanagan (1987, pp. 88-89).

3 Dean-Myrda and Cullen (1985, p. 26) have observed that "reformers would do well to reconsider whether it was a wise decision to have abandoned community corrections as their panacea when no alternative other than pessimism was at hand." Clear and Cole (1986) and Finckenauer (1982) also provide an excellent overview of the panacea problem in adult and juvenile corrections.

4 For a good overview of the movement of offenders between institutional and community control, see Byrne and Kelly (1989). See also Bureau of Justice Statistics (1984, 1988a, 1988b, 1988c).

5 A recent issue of the *Journal of Research in Crime and Delinquency* (Vol. 25, No. 4, 1988) was devoted to the concept of community in criminology. For an overview of this research, see Leighton (1988).

6 Ironically, decision makers have developed the new wave of intermediate sanctions in a manner that results in *lower-risk* — but apparently prison/jail bound — offenders being placed under higher levels of supervision than *higher-risk* offenders on regular probation. See Byrne and Kelly (1989) for a more detailed examination of this issue. See also Byrne (1986).

7 A detailed review of criminal career research is provided by Blumstein et al. (1986). For a critique of this body of research, see Gottfredson and Hirschi (1988).

8 The basic description of the case included here was adapted from a chronology prepared by Maryellen Fidrich of the Massachusetts Committee on Criminal Justice in June 1988.

9 The same pattern was identified when alternative criterion measures (e.g., any rearraignment, and any *felony* rearraignment) were employed. Importantly, there were no significant differences in the risk profiles of these two groups of offenders. See Byrne and Kelly (1988, 1989).

10 A detailed examination of racial disparities in the criminal justice system is provided by Petersilia (1983).

11 There is obviously considerable debate on this issue. A general overview of this research is provided by Gottfredson and Gottfredson (1988), but see also Lipton et al. (1975) and Gendreau and Ross (1987).

12 Of course, police administrators are also reconsidering their *own* recent past. Consider, for example, the resurgence of foot patrol. A good summary of advocacy, brokerage, and community — "The A, B, C's of probation and parole" — is provided by Dell'apa et al. (1987).

13 See also the recent evaluation of the Florida Community Control Program's diversionary impact (Baird, 1988). In this evaluation, Baird concluded that approximately half of the offenders referred to this "house arrest" program were *true* diversions.

14 In their recent analysis of the "hot spots" of predatory crime, Sherman, Gartin, and Buerger (1989) suggest a variety of techniques for changing *places* rather than people. "On a place-specific basis, targets may be made less suitable, guardianship may be increased, and the supply of potential offenders may be reduced" (Sherman, Gartin, and Buerger, 1989, p. 47).

15 Clear (1987) also emphasizes the need to clarify organizational purpose in this manner. A detailed discussion of the community control of offenders utilizing a *limited risk control* model is offered by Clear and O'Leary (1983). See also O'Leary and Clear (1984).

## References

Baird, Christopher. 1988. *Analysis of the Diversionary Impact of the Florida Community Control Program: Preliminary Report*. Madison, WI: National Council on Crime and Delinquency.

Bennett, Georgette. 1987. *Crime Warps: The Future of Crime in America*. Garden City, NY: Anchor.

Bidinotto, Robert J. 1988. "Getting Away With Murder." *Reader's Digest*, pp. 57-63.

Blumstein, Alfred. 1983. "Prisons: Population, Capacity, and Alternatives." In *Crime and Public Policy*, edited by James Q. Wilson. San Francisco, CA: Institute For Contemporary Studies.

Blumstein, Alfred, Jacqueline Cohen, Jeffrey A. Roth, and Christy A. Visher, eds. 1986. *Criminal Careers and "Career Criminals."* Washington, DC: National Academy Press.

Bureau of Justice Statistics. 1984. *Probation and Parole, 1983*. Washington, DC: U.S. Department of Justice.

_____ 1988a. *Report to the Nation on Crime and Justice*. 2nd ed. Washington, DC: U.S. Department of Justice.

_____ 1988b. *Probation and Parole 1987*. Washington, DC: U.S. Department of Justice.

_____ 1988c. *Prisoners in 1987*. Washington, DC: U.S. Department of Justice.

Bursik, Robert J., Jr. 1986a. "Delinquency Rates as Sources of Ecological Change." In *The Social Ecology of Crime*, edited by J. M. Byrne and R. J. Sampson. New York: Springer.

_____ 1986b. "Ecological Stability and the Dynamics of Delinquency." In *Communities and Crime*, edited by A. J. Reiss and M. Tonry. Chicago: University of Chicago Press.

_____ 1988. "Social Disorganization and Theories of Crime and Delinquency: Problems and Prospects." *Criminology* 26(4):519-52.

Byrne, James M. 1986. "The Control Controversy: A Preliminary Examination of Intensive Probation Supervision Programs in the United States." *Federal Probation* 50:4-16.

_____ 1989. "Restructuring Probation as an Intermediate Sanction: An Evaluation of the Massachusetts Intensive Probation Supervision Program." Final Report to the National Institute of Justice, Research Program on the Punishment and Control of Offenders.

Byrne, James M. and Linda Kelly. 1988. "Does Split Sentencing Increase an Offender's Risk of Recidivism? A Preliminary Review." Paper presented at the annual meeting of the American Society of Criminology, Chicago.

Byrne, James M. and Robert Sampson. 1986. "Key Issues in the Social Ecology of Crime." In *The Social Ecology of Crime*, edited by J. Byrne and R. Sampson. New York: Springer-Verlag.

Clear, Todd R. 1987. "The New Intensive Supervision Movement." Mimeographed. Rutgers University.

Clear, Todd R. and Christopher Baird. 1987. "In/Out Decisionmaking: A Conceptual Framework." *Perspectives* 10:14-26.

Clear, Todd R. and George F. Cole. 1986. *American Corrections*. Belmont, CA: Brooks/Cole.

Clear, Todd R. and Vincent O'Leary. 1983. *Controlling the Offender in the Community*. Lexington, MA: Lexington.

Cullen, Francis T. and Karen E. Gilbert. 1982. *Reaffirming Rehabilitation*. Cincinnati, OH: Anderson.

Currie, Elliot. 1985. *Confronting Crime: An American Challenge*. New York: Pantheon.

Dean-Myrda, Mark and Francis T. Cullen. 1985. "The Panacea Pendulum: An Account of Community as a Response to Crime." In *Probation, Parole, and Community Corrections*, edited by L. F. Travis III. Prospect Heights, IL: Waveland.

Dell'apa, Frank, Tom W. Adams, James D. Jorgensen, and Herbert R. Sigurdson. 1987. "Advocacy, Brokerage, Community: The ABC's of Probation and Parole." In *Corrections: An Issues Approach*, edited by Schwartz et al. Cincinnati, OH: Anderson.

Felson, Marcus. 1987. "Routine Activities and Crime Prevention in the Developing Metropolis." *Criminology* 25:911-32.

Finckenauer, James O. 1978. "Crime as a National Political Issue: 1964-'76." *Crime and Delinquency* 24:13-25.

_____ 1982. *Scared Straight! and the Panacea Phenomenon*. Englewood Cliffs, NJ: Prentice-Hall.

Gendreau, Paul and Robert R. Ross. 1987. "Revivification of Rehabilitation: Evidence from the 1980s." *Justice Quarterly* 4:349-408.

Gibbons, Don C. 1988. *The Limits of Punishment as Social Policy*. New York: Edna McConnel Clark Foundation.

Gottfredson, Michael R. and Don M. Gottfredson. 1988. *Decision Making in Criminal Justice: Toward the Rational Exercise of Discretion*. New York: Plenum.

Gottfredson, Michael R. and Travis Hirschi. 1988. "Science, Public Policy, and the Career Paradigm." *Criminology* 26:37-56.

Gottfredson, Stephen D. and Ralph B. Taylor. 1983. *The Correctional Crisis: Prison Populations and Public Policy*. Washington, DC: National Institute of Justice.

_____ 1986. "Person-Environment Interactions in the Prediction of Recidivism." In *The Social Ecology of Crime*, edited by J. M. Byrne and R. J. Sampson. New York: Springer-Verlag.

Greenberg, Stephanie W. 1986. "Fear and Its Relationship to Crime, Neighborhood Deterioration, and Informal Social Control." In *The Social Ecology of Crime*, edited by J. M. Byrne and R. J. Sampson. New York: Springer-Verlag.

Irwin, John and James Austin. 1987. *Its About Time: Solving America's Prison Crowding Problem*. San Francisco, CA: National Council on Crime and Delinquency.

Jamieson, Katherine M. and Timothy J. Flanagan, eds. 1987. *Sourcebook of Criminal Justice Statistics-1986*. Washington, DC: Bureau of Justice Statistics.

Kelling, George L. 1988. "Police and Communities: The Quiet Revolution."
    *Perspectives on Policing* 1:1-8.
Lauen, Roger L. 1988. *Community-Managed Corrections*. Washington, DC:
    American Correctional Association.
Leighton, Barry. 1988. "The Concept of Community in Criminology: Four Papers
    from Canada." *Journal of Research in Crime and Delinquency* 25:347-425.
Lipton, Douglas, Robert Martinson, and Judith Wilks. 1975. *The Effectiveness
    of Correctional Treatment: A Survey of Treatment Evaluation Studies*. New
    York: Praeger.
McGahey, Richard M. 1986. "Economic Conditions, Neighborhood Organization,
    and Urban Crime." In *Communities and Crime*, edited by A. J. Reiss, Jr.,
    and M. Tonry. Chicago: University of Chicago Press.
Michalowski, Raymond J. and Michael A. Pearson. 1987. "Crime, Fiscal Crisis
    and Decarceration: Financing Corrections at the State Level." In
    *Transcarceration: Essays in the Sociology of Social Control*, edited by J.
    Lowman, R. J. Menzies, and T. S. Palys. Brookfield: Gower.
Moore, Mark H., Robert C. Trojanowitz, and George Kelling. 1988. "Crime and
    Policing." *Perspectives on Policing* 1:1-15.
Morris, Norval. 1987. "Alternatives to Imprisonment: Failures and Prospects."
    *Criminal Justice Research Bulletin* 3:1-6.
Murphy, Christopher. 1988. "Community Problems, Problem Communities, and
    Community Policing in Toronto." *Journal of Research in Crime and
    Delinquency* 25:392-410.
O'Leary, Vincent and Todd R. Clear. 1984. *Directions for Community Corrections
    in the 1990's*. Washington, DC: U.S. Department of Justice, National Institute
    of Corrections.
Palmer, Ted. 1984. "Treatment and the Role of Classification: A Review of the
    Basics." *Crime and Delinquency* 30:245-68.
Pearson, Frank S. 1987. "Research on New Jersey's Intensive Supervision
    Program." Final report submitted to National Institute of Justice under Grant
    No. 83-IJ-CX-K027.
Petersilia, Joan M. 1983. *Racial Disparities in the Criminal Justice System*. Santa
    Monica, CA: RAND.
_____ 1987. *Expanding Options for Criminal Sentencing*. Santa Monica, CA:
    RAND. (preliminary report)
_____ 1988. *Conditions for Implementing Successful Intensive Supervision
    Programs*. Santa Monica, CA: RAND.
Petersilia, Joan M., Susan Turner, and Joyce Peterson. 1986. *Prison Versus
    Probation in California: Implications for Crime and Offender Recidivism*.
    Santa Monica, CA: RAND.
Reiss, Albert J. 1986. "Why are Communities Important in Understanding
    Crime?" In *Communities and Crime*, edited by A. J. Reiss and M. Tonry.
    Chicago: University of Chicago Press.
Schmidt, Peter and Ann Dryden Witte. 1988. *Predicting Recidivism Using
    Survival Models*. New York: Springer-Verlag.
Sherman, Lawrence W., Patrick R. Gartin, and Michael E. Buerger. 1989. "Hot
    Spots of Predatory Crime: Routine Activities and the Criminology of Place."
    *Criminology* 27:27-56.

Skogan, Wesley. 1986. "Fear of Crime and Neighborhood Change." In *Communities and Crime*, edited by A. J. Reiss and M. Tonry. Chicago: University of Chicago Press.

Smith, Douglas A. 1986. "The Neighborhood Context of Police Behavior." In *Communities and Crime*, edited by A. J. Reiss, Jr. and M. Tonry. Chicago: University of Chicago Press.

Spangenberg Associates. 1987. *Assessment of the Massachusetts Probation System*. Prepared for the Office of the Chief Administrative Justice of the Trial Court. Newton, MA: Spangenberg Group.

Stark, Rodney. 1987. "Deviant Places: A Theory of the Ecology of Crime." *Criminology* 25:893-910.

Tonry, Michael and Richard Will. 1988. "Intermediate Sanctions." Preliminary report to the National Institute of Justice.

Wasik, Martin and Andrew von Hirsch. 1988. "Non-Custodial Penalties and the Principles of Desert" *Criminal Law Review*, pp. 555-72.

Wilson, James Q. and George Kelling. 1989. "Making Neighborhoods Safe." *The Atlantic* 263:46-57.

# Epilogue

During the 1980s we witnessed a period of unprecedented change in the field of community corrections. The profession moved rapidly to adopt the popular ideology of offender punishment and offender accountability. Prison populations in many of the largest states escalated well beyond the ability to adequately house the growing population. State legislatures and Congress continued to appropriate funds, with a view toward addressing the problem of overcrowding. While the public debate over prison overcrowding and construction costs continued through the decade and into the 1990s, community corrections professionals were confronted with larger caseloads and a significant number of offenders who needed close supervision for the purpose of community safety on the one hand, and treatment and service on the other. The role of the community corrections professional changed over time, as reductions in funding for social and human service were coupled with public support for the use of prisons and jails as a mechanism to reduce crime.

As several authors have suggested, the role of the community corrections professional has changed. This has meant a deemphasis on offender treatment and service, though service delivery continues as an important feature of work within the profession, a tradition which is not likely to be totally eliminated. The fact that community corrections professionals continue to support treatment aims, in spite of public and political views, is an issue which is likely to become a subject for debate in years to come. As we prepare to move into the next century, ideological change in the way offenders and their crimes are viewed by legislators may well be influenced by the ability to fund the system of criminal justice and by the increasing severity of punishments being mandated into law.

The growth in the use of prisons has been slowed by the increased use of alternative forms of punishment, typically referred to as alternative sanctions, or alternatives to incarceration. Most states offer an array of intensive supervision programs for probationers and those released from prison, electronic monitoring for both pretrial releasees and those sentenced by the court. The use of house arrest as an alternative to jail and detention for both adults and juveniles has had a modest impact on the jail overcrowding. Day reporting, restitution, and community service requirements offer sentencing and release authorities options which did not exist twenty years ago.

In 1991, when the first edition of this book was being compiled, one of every 46 citizens in the United States was under some form of correctional supervision, whether it be probation, parole, jail or prison. As evidence of the continued expansion of the effect of the criminal justice system on the lives of Americans, that ratio today has shrunk to one in every 42 persons in the United States. We must again ask ourselves, from both a philosophical as well as a practical perspective, what is and what should be the mission of community corrections? Have we, as one author suggested, drifted away from the original intent? The use of alternative sanctions has given the community corrections system a stronger ability to meet the needs of both the offender and the community, a goal which has been somewhat elusive in the past where the only options were either probation or prison. Sentencing and release authorities must be mindful that alternative sanctions, while used as popular alternatives, should be treated as limited resources, and utilized when most needed. As we face an increased number of Americans under correctional supervision my fear is not an increase in the rate of crime, but the increased use of community punishments for offenders who, in years past, may have been diverted from the system.

In recent years, policymakers and scholars have given increased attention to identifying performance indicators and factors which influence system outcomes. Community corrections professionals will continue to operate in an era of diminished resources, continuing to do more with less, while meeting the needs of the "system" and those of the community. It has been more than twenty years since Martinson's "nothing works" thesis was published, leading to the demise of correctional treatment as a primary system goal. Today, program evaluation has become more commonplace, especially in newly funded initiatives designed to reduce jail overcrowding and to divert defendants from the criminal justice system. As community corrections continues to address both public and political aims, the results of program evaluation should serve as a guide for future development, including the identification of effective offender supervision strategies. As our knowledge of "what works" in the field of community corrections continues to grow, we must avoid the tendency to unilaterally reject program evaluation data because of jurisdictional or minor programmatic differences.